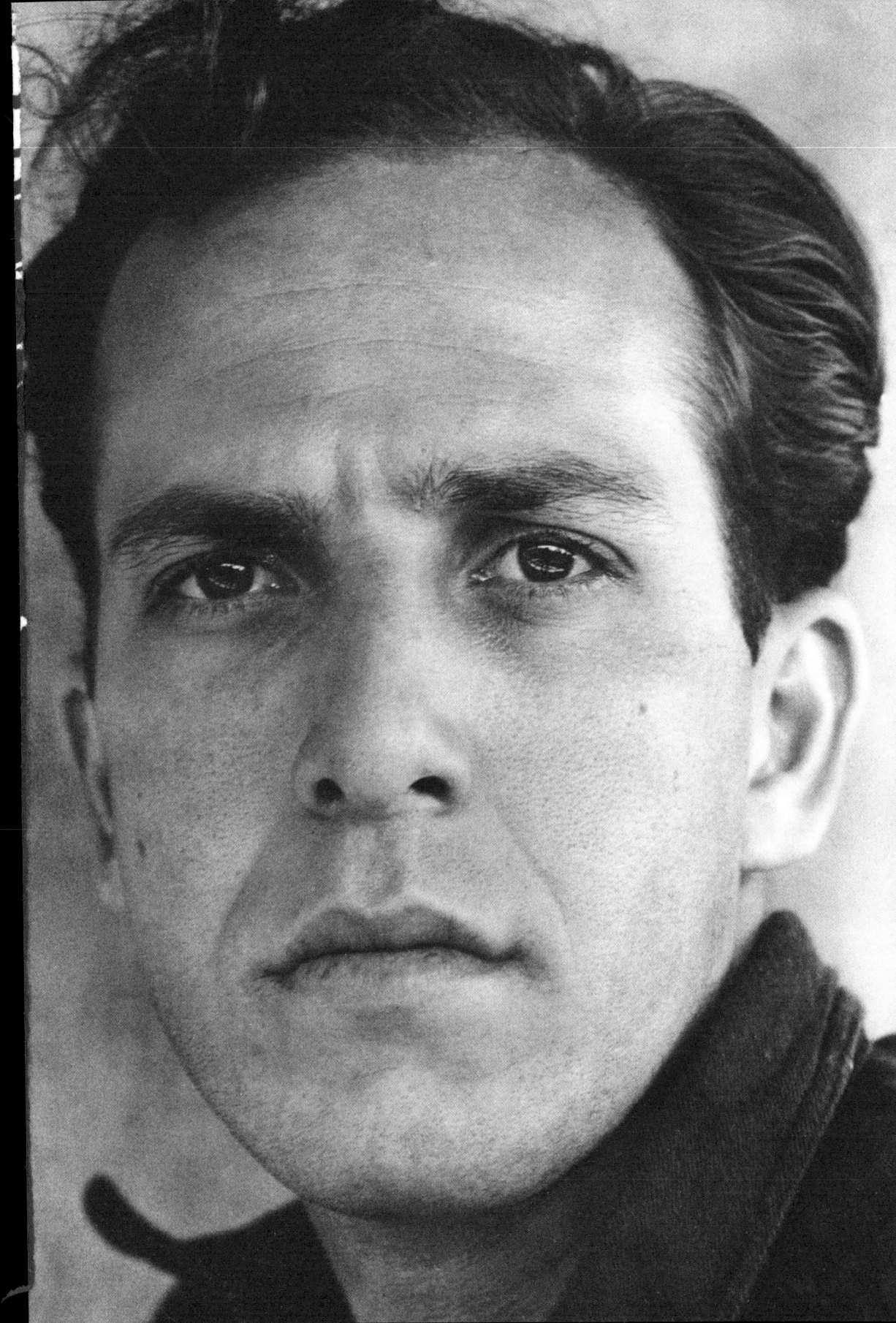

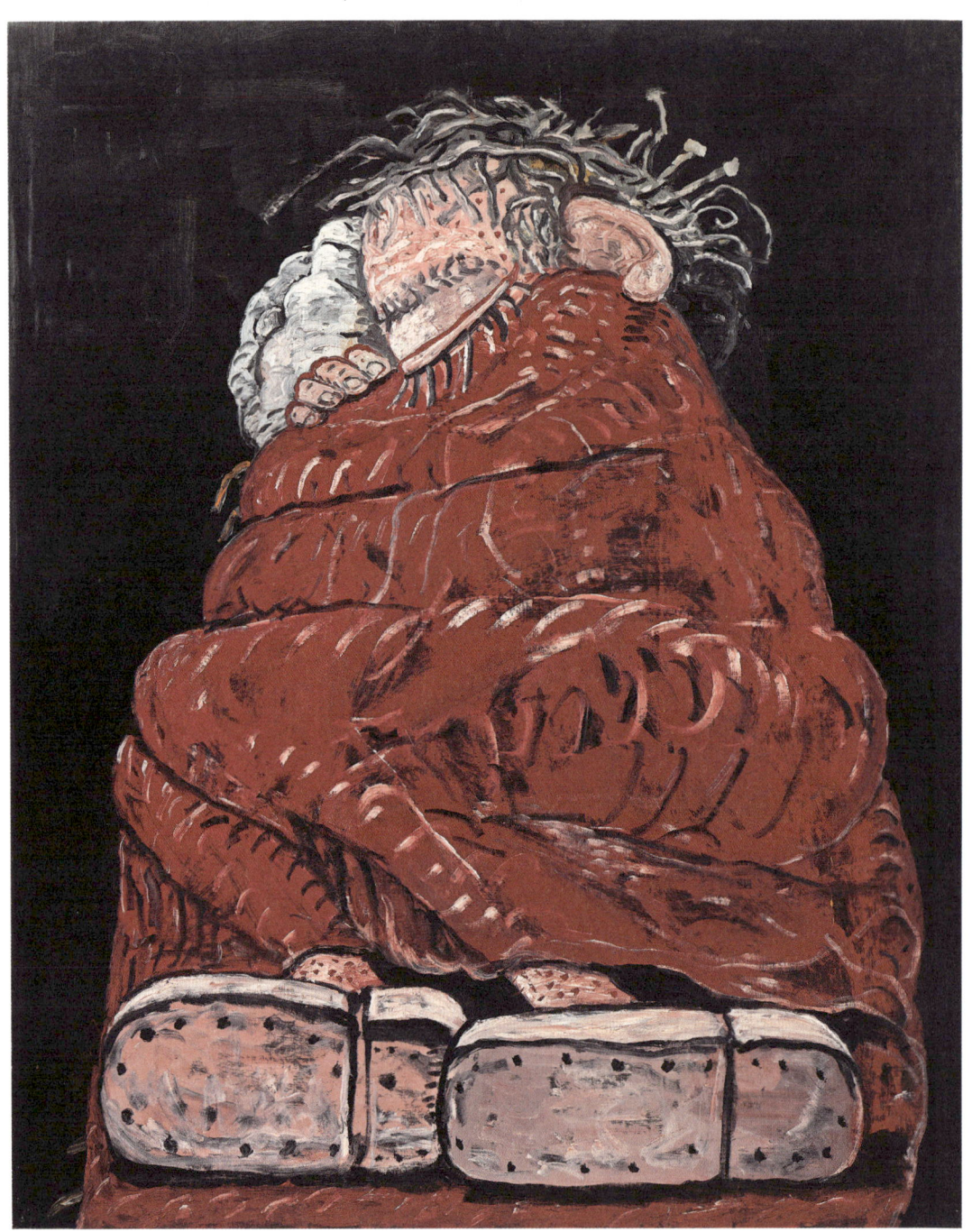

preceding page
1 — Edward Weston, *Philip Guston*, 1930
2 — *Sleeping*, 1977. Oil on canvas, 231.4×175.3 cm

PHILIP GUSTON

THE IRONY OF HISTORY

Gallimard
Musée Picasso-Paris

Philip Guston, the Irony of History

Recognized as a major figure of the New York School and of Abstract Expressionism, Philip Guston caused astonishment and created a scandal when he returned to figurative painting in the late 1960s, adopting a line inspired by comics. And yet prior to his New York period, the young Guston, influenced in particular by the Mexican muralists, painted canvases in a realist style that served as denunciations of social issues, such as racial segregation in the United States. By presenting works dating from the 1930s to the final period of his life, the exhibition at the Musée National Picasso-Paris thus makes it possible to trace the atypical career of this artist, whose work has rarely been exhibited in France and who was last given a retrospective in 2000.

This overview of his oeuvre reveals to a striking degree how, above and beyond stylistic variations, Guston's political activism and caustic tone were constant threads over the years. They are apparent in all of the works, from the creation of *Bombardment* in 1937 to his depiction, over the following decades, of ambivalent figures that evoke the Ku Klux Klan – the Jewish artist wearing a white hood in order to more effectively highlight the systemic and insidious racism of American society – via the exceptional ensemble of the *Nixon Drawings*, being shown here for the first time in France. A response to Philip Roth's *Our Gang* (1971), a pamphlet on President

Richard Nixon and his entourage, these seventy or so drawings feature an iconography that forms an extension to Picasso's 1937 series of prints titled *The Dream and Lie of Franco*, George Grosz's biting political drawings done for the magazine *Americana* in the 1930s, and the dark humor of the drawings of George Herriman that Guston admired in the American dailies.

These drawings emphasize the skillful permeability that Guston cultivated between his art and a satirical, caricatural verve that tends toward the grotesque. This transference of energy, which can be found in all of his works, endows his art with a black humor, making Guston a sort of pictorial Kafka. It also forms an invisible link—one suggested by the exhibition—that brings him into proximity with Philip Roth, his neighbor in Woodstock from 1969 until 1973, as well as with Picasso—the discovery of whose *Guernica* in the late 1930s formed one of the cornerstones of his artistic and political activism—and also, amongst the following generation, with Raymond Pettibon, a punk-rock artist who created an ironic and disturbing world that paints an acerbic portrait of a nihilistic and violent America, forcing the viewer to re-examine the American dream and, beyond that, their own values.

Skillfully devised by Didier Ottinger, a knowledgeable authority on the artist who initiated the project, and by Joanne Snrech, curator at the Musée National Picasso-Paris, this exhibition is a precious contribution to our knowledge about this artist who is still little known in France, while also highlighting the influence of Picasso on the American art scene in the 20th century. I would like to express my deepest gratitude to them, as well as to the entire team that worked on this project: Louise Rivet, project manager, Joris Lipsch (Studio Matters) for the exhibition design, Floriane Lipsch-Pic and Claire Cambier (Studio Matters) for the graphic design, and Vyara Stefanova (Aura Studio) for the lighting design.

Finally, I extend my warmest thanks to Renee Conforte McKee for her generosity and to the Guston Foundation for the invaluable support it provided for this exhibition. In particular, I would like to thank Musa Mayer, the artist's daughter and president of the Foundation, who demonstrated her trust in us by loaning the entire series of the *Nixon Drawings*, in addition to a number of unpublished works, and who made this exhibition and this book possible.

CÉCILE DEBRAY
President of the Musée National Picasso-Paris

Authors

Editorial Direction by
Didier Ottinger
General curator,
Centre Pompidou, Musée National
d'Art Moderne – Centre de Création
Industrielle, Paris

Agnès Desarthe
Writer

Joanne Snrech
Curator,
Musée National Picasso-Paris

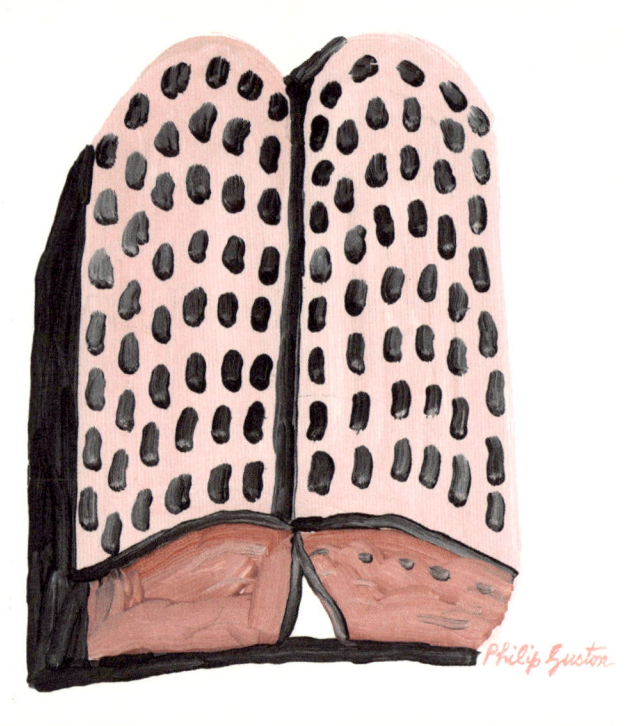

3 — *Tall Book*, 1968. Acrylic on panel, 50.8 × 45.1 cm

Table of Contents

Philip Guston, the Irony of History   4
CÉCILE DEBRAY

Philip Guston. A Counterlife in Pink   10
DIDIER OTTINGER

    Murals   46
    The action painting era   56
    The 10th Street gang   60
    Nixon Drawings   74

Philip Roth and the Grotesque   114
AGNÈS DESARTHE

Pictures by Guston PHILIP ROTH   127
Thought (or advice to myself) PHILIP GUSTON   131
The Appointment (A True Story) PHILIP GUSTON   131

    "A Mandarin Pretending to be a Stumblebum"   134

Picasso and the Grotesque   144
JOANNE SNRECH

    A tragicomic world   164
    Final work   174

Chronology   196
DIDIER OTTINGER

Select bibliography   210
List of illustrations   212
Index of names   220

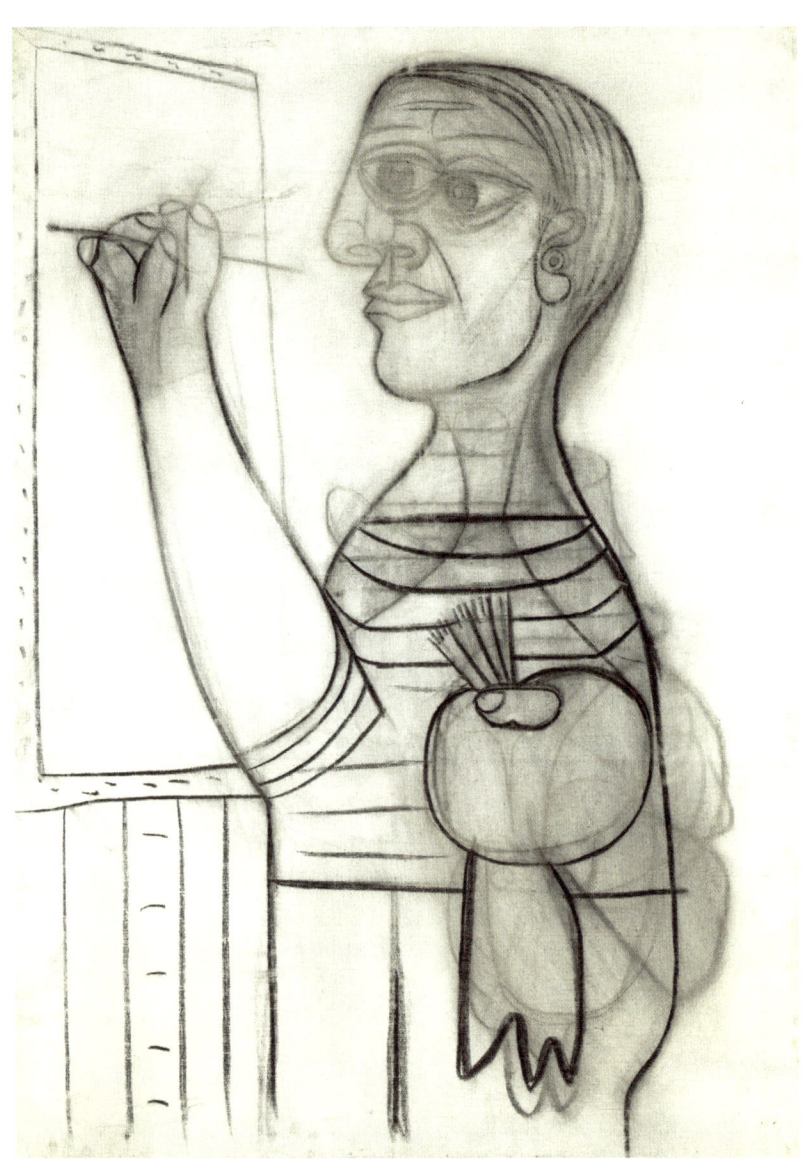

4 — Pablo Picasso, *The Artist before his Canvas*, 1938. Charcoal on canvas, 130×94 cm. Musée National Picasso-Paris

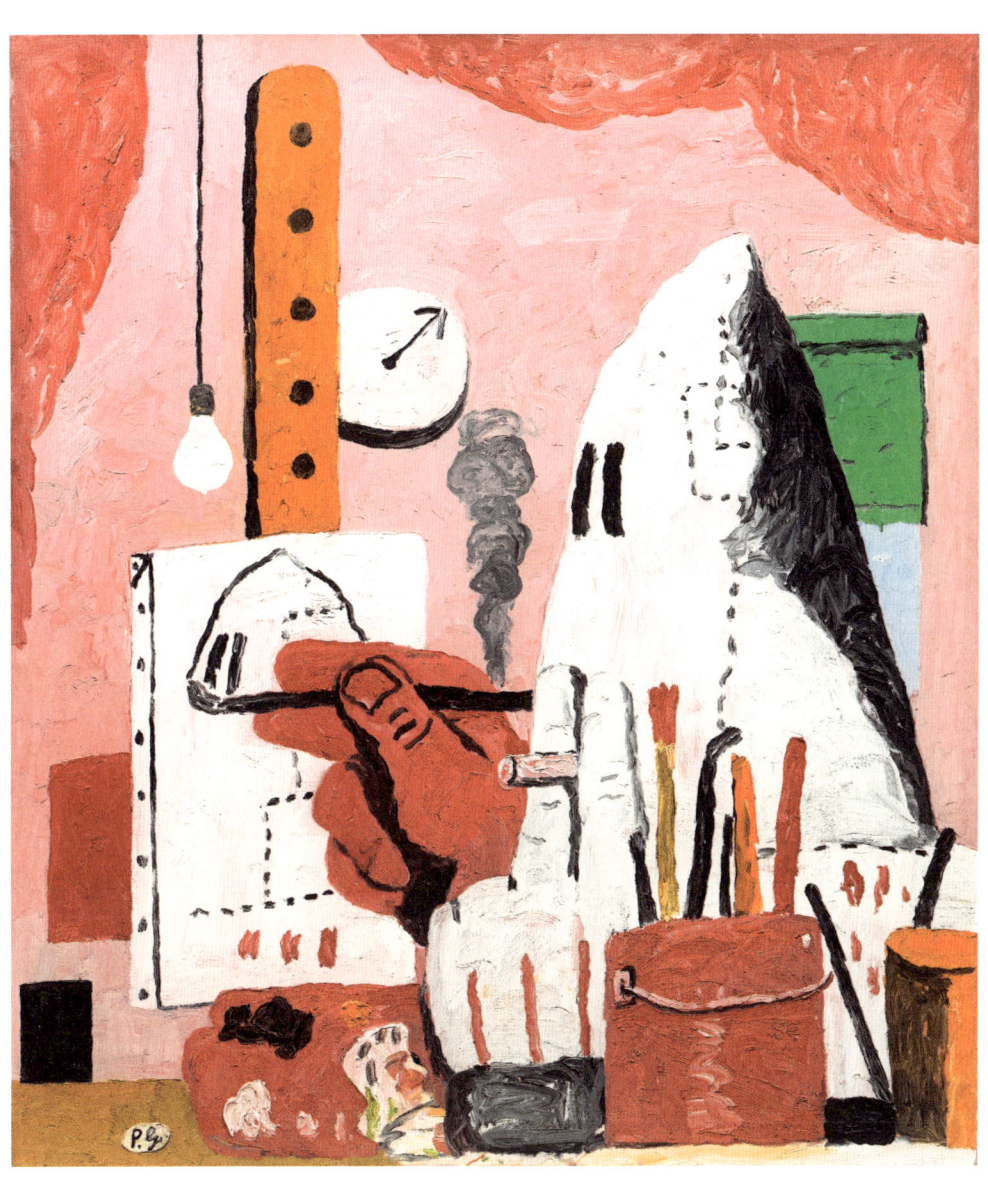

5 — *The Studio*, 1969. Oil on canvas, 121.9×106.7 cm

Philip Guston:
A Counterlife
in Pink

DIDIER OTTINGER

On Maverick Road, just outside the small town of Woodstock in upstate New York, in the heart of a forest of pines and maples, are scattered clapboard houses that remind you of trappers' cabins. One of them is flanked by a modern building with wide north-facing windows. These white walls house the studio Philip Guston first occupied in the winter of 1967.

A SANCTUARY IN WOODSTOCK

"I have a studio in the country—in the woods,"[1] he wrote in the year when, weary of the New York atmosphere he had been working in until then, he settled permanently in Woodstock. His self-imposed exile distanced him from a milieu whose values he no longer shared: "I'm almost going into a kind of figuration."[2] This shift in his painting cut him off from an artistic community within which he had contributed to the advent, and public recognition, of a "New York School" that had universally imposed the standards of an uncompromising abstraction. Nonetheless, Guston knew that solitude and incomprehension were the price to pay for the inexorable transformation to which he had committed his painting. His studio took him back to the "closet" where, as a child, he isolated himself from the turmoil of the world. "As a boy I would hide in the closet when my older brothers and sisters came with their families on Sunday afternoons. I felt safe. Hearing their talk about illnesses, marriages, and the problems of making a living, I felt my remoteness in the closet with the single light bulb. I read and drew in this private box.... I was happy in my sanctuary."[3]

Invited to teach at New College in Sarasota, Florida, during the winter term of 1967, Guston left his "sanctuary" and moved his studio there. The charcoal and brush drawings he now produced confirmed the figurative turn in his art: "I would one day tack up in the house a bunch of pure drawings, feel good about them, think that I could live with them. And that night go out to the studio to the drawings of objects—books, shoes, buildings, hands, feeling *relief* and a strong need to cope with tangible things. I would denounce the pure drawings as too thin and exposed, too much 'art,' not enough nourishment, and as an impossible direction with no future. The next day, or day after, back to doing the pure constructions and to attacking the other. And so it went, this tug-of-war, for about two years."[4]

The battle going on in the studio was all the more bitter in that it involved incompatible conceptions of art. While his "pure drawings" appear to be the cutting edge of an abstraction fueled by the aesthetics of Eastern philosophy, proceeding from an economy of means, and testifying to an attraction toward the "void," the objects he took as models in his figurative drawings made no secret of their triviality and their rootedness in a thoroughly material, human reality.

A few years earlier this incompatibility between abstract "purity" and everyday forms had taken the form of a memorable quarrel. Guston and his friends Rothko, Motherwell, and de Kooning had

1
Musa Mayer, *Night Studio: A Memoir of Philip Guston by His Daughter*, New York: Penguin, 1990, p. 104.
2
Idem.
3
Ibid., p. 24.
4
Ibid., p. 141.

stormed out of Sidney Janis's gallery when it decided to exhibit Pop artists. The "sublime" that went hand in hand with American abstract painting had no room for vulgarity, the celebration of objects, and images of mass consumption.

In the course of a repeat version Guston re-enacted this fight to the death in his Sarasota studio. Ultimately the Objects won out and soon migrated from paper to canvas in small, isolated formats. Rigorously stylized and formally pared down, books, old shoes, hands, and clocks discredited the obtuse mutism of "pure" drawings. Objects are vehicles for stories, inviting a volatility which soon became Guston's obsession: "You're painting a shoe, you start painting the sole, and it turns into a moon; you start painting the moon, and it turns into a piece of bread."[5]

In 1968, the first hooded figures made their appearance in Guston's pictures. In the early 1930s, when he brought them into his drawings and murals, the men of the Ku Klux Klan were as "real" as they come. In Los Angeles they were regularly harassing striking workers and vandalizing artworks they deemed "leftist." By the late 1960s, however, the hooded figures had become allegories of a more generic evil. Their appearance was tied in with a fresh episode of social and political violence in America. During the Democratic Convention held in Chicago in May 1968, student demonstrations opposing the Vietnam conflict were put down by police reinforced by the National Guard. The repression turned into a bloodbath. Gallerist David McKee[6] recalls the paintings he discovered in Guston's studio: "They reflected so much of what was happening in the world at that time in America, the civil rights disturbances and the marches and the fires and the anger and the disruption of everything. And we would talk about his own early interests in taking a position against social injustice."[7]

For Guston, the "evil" symbolized by the Klan figures was not just social and political. "They are self-portraits,"[8] he said The "little bastards," as he called them, soon multiplied (ill. 146 to 149). They engaged in aesthetic debates, commented on paintings, exchanged studio talk, and were part of the artistic community. These "self-portraits" condensed the strata of an introspection mingling irony, disillusionment, provocation, and playful innocence.

The hooded figures simultaneously embodied an "evil" that Guston had long refused to face: the irrelevance of an abstract art alienated from social and political realities, of an aesthetic that had evolved into a new academicism, which in turn had become authoritarian and intransigent.

The "little bastards" soon broke free of their creator and began leading a life of which Guston became the amused chronicler: "What would it be like to be evil? To plan, to plot."[9]

The Klansmen were given pink as the color of their movement. A pink that became emblematic of Guston's painting. It was the unmistakable sign of the "evil" his painting aligned itself with, not

5
Ibid., p. 148.
6
Working with his wife Renee at the Marlborough Gallery when Guston was "ejected" following his figurative turn, David McKee founded his own gallery dedicated to supporting the painter's work.
7
See "1968" in the biography accompanying the online catalogue raisonné of Guston's work: https://www.philipguston.org/home/chronology.
8
Musa Mayer, *Night Studio*, op. cit., p. 148.
9
Idem.

only by telling grotesque stories, but by choosing to do so in a style derived from the comic strip.[10] As soon as it appeared in the late Middle Ages pink, associated with the incarnate, became the color of choice for the representation of flesh and the dominant color of a hedonistic, Rococo eighteenth century, which had made its art a celebration of the feminine, of gentleness, pleasure, and happiness. It's hardly surprising that it became the target of revolutionary rigor and purity. Denis Diderot heralded this puritanism when he denounced pink as "frivolous, silly, and effeminate."[11] Posterity was to make it the color of the monarchy's decadence: "Rococo is associated with an innately feminine smallness of mind and love of adornment and artificiality and also with an effeminized, arriviste aristocracy, both of which are markers of inferiority and the decline of French culture."[12]

The virile revolutionary ideal that fueled the avant-garde ethos was bound to cast suspicion on a pink historically associated with mawkish, flaccid femininity. Futurism, the first of the historical avant-garde movements, banned a color so contrary to its masculinist warrior ideal: "We've already said several times how much we despise this tendency towards the feminine, the soft, the tender," declared the Italian Futurist painter Carlo Carrà.[13]

Guston was well aware of pink's ill repute when he decided to make it his preferred color. In doing so he affirmed the heresy of his art and its roots in an unreservedly prosaic and "impure" reality. Armed with the pink that flooded his studio, he transformed himself into the director of a seemingly burlesque film, in which the actors are recast as artists and critics, putting art on trial.

With a touch of irony he confided to the writer Ross Feld, "People, you know, complain that it's horrifying. As if it's a picnic for me, who has to come in here every day and see them first thing. But what's the alternative? I'm trying to see how much I can stand."[14]

MEETING AT WOODSTOCK

For some time to come Guston's heretical works would remain confined to his studio, where writer Philip Roth was among the first to discover them: "I turned my back on New York to hide out in a small furnished house in Woodstock, across town from Philip, whom I didn't know at the time. I was fleeing the publication of *Portnoy's Complaint*. My overnight notoriety as a sexual freak had become difficult to evade in Manhattan."[15]

Unlike Guston, who identified with his hooded characters, Roth never ceased to assert that he was in no way the monomaniacal masturbator of *Portnoy*. But to no avail. He was roundly attacked by New York's most respected rabbis for humiliating the Jewish community. The watchdogs of virtue were outraged by a book whose chapter headings included "Whacking Off" and "Cunt Crazy." *Portnoy* seemed as intolerably immoral and over the top as Guston's little ghosts were soon to be.

10
To gauge the transgressive character of Guston's new paintings, see Clement Greenberg, "Avant-Garde and Kitsch," *Partisan Review*, 1939, whose catechism of modernist art castigated the bad taste of popular culture and took particular aim at comics.

11
See Hayley Edwards-Dujardin, "Apparences, apparat et féminité: le goût et la postérité de la mode rococo," in Hélène Jagot et al. (eds.), *L'Amour en scène! François Boucher, du théâtre à l'opéra*, Paris: Éditions Snoeck, 2022, p. 217.

12
Melissa Hyde, *Making up the Rococo: François Boucher and his Critics*, Los Angeles: Getty Publishing, 2006, p. 47.

13
Carlo Carrà, "La peinture des bruits, des sons et des odeurs," Futurist leaflet, Milan: August 11, 1913, reprinted in *Cahiers d'Art*, January 1, 1950, p. 76.

14
Musa Mayer, *Night Studio*, op. cit., p. 182.

15
"Pictures by Guston," in Philip Roth, *Shop Talk*, London: Vintage, 2002, pp. 131–32.

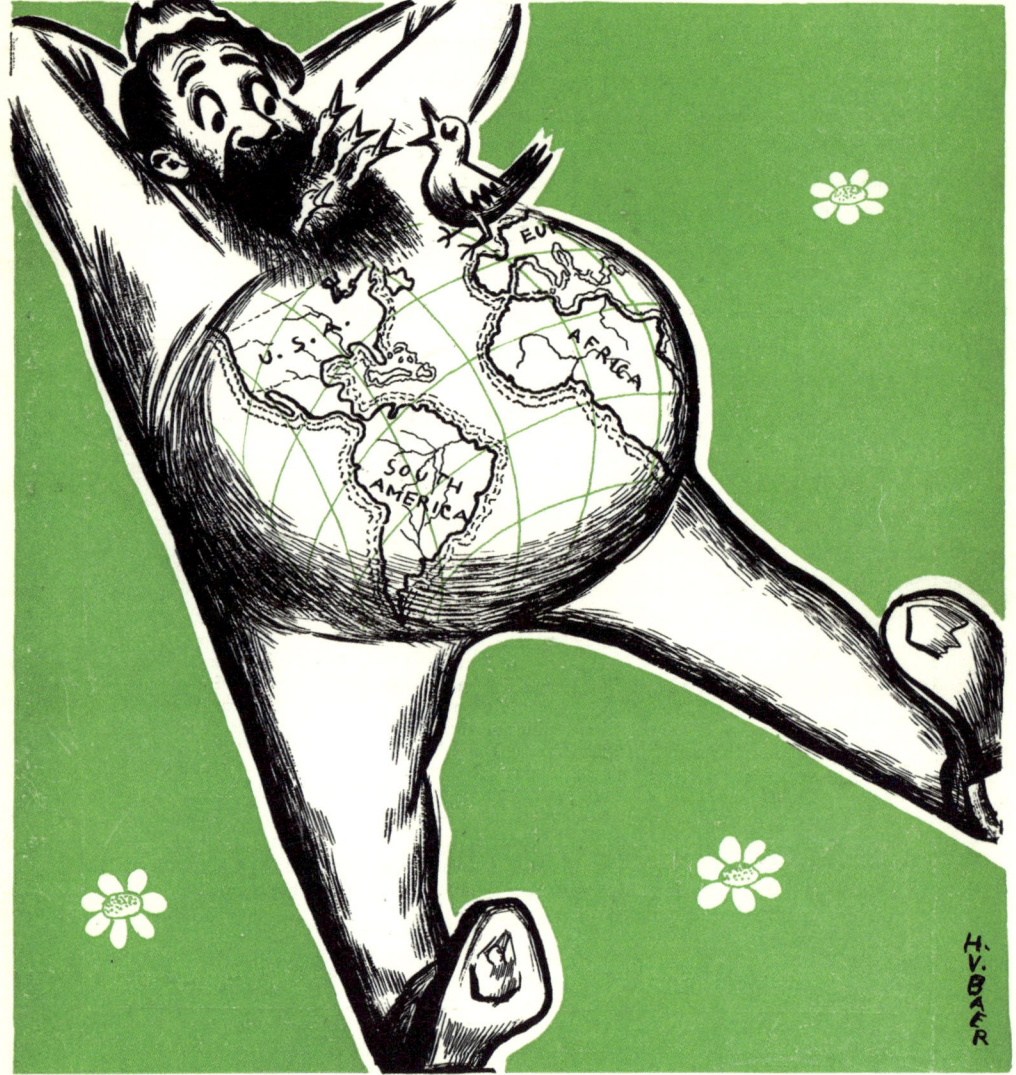

AMERICANA

APRIL   SATIRE and HUMOR   **15 cents**

GILBERT SELDES ● LAWRENCE DENNIS ● GEORGE GROSZ ● CHARLES D. YOUNG

6 — Cover of *Americana: A Magazine of Pictorial Satire,* April 1933.
Courtesy of the Robert D. Farber University Archives & Special Collections Department,
Brandeis University

Roth's description of the painter he met speaks of "the bulky torso of the heavy-drinking, somewhat august-looking white-haired personage into whom darkly, Jewishly, Don Juanishly handsome Guston had been transformed in his fifties."[16] And recognizes his immense solitude: "Cut off from New York and living apart from the Woodstock community of artists, with whom he had little in common, Philip often felt out of it: isolated, bitter, uninfluential, out of place."[17]

Their shared passion for Russian literature and their cheerful disregard for the hierarchies of taste brought the painter and writer closer together. "What caused our friendship to flourish was, to begin with, a similar intellectual outlook, a love for many of the same books as well as a shared delight in what Guston called 'crapola', starting with billboards, garages, diners, burger joints, junk shops, auto body shops—all the roadside stuff we occasionally set out to Kingston to enjoy."[18]

Roth had Guston read the first chapter of *Our Gang*,[19] his work-in-progress, published in the *New York Review of Books*, and kept him up to date on the novel's progress. This violent satire of the Nixon administration was the catalyst for Guston's desire to give shape to his aversion to a government that was waging an iniquitous war and riding roughshod over the civil rights of the African-American community.

The *Nixon Drawings* harked back to the comics of his childhood, and the illustrations in the magazine *Americana* (ill. 6) which, in the early 1930s, was publishing drawings by George Grosz.

In shaping his Nixon character, Guston was reminded of Picasso's *Dream and Lie of Franco* (ill. 165, 166). Like Picasso, he transformed his "hero" into a phallus-like creature. The *Poor Richard* drawings took him back to the distant days of his Californian childhood and his dream of being a cartoonist (ill. 65 to 137).

EARLY YEARS

Like many young Americans at the dawn of the twentieth century, Guston was fascinated by George Herriman's drawings, and his facetious, libertarian *Krazy Kat*, whose adventures had been featured in the *New York Evening Journal* since 1913.

He was thirteen when his mother enrolled him in a cartoon-drawing correspondence course. Since 1920 he had been living in Los Angeles, where his parents had settled after spending time in Montreal. Originally from Odessa, his family had left Russia to escape its persistent anti-Semitism. Russian literature and memories of the shores of the Black Sea would haunt the works of Guston's mature years, and resurfaced constantly in his late paintings.

After two years of correspondence courses some of his drawings, still bearing the family name Goldstein, were reproduced in the pages of the *Los Angeles Times*. Despite this relative success, he decided to turn to a more traditional art form and in 1927 he entered the Manual

16
Ibid., p. 134.
17
Idem.
18
Ibid., p. 135.
19
Philip Roth, *Our Gang*, New York: Random House, 1971.

Arts High School in Los Angeles, where he became friends with the young Jackson Pollock. Thereafter, their destinies constantly intersected. Their respective artistic trajectories summed up the issues of American painting, oscillating between the realist, popular roots of the country's first independent movement—the Ashcan School, largely the work of newspaper illustrators from Philadelphia—and aspiration toward the formalist project of the European avant-garde movements.

At the Manual Arts High School the pair were excited by the harangues of their teacher, Frederick John Saint-Vrain Schwankovsky. Schwankovsky was an adept of the guru Jiddu Krishnamurti, who preached a mystically tinged individual wisdom; the leitmotif of his teaching—an enduring spirit of revolt—would ring in the ears of his young pupils for a long time to come. This injunction was given a comical twist in Guston and Pollock's caricatures against sports, which earned them expulsion from the school.

In 1930, Guston enrolled at the Otis Art Institute of Los Angeles, where the stringent study program required students to copy antique plaster casts. Here he was confronted with a different kind of antiquity: to make ends meet he signed on as an extra in Hollywood, and would later boast of having taken the Bastille and contributed to the fall of Babylon. Discovering the films of Eisenstein and Dovzhenko, he equipped himself with a camera and even made a short film influenced by Soviet cinema.

These early, hands-on contacts with the movies spurred Guston's imagination, reinforcing his leaning toward the forms of popular culture. This attraction was reinforced by his reading of Mexican painter Diego Rivera's essay on Walt Disney, "Mickey Mouse and American Art" (1932), in which Rivera describes Mickey Mouse as "one of the genuine heroes of American art in the first half of the 20th Century."[20] The social force of art and its flair for reaching the public at large were forging values to which Guston's work would remain faithful.

Reuben Kadish, one of Guston's closest friends, was attending the life classes of Lorser Feitelson, a teacher highly reputed for having made a long stay in Paris during which he had assimilated the lessons of Cubism and witnessed the birth of Surrealism. Kadish advised Guston to show Feitelson the nude studies he had copied from Michelangelo's drawings and Piero della Francesca's frescoes in art books. Feitelson became his artistic mentor for a time and gained Guston an entry to the Arensberg collection, which offered a panorama of modern European art unmatched by any American museum of the time. An expert on Dante and translator of Mallarmé, Walter Arensberg had built up his collection with the help of Marcel Duchamp, whose main patron he had been in New York in the mid-1910s. On the walls of his Los Angeles home hung paintings by Picasso, Le Douanier Rousseau, and Chagall. Above all it was de Chirico's

20
Diego Rivera, "Mickey Mouse and American Art," *American Quarterly Review*, vol. 1, February 1, 1932.

paintings that caught Guston's eye. He would never forget the complex perspectives, the obsession with the monumental, and the "metaphysical" dimension of the Italian's paintings.

Dating from these formative years, *Mother and Child* (ill. 7) provides an insight into Guston's culture and range of curiosity. Against an architectural backdrop reminiscent of de Chirico, he sets a figure whose mannerist rendering echoes Feitelson's part-neoclassical, part-Surrealist style. Its monumentality recalls Picasso and Michelangelo, while the clouds gliding across a limpid sky bring to mind Piero della Francesca's *Baptism of Christ*, whose reproduction had a permanent place in Guston's studio. Nor was Feitelson's role as mentor restricted to the artistic realm. He also triggered Guston's political awareness and introduced him into the circle of Californian communist sympathizers.

MURALS

Expelled from Mexico in 1932 for his radical political activism, painter David Alfaro Siqueiros spent several months in Los Angeles, where he was offered a teaching position at the Chouinard Art Institute. There he painted the vast mural *Street Meeting* (Workers' Meeting) for the school (ill. 9).

Siqueiros's courses and lectures drew a young audience fascinated by his charisma and his already legendary biography. A former fighter in the Mexican Revolution and its military attaché in Europe, he was, alongside Rivera and Orozco, one of the key figures in the mural program launched by President Obregón's government. When Siqueiros undertook a second mural in California, *Portrait of Mexico Today* (Santa Barbara Museum of Art), Guston kept track of the work in progress, enquiring about the Mexican painter's daring techniques, which included sprayguns and photographs of his sketches projected onto the wall.

With Siqueiros's advice in mind, Guston set about his first mural, destined for the John Reed Club in Los Angeles. These "clubs," named in honor of journalist and political activist John Reed, were open to artists, writers, and intellectuals sympathetic to the American Communist Party throughout the United States. For the Los Angeles club's meeting room Guston came up with a painting inspired by the death sentence handed down in Alabama to nine black teenagers wrongfully accused of raping two white women (*The Scottsboro Case*, 1931).

The painting showed the torture of an African-American by a Ku Klux Klan member. On February 11, 1933, the Los Angeles Police Department's "Red Squad"—an unofficial "anti-communist" offshoot of the local police—raided the club, assaulted the participants at a meeting attended by two hundred people, and vandalized the murals embellishing the meeting rooms. Guston's work did not escape the devastation.

The economic crisis of 1929 and the ensuing fallback on nationalism swelled the ranks of the KKK, which soon numbered 4.5 million members, most of them in and around Los Angeles. Guston had already had dealings with hooded men come to beat up strikers at a plant where he was working. In a further sign of the violent political tensions in America in the 1930s, *Mother and Child* (1931), presented at the Los Angeles County Museum's 14th annual exhibition and in no way subversive in subject or form, came under attack from a group of militantly regionalist landscape painters. Deemed "un-American," the painting was accused of "endangering American values."

In this climate of intolerance, the National Legion of Decency, a Catholic pressure group founded in 1934, set about purging the cinema of all its members "contaminated" by Marxist theories.

The mural Reuben Kadish created for the International Ladies' Garment Workers Union in Los Angeles bears witness to this political tension. Marx himself appears alongside Lenin, in a composition that shows proletarian hammers and sickles striking down the symbols of totalitarianism, including a swastika.

Next, far from any political commitment, Guston and Kadish imagined a mural illustrating "the rise of technology and trade from Egyptian times" for a Los Angeles school of applied art. The rejection of this project led the two painters to look around for a sponsor better disposed to their political aims. Kadish appealed to Siqueiros, whose assistant he had been. Encouraged by their mural for the Garment Workers Union, Siqueiros persuaded the Mexican authorities to entrust the young artists with a wall at the University of St. Nicholas of Hidalgo in Morelia. The only constraint was that the project had to be completed within six months. Guston and Kadish set to work. Their subject, *The Struggle Against Terrorism*, was a form of revolutionary "last judgment" (ill. 29). *Time* magazine's report on the fresco presented Guston, aged only twenty-two at the time, as a young mural prodigy. Disregarding the political content of his fresco, this endorsement earned him a federal government commission for a mural for the City of Hope, the sanatorium in the town of Duarte, Los Angeles County.

In the winter of 1936, Guston left Los Angeles for New York. Pollock had told him that the Roosevelt government was setting up a vast program to help artists hit by the continuing economic crisis. On August 27, 1936 he wrote to Kadish that this program was "the best thing that is new with me . . . [and] now I'm going to New York in 3 weeks. I saw Tolegian [a member of the Manual Arts group] and he tells me that I will have a better chance to get on the project around this time than later in the fall."[21]

For him the trip to the East Coast was a new beginning. In New York he gave up the family name of Goldstein and adopted that of Guston.

21
Dore Ashton, *A Critical Study of Philip Guston*, Oxford: University of California Press, 1990, pp. 32–33. It has been confirmed as 1936.

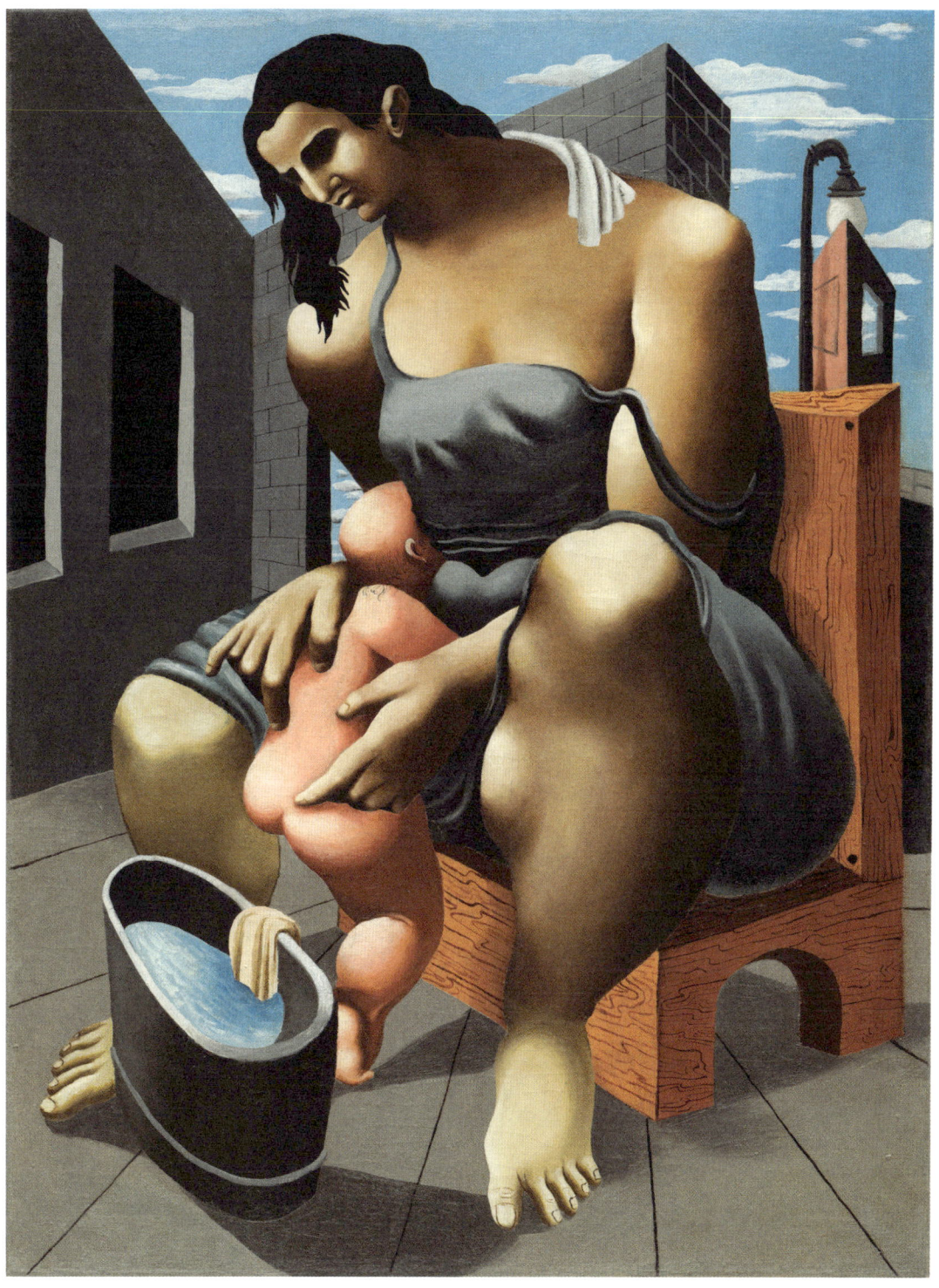

7 — *Mother and Child*, c. 1930. Oil on canvas, 101.6 × 76.2 cm

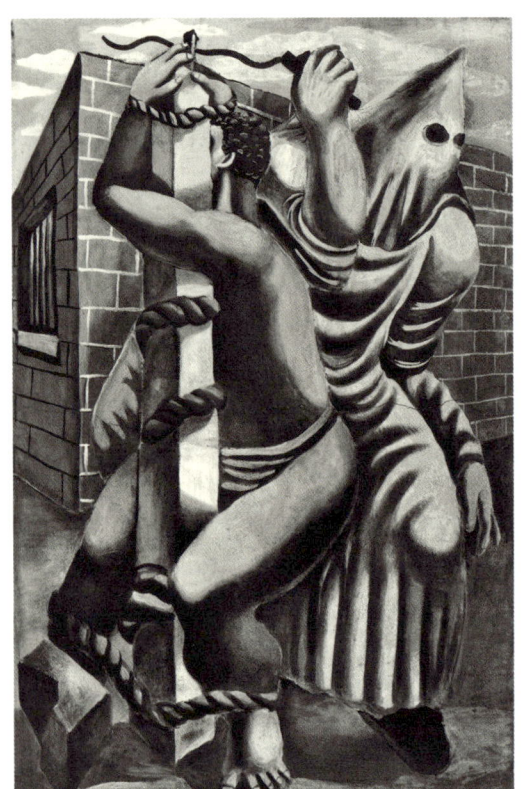 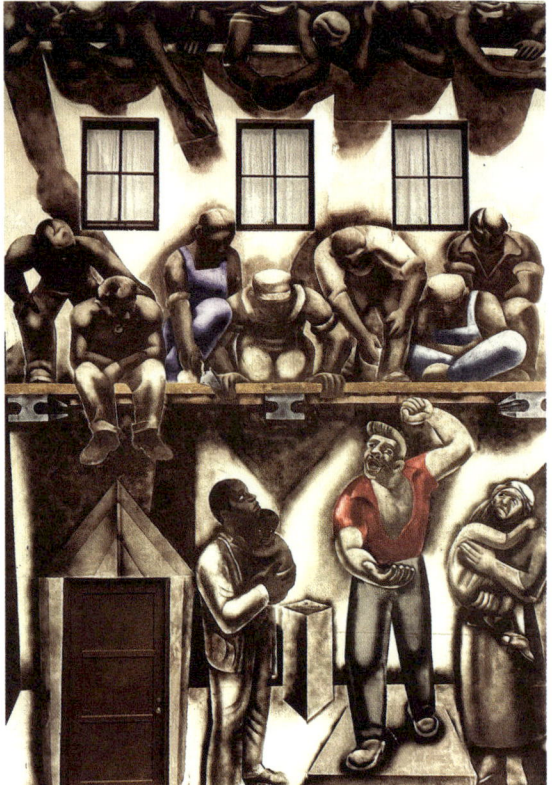

8 — *John Reed Club Panel*, c. 1931. Fresco, dimensions unknown, destroyed in February 1933
9 — David Alfaro Siqueiros, *Street Meeting*, 1932. Mural, 731.5 × 579.1 cm. Chouinard Art Institute
(today the Chouinard Foundation), Los Angeles

On his arrival in New York Guston went to live with Jackson Pollock's brother. At MoMA he discovered the *Cubism and Abstract Art* exhibition, a statement of the museum's commitment to the study and backing of the American development of abstract formalism, initiated by Cubism. A message that Guston was not ready to hear, obsessed as he was by his determination to produce a figurative social art inspired by the Mexican revolutionary painters. For him this issue was all the more topical in a city still reeling from the scandal caused by Diego Rivera's Rockefeller Center frescoes (ill. 10).

The Rockefeller commission had nonetheless been quite clear. The mural was to illustrate "Man at the Crossroads Looking with Hope and High Vision to the Choosing of a New and Better Future."[22] Matisse and Picasso had been considered for some time, but declined, leaving the way open to Rivera, the canonized master of mural painting, who submitted the following interpretation of the specifications to the Rockefellers: "On the right, the cinema and a group of young women enjoying themselves. On the left, a group of unemployed. Above the group, the television broadcasts images of war illustrating the ravages of technology not directed by an ethic."[23] Raymond Hood, the building's architect, accepted the project. In the course of its creation, the fresco was enriched by unexpected details: on the right-hand side the red flags of a demonstration unfurled, while on the left Rivera associated an evocation of fascism with representations of the plague and syphilis viruses. And as if that weren't enough, in the center of the composition there blossomed a portrait of Lenin.

The scandal erupted in the columns of the *New York World-Telegram*, which headlined: "Rivera Paints Scenes of Communist Activity and John D. Jr. Foots the Bill."[24] The ensuing outrage led to the destruction of the monumental fresco. It was in this context of political paranoia, in order to curb a probable "Marxization" of the American intelligentsia, that the Roosevelt government launched a new program of aid to artists.

In 1934 the federal government began funding traveling theaters and public drama classes. This support for the living arts inspired the College Art Association to champion the cause of visual artists. In an appeal to the American authorities, it estimated the number of artists in urgent need of material assistance at 1,400. George Biddle, Roosevelt's former classmate turned painter, relayed this plea to the president in a letter on May 9, 1933: "The Mexican artists have produced the greatest national school of mural painting since the Italian Renaissance. Diego Rivera tells me that it was only possible because Obregón allowed Mexican artists to work at plumber's wages in order to express on the walls of the government buildings the social ideals of the Mexican revolution. The younger artists of America are conscious as they never have been of the social revolution that our

22
Diego Rivera, quoted by Lucienne Bloch in "On location with Diego Rivera," *Art in America*, no. 2, February 1986, p. 108.
23
Ibid.
24
https://www.npr.org/2014/03/09/287745199/destroyed-by-rockefellers-mural-trespassed-on-political-vision.

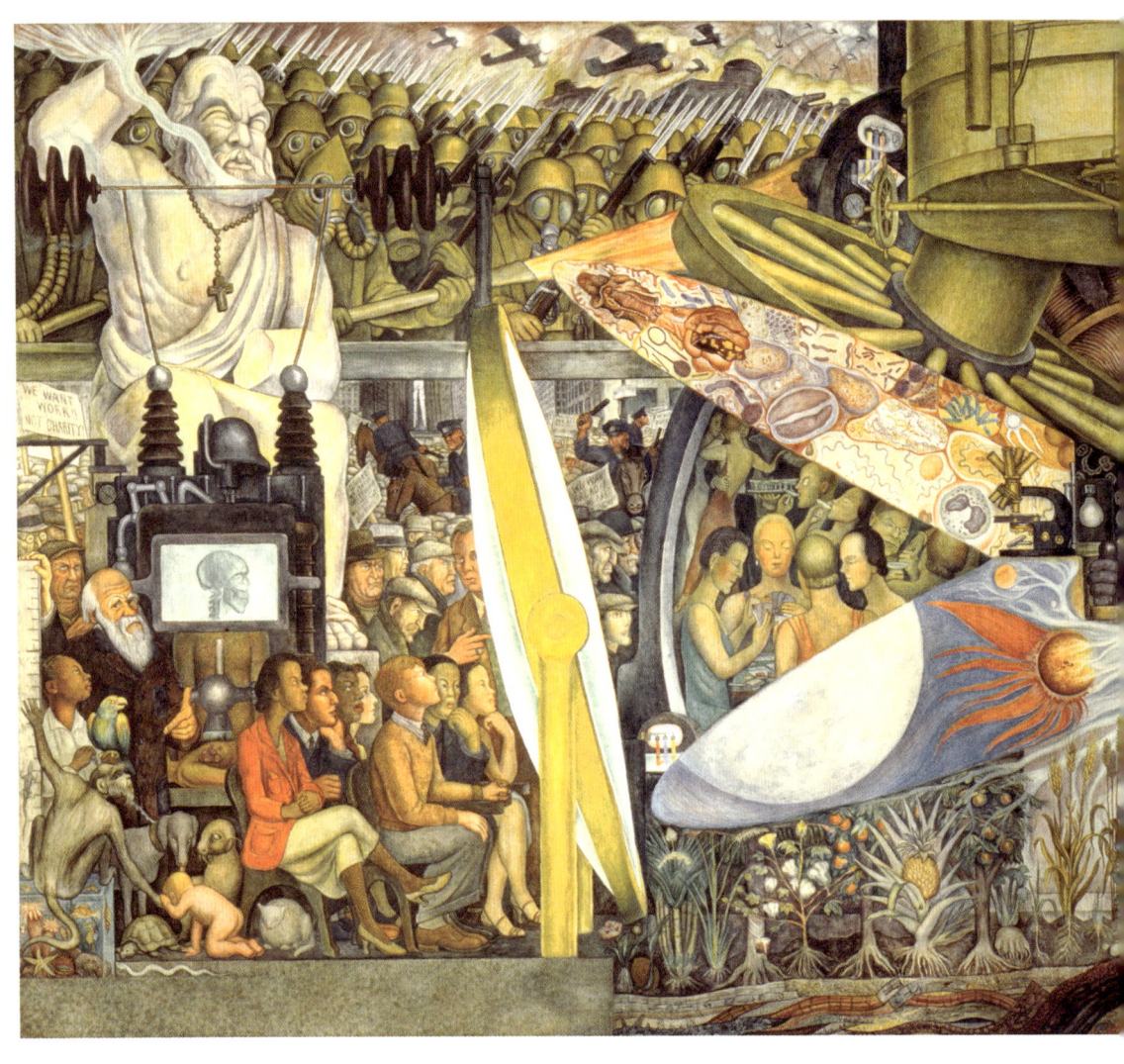

10 — Diego Rivera, *Man, Controller of the Universe* or *Man in the Time Machine*, 1934.
Replica of the fresco rejected and destroyed by the Rockefeller Center, 48.5×114.5 cm.
Palacio de Bellas Artes, Mexico City

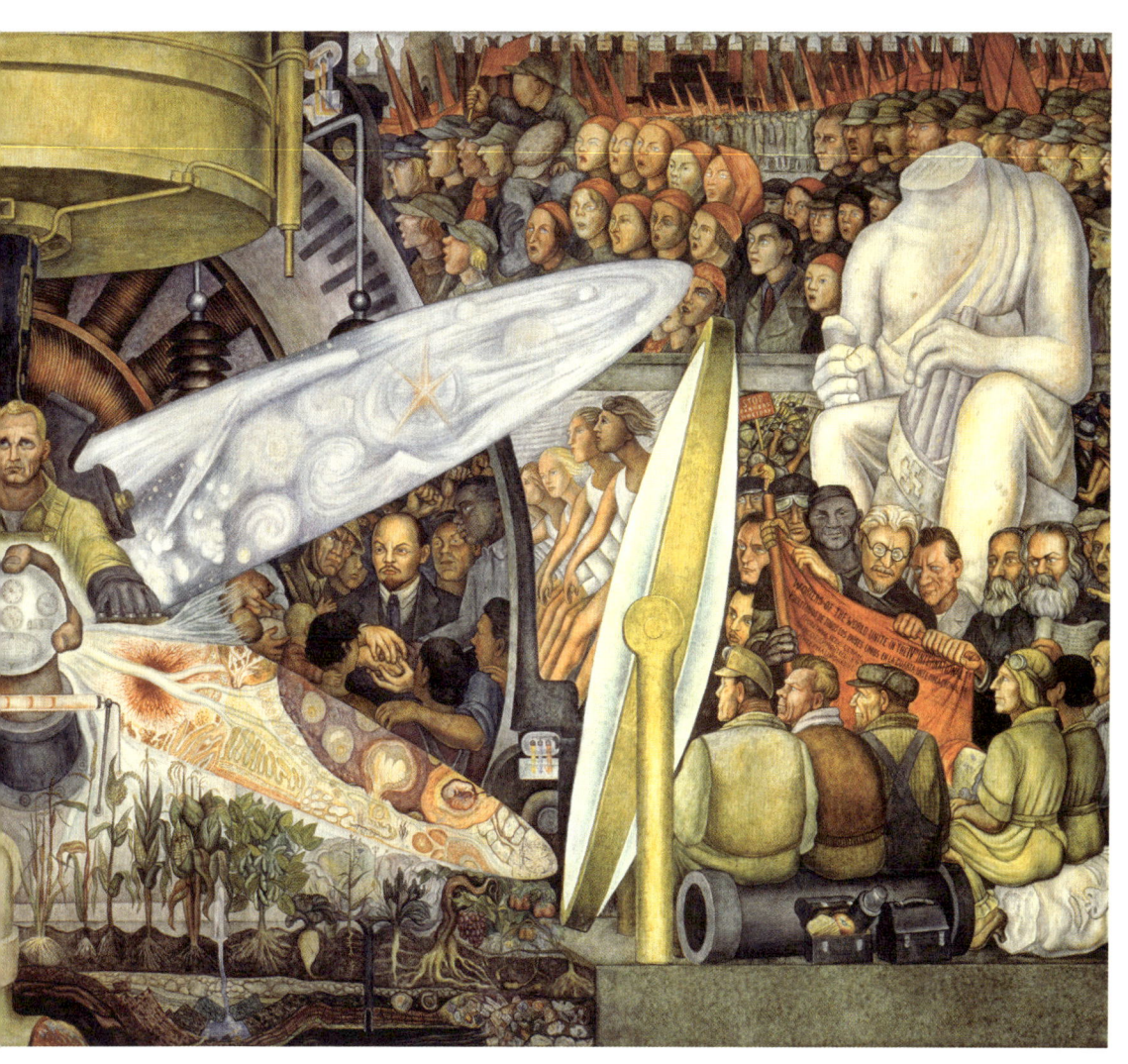

country and civilization are going through; and they would be very eager to express these ideals in a permanent art form if they were given the government's co-operation."[25]

In response to this demand and to appeals from painters' unions and associations, a vast aid program launched under the direction of painter Edward Bruce enabled the employment of 1,700 artists. Over 15,000 works were acquired by the US government. A year later a new program, this time from the Department of Treasury, introduced a measure to devote 1% of the cost of public buildings to financing their decoration with works of art. This measure benefited regionalist artists in the various American states.

The artistic emphasis of these grants changed radically with the new program implemented by the Roosevelt government in 1935. The WPA (Works Progress Administration) was overseen by Holger Cahill, a former neo-Dadaist activist who had worked for several years at the Newark Museum, New Jersey, where he had steered policy toward the most innovative art forms. His connections and friendships were rooted in the East Coast, and of the 1,499 artists who benefited from the WPA program 1,090 were New Yorkers. Cahill organized and protected an "artistic nursery" from which the postwar New York School would emerge. Gorky, de Kooning, Reinhardt, Rothko, Gottlieb, and Guston owed their survival as artists to the WPA. For ninety-five dollars a month they were theoretically required to provide ninety-six hours of work. Most of them did this in the context of the murals they were commissioned to paint. De Kooning worked on an urban planning project, Gorky designed paintings for Newark airport, and Stuart Davis provided a fresco for the 1939 World's Fair in New York—at which Guston was commissioned to paint a mural for the façade of the WPA pavilion. The obligatory subject was *Maintaining America's Skills* (ill. 28). The workers Guston painted—a scientist, a foreman, a mechanic, a farmer—met the mural's specifications.

GUERNICA

The political tensions that were rending the world reached an America that was pinning its hopes for social peace on economic growth. December 1937 brought "An exhibition in defense of world Democracy: Dedicated to the people of Spain and China" in New York. The event was organized by the American Artists' Congress, founded by the Communist Party in 1936 and devoted to supporting the Spanish people, victims of the civil war, and China, threatened by Japanese aggression. In a telephone message, Pablo Picasso addressed the organizers: "Artists who live and work with spiritual values cannot and should not remain indifferent to a conflict in which the highest values of humanity and civilization are at stake."[26] In addition to his statement, he supported the exhibition by displaying the plates from his *Dream and Lie of Franco* series of prints. For the first time Guston was to be found alongside Picasso: his

25
George Biddle, quoted in Dore Ashton, *The New York School: A Cultural Reckoning*, New York: Viking, 1973, p. 46.
26
See "Chronology of the Artist's Life": https://reader.digitalbooks.pro/content/preview/books/128403/book/OEBPS/Text/gm_picasso_eng_split_003.html

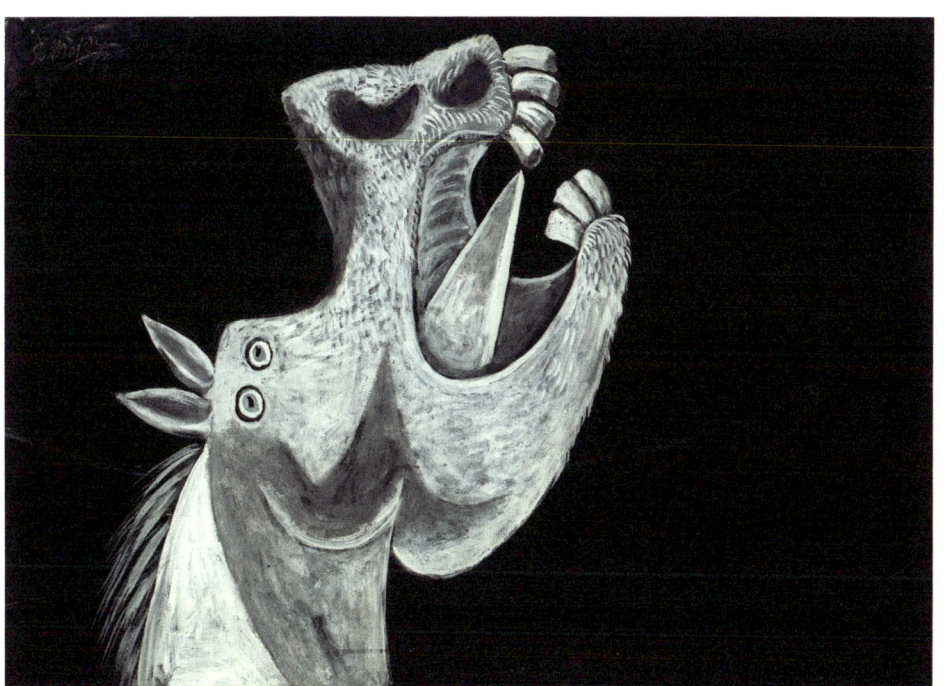

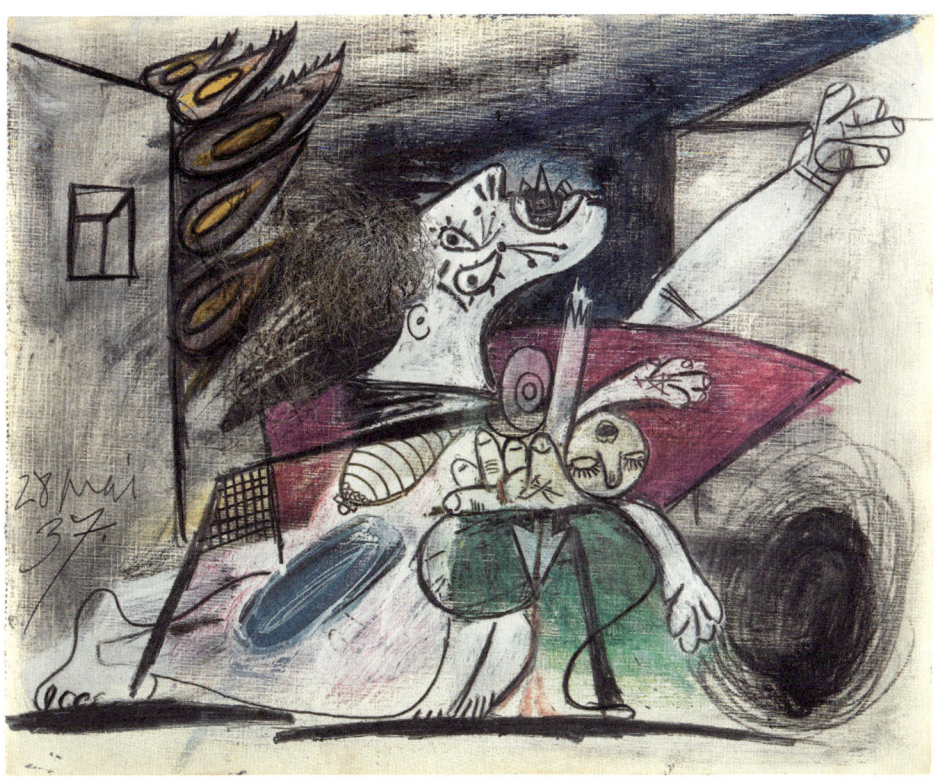

11 — Pablo Picasso, *Horse Head. Sketch for "Guernica,"* 1937. Oil on canvas, 65×92 cm. Museo Nacional Centro de Arte Reina Sofía, Madrid

12 — Pablo Picasso, *Mother with Dead Child (IV). Sketch for "Guernica,"* 1937. Graphite, gouache, collage and crayons on tracing paper, 23.1×29.2 cm. Museo Nacional Centro de Arte Reina Sofía, Madrid

Bombardment was inspired by the destruction of Basque villages by the German air force (ill. 13).

After *Dream and Lie*, Guston discovered *Guernica* (Reina Sofía Museum, Madrid) in 1939, when it was shown in various American cities as part of a fundraising "tour" for Spain's Republican government. *Guernica* convinced Guston that a "militant" work could convey a political message without resorting to literal illustration. Poetically and politically, the allegory and the myth interwoven in this great painting proved more effective than documentary realism. For many American artists, *Guernica* was the antidote to realism, to the neoclassicism of Rivera, and to the expressionism of Orozco and Siqueiros. This revelation of the powers of allegory and myth was reinforced in 1939 by Guston's discovery of the work of Max Beckmann at the Buchholz Gallery in New York. The German painter also used mythology and allegory to translate the tragedy of history.

Psychologically devastated at the end of World War I, Beckmann had dealt with his trauma by making the violence of war look like a children's fight (ill. 14). In 1940, when war had just broken out in Europe, Guston resorted to a similar transposition. Children turned into "gladiators" became the message-bearers of his anguish (ill. 15).

In the early 1940s Guston felt the need to escape the demands and the hustle and bustle of New York. Bent on absorbing the lessons learnt from Beckmann and Picasso, he left the city to take refuge in the artists' colony in Woodstock. It was here that he produced the work he considered his first success (to be taken as meaning his first truly personal easel painting): *Martial Memory* (ill. 16).

From *Guernica*, *Martial Memory* retained the shades of gray and the geometric volumes of folded paper headgear that punctuate the work. From Beckmann it borrowed the "compression" of entangled figures. While *Gladiators* still tended toward a flatness inherited from Cubism, *Martial Memory* no longer hesitated to reclaim the space, the illusionistic depth, in which Beckmann saw "the palace of the gods."[27]

INTERIOR EXILE

In 1942 Guston, twenty-eight years old, accepted a teaching position at the State University of Iowa in Iowa City, in the heart of the Midwest. He had just completed his last mural, *Reconstruction and The Well-Being of the Family* (ill. 37), for the auditorium of the Social Security Building in Washington D.C. America had been at war since December 7, 1941. For *Fortune* magazine, he created a series of gouaches to illustrate an article on the defense industry and air force training programs (ill. 18).

These gouaches were Guston's last ties to the world and its progress, which he had hitherto insisted on approaching as a witness. Introspection, withdrawal, and immersion in the history of art were the hallmarks of the works he undertook in Iowa City. This "Athens of America," as it was characterized by Regionalist painting apologist

27
"For, in the beginning was space, that frightening and unthinkable invention of the Force of the Universe. Time is the invention of mankind; space or volume, the palace of the Gods." Max Beckmann, "Letters to a Woman Painter," quoted in Peter Selz, *Max Beckmann*, New York: Museum of Modern Art, 1964, p. 94.

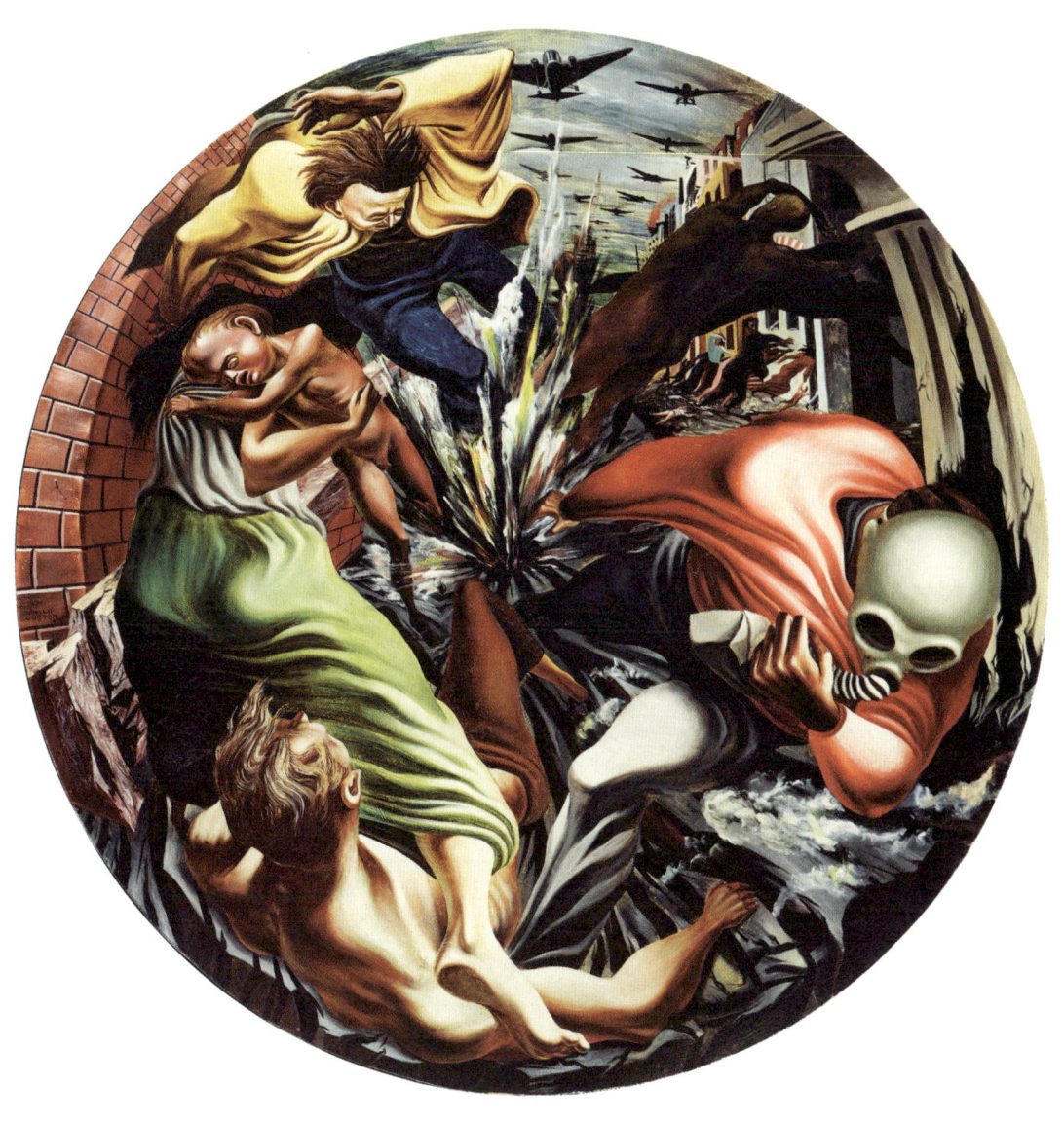

13 — *Bombardment*, 1937. Oil on Masonite, diam. 106.7 cm. Philadelphia Museum of Art

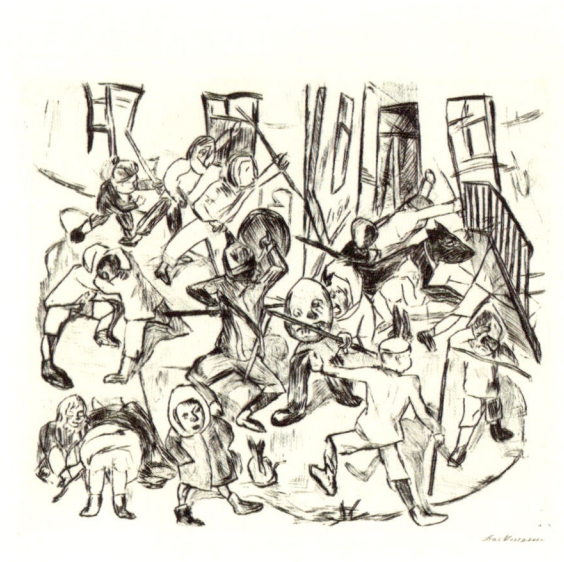

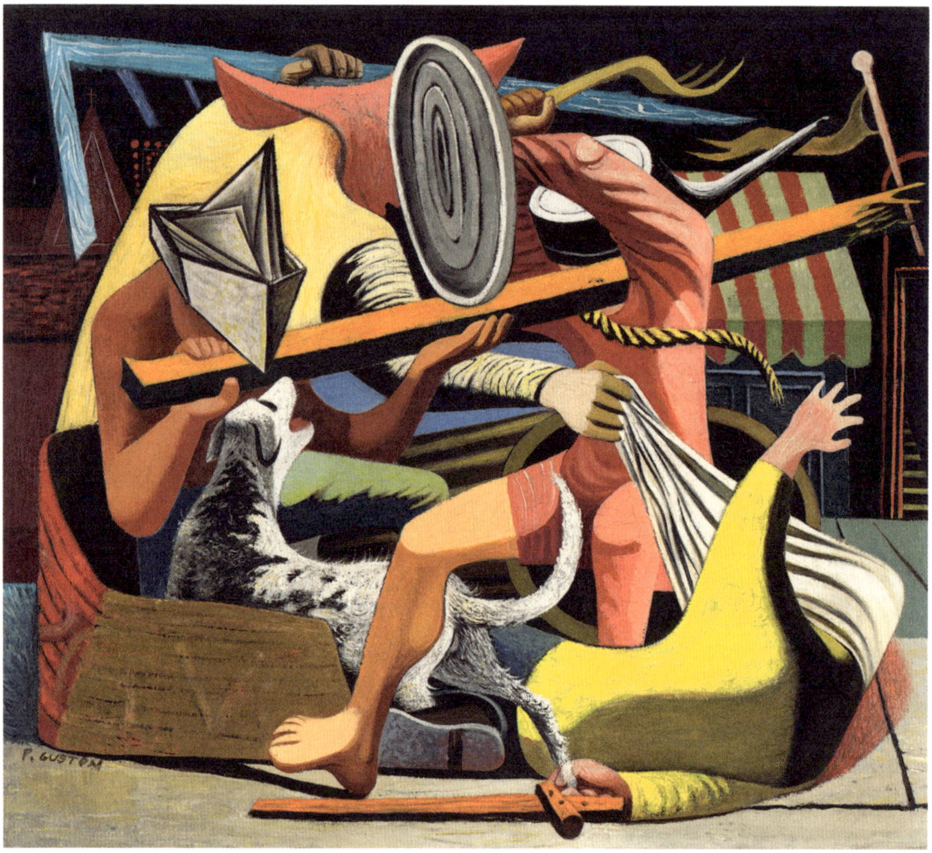

14 — Max Beckmann, *Playing Children*, 1918. Drypoint on laid paper, 37 × 36.9 cm. Sprengel Museum Hannover

15 — *Gladiators*, 1940. Oil and pencil on canvas, 62.2 × 71.4 cm. MoMA, New York

Grant Wood, gave rise in him to a deep depression. Wood, who had preceded Guston in his teaching post from 1934 to 1941, had made the city the epicenter of an aesthetic that condemned "European cultural colonialism" and extolled the virtues of rural America.[28] Iowa City had become a bastion of resistance to the values brought by the European modernists exiled to the United States by the war. In the heart of this conservative America Guston, deprived of the stimulating cut and thrust of New York's Cedar Tavern in Greenwich Village, was overcome by a melancholy whose history and iconographic potential he explored in his assiduous reading of the works of Erwin Panofsky.[29] (A reproduction of Dürer's *Melancholy* would feature in the little imaginary museum he set up in the kitchen of his Woodstock home.) Guston's figures set against the backdrop of the neoclassical theater set of Iowa City's Main Street are marked by worried, bored gazes receding into the void (ill. 19).

In what looked to him like a "Potemkin city," he experienced the strangeness and absurdity of the world described in Kafka's *The Trial* and *The Castle*. The arcades of Iowa City's buildings reminded him of de Chirico's paintings from another war, executed in the solitude of a barracks in Ferrara. *Sanctuary* (1944), the climax of this alienation, is the image of a seemingly infinite insomnia, of a melancholy bordering on breakdown (ill. 21).

If This Be Not I, dating from 1945 (ill. 17), is an erudite, crepuscular condensation of Guston's feelings about his stay—his exile?—in Iowa City. Its complex combination of children's games with memories of Piero della Francesca—those columns reminiscent of the *Flagellation of Christ*—and Beckmann's bodies compressed by the picture space, transposes, once again, the anguish triggered in Guston by the shadow of war. While the African masks and cut-out or folded newspapers are reminiscent of Picasso, the tawdry actors and kings in the painting inevitably call up the actors and acrobats of Beckmann's triptychs. With its silvery tones, its palette combining evanescence and vivid punctuations, and its melancholy theatricality, *If This Be Not I* is also indebted to Tiepolo and Watteau.

The title of the painting gives it its psychological "coloring." Guston's wife Musa suggested the title of a ditty inspired by the fairy tales of Charles Perrault, recounting the story of an old woman who has lost her identity. Fear, bewilderment, and the quest for meaning to be wrested from the dark realm of history shape *If This Be Not I*.

Interviewed in 1943 by *Art News* magazine about his work as a muralist, Guston declared: "I would rather be a poet than a pamphleteer."[30] Traumatized by the anxieties precipitated by the echo of world events and overwhelmed by loneliness, he had misgivings about the project of social emancipation that had hitherto driven his work and given it meaning. His facial expression in a self-portrait from 1944 testifies to this bewilderment, making him the double of Watteau's haggard *Gilles* (ill. 20).

28
See Wood's 1935 essay, "Revolt Against the City", https://interarts.org/ CW%20Wood%20 Essay%20Revolt.pdf
29
See, for example, Raymond Klibansky, Erwin Panofsky, and Fritz Saxl, *Saturn and Melancholy*, New York: Basic Books, 1964.
30
Dore Ashton, *Philip Guston*, op. cit., p. 61.

The erudite, complex, sentimental paintings produced by Guston in Iowa earned him his first critical successes, among them the Carnegie Prize, the highest American distinction awarded to a painter.

BACK TO BEDLAM

On January 15th, 1945, an exhibition of Guston's Iowa City paintings opened at the Midtown Gallery in New York. Back with Pollock, Gorky, and de Kooning after his long period of isolation, he saw their work as the antithesis of the learned historicism of his recent canvases. During the war years, the New York artists had absorbed the lessons of the Europeans: the automatism of Masson, Ernst, and Matta, and the plunge into the personal or collective unconscious summoned by Surrealism, had liberated their gestures, sparking an emergence of forms that no longer owed anything to the museum ethos. Pollock, who had just painted pictures in which "ideograms," evenly distributed across the canvas, announced the lineaments of the "drippings" to come, made a point of letting Guston know just what he thought of his recent paintings. Stephen Greene, one of Guston's former students in Iowa City, recounted how, on the evening of the opening of the Midtown Gallery exhibition, "Pollock wandered in, ragingly drunk, and upbraided Philip for some form of aesthetic betrayal."[31]

In their excessiveness Pollock's reproaches underscored the divergent trajectories of Guston's work and that of his New York friends during the war years. However, the impassioned discussions he returned to in bars and studios soon tore him away from his melancholy and the nostalgia of his aesthetic reveries.

The photograph illustrating *Life* magazine's article on Guston in May 1946 shows him standing at an easel with a painting that, with its almost abstract character and rigorous flatness, stands in stark contrast to the Iowa paintings (ill. 191). Answering a journalist's question about the work that won him the Carnegie Prize, Guston disappointed the interviewer, describing it as "too literal." *Life* had no choice but to headline the article, "Carnegie Prize winner is abstract and symbolic." A new page had been turned.

With this fresh episode in his artistic "counterlife," Guston let down those who had seen him as one of the most promising painters on the American scene, and disappointed both the market and the collectors who had pledged to support his work.

SAINT LOUIS

In retrospect, Guston would describe his two years in Saint Louis, Missouri, where Washington University offered him a teaching post, as a "breakdown." During this period of profound questioning, as with the one he had gone through in the late 1920s, it was Picasso's work that opened up new avenues for him. He studied paintings by the Spanish artist in the collections of Vladimir Golschmann, conductor of the Saint Louis Symphony Orchestra, and Saint Louis-based press

31
Musa Mayer, *Night Studio*, op. cit., p. 37.

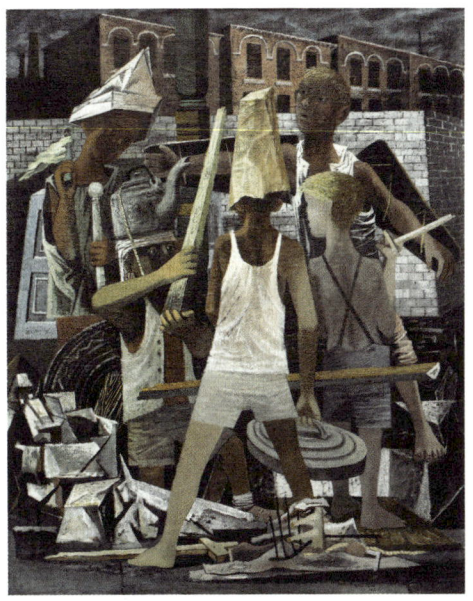

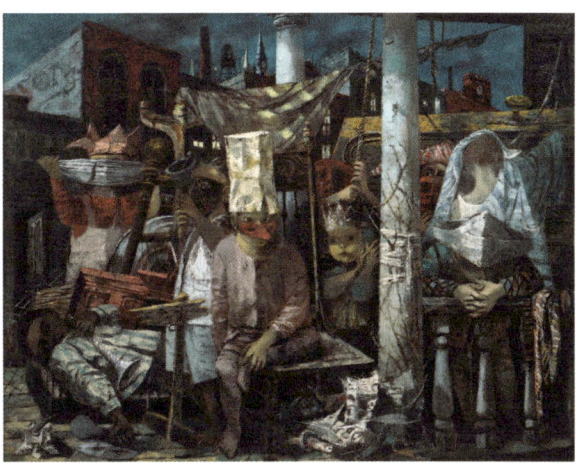

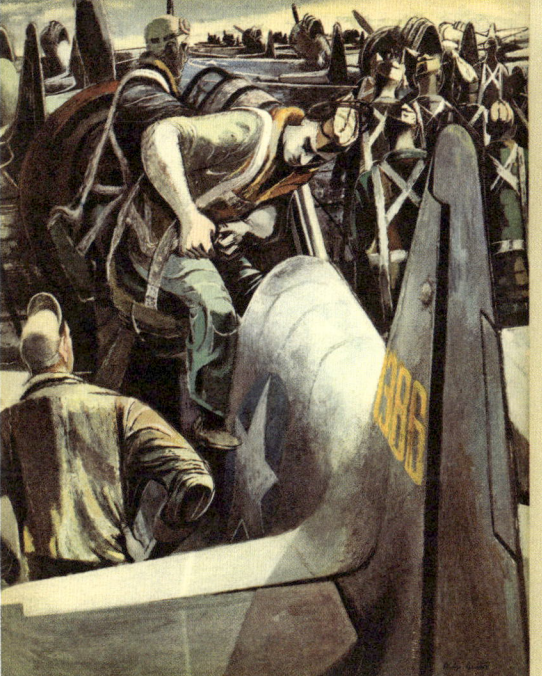

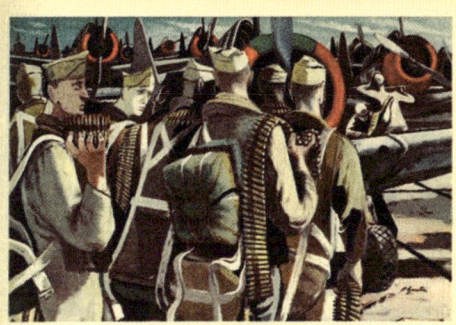

16 — *Martial Memory*, 1941. Oil on canvas, 101.9 × 81.9 cm. Saint Louis Art Museum
17 — *If This Be Not I*, 1945. Oil on canvas, 107.3 × 140.3 cm. Mildred Lane Kemper Art Museum,
Washington University in Saint Louis
18 — *Fortune*, "The Air Training Program," February 1944, *Advanced Fighter Training*
and *The Air Training Program (Advanced Pilot Training)*, 1943. Private collection

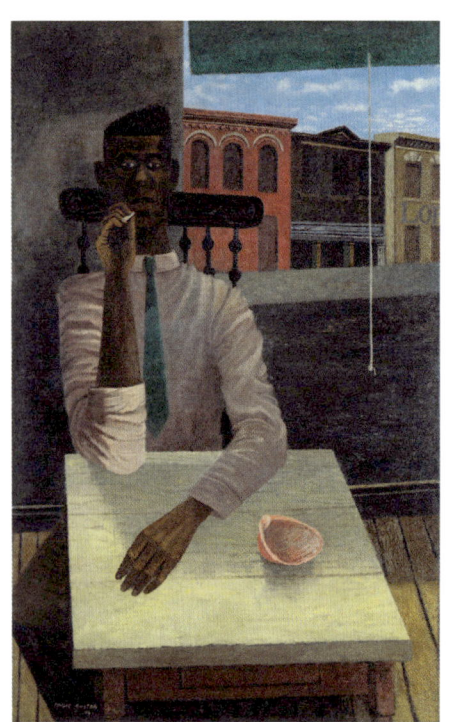

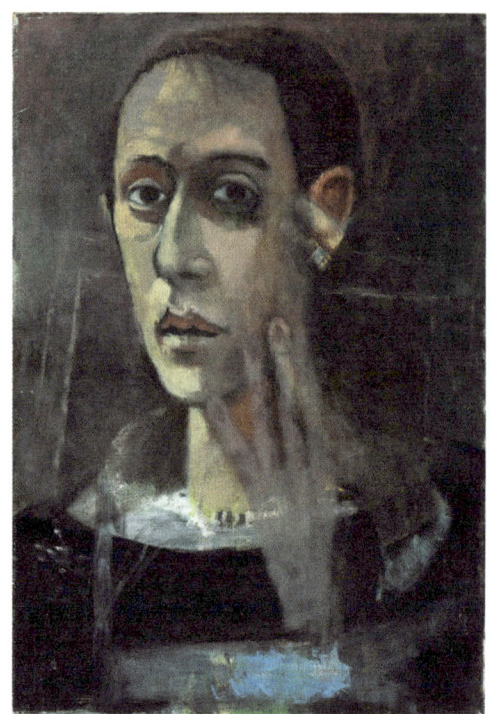

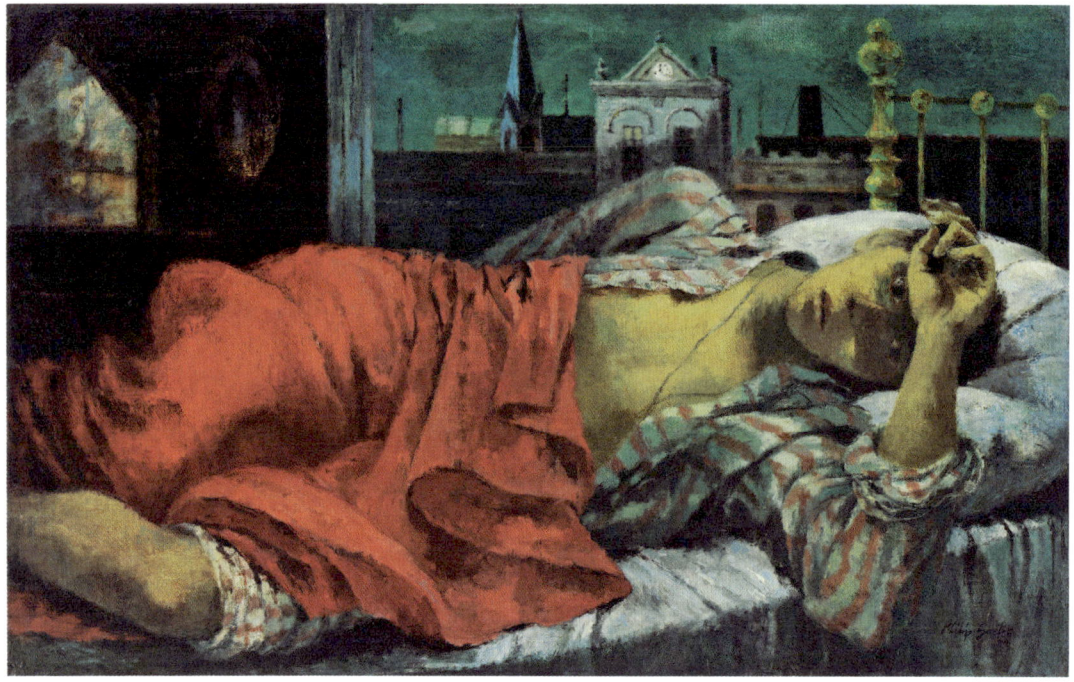

19 — *Sunday Interior*, 1941. Oil on canvas, 96.5 × 61 cm. Private collection

20 — *Self Portrait*, 1944. Oil on canvas, 66 × 45.7 cm

21 — *Sanctuary*, 1944. Oil on canvas, 56.2 × 91.1 cm

baron Joseph Pulitzer Jr. From Cubism Guston borrowed a palette reduced to a few hues (red, black, yellow), a rigorous geometry, and a two-dimensionality that integrated his figures into a pictorial order devoid of depth (ill. 22).

While the memory of Beckmann hovers over his claustrophobic compositions, the images of the Nazi camps discovered by Guston and America also played their part. The figures in *The Porch II* embody a malaise, an anguish, fueled by the horror of Holocaust images that left an enduring mark on his imagination (ill. 23). Years later, the piles of legs and shoes would reappear obsessively in his pictures.

The "breakdown" that Guston associated with his stay in Saint Louis came to an end in the spring of 1947, when he left Missouri for New York. Rather than a lull, this interlude was the moment of a transformation: one that would lead his painting down the path of abstraction.

MAVERICK ROAD

Guston returned to live in Woodstock, where his New York friends filled him in on the effervescent New York art scene. Having definitively turned its back on the conservative values of the prewar Regionalist painters, America was celebrating the generation of artists who had taken up the torch of European modernity. "The main premises of Western art," wrote Clement Greenberg, New York's most influential critic, "have at last migrated to the United States . . . . [along with] political power."[32]

In 1948 William Baziotes, Mark Rothko, and Clyfford Still set up "The Club" on 8th Street as a venue for artistic practice and ideas. Every Friday guest speakers, including Hannah Arendt, John Cage, and Harold Rosenberg, commented on the state of the world and the arts. Guston's Woodstock neighbor, the painter Bradley Walker Tomlin, an abstractionist inspired by Oriental art, acted as an intermediary between Guston and the new energy driving New York's artistic community. As if echoing the formal radicalism being invented at the Club, and despite a subject still imbued with memories of the horrors of war, Guston's *The Tormentors* (1947–48) is figurative only in its title (ill. 24).

Guston's visit to Italy in October 1948 had no effect on the trajectory of his art toward radical abstraction. Neither Piero's frescoes, nor those of the Lorenzetti brothers and Masaccio, diverted him from an abstraction that had become inexorable. From his stay in Italy he brought back just a few drawings, one of which, inspired by the island of Ischia, reduces its subject in the Bay of Naples to a grid that looks as if it has been lifted from a Mondrian work of the 1910s (ill. 25).

Back in the United States, Guston became convinced that his painting needed the spirit of stimulation that fired the Greenwich Village artists' community. For a time he shared a studio with Tomlin, before settling on 10th Street, close to the Cedar Tavern and the Club, whose minutes testify to his active participation in its debates.

32
Clement Greenberg, "The Decline of Cubism," *Partisan Review*, May 1948, p. 139.

The abstract asceticism he imposed on his art culminated in *Red Painting* (1950), reduced to a set of perpendicular strokes. Presented at MoMA, the work was likened by critics to an "abyss" and a "point of no return."[33]

In the course of endless discussions, the Club artists mulled over the meaning and purpose of the painting being invented in their studios. In the winter of 1952 de Kooning put forward a hypothesis whose assumptions were shared by all the participants in the debate, Guston included. De Kooning cited as an example van Gogh's potato paintings, in which he saw "open-ended," perpetually changing forms.

Among the art historians Guston had discovered during his time in Iowa City was Henri Focillon, whose *Life of Forms* (1934) he pondered at length. In an organic, materialist history of art, Focillon posited the development of forms which invent their own laws, in dynamic interaction with the historical context in which they flourish. From the self-generation of forms, deducible from Focillon's writings, to the Surrealist automatism reinvented in New York, Guston forged the idea of a self-sufficient art born of its technical and material conditions.

His biographers note that in the late 1940s, "the idea of art as *process* began to obsess him."[34] *White Painting II* of 1951 (ill. 38) is the fruit of this method and its postulation of growth and metamorphosis: "The desire for direct expression finally became so strong that even the interval necessary to reach back to the palette beside me became too long; so one day I put up a canvas and placed the palette in front of me. Then I forced myself to paint the entire work without stepping back to look at it. I remember that I painted this in an hour."[35] This narrative could have been made by Pollock to account for the realization of his *drippings*. It literally transcribes the definition of "action painting," that "direct expression," that existentialism in action, theorized by Harold Rosenberg to define the art of the painters of the New York School.

While Existentialism, championed by Rosenberg during discussions at the Club, was a major philosophical reference for artists of the New York School, it was Eastern thought that Guston favored in his works of the early 1950s. "It's wonderful to be able to paint about *nothing*,"[36] remarked composer John Cage when confronted with Guston's recent paintings. Cage's "nothing" references the "void" he made the alpha and omega of his own work—including that of his composition *4'33"*, which consists in rendering all music silent for the time imposed by the score. Fascinated by Zen Buddhism, Cage communicated his passion to Guston when the painter and the musician met in Rome. Later, in discussions at the Club, they pursued their exchanges, fueling them with lectures on Zen Buddhism given at Columbia University by Professor Suzuki. A close friend of Cage's, Morton Feldman became one of Guston's closest companions.

33
H. H. Arnason, *Philip Guston*, exhibition catalog, New York: Solomon R. Guggenheim Museum, 1962, p. 20.
34
Robert Storr, *Philip Guston: A Life Spent Painting*, London, Laurence King Publishing, 2020, p. 25.
35
Guston, quoted in Robert Storr, *Philip Guston*, op. cit., p. 25.
36
John Cage quoted in Robert Storr, *Philip Guston*, op. cit., p. 31.

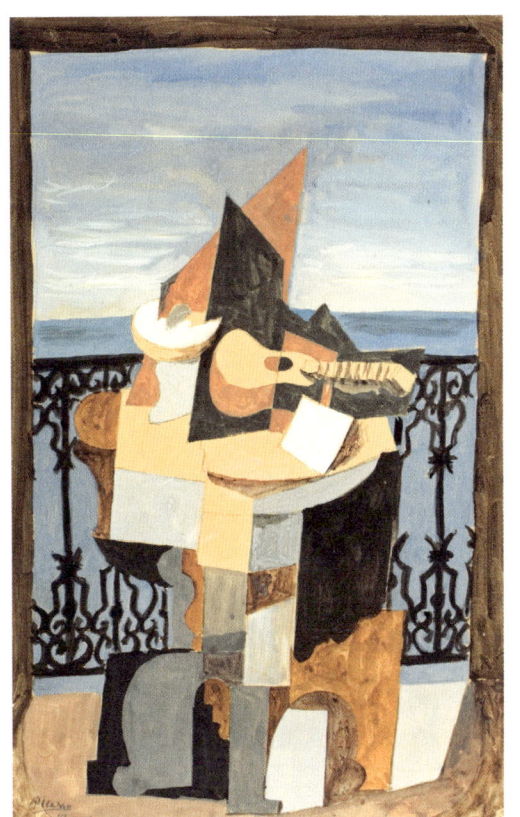
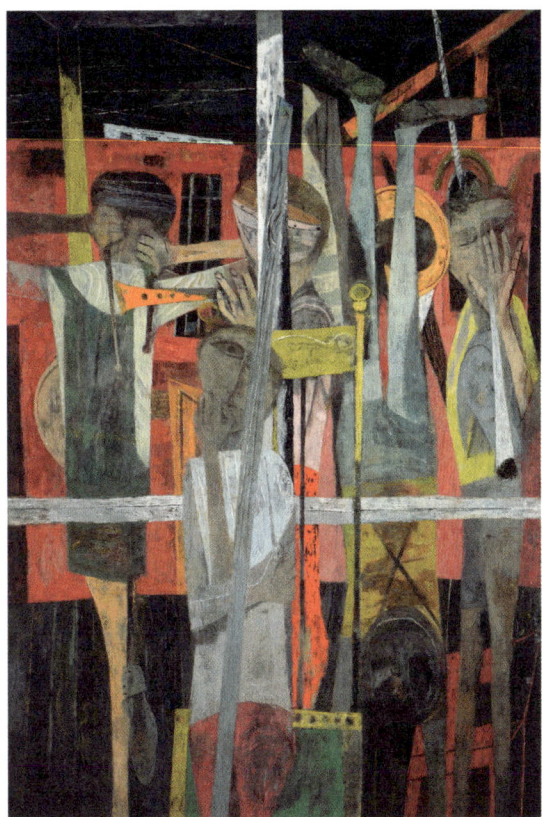

22 — Pablo Picasso, *Still Life on a Pedestal Table in Front of a Window*, 1919.
Gouache and pencil on paper, 49×30.9 cm. Los Angeles County Museum of Art
23 — *The Porch II*, 1947. Oil on canvas, 158.8×109.2 cm. Munson Museum of Art

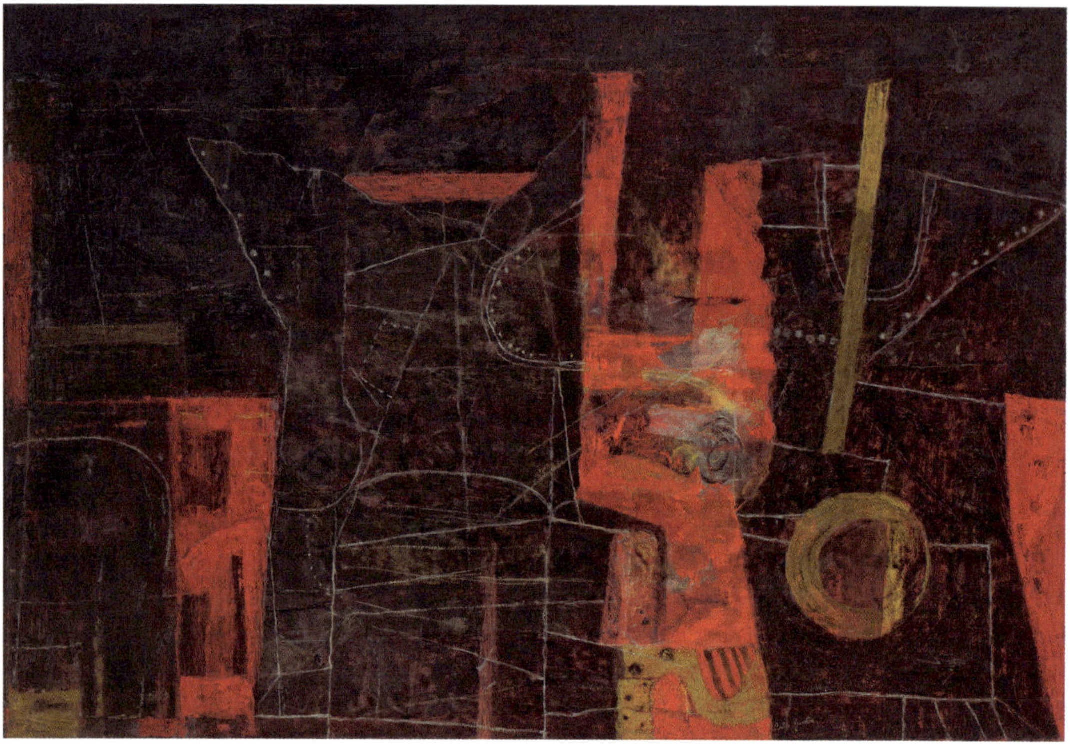

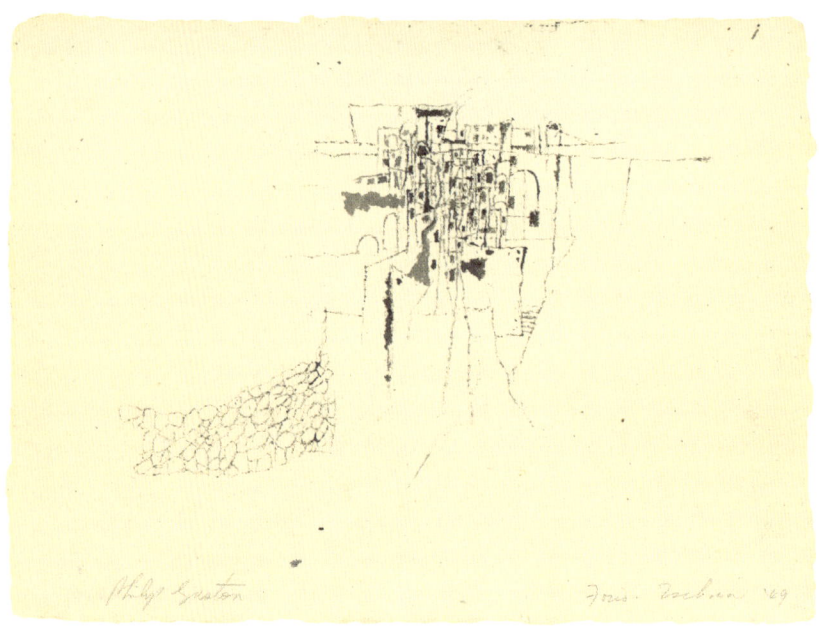

24 — *The Tormentors*, 1947–48. Oil on canvas, 103.84×153.67 cm. San Francisco
Museum of Modern Art

25 — *Drawing No. 2 (Ischia)*, 1949. Ink on paper, 27.9×38.1 cm

In his musical compositions, he too bears witness to his interest in the "void" of Zen Buddhism.

Whether it refers to Eastern *emptiness*, or submits to the principle of *self-purification* to which Greenberg invites it, American painting was striving to get closer to its essence.[37] It was at this point in its history, when American painting was aspiring to its most ethereal manifestation, that de Kooning and Guston reacted to this asceticism. Comparing painting to a "stew," de Kooning said he only liked surfaces that are "greasy and juicy."[38] When Morton Feldman praised the whiteness of his paintings, Guston told him he only worked with "colored dust." Years later, he would return to this moment in the art of the 1950s: "There is something ridiculous and miserly in the myth we inherit from abstract art. That painting is autonomous, pure and for itself, therefore we habitually analyze its ingredients and define its limits. But painting is 'impure'. It is the adjustment of 'impurities' which forces its continuity."[39]

His fascination with the Zen "void" had come to an end. His brushstrokes gained in density, prompting critic Paul Brach to write of his "searching and extremely tactile brush work."[40] His color evolved from "impressionistic" strokes to flat tints that converged on the center of his canvases, sketching what increasingly resembled "figures" that stood out against a background. Finally, the titles he gives his paintings, such as *Fable, The Mirror, Cythera*, and *The Clock*, suggest narratives and figures.

Despite the figurative impulse in his work, Guston remained an abstract painter and a central figure in the New York School. He joined the Sidney Janis Gallery, whose stable included Kline, Pollock, and Rothko. His paintings were included in the *New American Painting* exhibition, which toured European capitals and officialized the worldwide "triumph of the New York School."[41] In 1962 Guston's work was the subject of a major retrospective at the Guggenheim in New York.[42] Its curator, H. H. Arnason, remarked that "Guston's painting has become a stage on which figure-forms play comedy or tragedy."[43] For Harold Rosenberg, the painting of the Abstract Expressionists was comparable to an "arena," within which the painter played out his existence. In the early 1960s, Guston transformed this arena into a theater stage, a movie screen. In a renunciation of color, broad strokes of gray were amassed in his compositions, to become what he described as his "last mask" (ill. 26).

In 1966, the Jewish Museum in New York presented Guston's most recent works. The exhibition's critical reception reflected the weariness of the American art world with a painting style rendered obsolete by the changing sensibilities evidenced by the emergence of Pop art. New York yawned with boredom at the countless canvases featuring the "10th Street touch," the vehement brushstrokes emblematic of what had become Abstract Expressionism.[44] In *The New York Times*, Hilton Kramer denounced the "much-repeated

37
"Thereby each art would be rendered 'pure', and in its 'purity' find the guarantee of its standards of quality as well as its independence. 'Purity' meant self-definition, and the enterprise of self-critism in the arts became one of self-defintion with a vengeance." Clement Greenberg, "Modernist Painting" [1965], reprinted in Francis Frascina and Charles Harrison (eds.), *Modern Art and Modernism: A Critical Anthology*, New York: Harper & Row, 1982.
38
Quoted in Thomas B. Hess, "De Kooning Paints a Picture," *Art News* 52, March 1953, p. 33.
39
Guston in 1960, quoted in Robert Storr, *Philip Guston*, op. cit., p. 34.
40
Paul Brach on Guston's 1953 exhibition at the Egan Gallery, quoted in Dore Ashton, *Philip Guston*, op. cit., p. 101.
41
The Triumph of American Painting is the title of a 1970 book by art historian Irwin Sandler.
42
After New York, the exhibition went on to Amsterdam, London, Brussels, and Los Angeles.
43
H. H. Arnason, *Philip Guston*, op. cit., p. 35.
44
A "mannerism" mocked by Roy Lichtenstein with his *Brushstrokes*.

visual vocabulary" of Guston's paintings, and their content as "so limited in range of feeling."[45]

A new chapter began in New York. De Kooning left the city to set up his studio in East Hampton. Pollock had died in 1956, Kline in 1962. Guston in turn quit Manhattan: in 1967, he moved permanently to Woodstock. This time, there was no turning back.

ONE-WAY TICKET TO WOODSTOCK

After tirelessly reproducing everyday objects, Guston amassed hooded figures, old shoes, childlike cars, and electric light bulbs, becoming a stage director and storyteller. "The paintings came so fast I had to make memos to myself, at a table drinking coffee. 'Paint them.' I felt like a movie director, like opening a Pandora's Box and all those things came out."[46] After two years of intense work, thirty-three of his paintings and eight of his recent drawings were ready to be exhibited at the Marlborough Gallery.

The exhibition scandalized the New York art world. Critic Hilton Kramer reflected the general feeling, titling his review "A Mandarin Pretending to be a Stumblebum" and commenting, "Mr. Guston is clearly seeking such a rejuvenation in turning to the popular visual slang of the old cartoonists as the basis of a new pictorial style."[47]

Inspired by press cartoons and comic strips, Guston's "new pictorial style" was akin to that of Pop Art, the sworn enemy of Abstract Expressionism. The indignation provoked by his paintings was not, however, due solely to their form. In a "self-portrait," he shows himself in his studio, his head covered with a Klan hood. Identifying himself with the Klansmen, Guston insidiously connected the "modern" painter, the avant-garde artist he had been until then, with the Klan torturers.

In his view, the reactions to his paintings justified his daring short-circuit: "I've been struck, because of certain developments of my thinking and painting which have occurred over recent years and the reception of this work, with how bigoted, which maybe isn't the right word, or how doctrinaire the so-called modern movement is."[48]

The hooded artist surrendering to the forces of "evil" is an allegory of tragic disillusionment. It is similar to that described by Walter Benjamin, who made Paul Klee's *Angelus Novus* the emblem of progress, of a time of hope, set in motion by a storm "caught in his wings with such violence that the angel can no longer close them. The storm irresistibly propels him into the future to which his back is turned, while the pile of debris before him grows skyward. This storm is what we call progress."[49]

That a monument of culture can also be a monument of barbarism, as Benjamin would again write, is what the modern artist ironically says as a Klansman: "My attempt was really not to illustrate, to do pictures of the KKK, as I had done earlier. The idea of evil fascinated me, and rather like Isaac Babel who had joined the Cossacks, lived

45
Hilton Kramer, "Art: Abstractions of Guston Still Further Refined," *The New York Times*, January 15, 1966.
46
Philip Guston, quoted in Robert Storr, *Philip Guston*, op. cit., p. 52.
47
Hilton Kramer, "A Mandarin Pretending To Be A Stumblebum," *The New York Times*, October 25, 1970.
48
Clark Coolidge (ed.), *Philip Guston, Collected Writings, Lectures and Conversations*, Los Angeles: University of California Press, 2011, p. 168.
49
Walter Benjamin, "Theses on the Philosophy of History," in *Illuminations*, trans. Harry Zohn, New York: Schocken Books, 1969, p. 249.

with them and written stories about them, I almost tried to imagine that I was living with the Klan."[50]

Tragedy and the irony of history transformed promises of emancipation into authoritarian dogma. The laughter that Guston's new paintings provoked was due to the explosive mixture and clash of opposing feelings out of which they were woven.

For Baudelaire, laughter stems from the telescoping of "an infinite grandeur and an infinite misery." The *grandeur* of Guston's paintings lies in their implacable form, inherited from Mondrian's geometry, Piero de la Francesca's compositions, and a painterly technique honed over years of abstract practice. Their *misery* is that of their characters, taken from the comic strips and the crass banality that provide their subjects.

Once again, Guston had burned his bridges. He was not afraid to set his art against the tide of the amiable, comforting complicity brought by commercial success.

His paintings, however, repelled even his closest friends. Morton Feldman rejected him: Guston's 1978 portrait explicitly shows Feldman turning away. The only one to escape the "prevailing bigotry" was de Kooning, who confided in him, "Do you know Philip what the real subject of your painting is? It's freedom!"[51]

THE BURROW

An apostate condemned to the solitude of his Woodstock "sanctuary," Guston dug his own burrow. "It feels strange to be completely cut off from the city. I feel like burrowing in again—to be a miner and not surface for a while."[52] As Philip Roth put it, "He couldn't leave the cave in which he hibernated because his nerves were too raw to work in the open air. He was too wounded."[53]

When asked to name his masters, Guston used to reply, "Dostoevsky and Kafka." From Dostoevsky he borrowed the fiction of the "underground man" cultivating his negativity, and from Kafka his fable of the *Burrow* dug by an animal that turns out to be the writer himself, shaping the labyrinth of his own thoughts. From this moment of crisis, in which his muses were paranoia and guilt, came *Studio Landscape* (ill. 152) and *Allegory*, which show the painter self-flagellating, or indulging in the vices of alcohol and tobacco (ill. 170).

The obsession with "purity" that Guston associated with modernism became the target of his new paintings. "American Abstract art is a lie, a sham, a cover-up for a poverty of spirit. A mask to mask the fear of revealing oneself. A lie to cover up how bad one can be. Unwilling to show this badness, this rawness. It is laughable, this lie. Anything but this! What a sham! Abstract art hides it, hides the lie, a *fake*! Don't! Let it show! It is an escape from the true feelings we have, from the 'raw,' primitive feelings about the world."[54] His antidote was what he called "crapola"—kitsch, the bad taste of popular culture.

50
Quoted in Robert Storr, *Philip Guston*, op. cit., p. 56.
51
Dore Ashton, *Philip Guston*, op. cit., p. 186.
52
Musa Mayer, *Night Studio*, op. cit., p. 173.
53
Quoted in Musa Mayer, Sally Radic, *Philip Guston, Nixon Drawings*, New York: Hauser & Wirth, 2017, p. 92.
54
Musa Mayer, *Night Studio*, op. cit., p. 170.

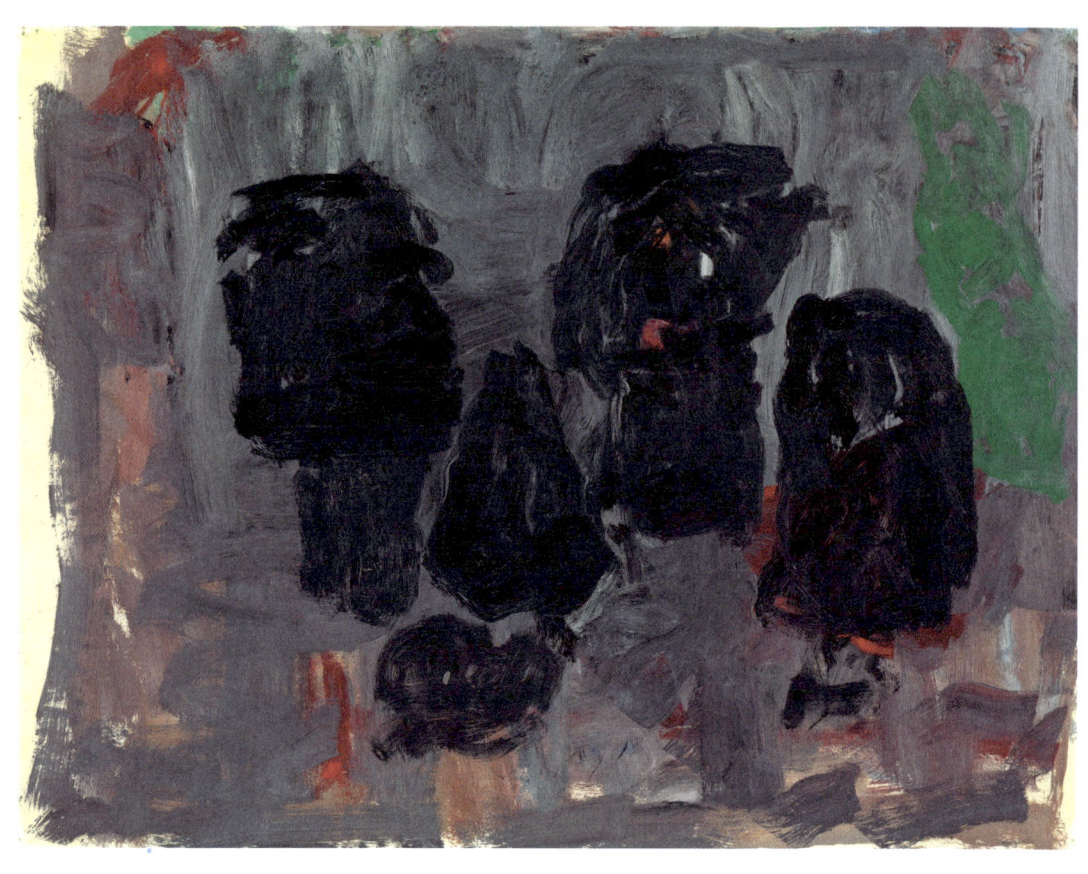

26 — *The Actors V*, 1962. Oil on paper mounted on panel, 76.2×101.6 cm.
Private collection, London

The years 1974 to 1979 were among Guston's most prolific. Never before had he painted with such ease. In 1976, he testified to his exaltation: "I've been painting around the clock, 24 hours or more—sleep a bit and go back—it is totally uncontrollable now.... Phone has been off for months and I look at mail only when a painting is done. They are large, ten feet or so, and take complete possession of me.... It is a new 'real' world now that I am making—and I can't stop."[55] *Painter's Forms II*, which shows the objects and forms of his painting gushing from the artist's mouth, evokes the overwhelming flood of images keeping him in the studio day and night: an outpouring matched only by that of Picasso's studio in the late 1960s, an invasion by an army of musketeers and swaggering burlesque characters from the Golden Age.

A first-hand witness to this frenzy, Philip Roth analyzed its psychological underpinnings: "Although painting monopolized just enough of his despair and seismic moodiness to make the anxiety of being himself something even he could sometimes laugh at, it never neutralized the nightmares entirely."[56]

In the early 1970s the torrent of images that swept away the work of two of the greatest figurative painters of the time resembled the "film" of an entire life; the life of a manner of painting abruptly passing from existence to death. At the time, painting was considered moribund. The musketeers Picasso pinned on the walls of the Papal Palace in Avignon in 1970 and 1973 outraged both artists and critics, who saw them as "calamitous daubs,"[57] and "Incoherent scribbles executed by a frantic old man in death's waiting room."[58] For the new generation of artists and critics, painting, as still practiced by Picasso and Guston, belonged to a bygone age.

THE DELUGE

Did Guston's melancholy stem from this "Russian soul," supposedly bequeathed to him by his Odessa ancestors? Discovering a new edition of Nadezhda Mandelstam's memoirs,[59] Guston could readily subscribe to this atavistic interpretation: "Madame Mandelstam should be believed when she speaks of the moral degradation of mankind and says that this degradation is devoid of national character and is not determined by concrete political processes. To justify existence, I repeat, Russian literature has done more than any other, and if a Russian writer says today that we are all criminals, it pays to listen carefully. When a Russian refuses consolation, it means that things are bad, it means that there really is no consolation. This is a book about how to live without consolation. Without consolation one can live only on love, memory and culture."[60]

The atrocities of the camps convinced Guston of the "moral degradation of mankind": "We are the witnesses of hell. When I think of the victims, it is unbearable.... To paint, to write, to teach in the most dedicated sincere way is the most intimate affirmation of creative life we possess."[61] The *Deluge* series expresses this "degradation." (ill. 171)

55
Ibid., p. 179.
56
Philip Roth, "Pictures by Guston," in *Shop Talk*, op. cit., p. 133.
57
Robert Hughes, *Time* magazine, June 18, 1973.
58
Douglas Cooper, *Connaissance des arts*, Paris, July 1973.
59
Wife of the poet Osip Mandelstam, victim of Stalinist terror, Nadezhda wrote her memoirs—*Hope Against Hope*—which were published in English in 1970.
60
Dore Ashton, *Philip Guston*, op. cit., pp. 177–78.
61
Philip Guston, in *Philip Guston: Nixon drawings*, op. cit., p. 95.

"Memory, culture and love" saturated the paintings piling up in his studio. Memory: the searing horror of the images of the camps, of the masses of shoes, of the bulldozed "heaps" of entangled bodies. Culture: memories of museum images, of Signorelli's swarming bodies of the damned, of those painted by Goya in his "deaf man's room".

The "seismic moodiness" that Philip Roth attributed to Guston drove the paintings of his last years, in which images of the utmost lyricism alternate with figures of annihilation and desolation. *Anxiety* (1975), *Melancholy Studio* (1977), *Martyr* (1978), *Solitary II* (1978), and the *Deluge* series reflect the depressive phase of this polarity, which is immediately contradicted by paintings that express the hope of new times: *Dawn* (1979) and *Sunrise* (1979) still want to believe in the possible salvation of *Ladder* (1978).

Wheel from 1980 (ill. 180) sums up this oscillation. It suggests an inspiration that begins at rock-bottom, elevates what it plucks from it, and projects it into the firmament. "To become an artist," Friedrich Schelling wrote, "means nothing other than to consecrate oneself to the subterranean divinities. In the enthusiasm of annihilation, the meaning of divine creation first reveals itself. Only in the midst of death is the spark of eternal light ignited."[62]

Guston brought together the cycles of his "cyclothymia" in a single image. *Above and Below* (1975) and *Pit* (1976) show how his painting recycles the most painful memories and "rock-bottom" values, and sets up their transmutation as a method.

Years of smoking and drinking—always that "Russian atavism," which convinced him for a time to treat his ailments with a cocktail of vodka and milk—had taken their toll on Guston's health. A violent heart attack in early 1979 left him hospitalized for several weeks. *East Coker-T.S.E.* (ill. 172) integrates the image of the painter as he "saw" himself, on the verge of death after a heart attack. "I wanted to paint a man dying, because that was what had happened to me."[63] Back in his "sanctuary," he complained that he could no longer paint big pictures. At the work table he was now confined to, he set about a series of twenty-six paintings on paper, the final chapter in his oeuvre.

Two years earlier,[64] he had declared: "I think in my studies and broodings about the art of the past my greatest ideal is Chinese painting, especially Song painting from about the 10th or 11th centuries. Song period training involves doing something thousands and thousands of times—bamboo shoots and birds—until someone else does it, not you, and the rhythm moves through you. I think this is what the Zen Buddhists called *satori*, and I have had it happen to me. It is a double activity, when you know and you don't know."[65]

His twenty-six paintings are indeed the result of a kind of *satori*. They are the culmination of "thousands and thousands" of drawings inspired by his old coffee pot, flat irons and rusty nails: trivial, everyday objects whose study had led him to a new figuration, whose

62
Quoted in James D. Reid, *Novalis: Philosophical, Literary, and Poetic Writings,* New York: Oxford University Press, 2024, p. 284.
63
Musa Mayer, *Night Studio,* op. cit., p. 237.
64
Lecture at the University of Minnesota.
65
Dore Ashton, *Philip Guston,* op. cit., p. 186.

form he synthesized to the point of reducing them to constructions as simple and monumental as the figures he admired in Piero della Francesca.

From this inventory of human banality emerged the motif of the slope, formed by the accumulation of discarded trash as a reminder of the rubbish dumps Guston and Roth enjoyed contemplating. A monumental sphere—Guston's own painting—"climbs" this ravine, aggregating as it goes old shoes and bent nails in a snowball effect.

Elsewhere, it was the bloated, patched-up heads of Guston's "self-portraits" that were making a comeback. During the 1950s, he had been an avid reader of Albert Camus, and his battered head, inseparable from its hill, was his version of the French novelist's "Myth of Sisyphus." Like the Greek hero, Guston endlessly climbed up and tumbled down the mountain of art (ill. 189), rummaging through the banality of reality for the forms and objects to be brought to light. The vivid brilliance of the ideal was enough to plunge him into the depths of the abyss. The endless cycle driven by his passion is the very movement of art.

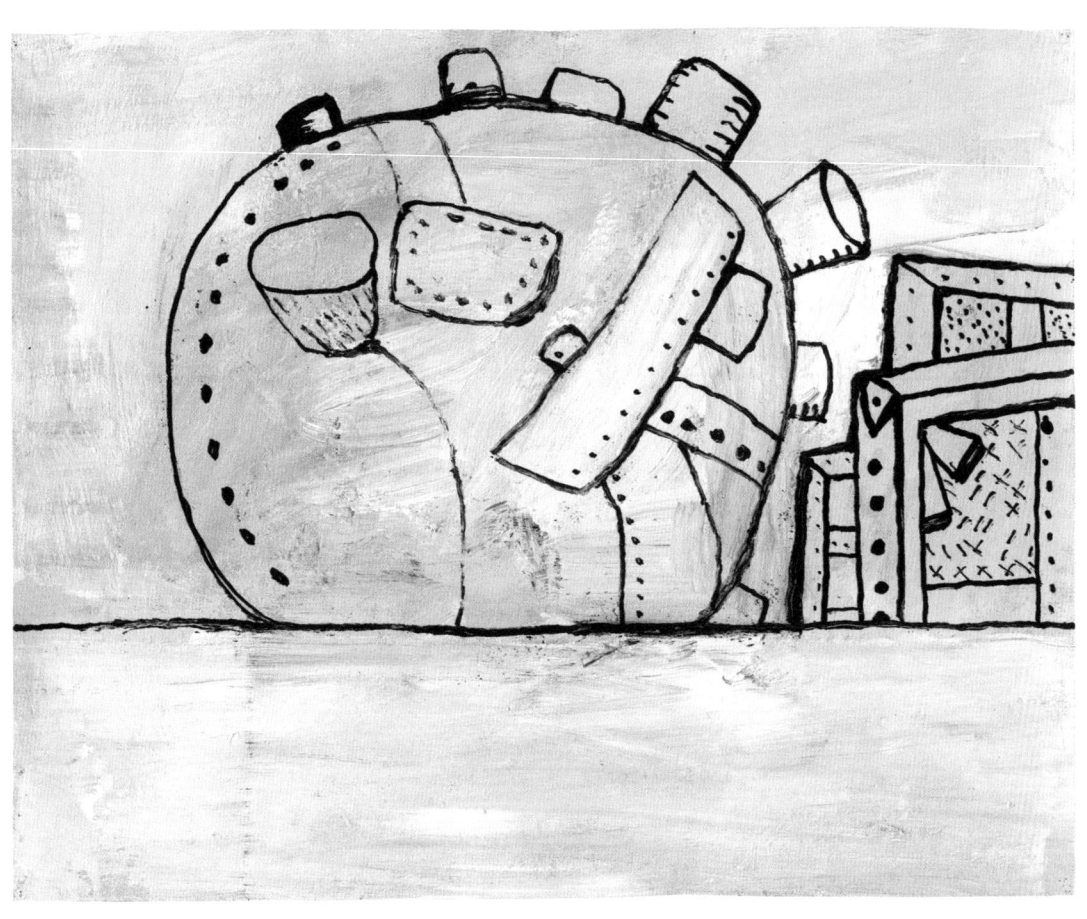

27 — *Untitled*, 1980. Acrylic and ink on paper, 57.1×74.9 cm

Murals

After leaving art school in Los Angeles, Philip Guston presented in 1931 a series of drawings in which he depicts for the first time members of the Ku Klux Klan and denounces the "judicial lynching" of the "Scottsboro Boys"—nine young African Americans wrongly accused of rape and sentenced to disproportionate prison terms and death. A year later, Mexican muralists José Clemente Orozco and David Alfaro Siqueiros were in California to create murals, and Guston followed every step of the process. With their support, he obtained a commission from the Mexican authorities for a large fresco, *The Struggle Against Terrorism* (ill. 29), a masterful warning against the rise of fascism in Europe and the United States. When the U.S. government set up a program to assist artists affected by the economic crisis—the Federal Art Project of the Works Progress Administration—Guston was commissioned to produce a series of murals extolling the virtues of the federal government's social policy. From then on, in whatever form it took, Guston's painting always had a political dimension, reflecting his social commitment. D. O.

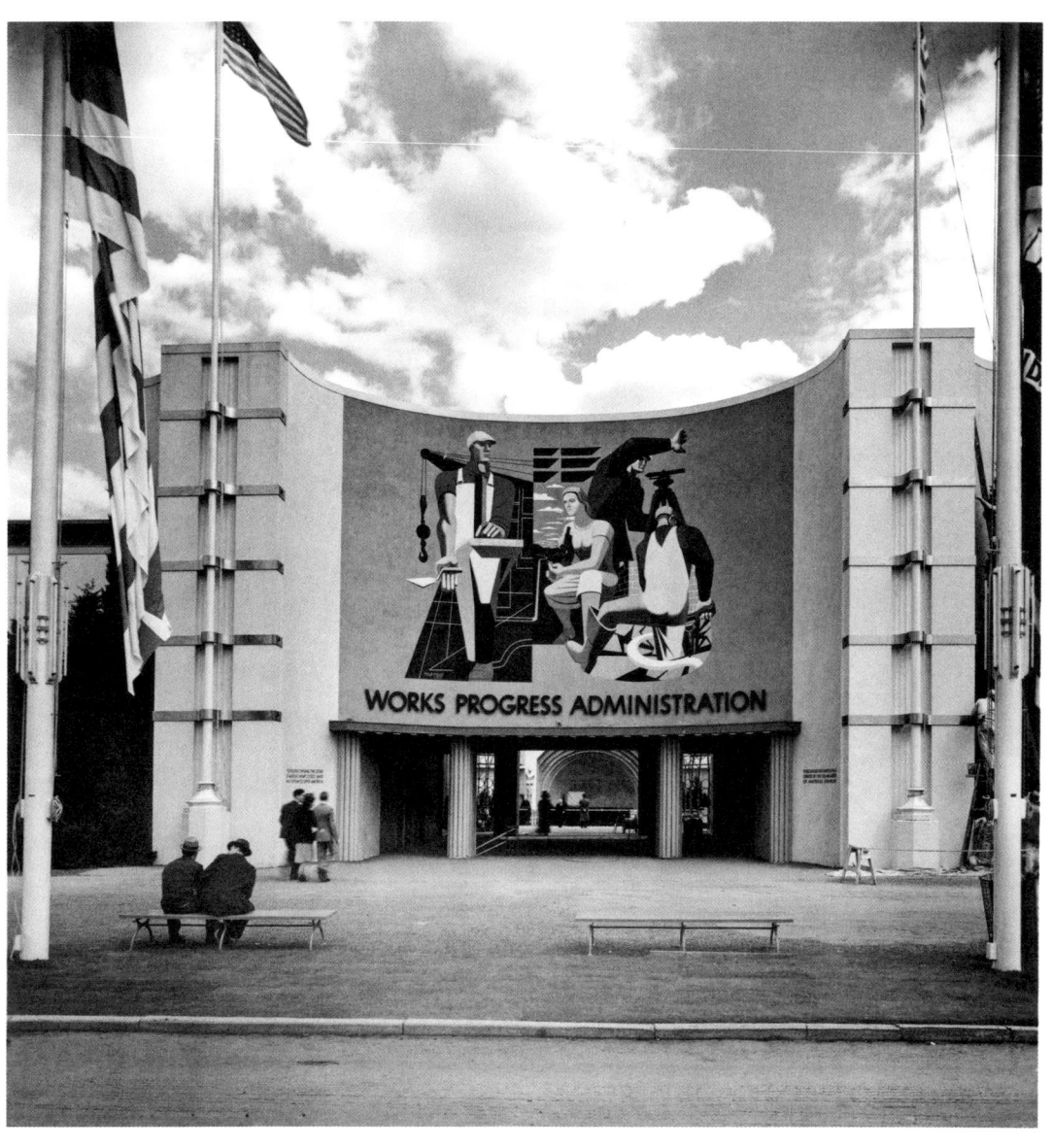

28 — David Robbins, *Chlorinated rubber paint on cement by Philip Guston "Work the American Way (Maintaining America's Skills),"* 1939. Courtesy of The Estate of Philip Guston Archives

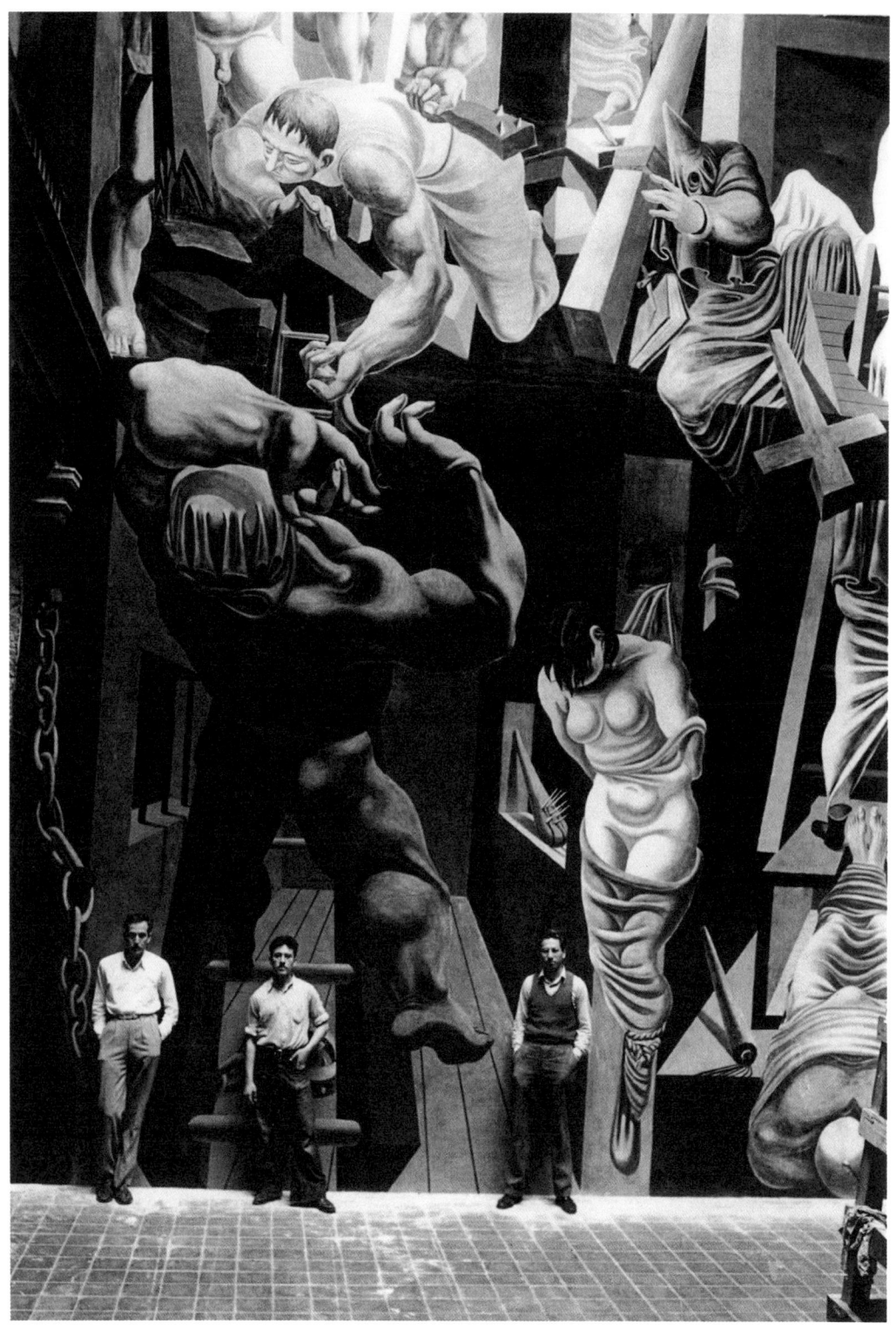

29 — *Philip Guston, Reuben Kadish and their friend Jules Langsner before the mural*
"The Struggle Against Terrorism," 1935. Museo Regional Michoacano, Morelia, Mexico

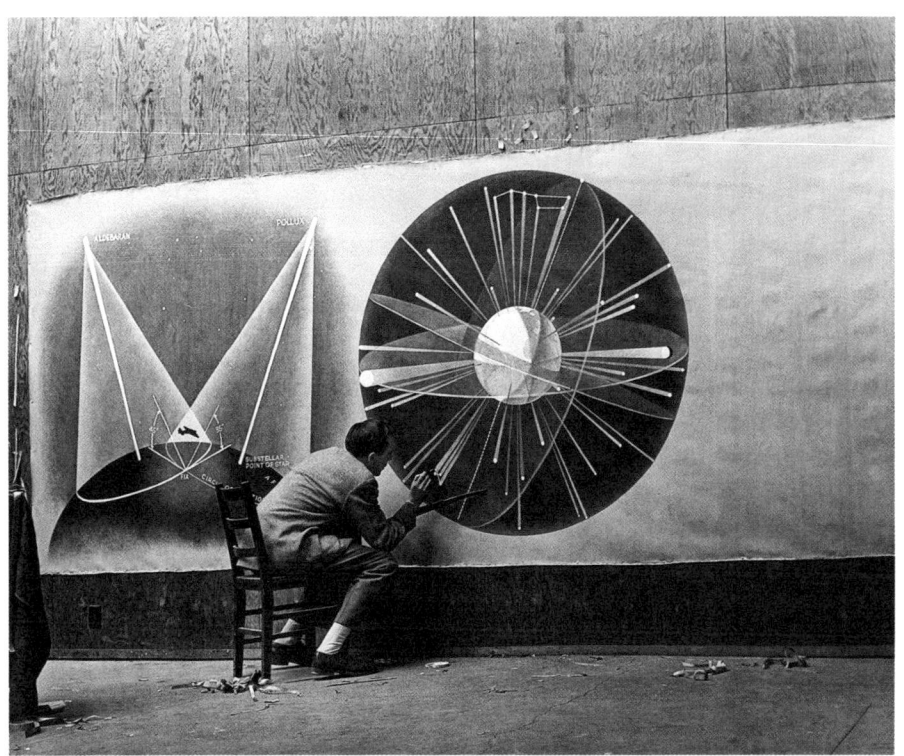

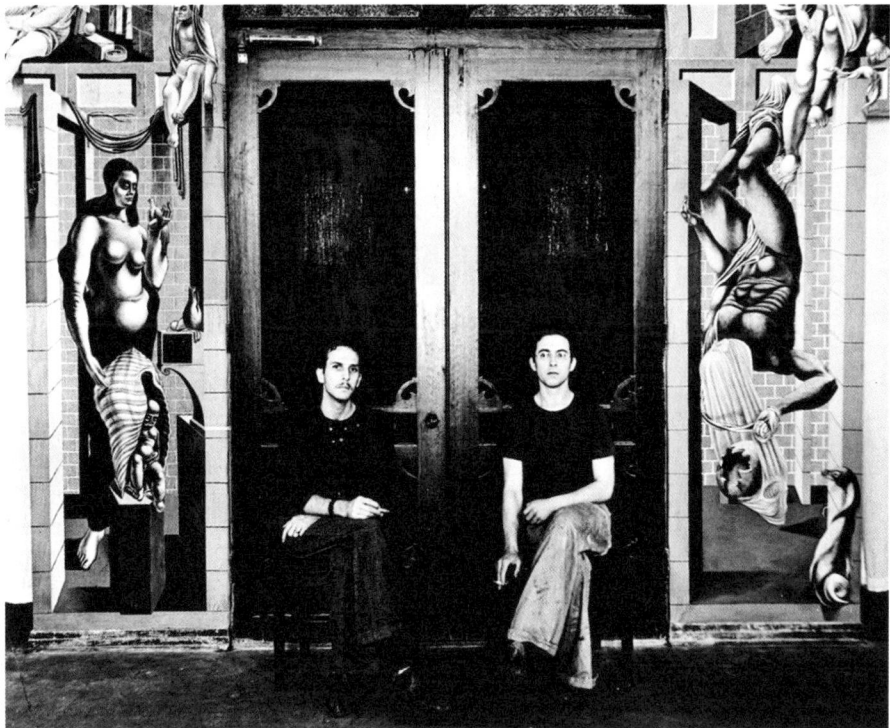

30 — Philip Guston working on *Untitled (Mural on Navigation, for Naval Preflight Training)*, 1942–43. Courtesy of The Estate of Philip Guston Archives

31 — *Philip Guston and Reuben Kadish, sitting in a doorway, under their fresco representing Physical Growth of Men, at the City of Hope sanatorium in Duarte (California)*, c. 1936. Courtesy of the Estate of Philip Guston Archives

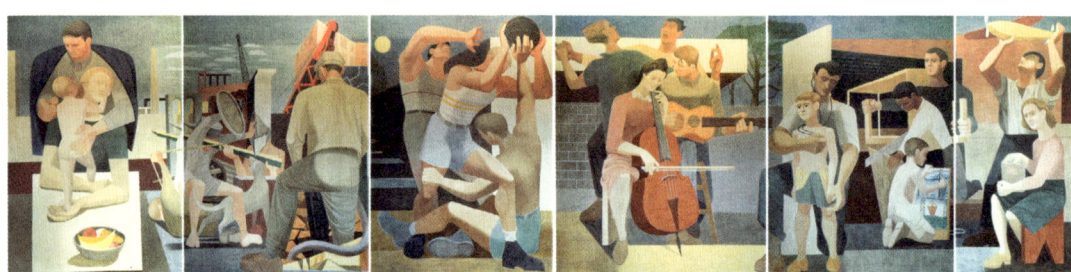

32

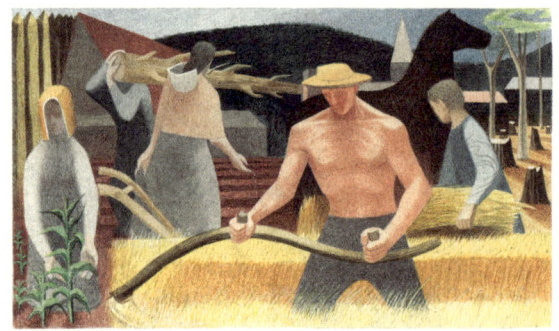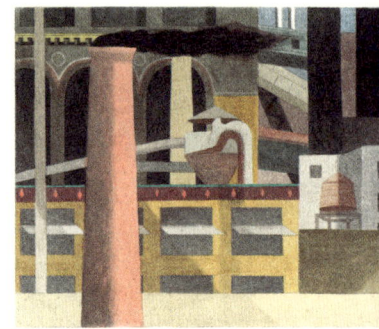

33

32 — *Work and Play (Queensbridge Housing Project Mural)*, 1940. Casein-glyptol tempera on gesso, 1219.2 × 175.3 cm. Queensbridge Community Center of the Queensbridge Houses
33 — *Untitled (preliminary study for "Reconstruction and The Well-Being of the Family")*, c. 1940. Fresco, 32.1 × 171.1 cm
34 — *Study for "Work and Play" (Queensbridge Housing Project Mural)*, 1939. Colored pencil and ink on paper, 38.1 × 62.9 cm

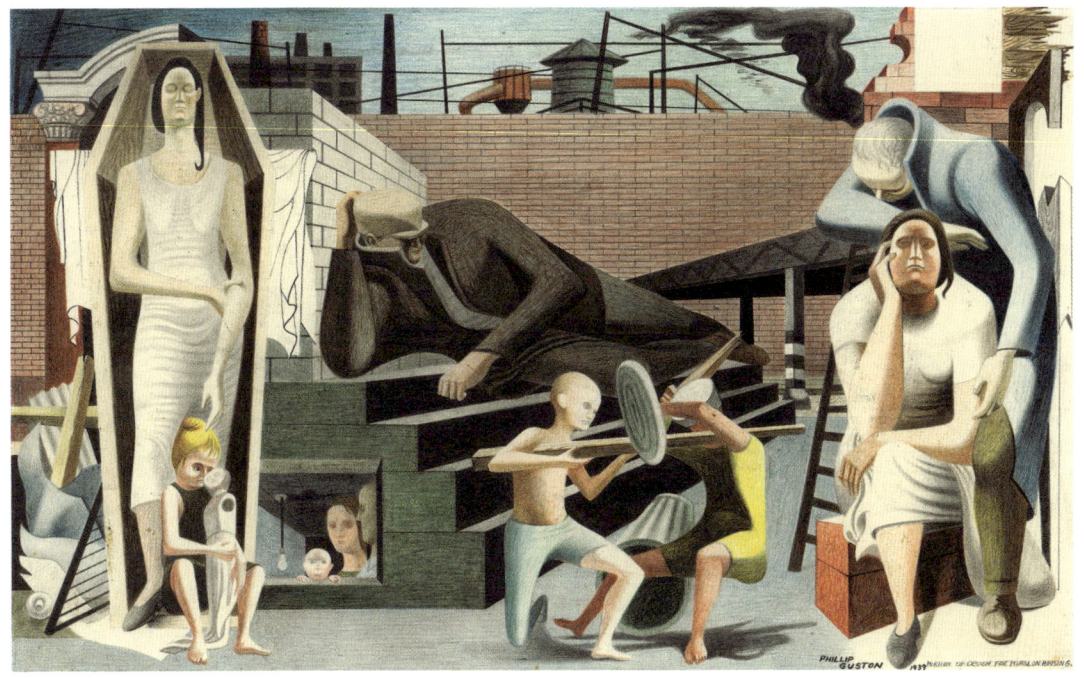

34

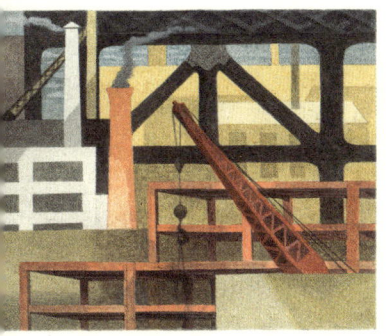

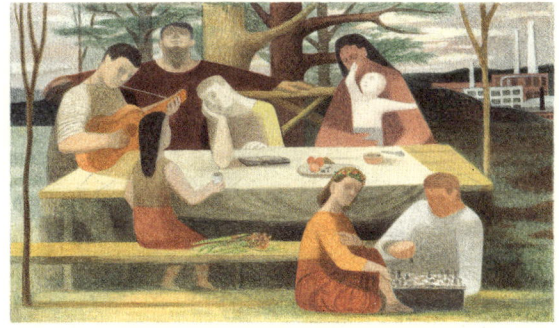

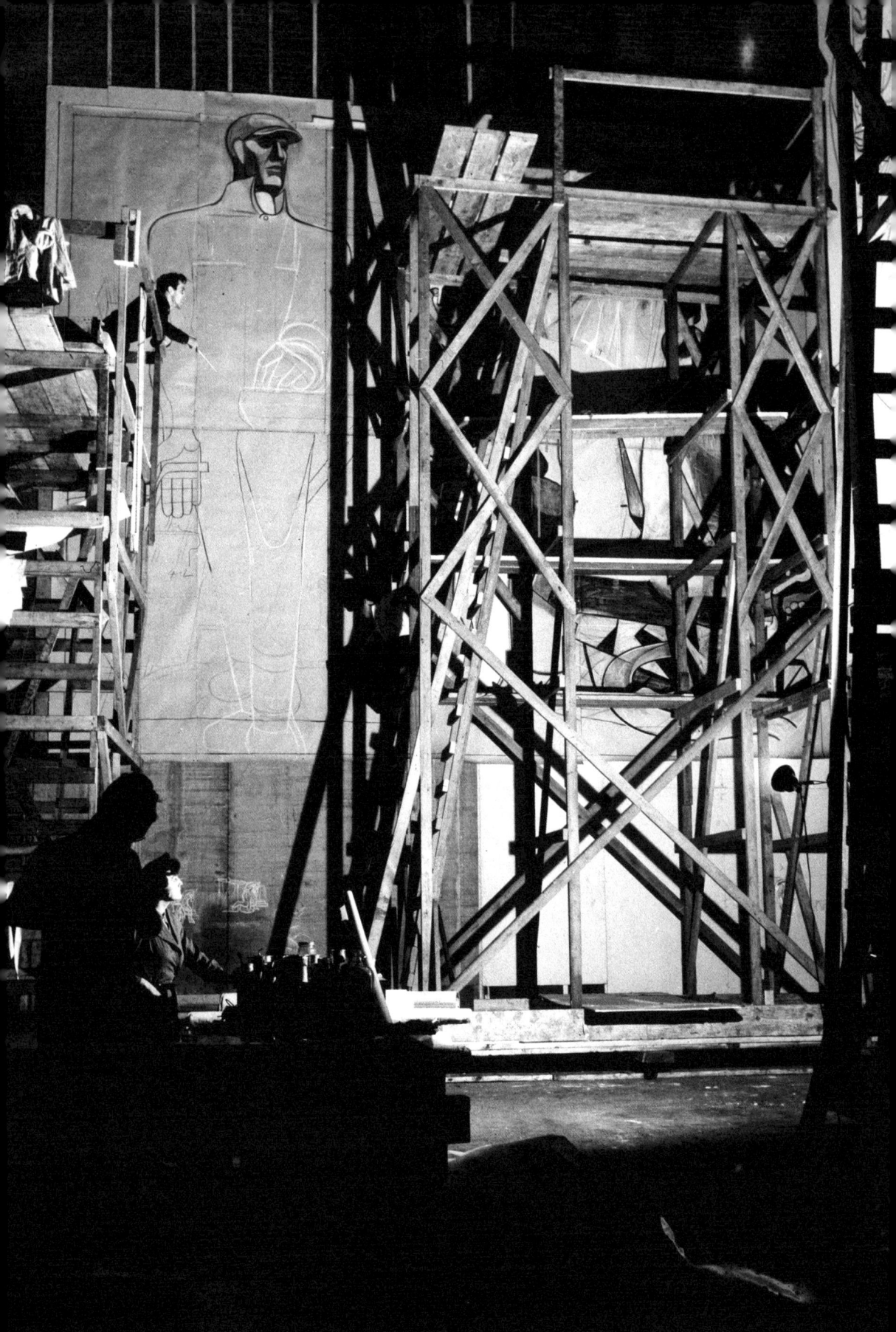

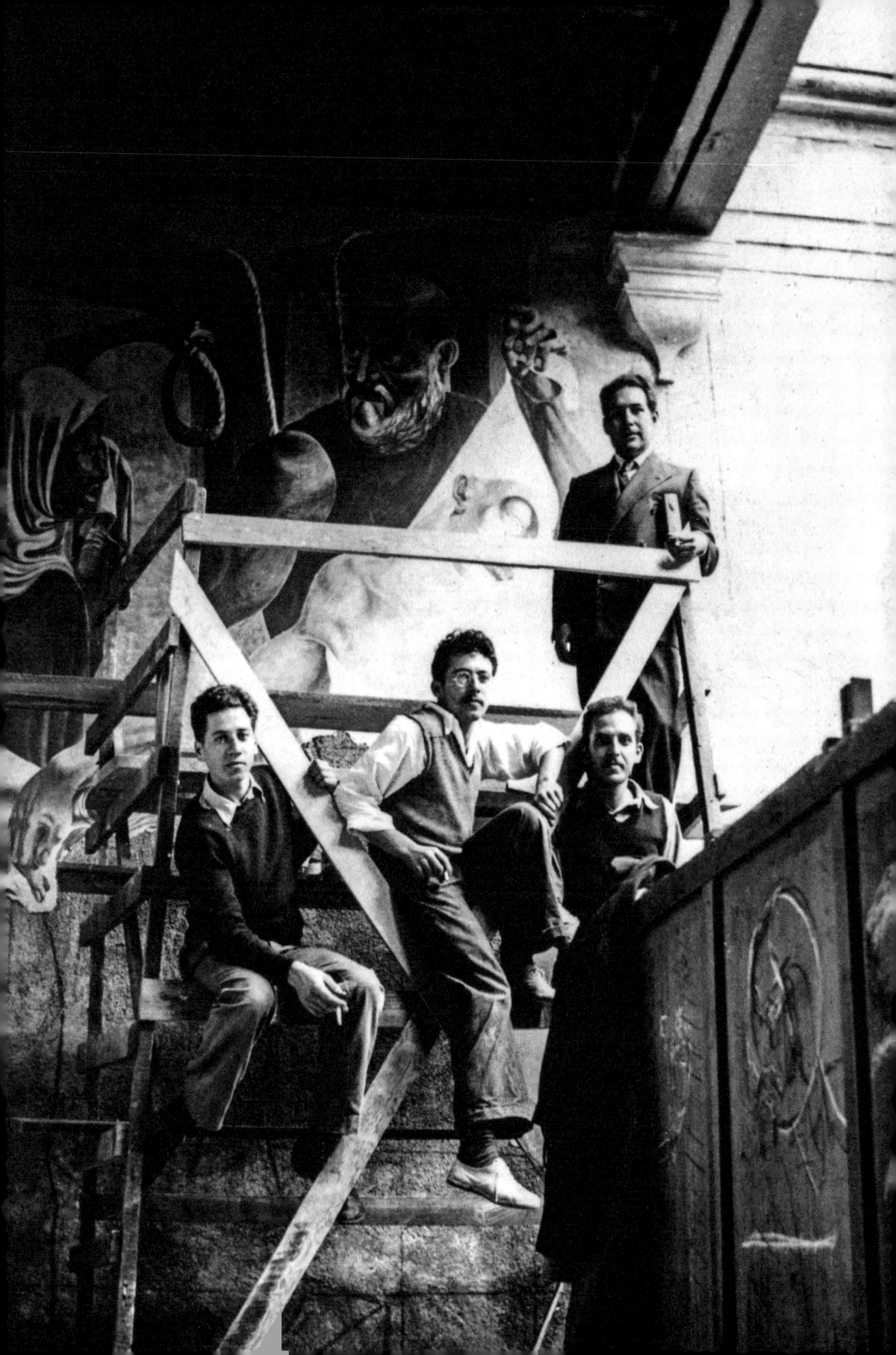

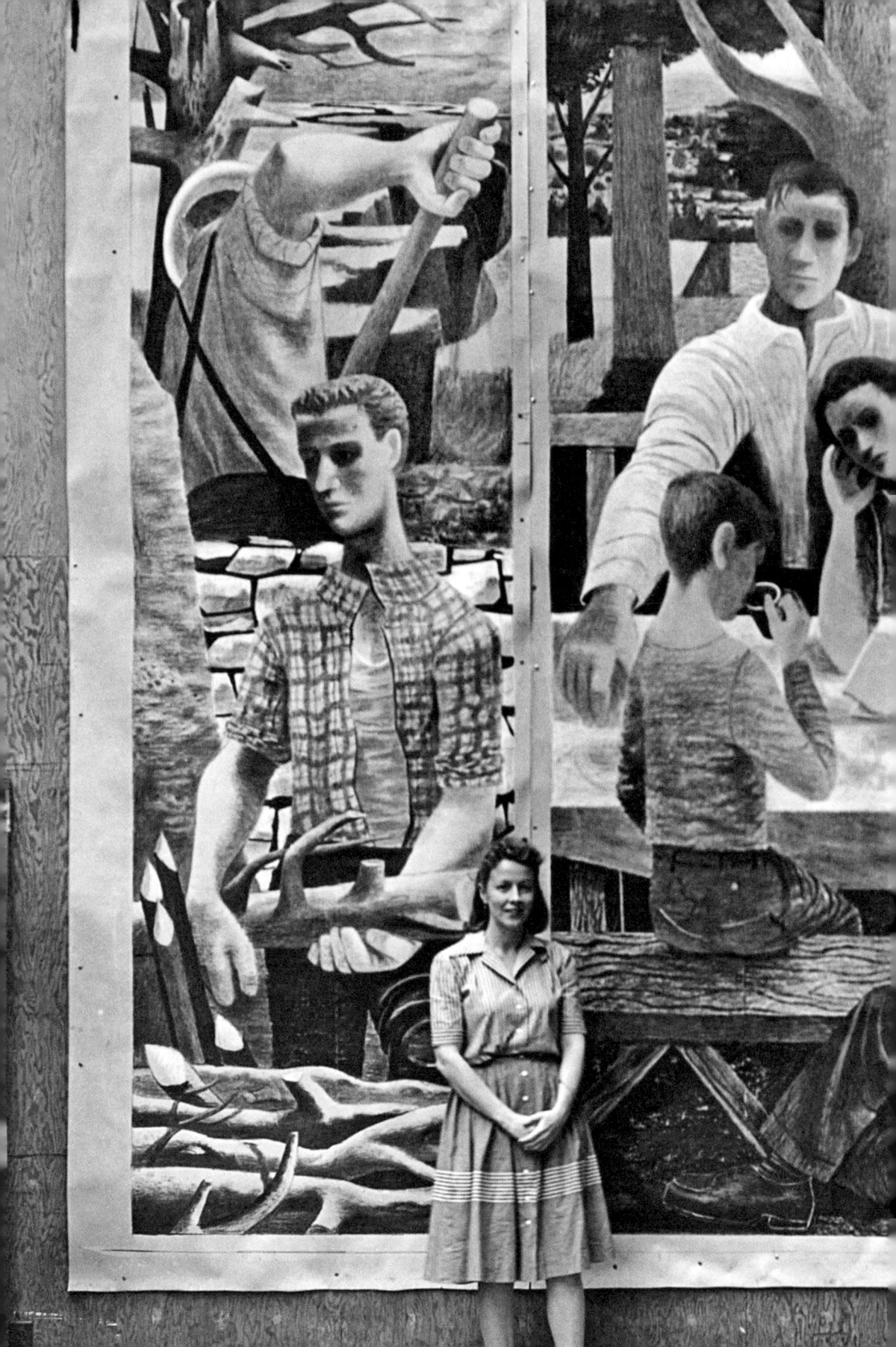

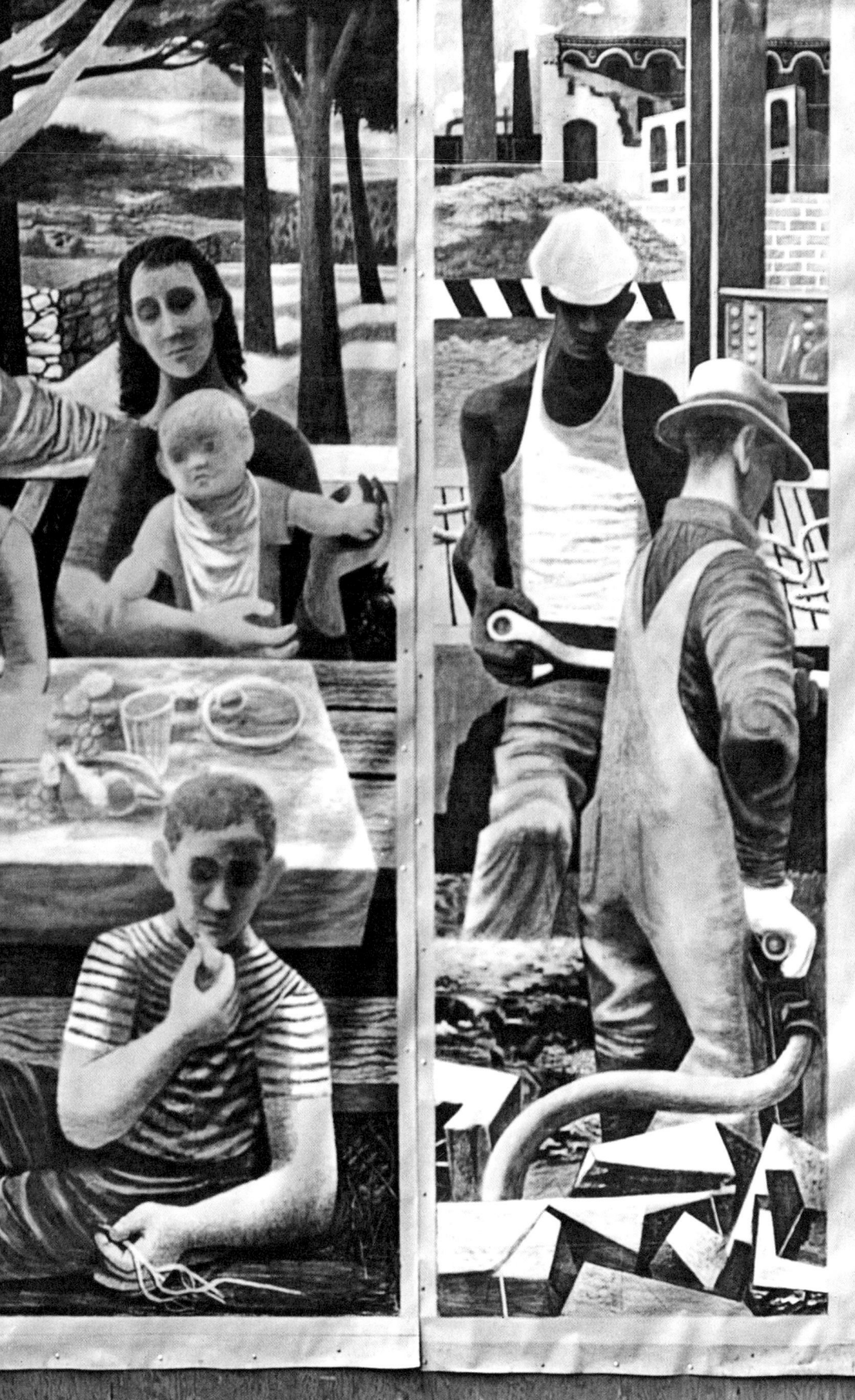

The action painting era

After teaching for several years at universities in the Midwest, Philip Guston went to Italy from 1948 to 1949 and returned to New York in 1949. Straightaway, he reconnected with Jackson Pollock, his former classmate at art school in Los Angeles, who created his first drip painting that year. Guston soon joined the group of painters who gathered at the Cedar Tavern in Greenwich Village, including Willem de Kooning, Mark Rothko, and Pollock. Guston's paintings were now entirely abstract and he became one of the pillars of what would soon be known as the New York School. He shared the interest in traditional Japanese culture of his friends, composers John Cage and Morton Feldman. His drawings and paintings were inspired by calligraphy, as well as the "grids" he admired in the works of Piet Mondrian. His paintings were included in the touring exhibition *The New American Painting* (1958), organized by the Museum of Modern Art in New York, which introduced postwar Europe to American Abstract Expressionist painting. D. O.

pages 52, 53
35 — *Philip Guston sketching a fresco for the World's Fair in New York*, February 15, 1939. Archives of American Art, Smithsonian Institution
36 — *Reuben Kadish, Jules Langsner, Philip Guston, and Gustavo Corona posing in front of the fresco "The Struggle Against Terrorism" in Morelia, Mexico*, c. 1934. Courtesy of the Estate of Philip Guston Archives
pages 54–55
37 — *Musa Guston in front of "Reconstruction and The Well-Being of the Family," oil painting for the Social Security Building*, c. 1940. Courtesy of the Estate of Philip Guston Archives

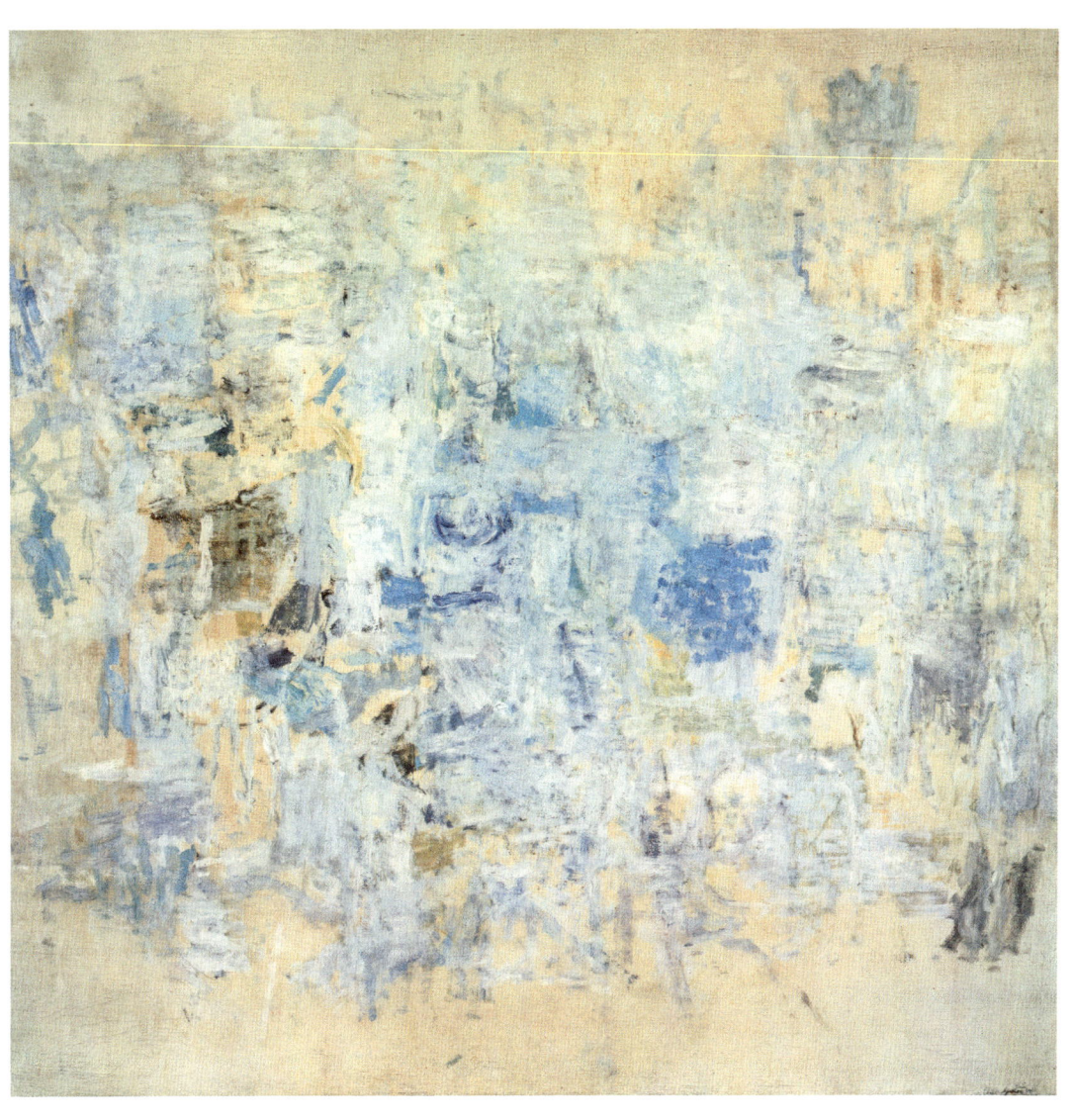

38 — *White Painting II*, 1951. Oil on canvas, 127 × 129.2 cm. Private collection, London

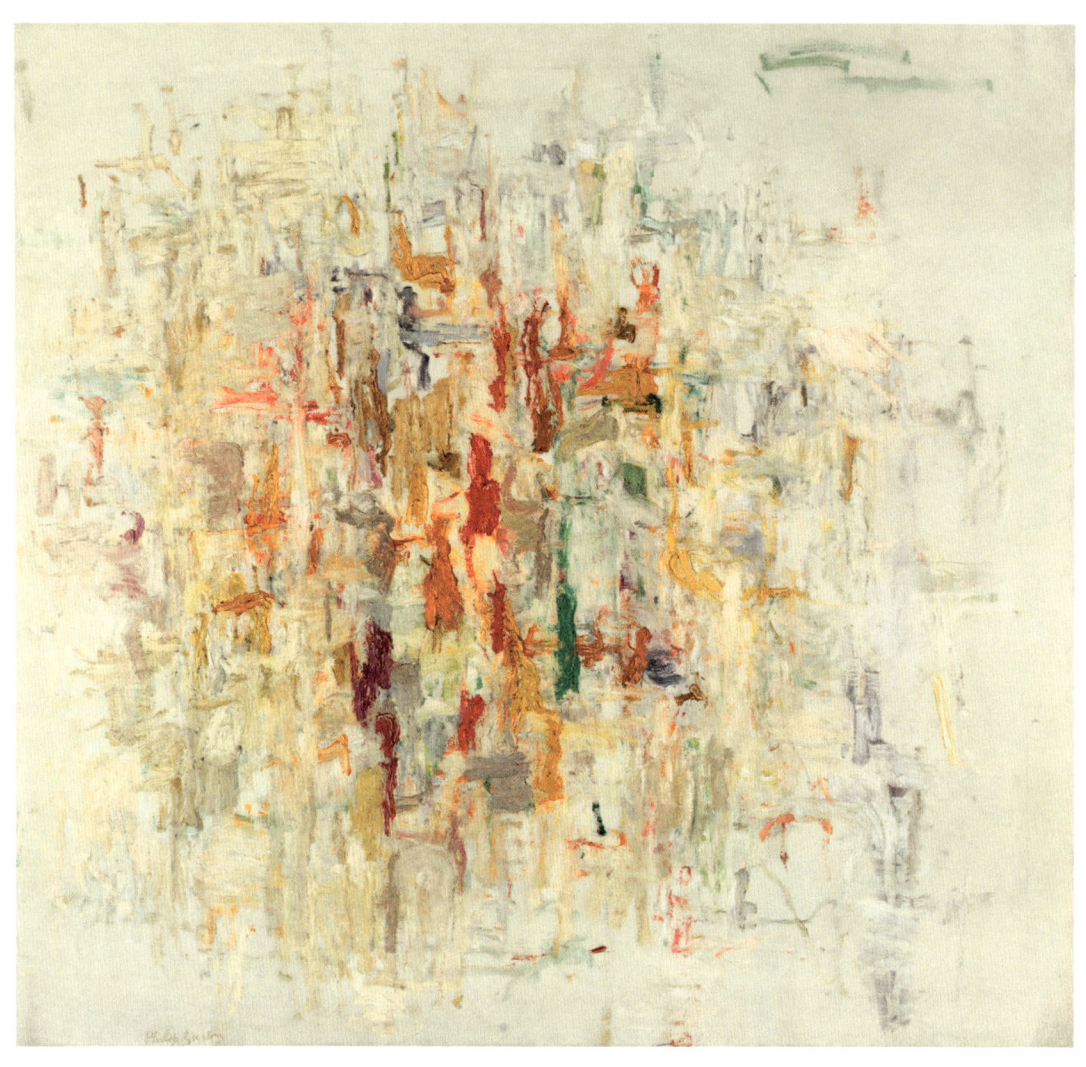

39 — *Painting*, 1952. Oil on canvas, 121.9×129.5 cm. Metropolitan Museum of Art, New York

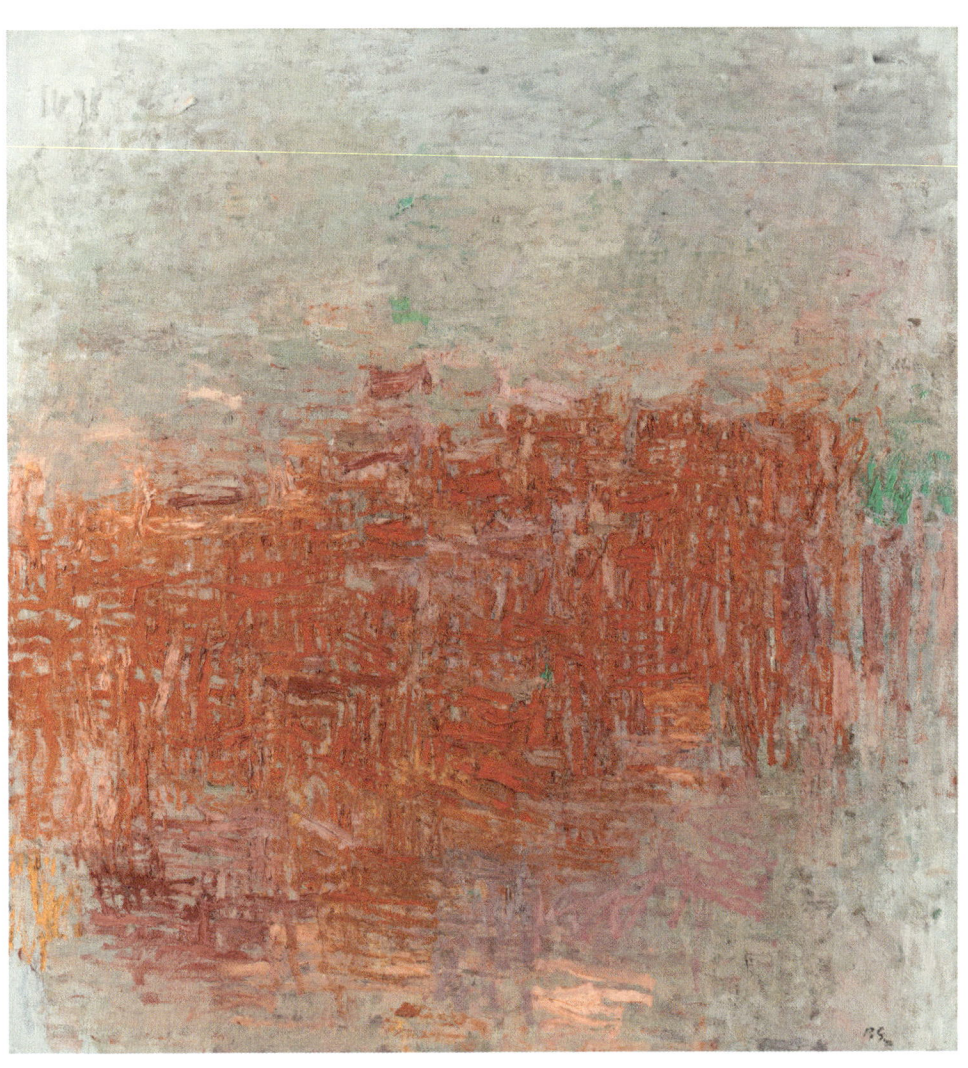

40 — *Painting*, 1954. Oil on canvas, 160.6 × 152.7 cm. MoMA, New York

The 10th Street gang

Philip Guston's passion for comic strips published in American dailies prompted his mother to enroll him in a cartoon-drawing correspondence course. His cartoons won prizes and his first strips were printed in *The Junior Times*. Later on, as an art school student, his irrepressible graphic verve led him to caricature the teaching staff, resulting in his expulsion. As an "artist," he was more inspired by the frescoes of Piero della Francesca and the drawings of Michelangelo than by George Herriman's *Krazy Kat* and Bud Fisher's *Mutt and Jeff*. His conversion to abstract art in the late 1940s seemed to shield him from popular culture, from the comic strip and caricature, deemed a corrupting influence on the "purity of art." But it was nothing of the sort. The Guston archives reveal his unwavering attraction to humorous drawing and caricature, which he applied to the most respectable figures of the New York School. D. O.

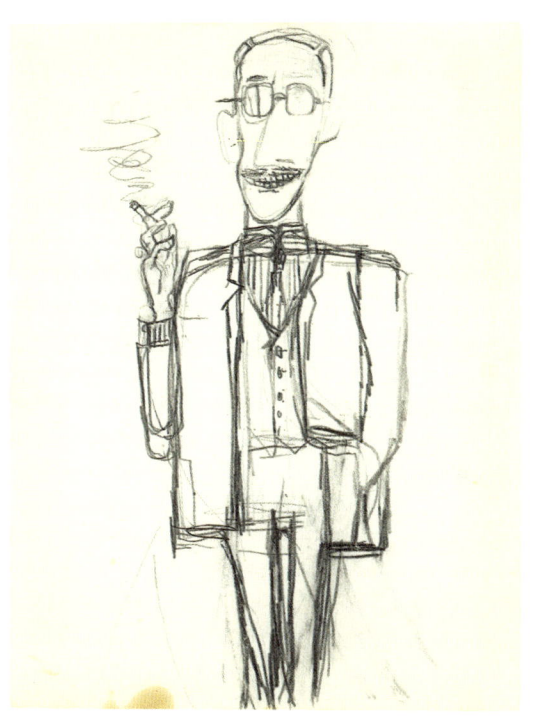
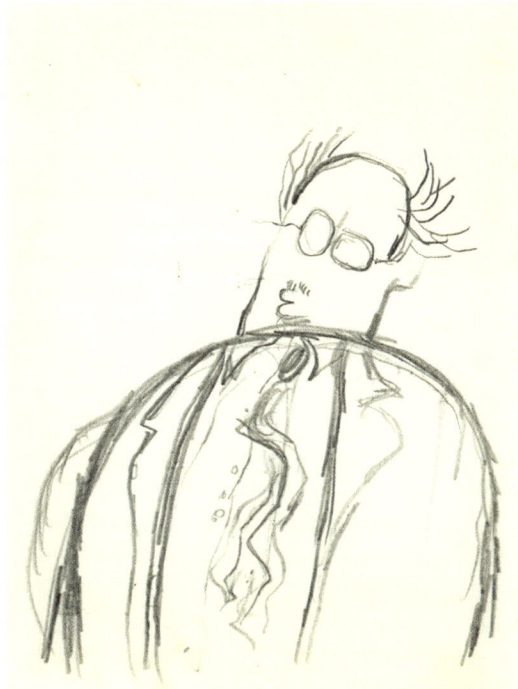
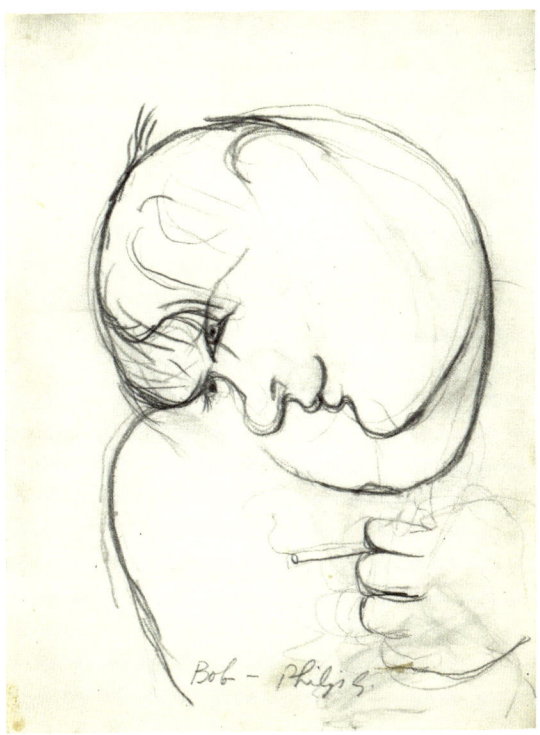
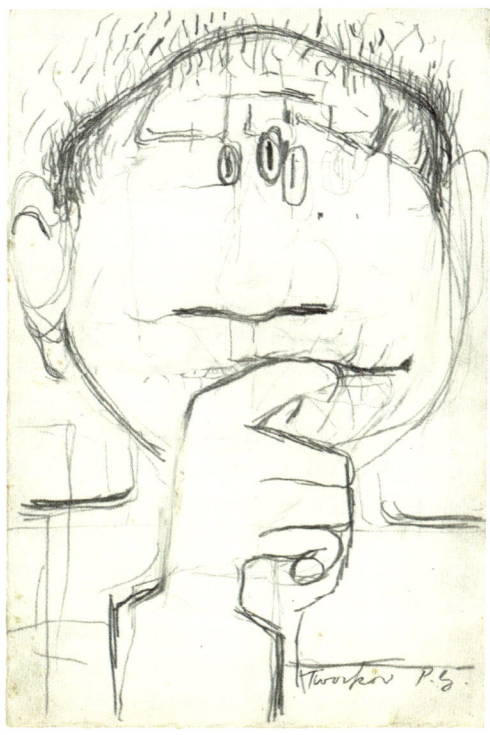

41 — *Saul Steinberg*, c. 1955. Pencil on paper, 28 × 21.6 cm. Private collection
42 — *Mark Rothko*, c. 1955. Pencil on paper, 28 × 21.6 cm. Private collection
43 — *Robert Motherwell*, c. 1955. Pencil on paper, 26.7 × 20.3 cm. Private collection
44 — *Jack Tworkov*, c. 1955. Pencil on paper, 24.1 × 16.5 cm. Private collection

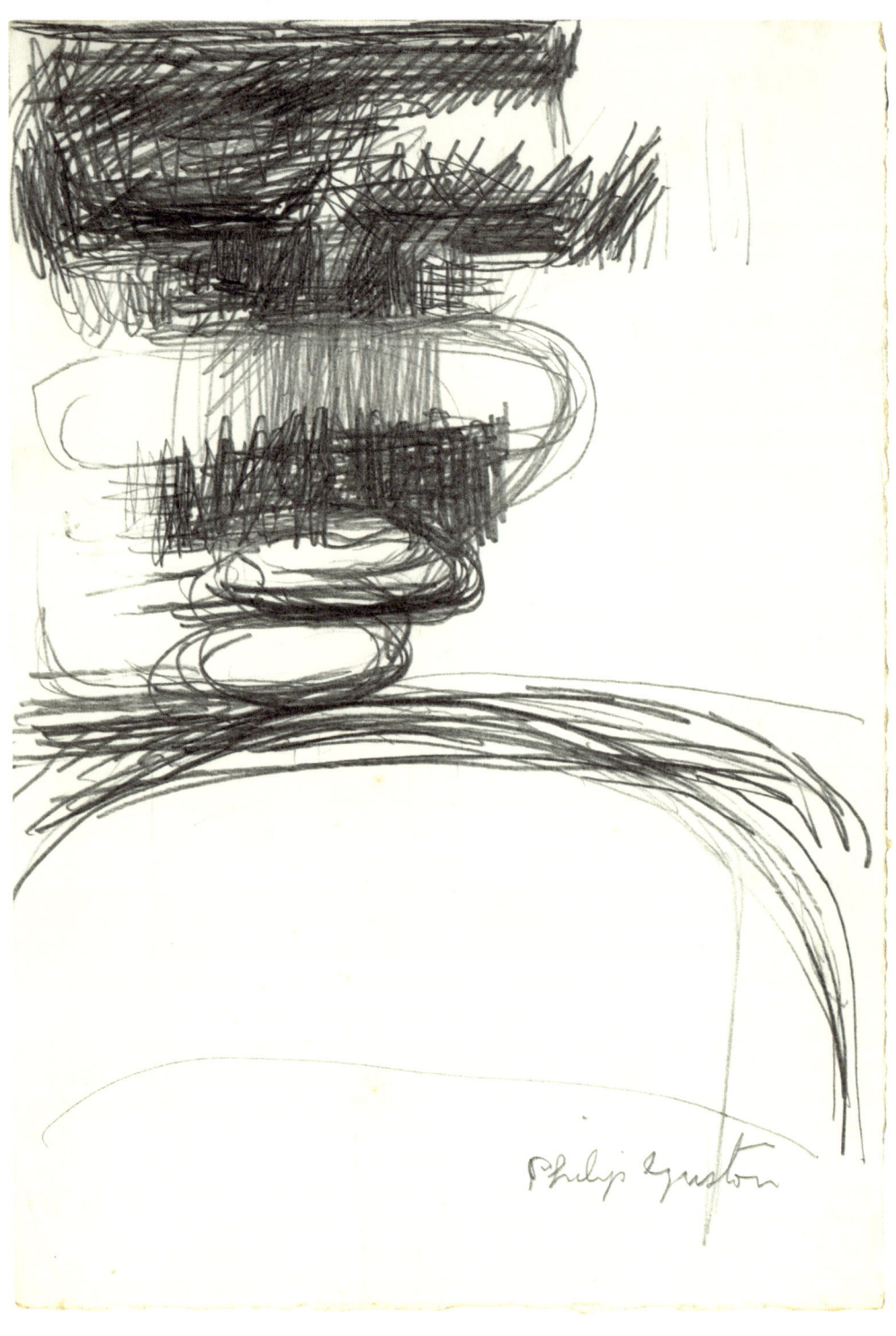

45 — *Harold Rosenberg*, 1955. Pencil on paper, 24.1×16.5 cm. The Guston Foundation, West Hurley (New York)

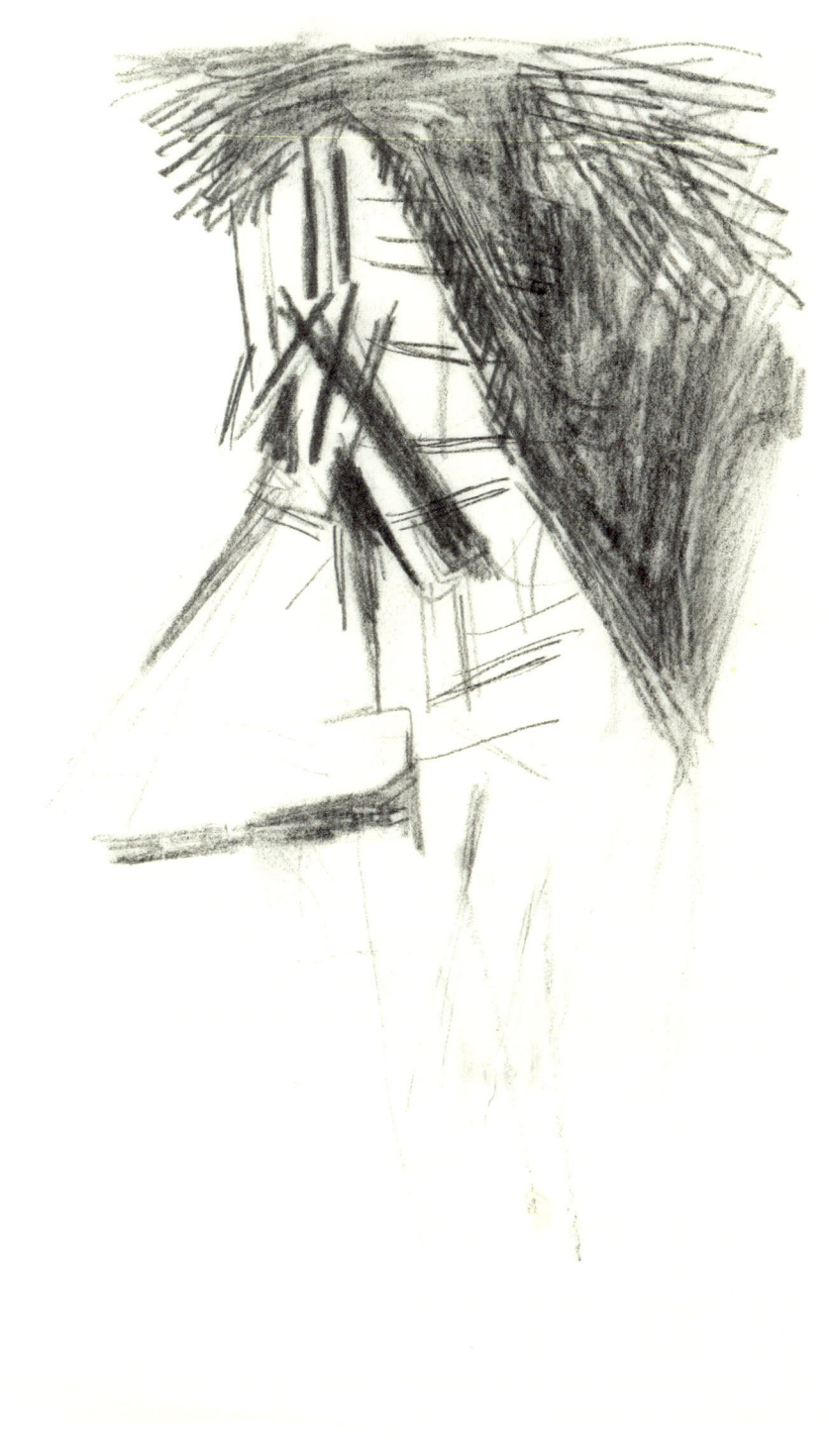

46 — *Franz Kline*, c. 1955. Pencil on paper, 27.9 × 21.6 cm. Private collection

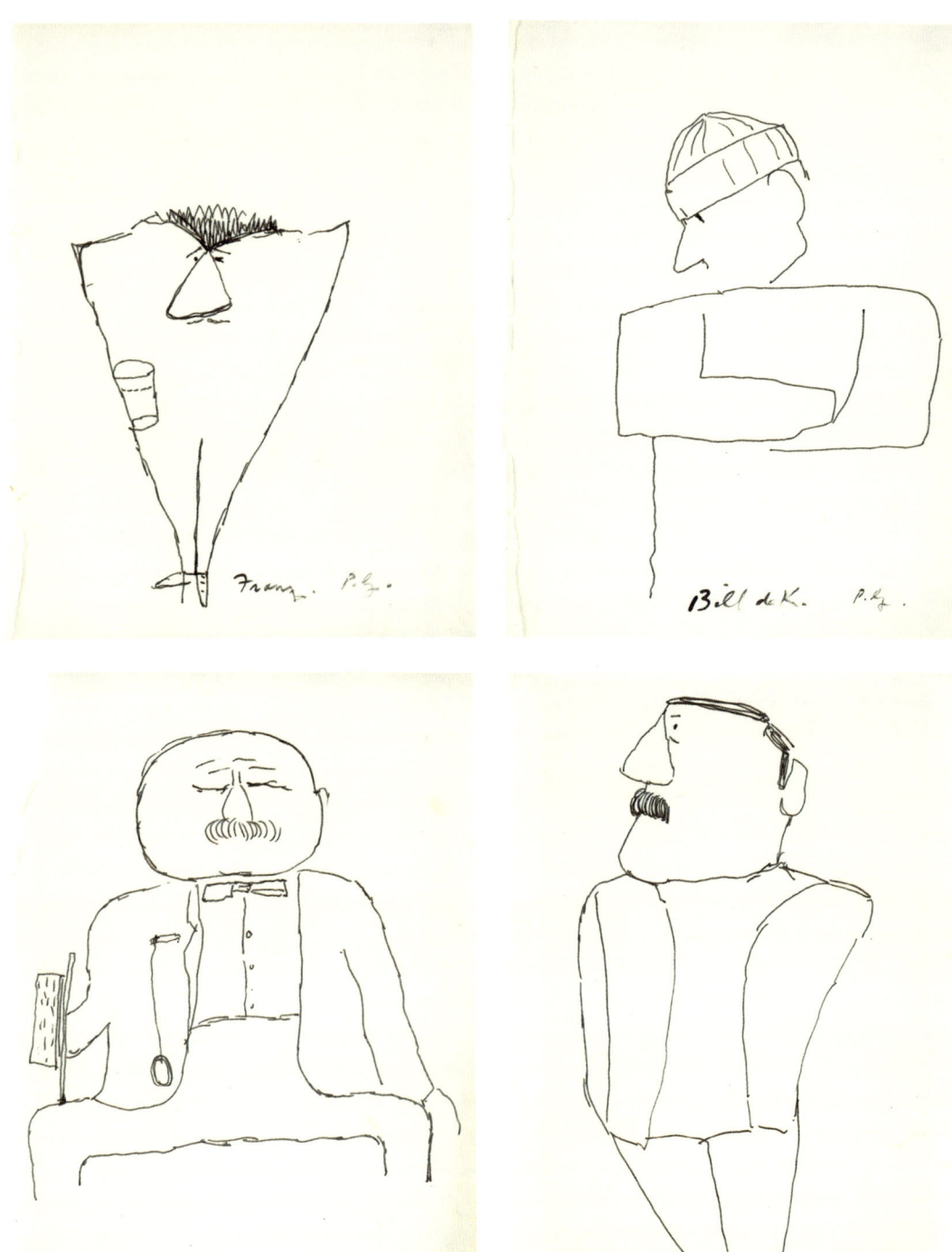

47 — *Franz Kline*, 1955. Ink on paper, 27.9×21.6 cm. Private collection
48 — *Willem de Kooning*, 1955. Ink on paper, 27.3×21.6 cm. Private collection
49 — *Barnett Newman*, 1955. Ink on paper, 27.3×21 cm. Private collection
50 — *Barnett Newman*, 1955. Ink on paper, 27.3×21 cm. Private collection

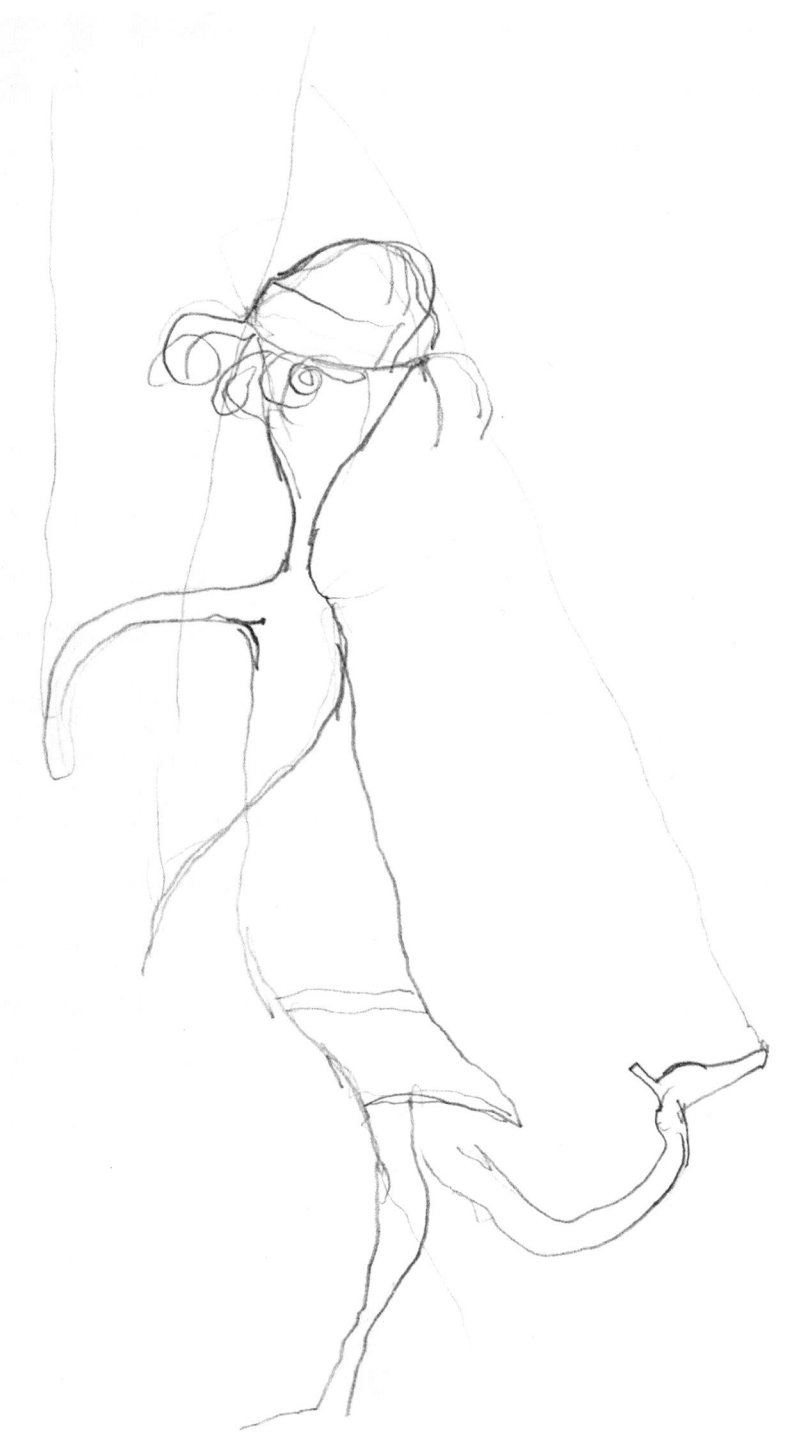

51 — *Elaine de Kooning*, c. 1955. Pencil on paper, 27.9 × 21.6 cm. Private collection

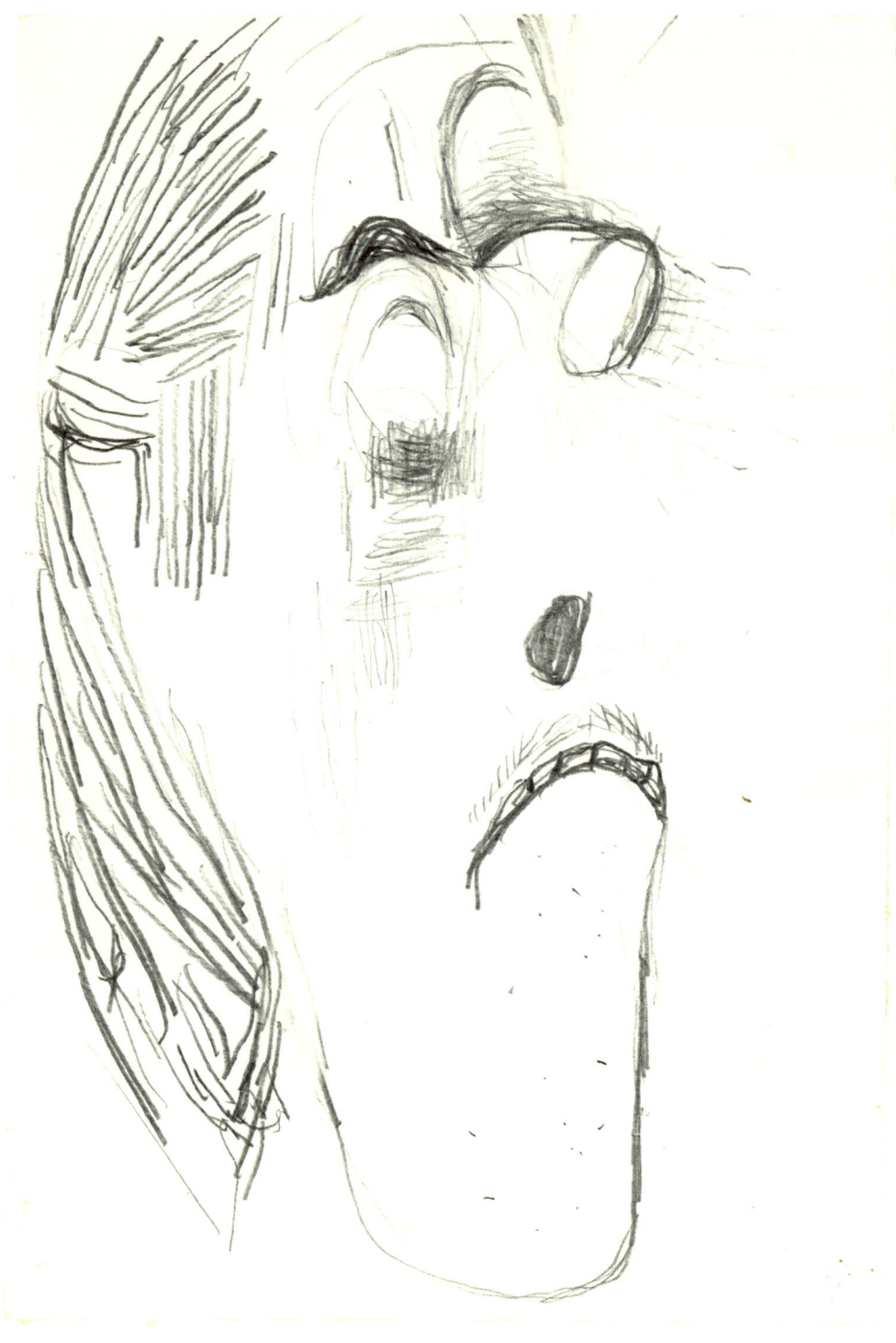

52 — *Esteban Vicente*, c. 1955. Pencil on paper, 24.1×16.5 cm. Private collection

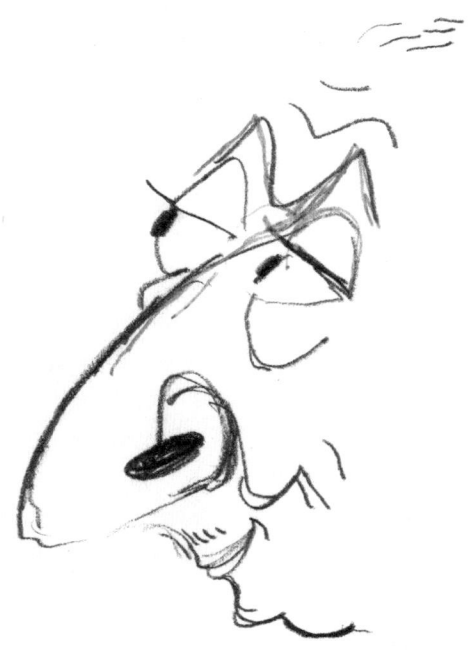

53 — *Stanley Kunitz*, c. 1955. Ink and pencil on paper, 26.7×21.6 cm. Private collection

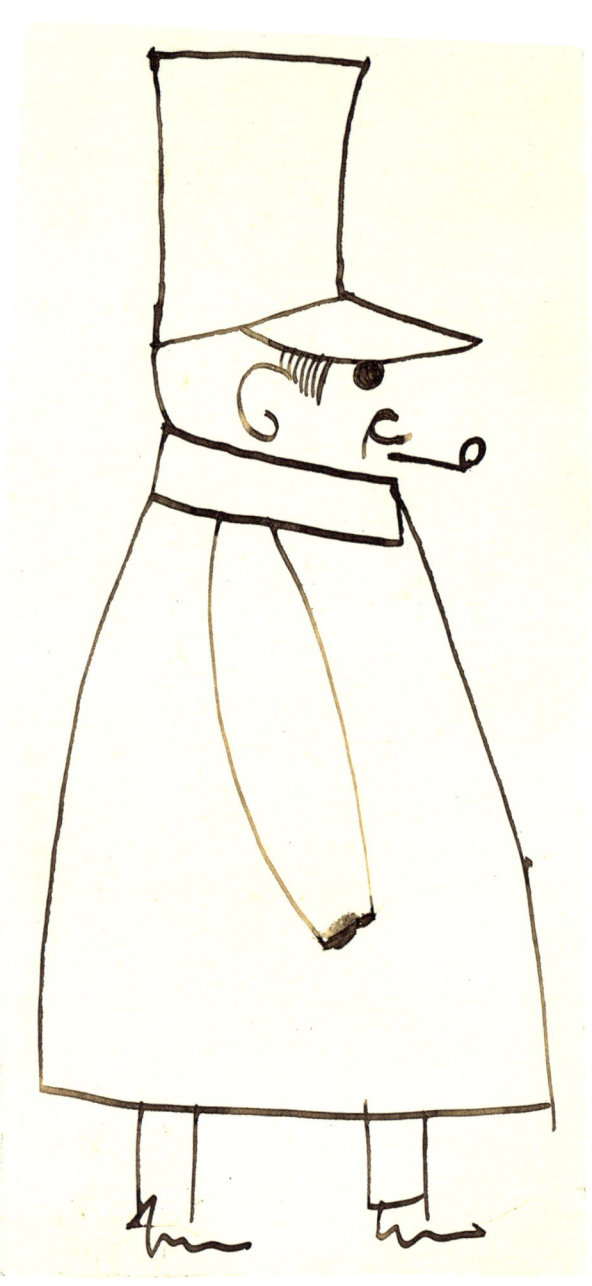

54 — Pablo Picasso, *Caricature (Self-Portrait?)*, [1917–18]. Ink on paper, 17 × 8.5 cm.
Musée National Picasso-Paris

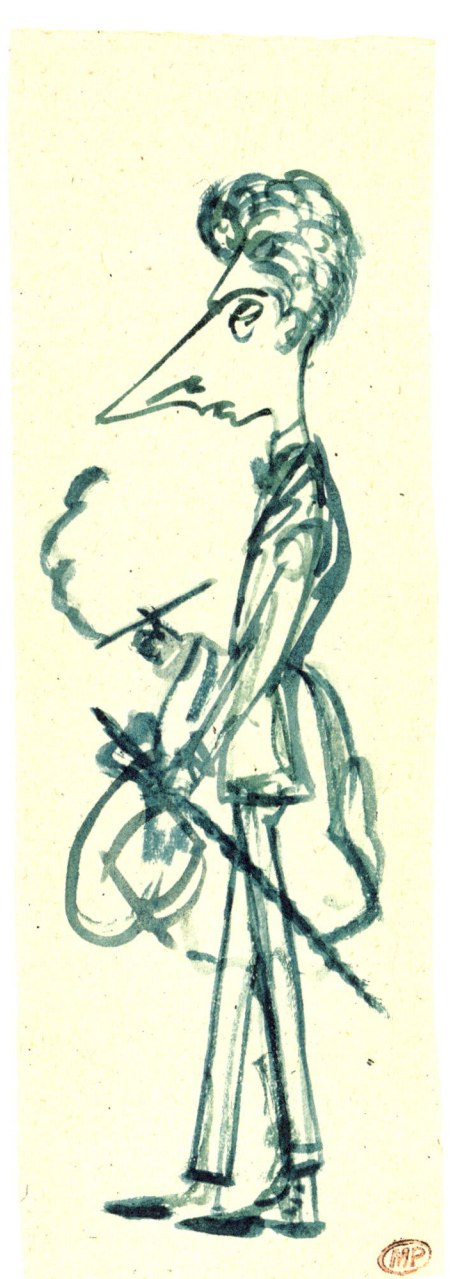

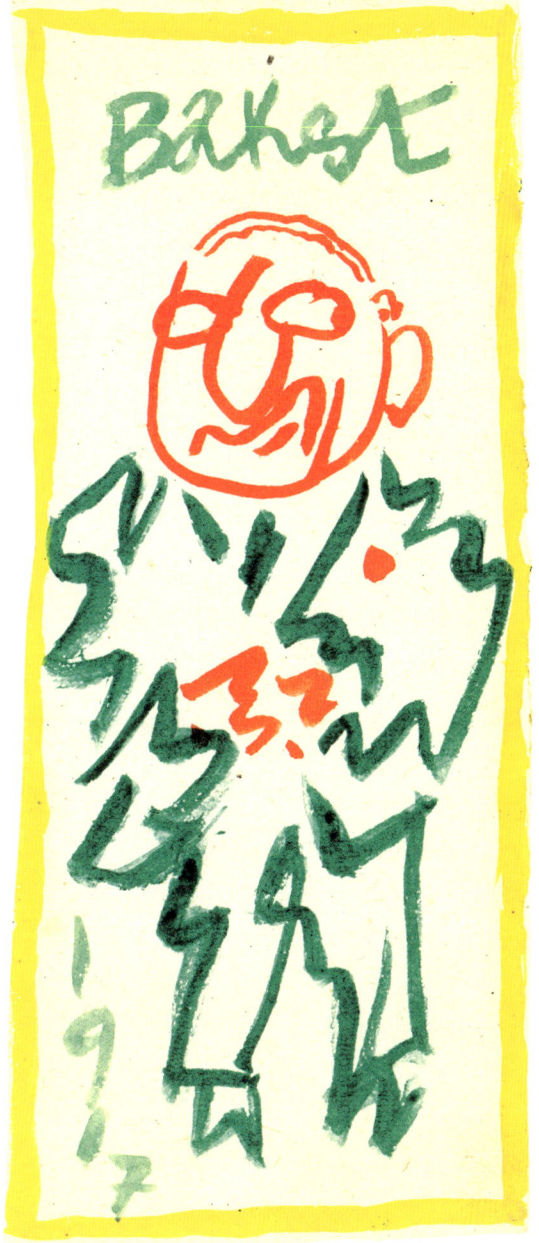

55 — Pablo Picasso, *Caricature of Jean Cocteau*, 1917. Gouache on paper, 19.7 × 6.8 cm.
Musée National Picasso-Paris
56 — Pablo Picasso, *Caricature of Léon Bakst*, 1917. Gouache on paper, 13.9 × 5.7 cm.

Musée National Picasso-Paris

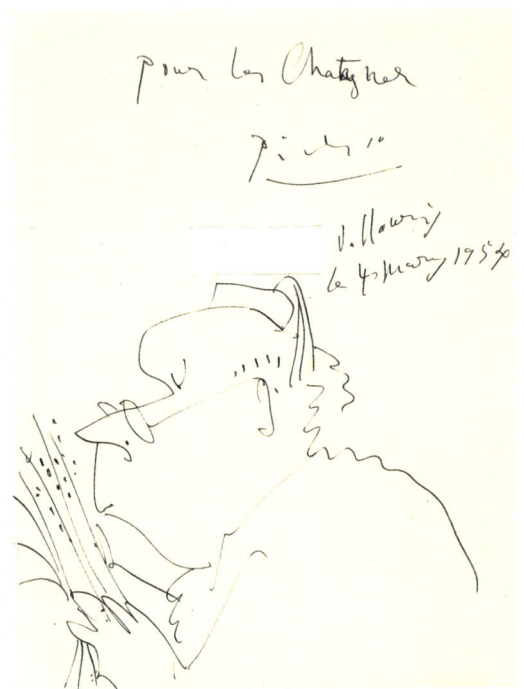

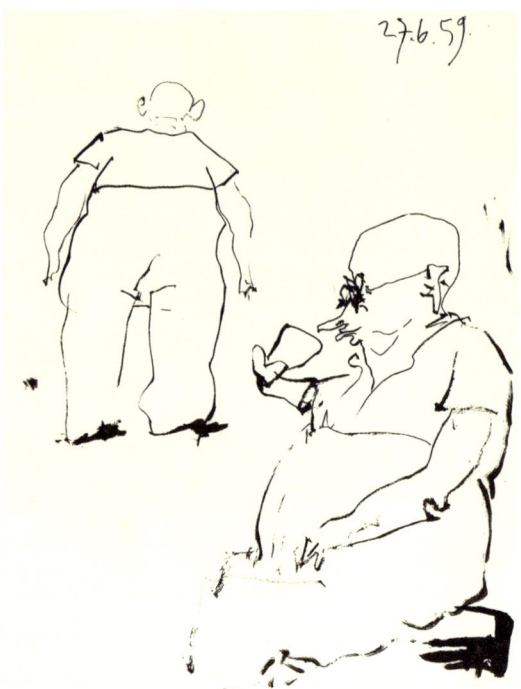

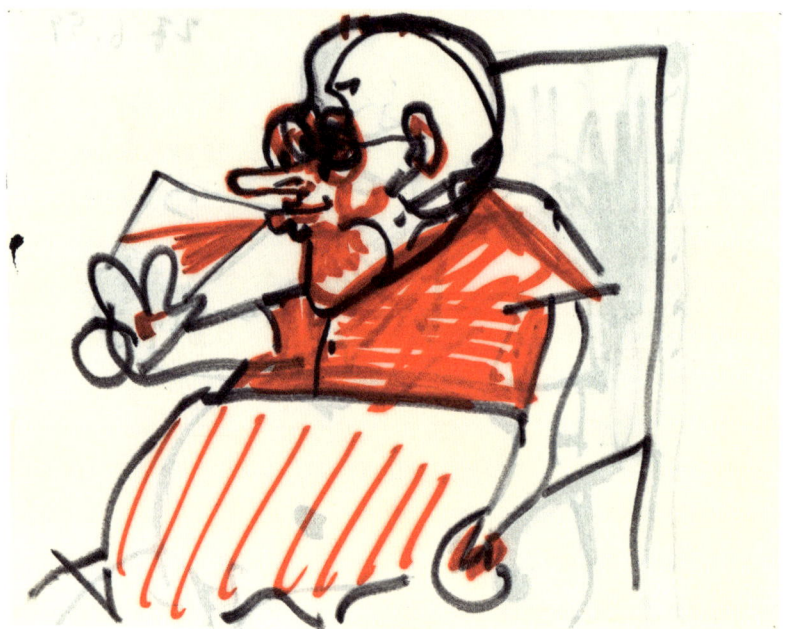

57 — Pablo Picasso, *Caricature of Jaime Sabartés*, 1954. Ink and collage on card
with gouache on paper, 32 × 24.5 cm. Musée National Picasso-Paris
58 — Pablo Picasso, *Caricature of Jaime Sabartés*, 1959. Ink on paper, 27 × 21 cm.
Musée National Picasso-Paris
59 — Pablo Picasso, *Caricature of Jaime Sabartés*, 1959. Ink and soft pencil on paper,
21 × 27 cm. Musée National Picasso-Paris

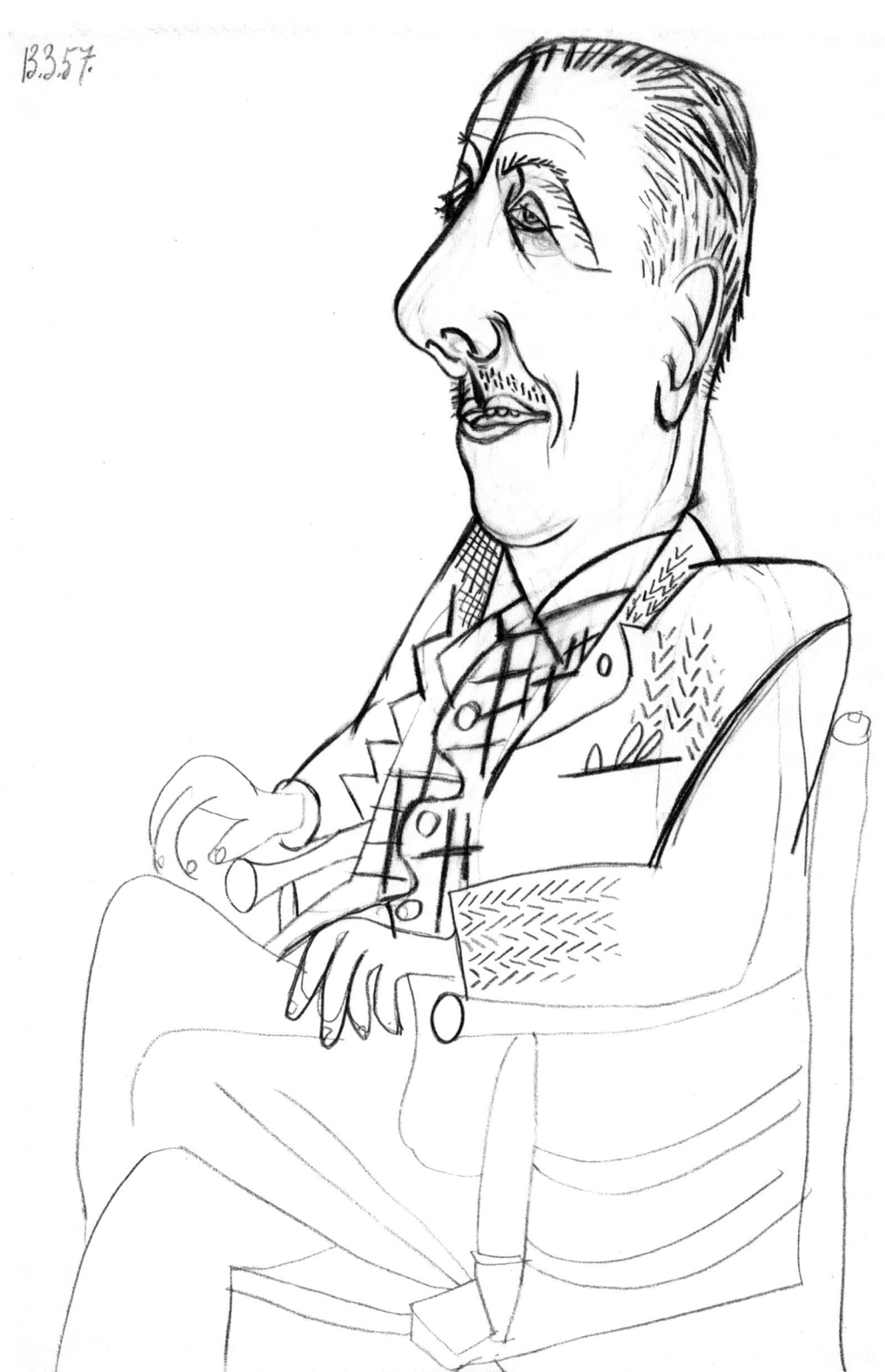

60 — Pablo Picasso, *Portrait of Francis Poulenc*, 1957. Graphite pencil on paper,
54 × 37 cm, 1979. Musée National Picasso-Paris

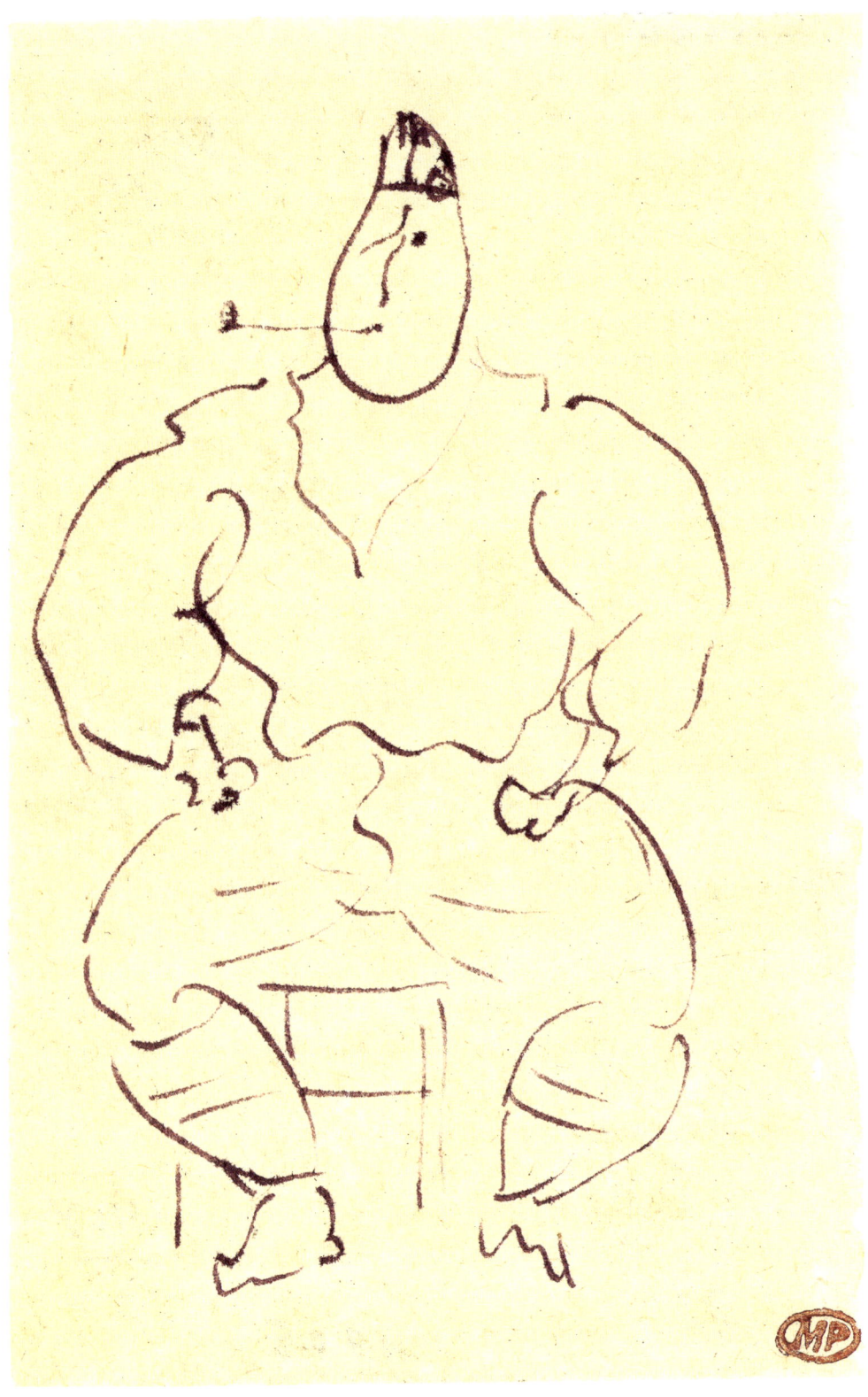

61 — Pablo Picasso, *Portrait of Guillaume Apollinaire*, 1918. Ink on paper, 13.6 × 8.7 cm.
Musée National Picasso-Paris

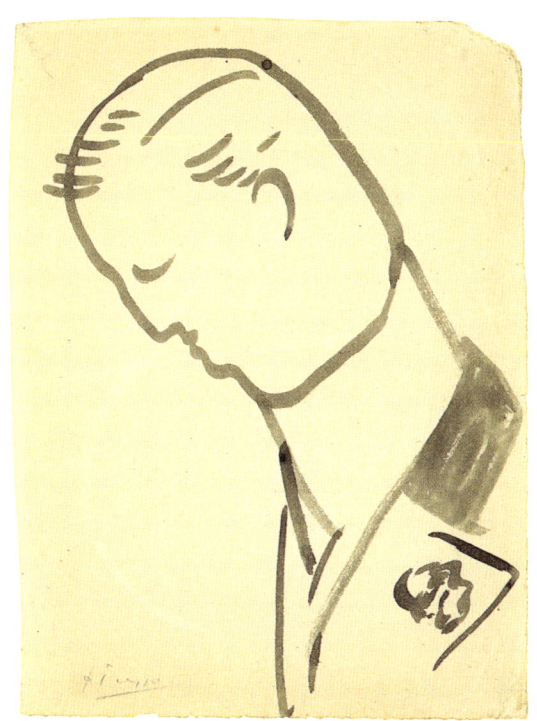

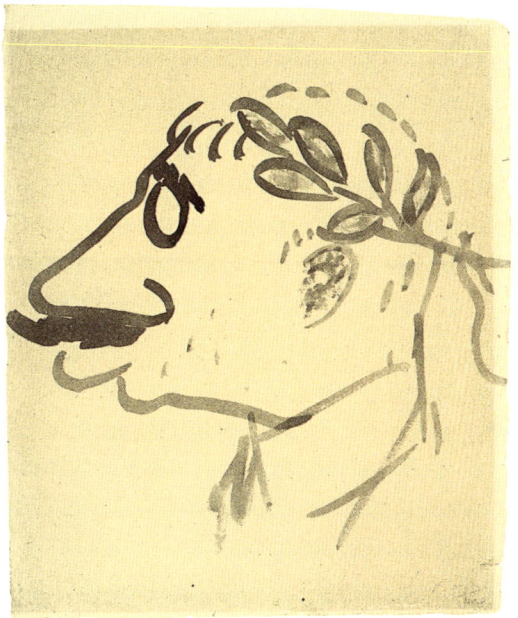

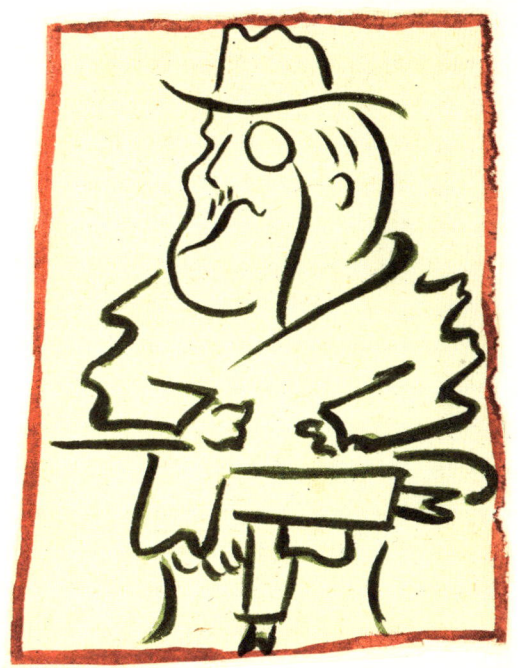

62 — Pablo Picasso, *Caricature of Henri Delormel*, [1905]. Ink on paper, 29.7×22.7 cm.
Musée National Picasso-Paris
63 — Pablo Picasso, *Caricature of Jean Moréas*, Paris, [1905]. Ink on paper, 29.2×24.9 cm.
Musée National Picasso-Paris
64 — Pablo Picasso, *Caricature of Sergei Diaghilev*, 1917–18. Gouache on paper, 8.6×6.7 cm.
Musée National Picasso-Paris

Nixon Drawings

The divisions of a still-segregationist America and the fractures caused by the Vietnam War in the late 1960s led writer Philip Roth to develop what he called "an obscene and delirious satire that soon challenged the sacrosanct rules of propriety."[1] Obscenity and satire crystallized in *Portnoy's Complaint*, published in 1969, and then in *Our Gang*, his scathing attack on the deeds and misdeeds of the Nixon administration, which he began working on soon after. Fleeing New York to escape the scandal caused by *Portnoy*, Roth settled in the small town of Woodstock. He soon became acquainted with Philip Guston, who had moved there permanently two years earlier. The painter and writer shared a taste for what they called "the crapola"—an interest in popular and trivial forms. A direct witness to the genesis of *Our Gang*, Philip Guston began work on a series of drawings entitled "Poor Richard." Caricaturing the thirty-seventh president of the United States as a phallic creature, he echoed Picasso's *Dream and Lie of Franco*. D. O.

1
Blake Bailey, *Philip Roth: The Biography*, New York: W. W. Norton & Co., 2021.

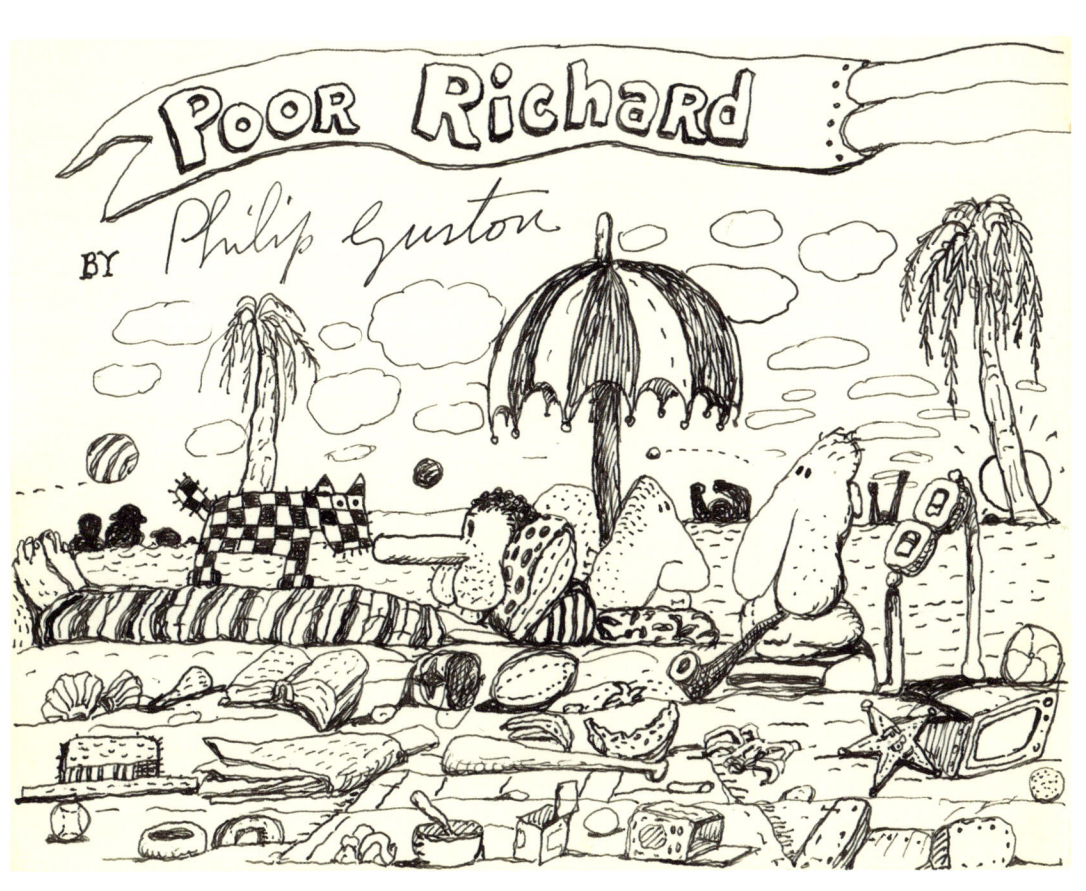

65 and following pages 66–137 — *Poor Richard*, 1971. Ink on paper, 26.7 × 35.2 cm.

The Guston Foundation, Promised Gift to the National Gallery of Art, Washington, D.C.

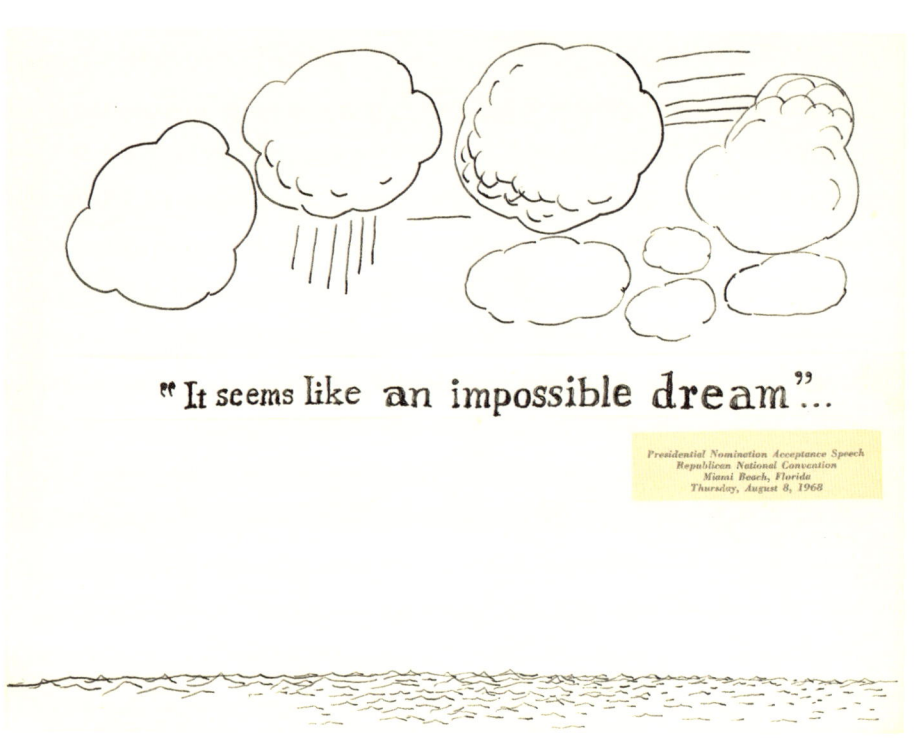

"It seems like an impossible dream"...

Presidential Nomination Acceptance Speech
Republican National Convention
Miami Beach, Florida
Thursday, August 8, 1968

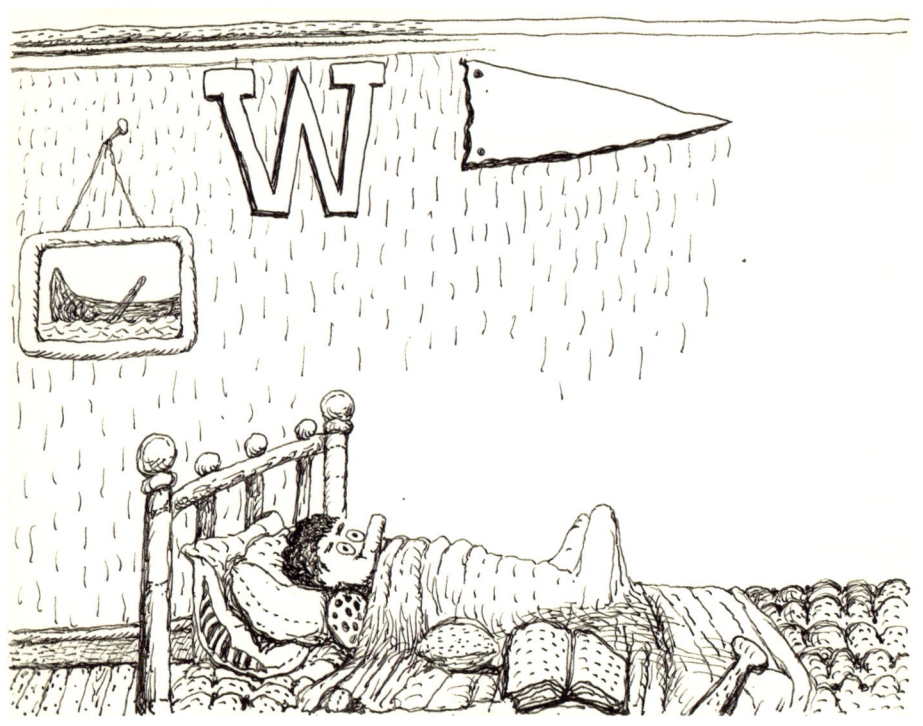

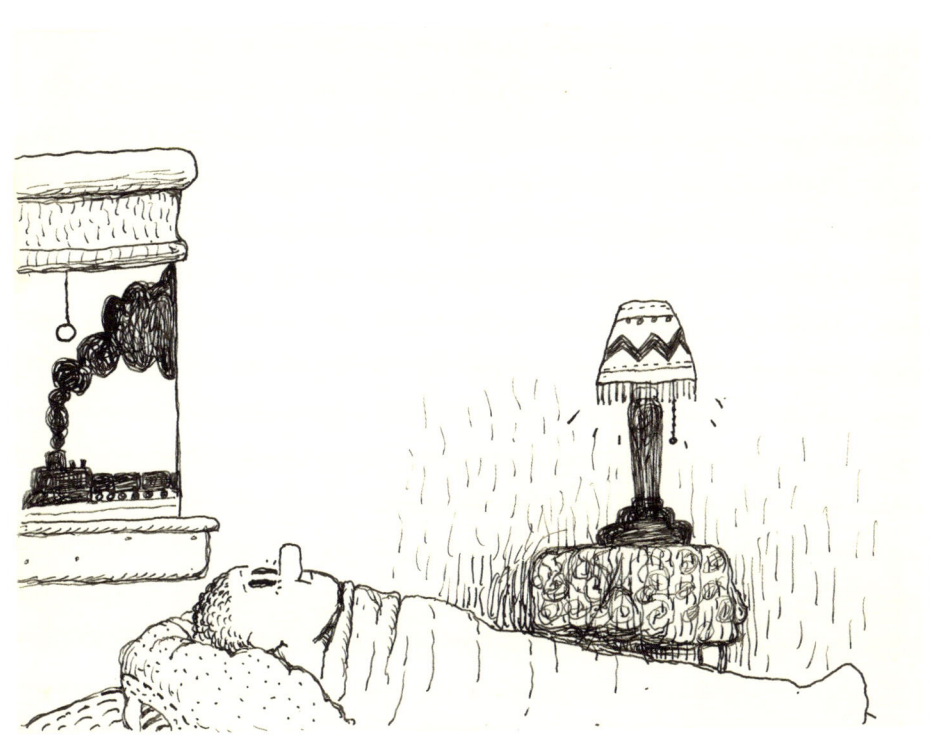

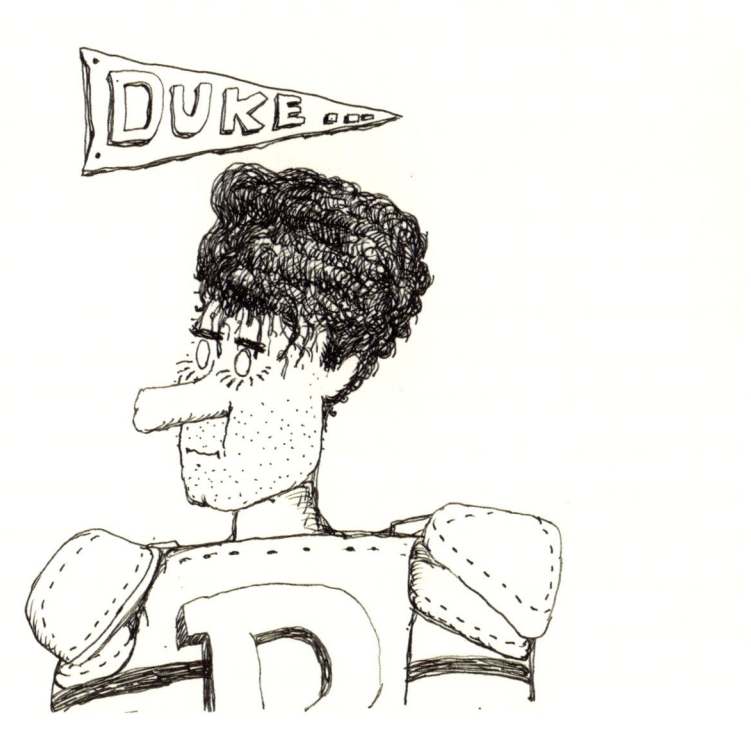

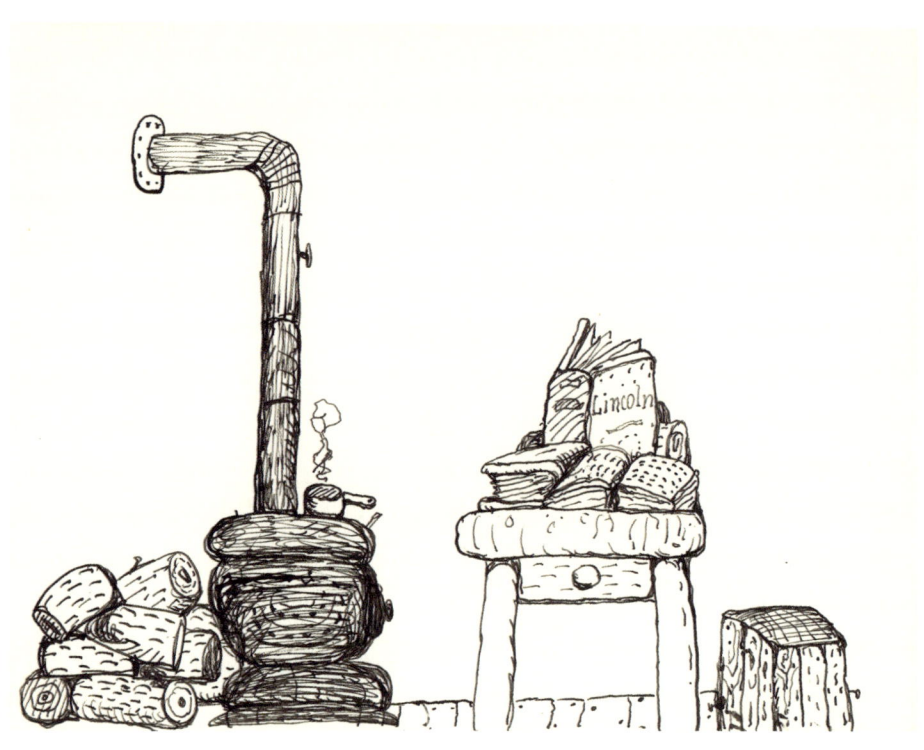

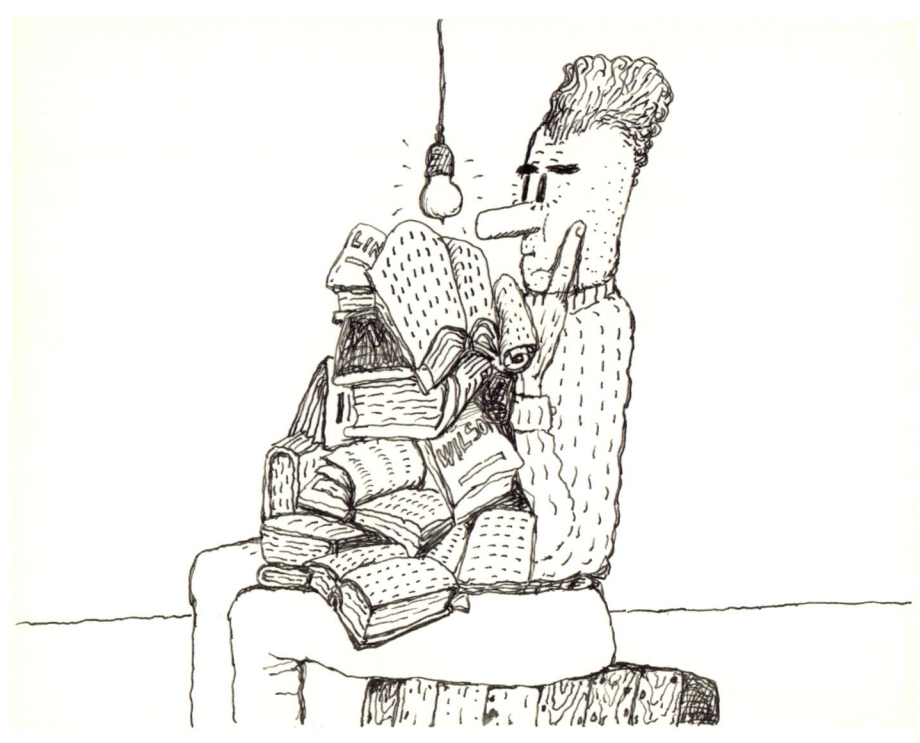

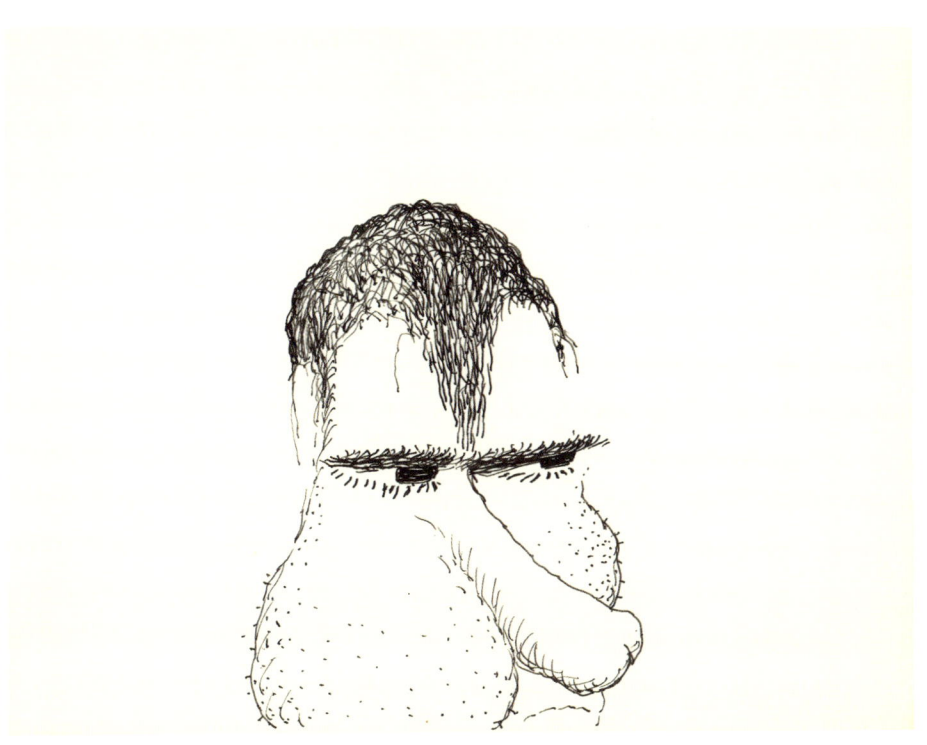

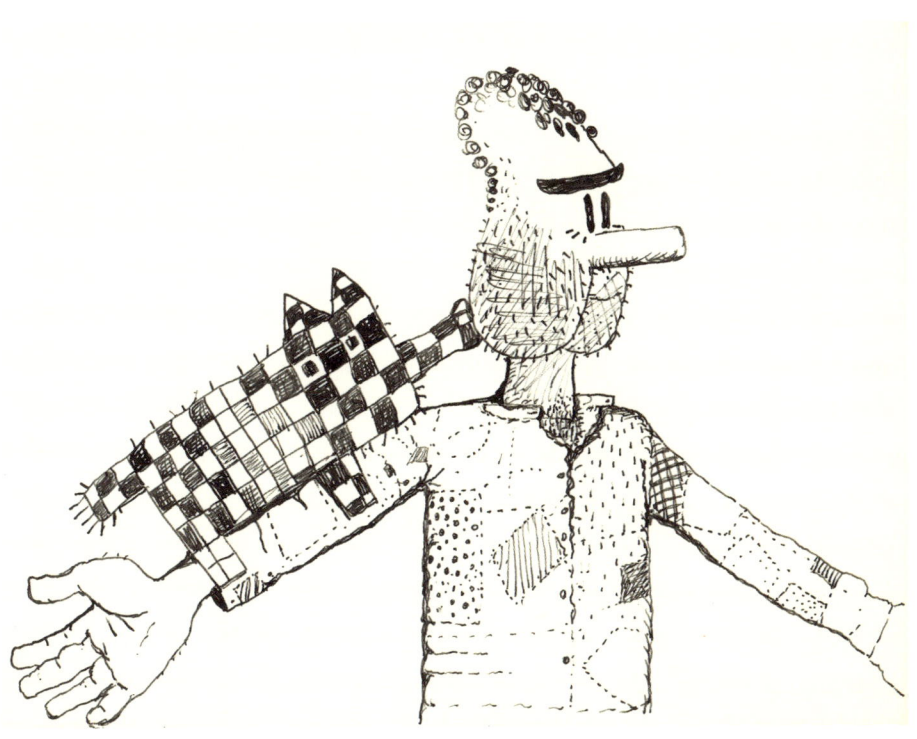

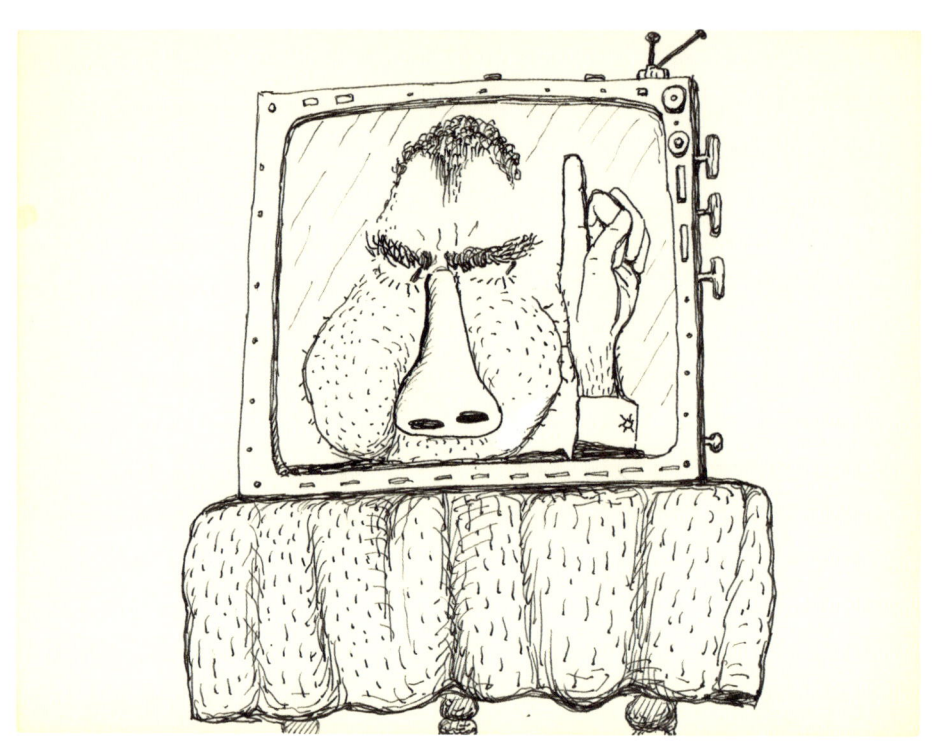

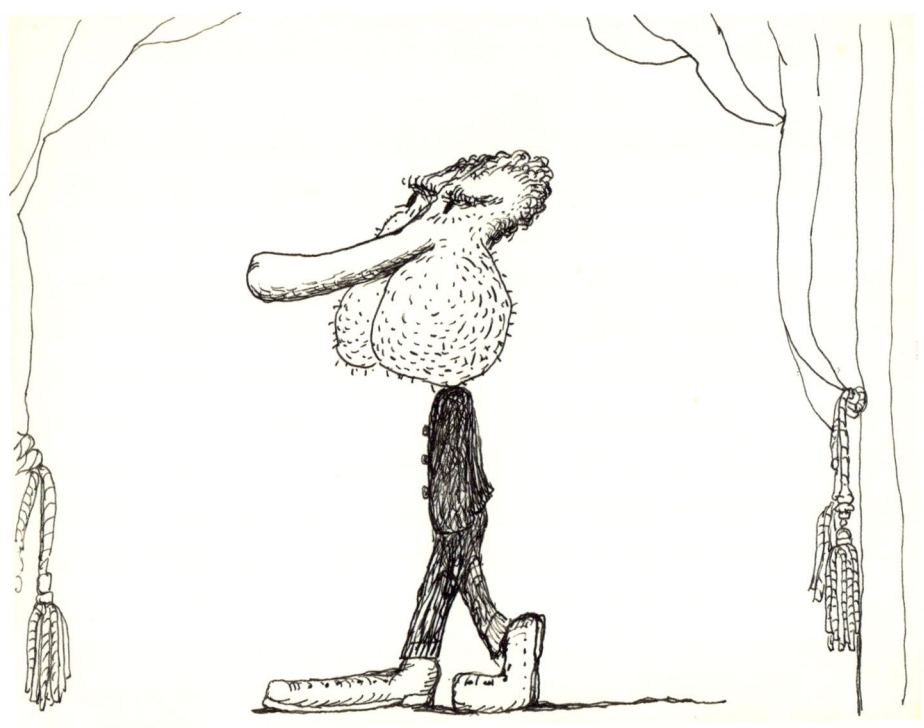

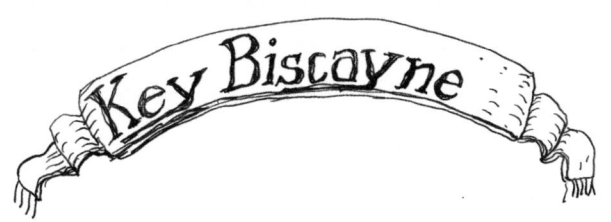

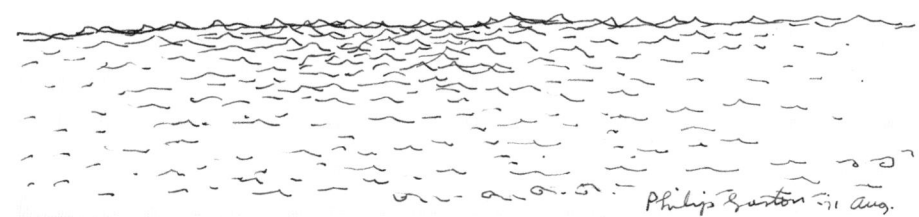

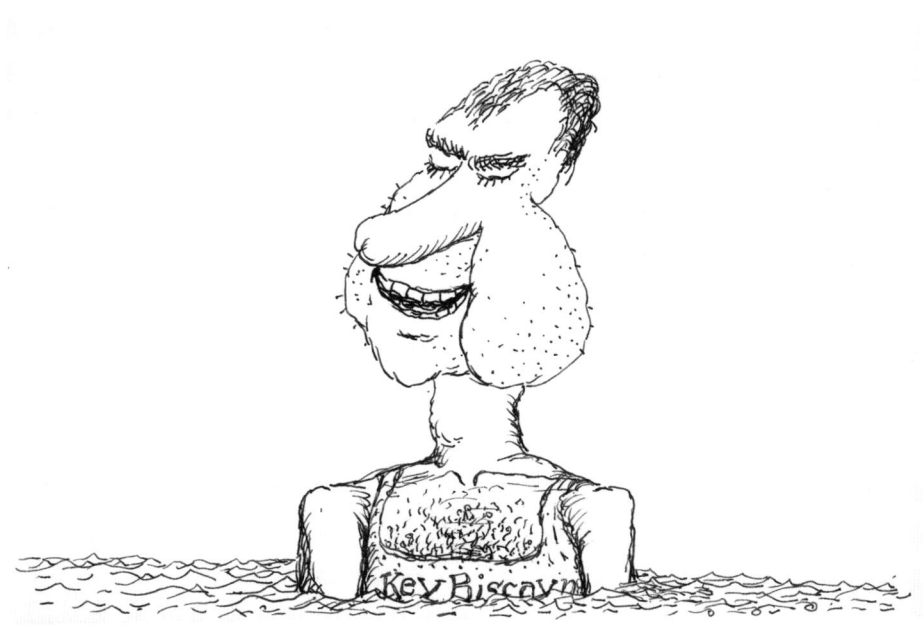

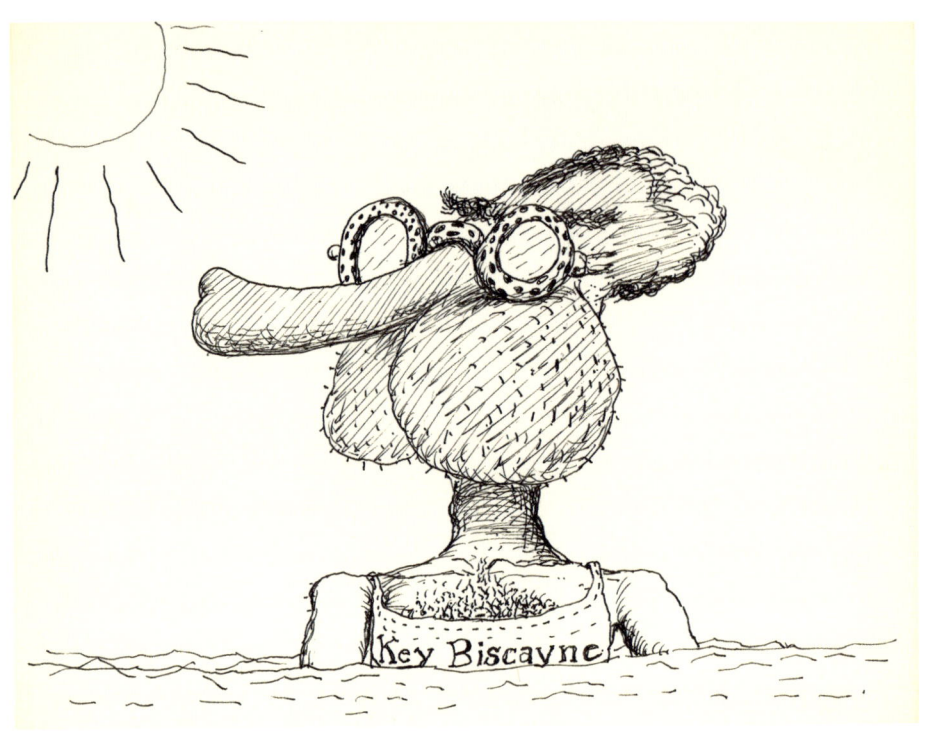

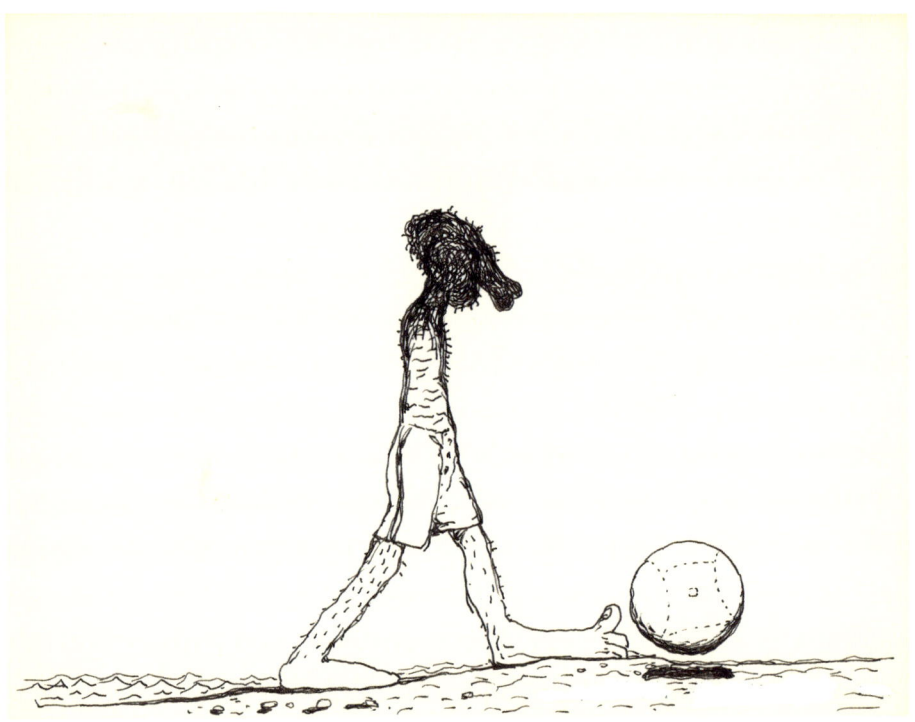

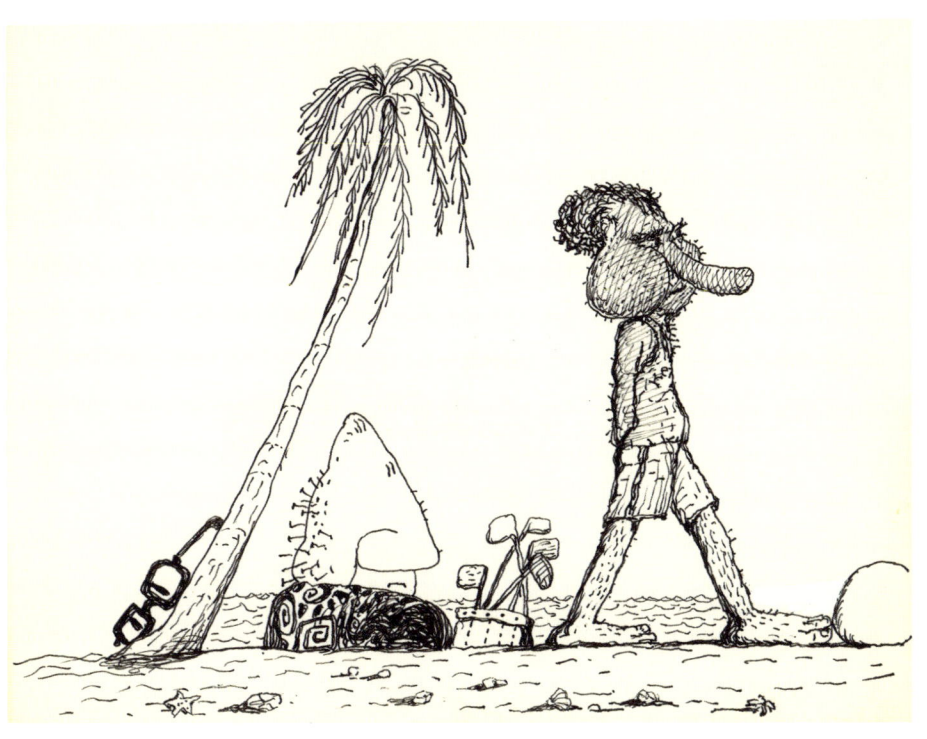

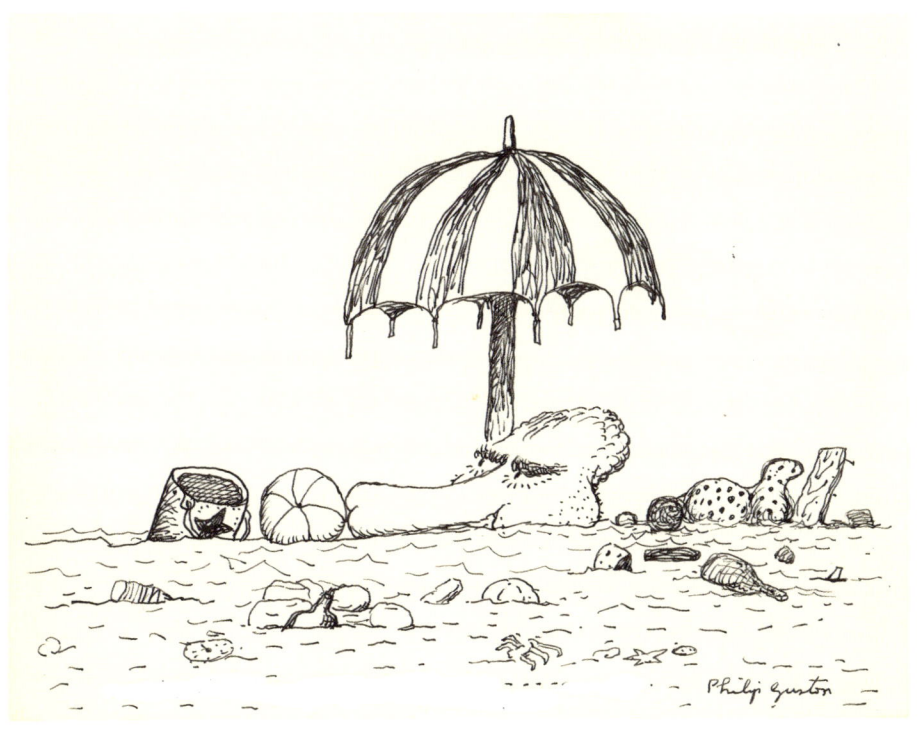

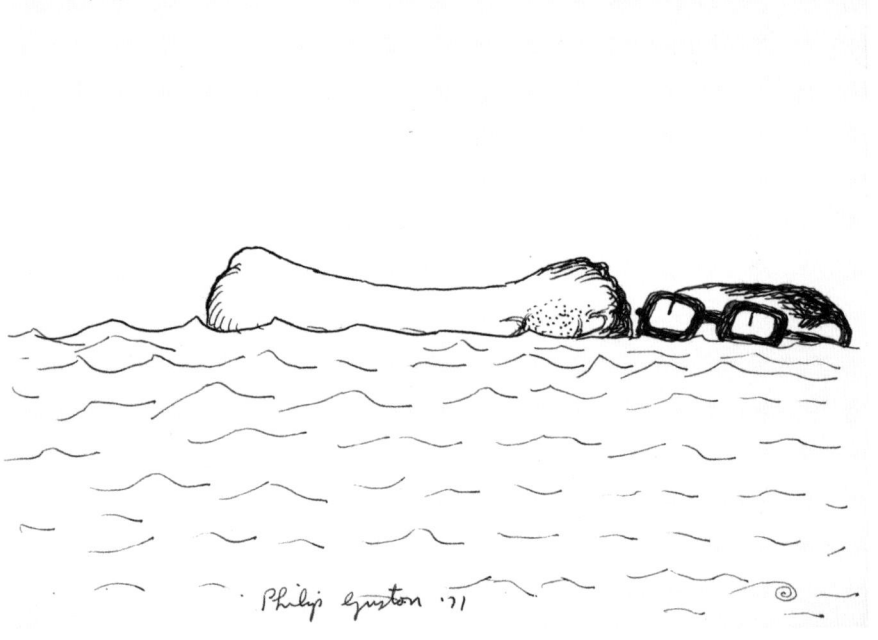

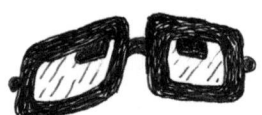

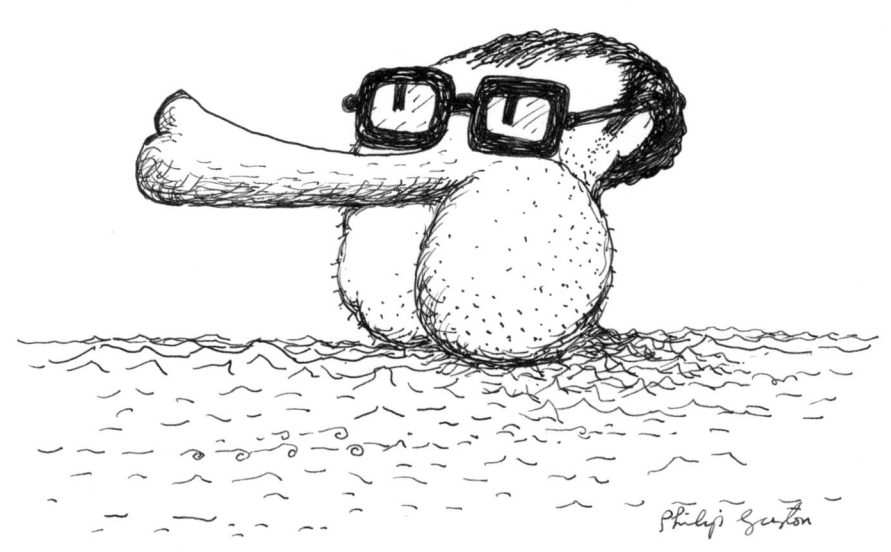

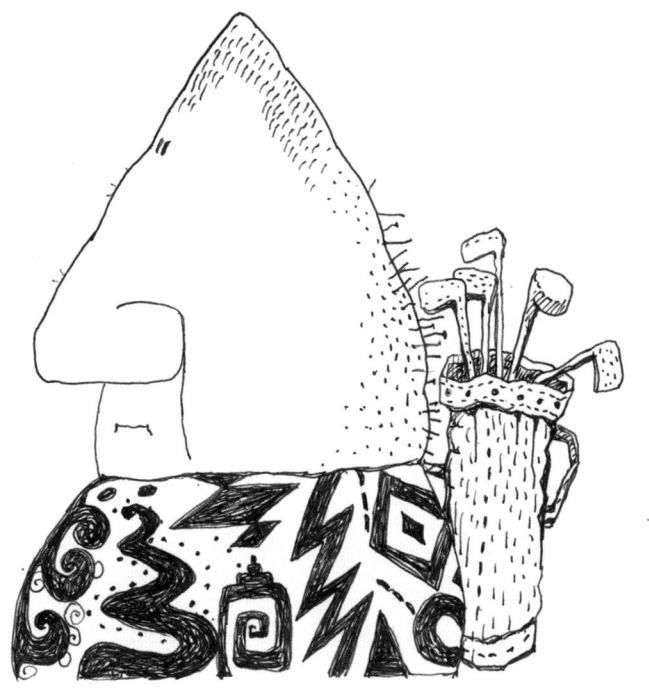

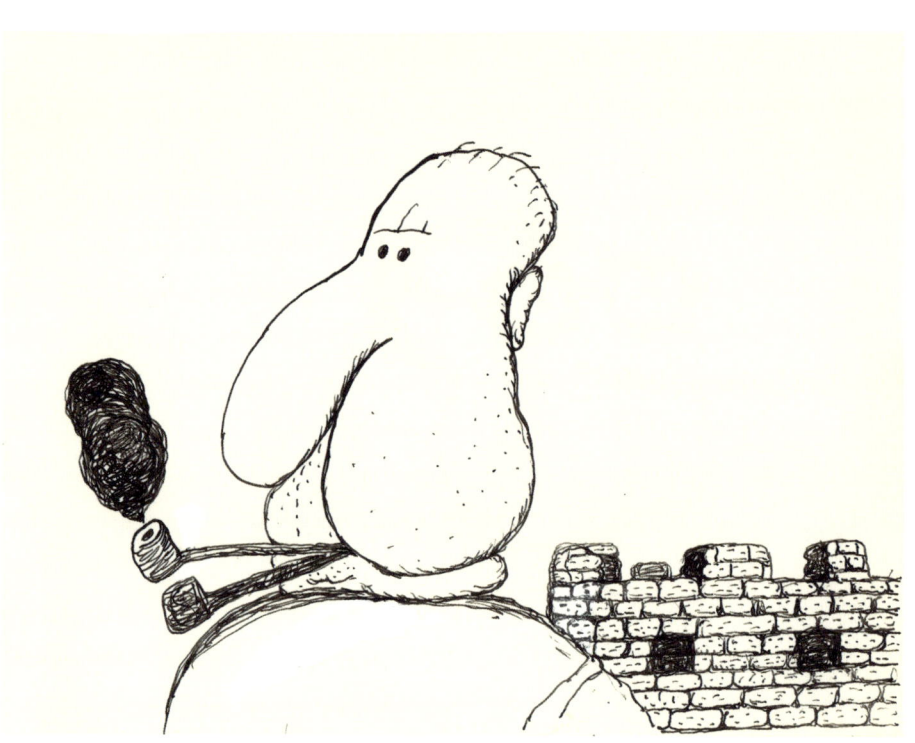

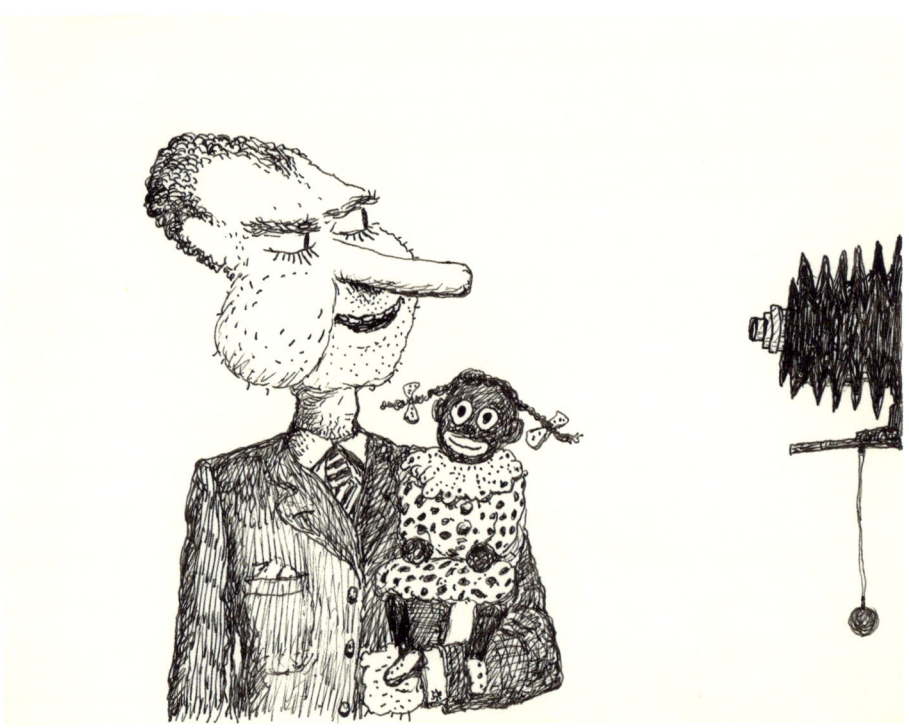

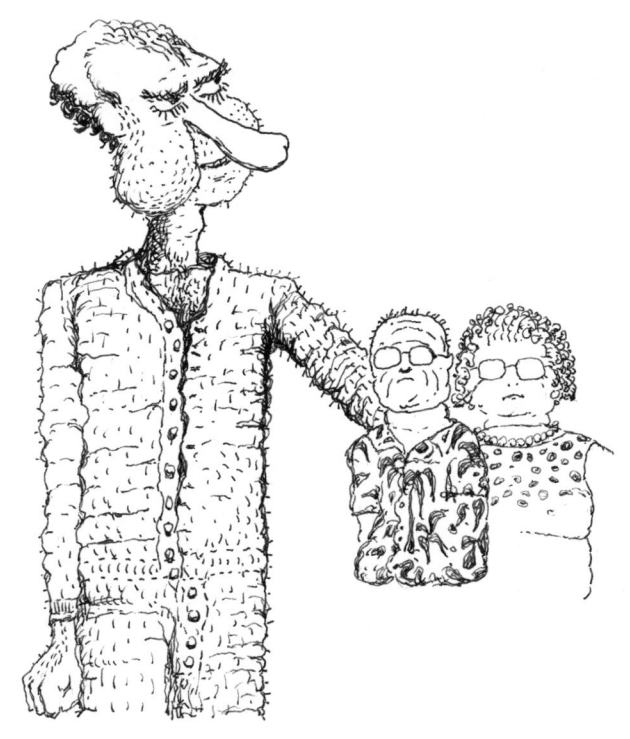

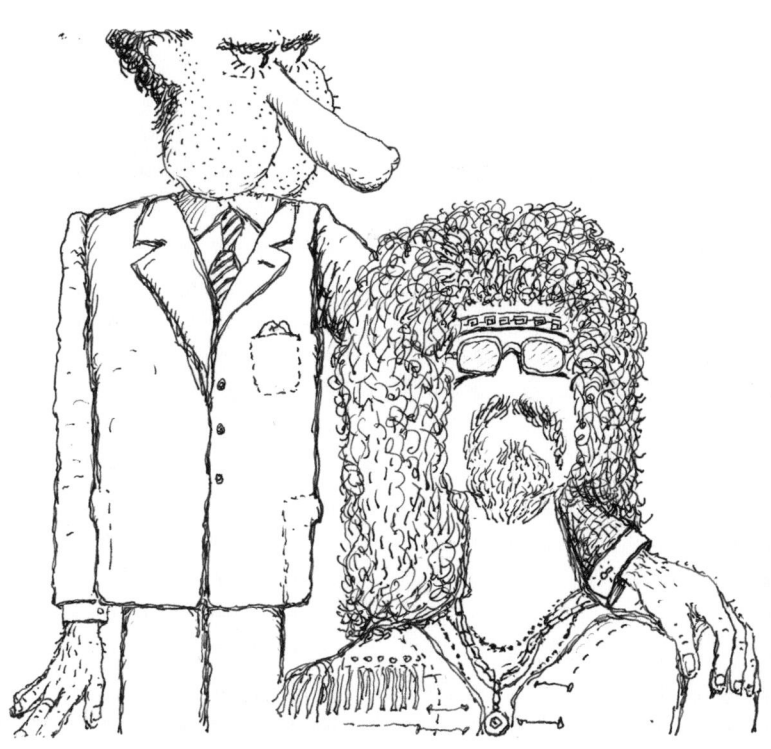

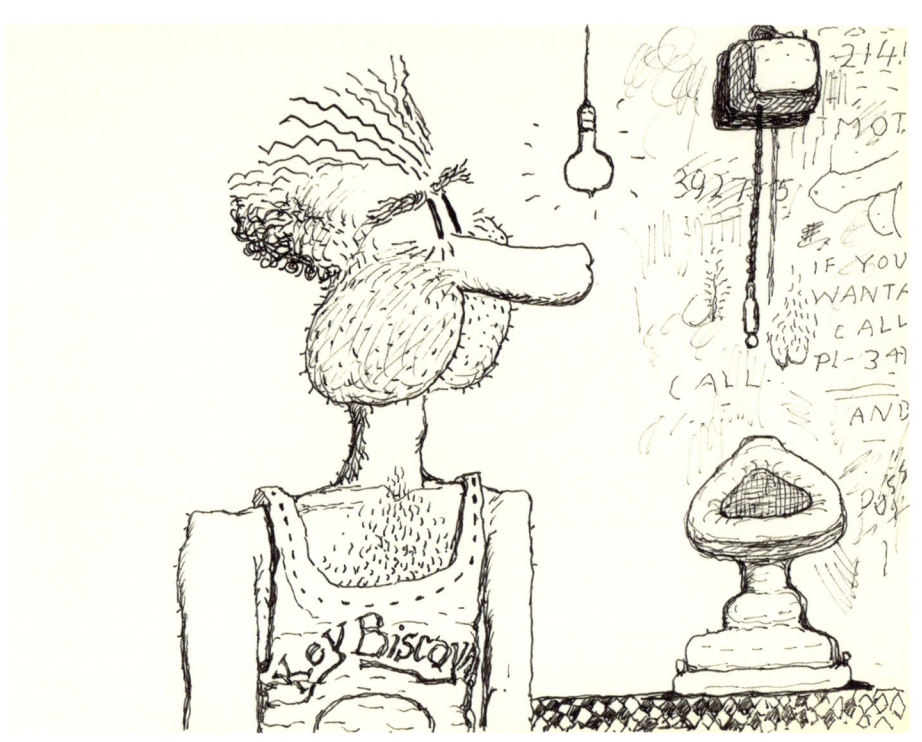

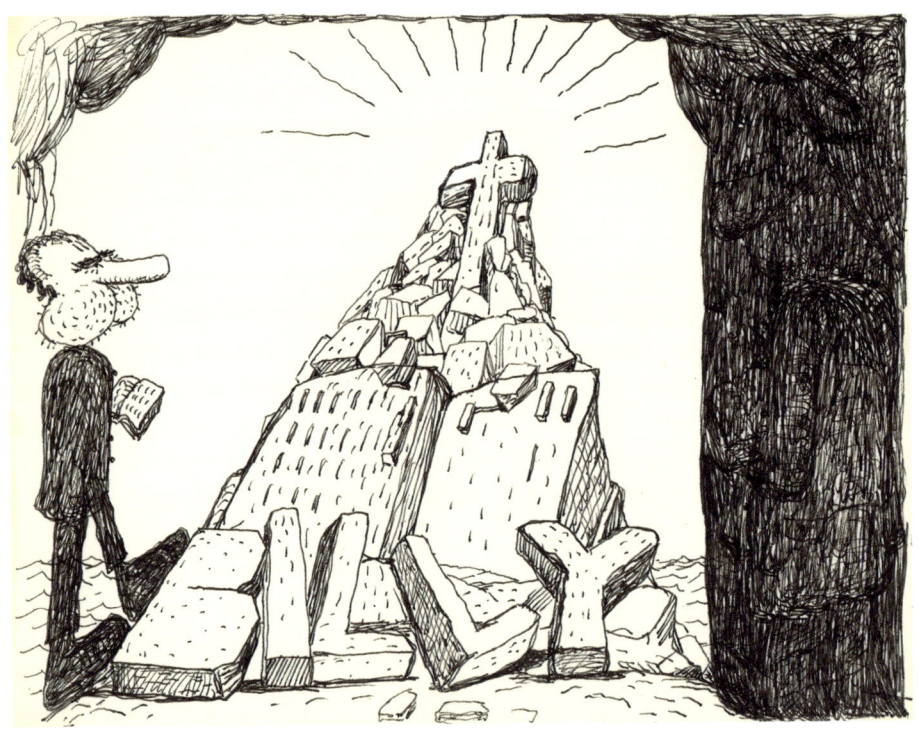

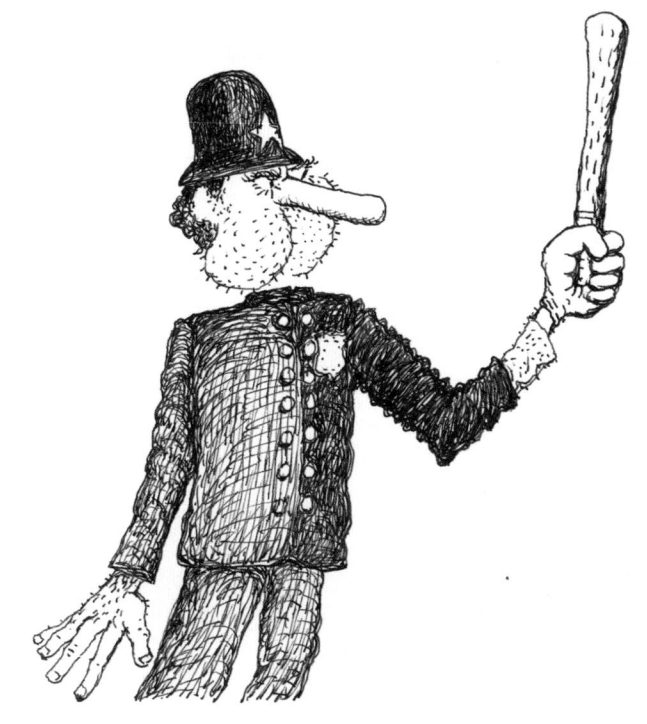

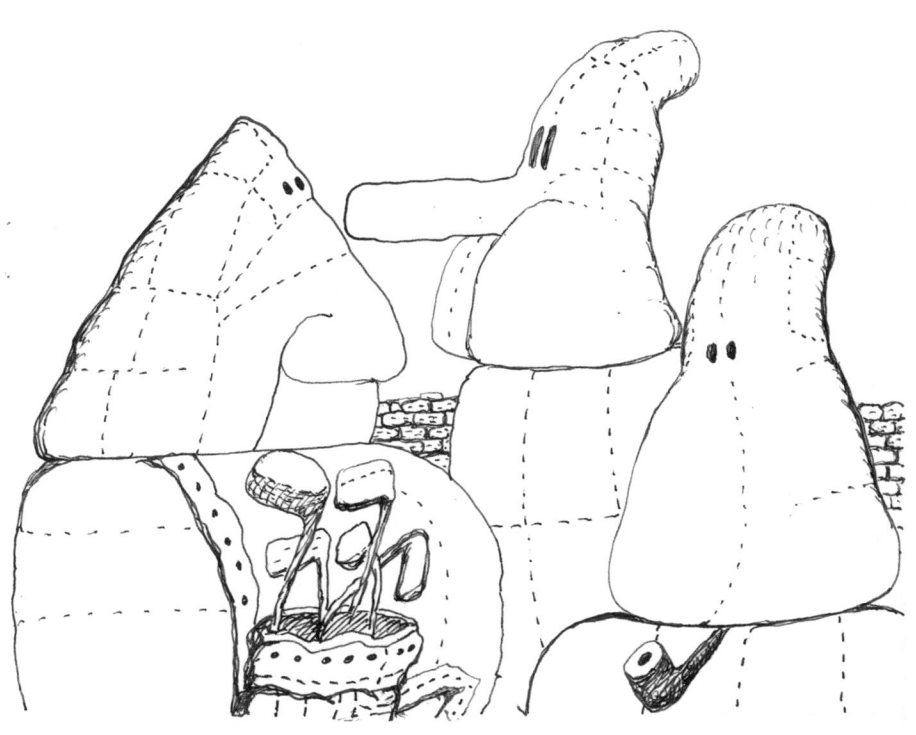

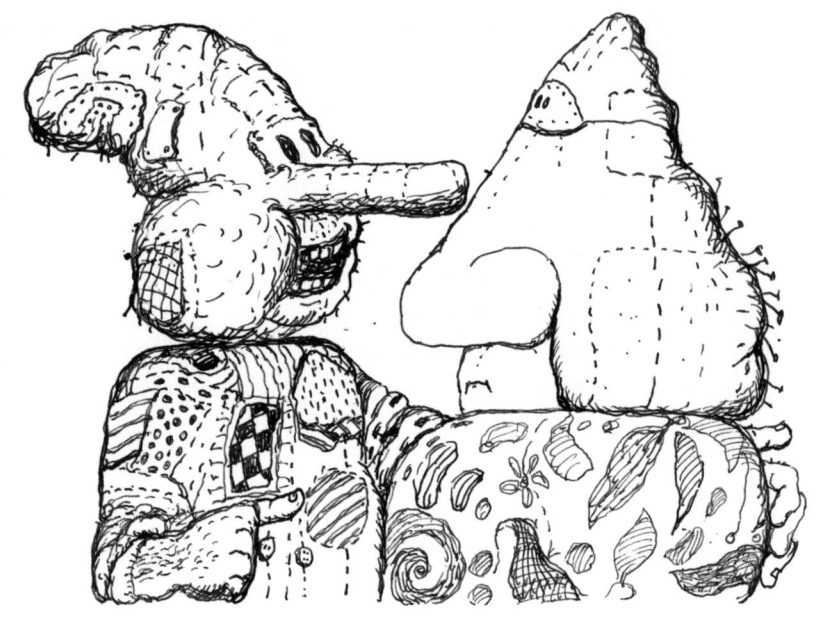
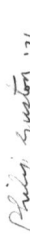
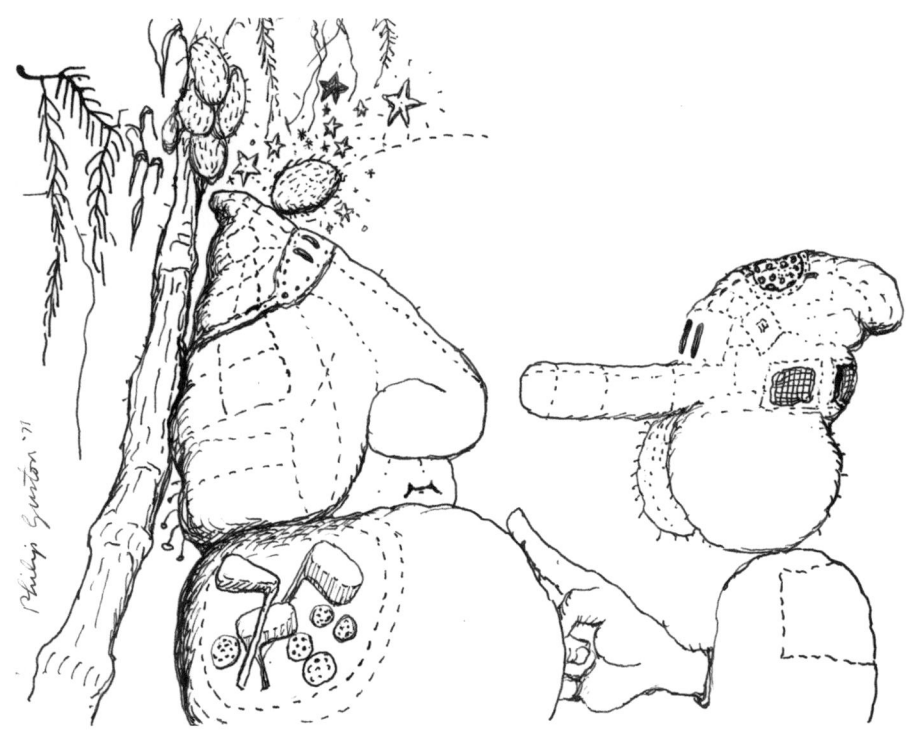

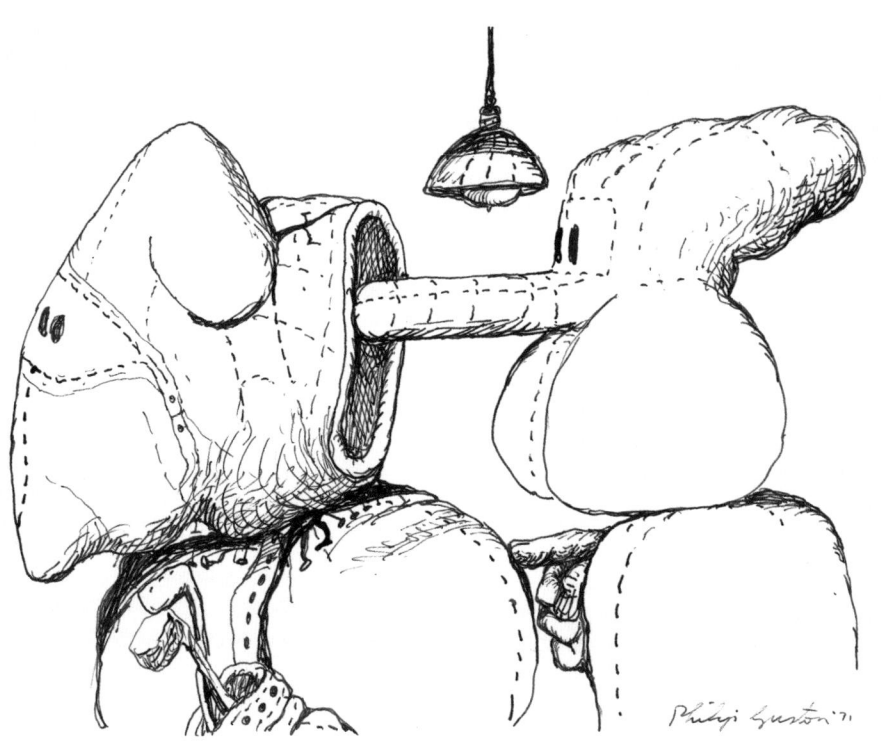

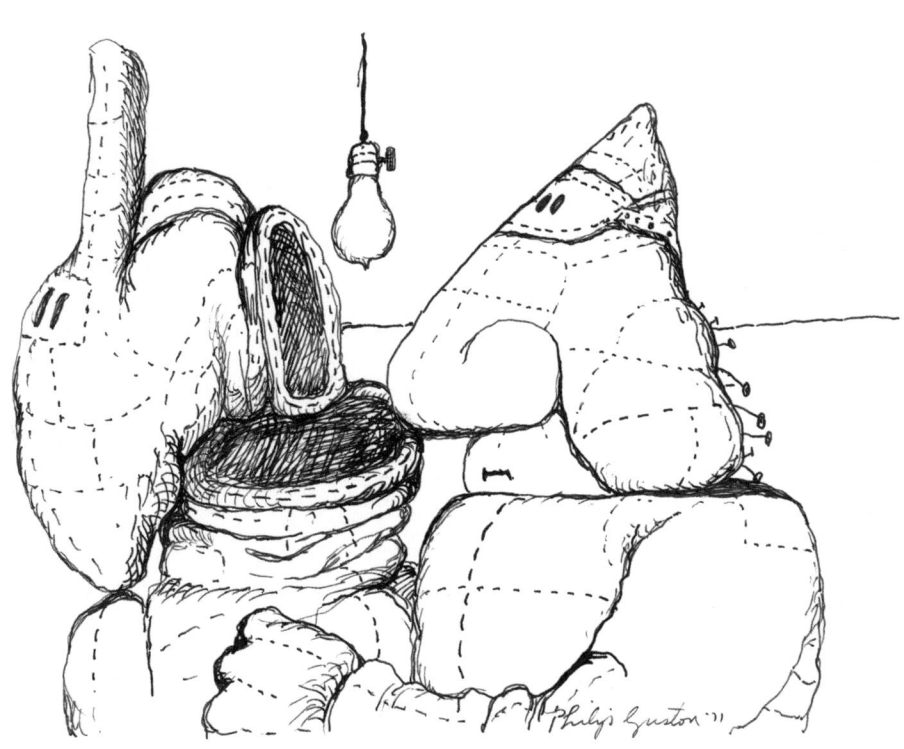

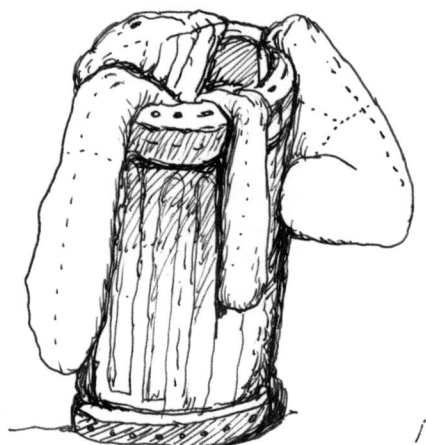

Philip Guston '71

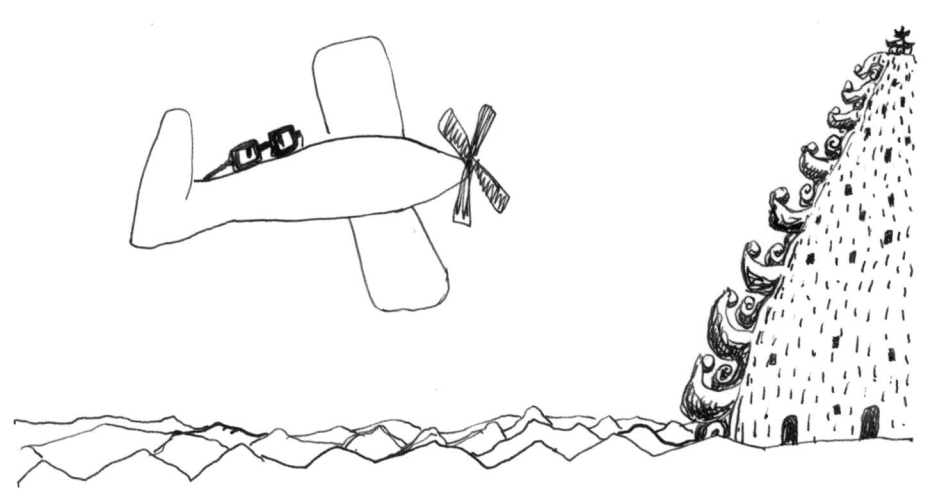

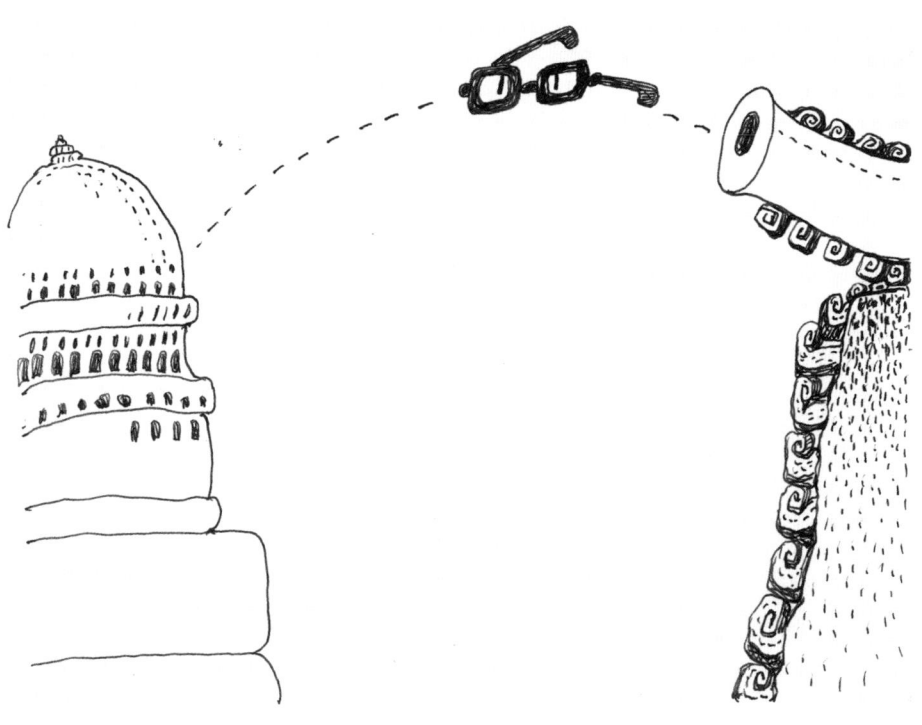

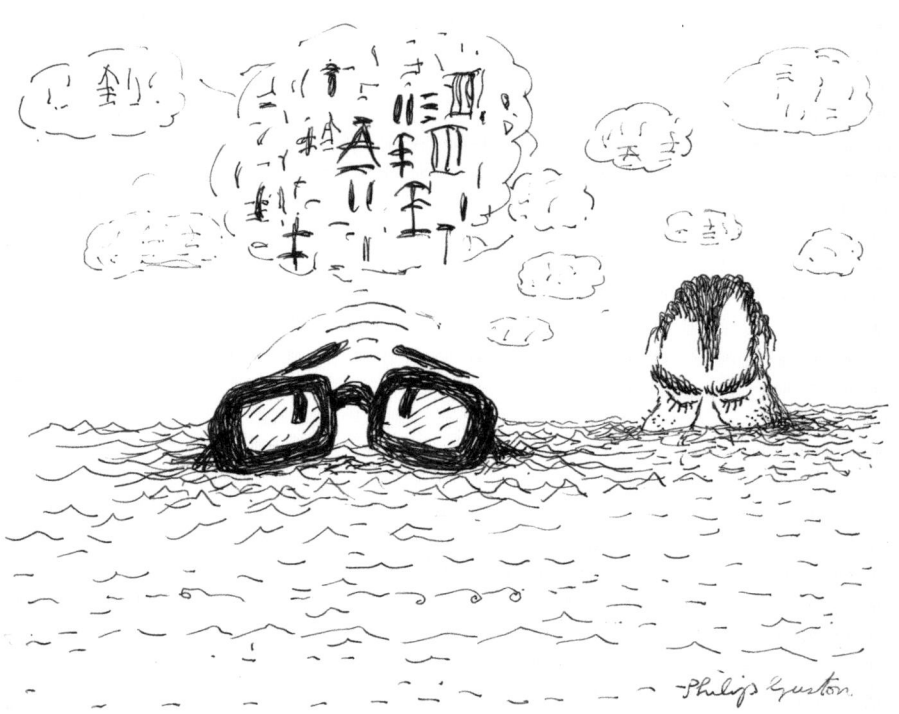

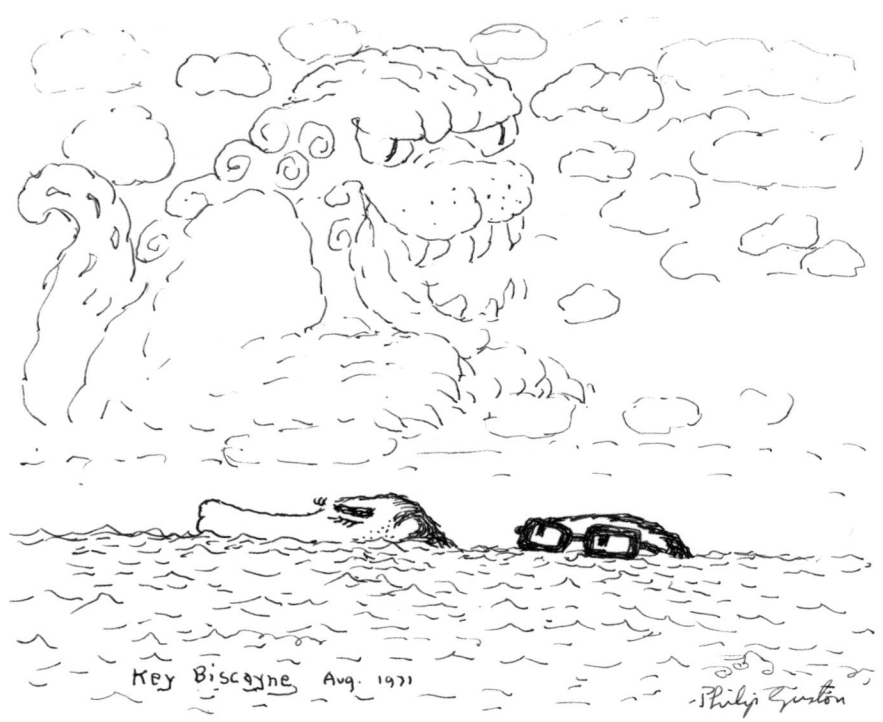

Key Biscayne Aug. 1971

Philip Guston

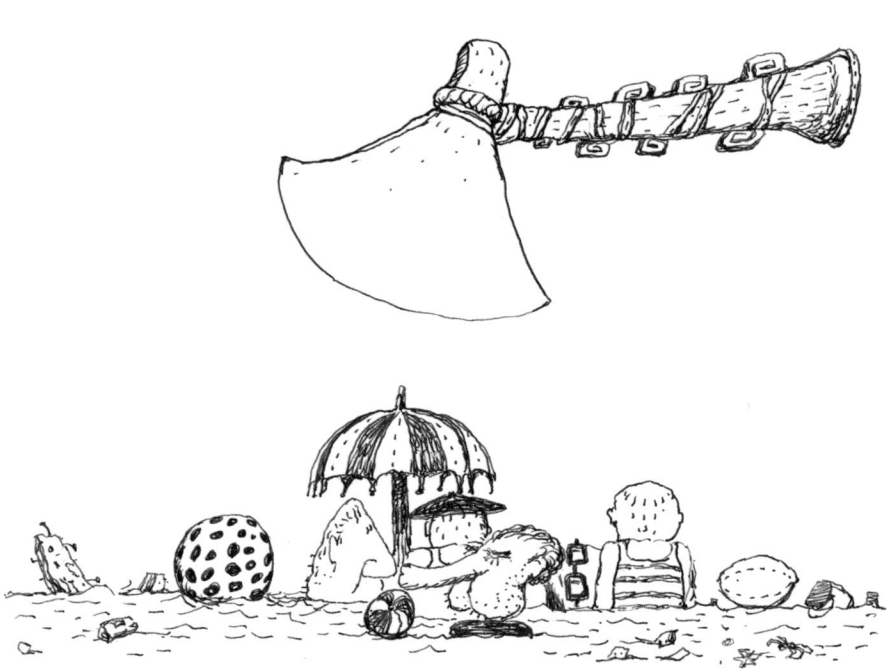

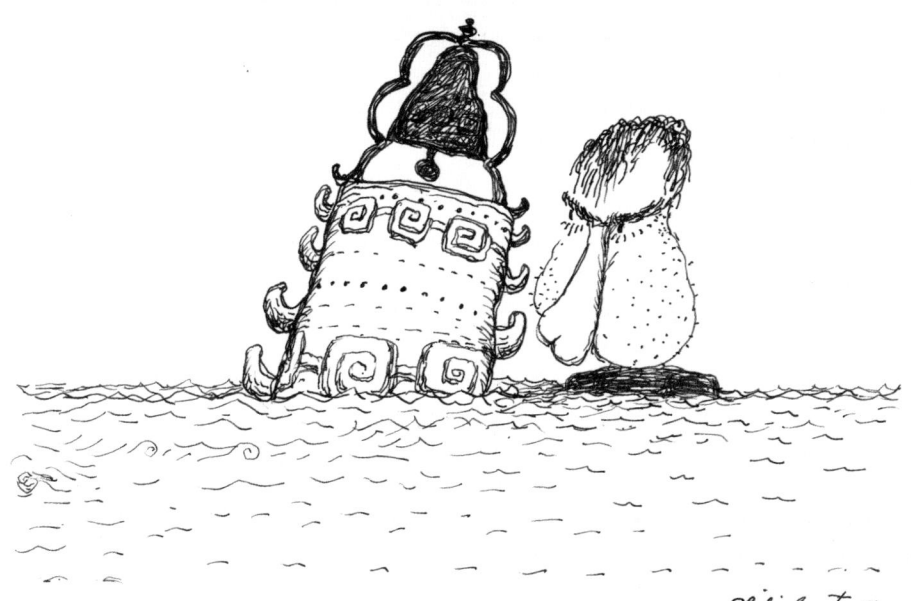

Philip Guston '71

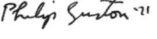

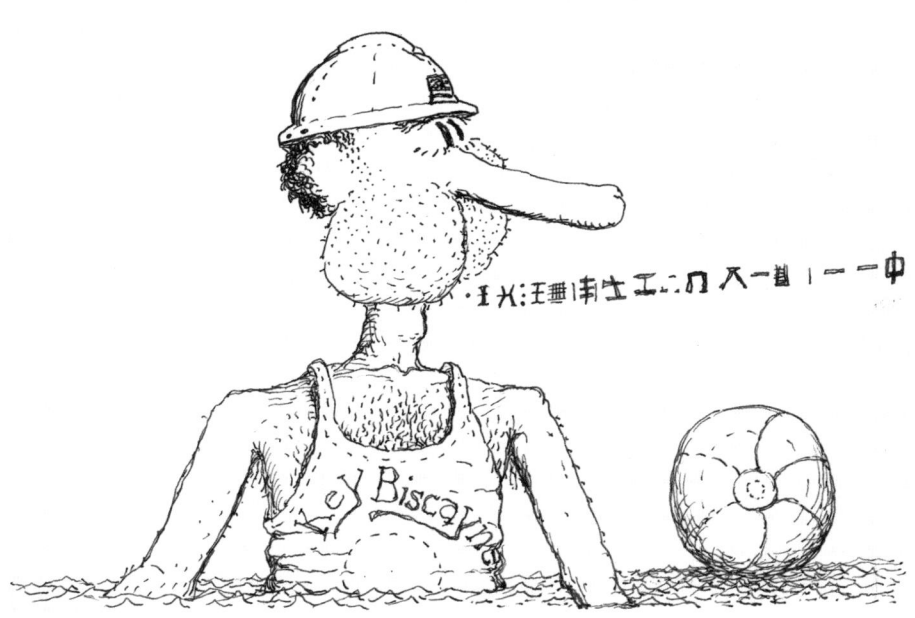

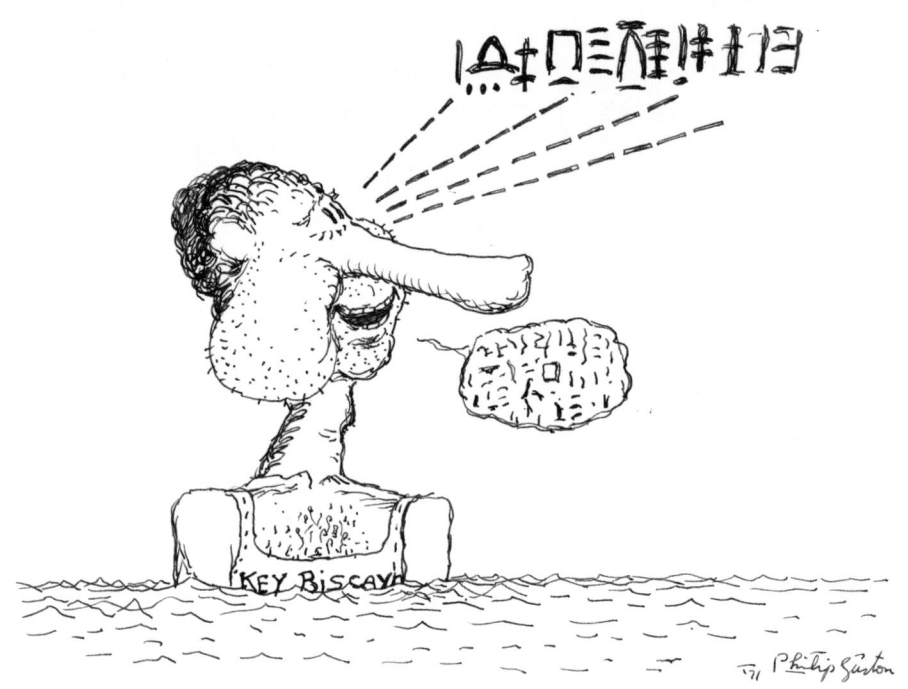

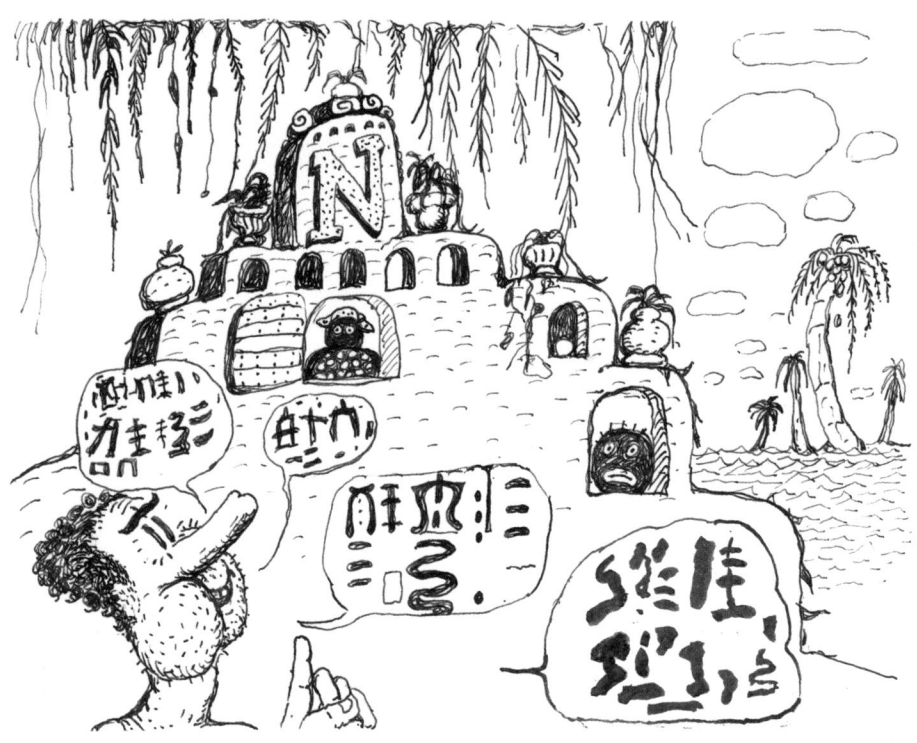

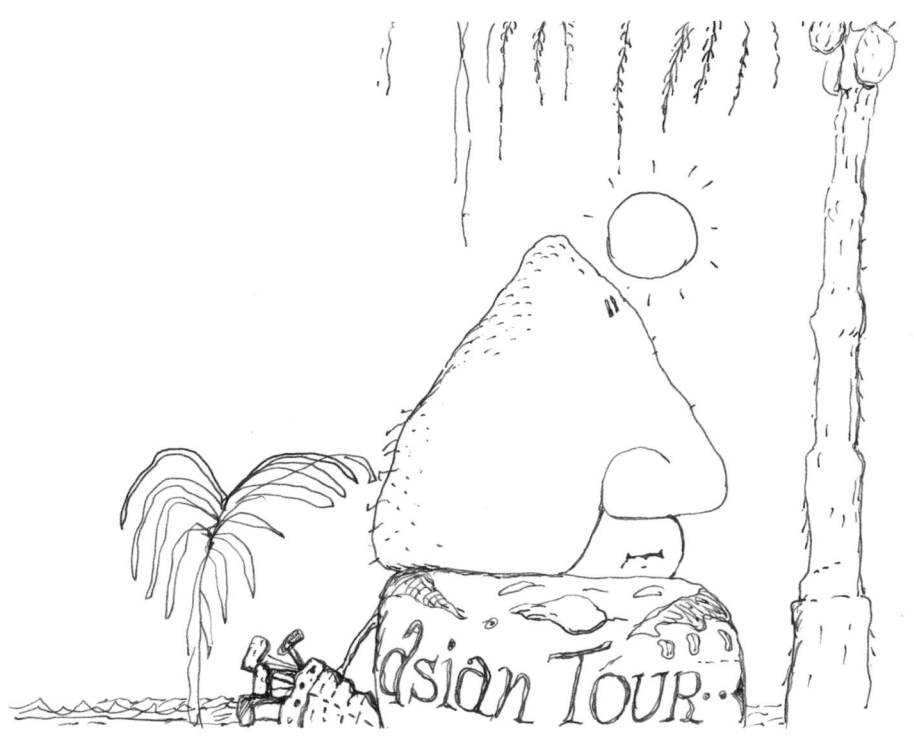

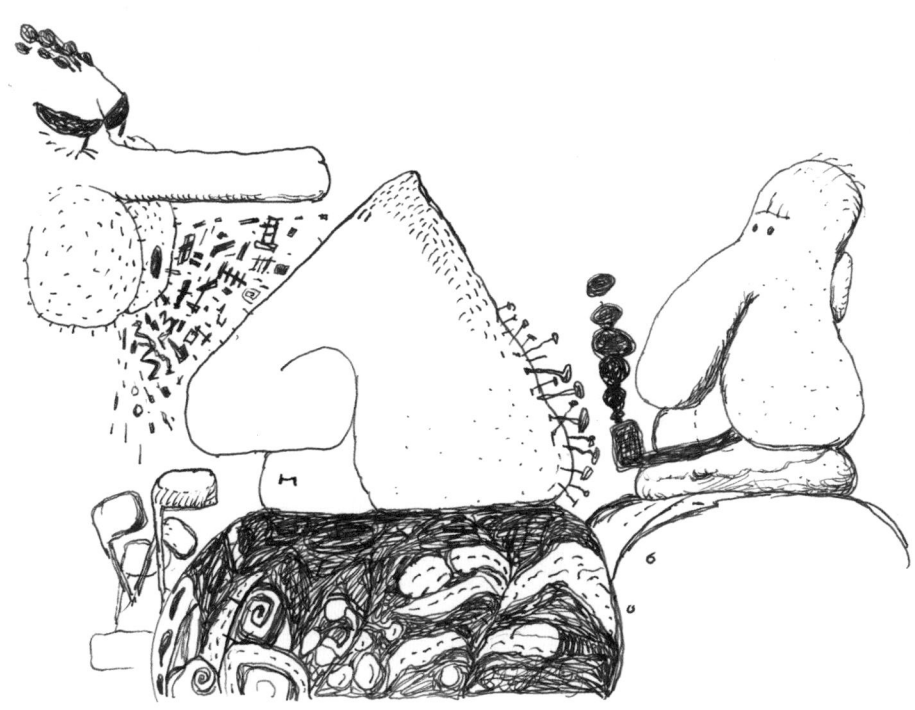

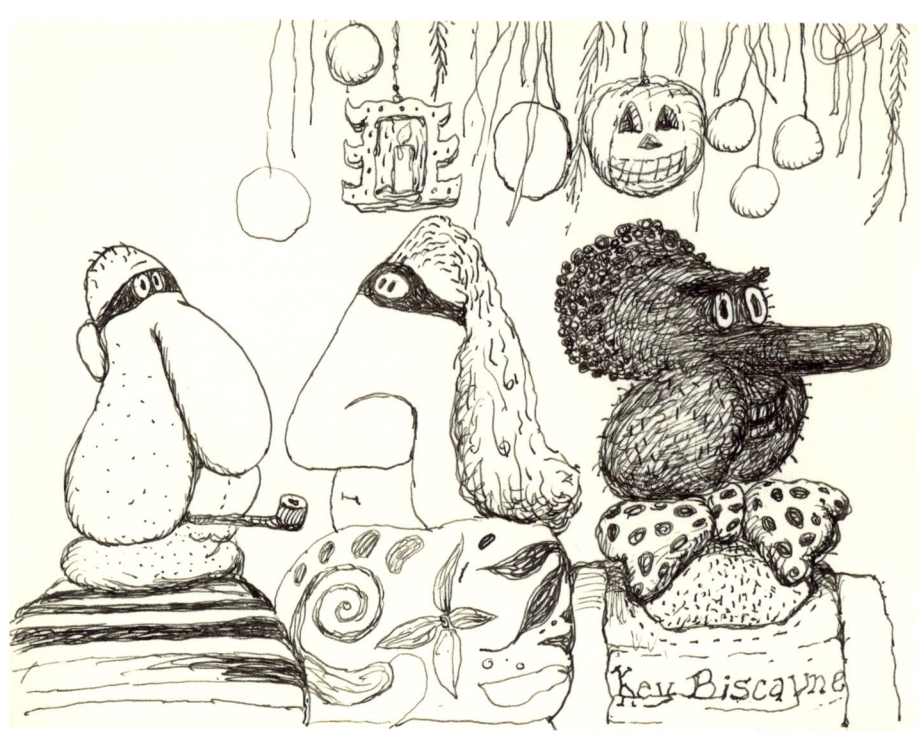

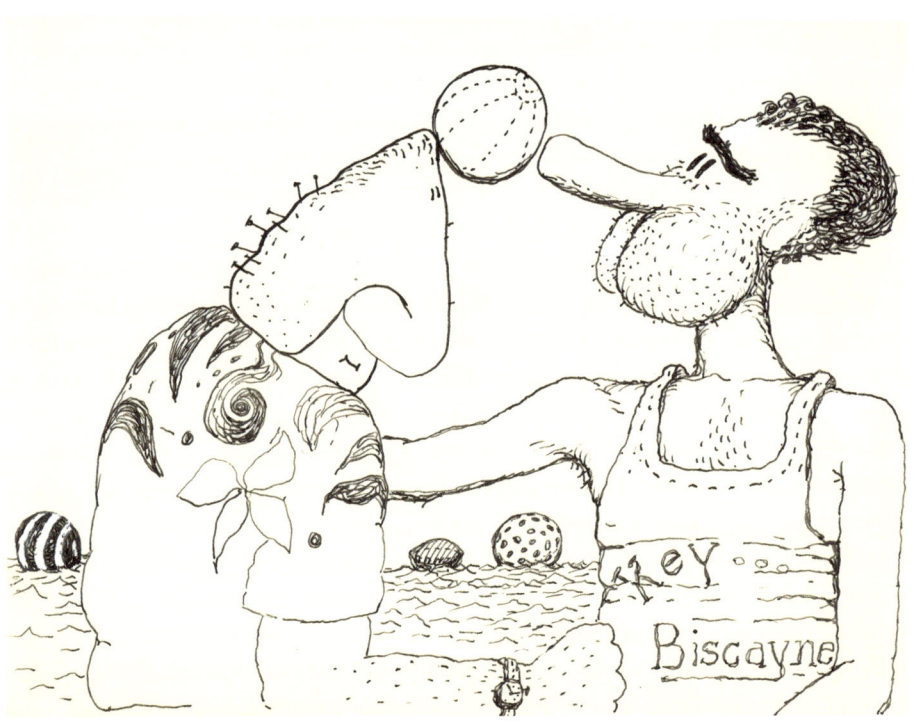

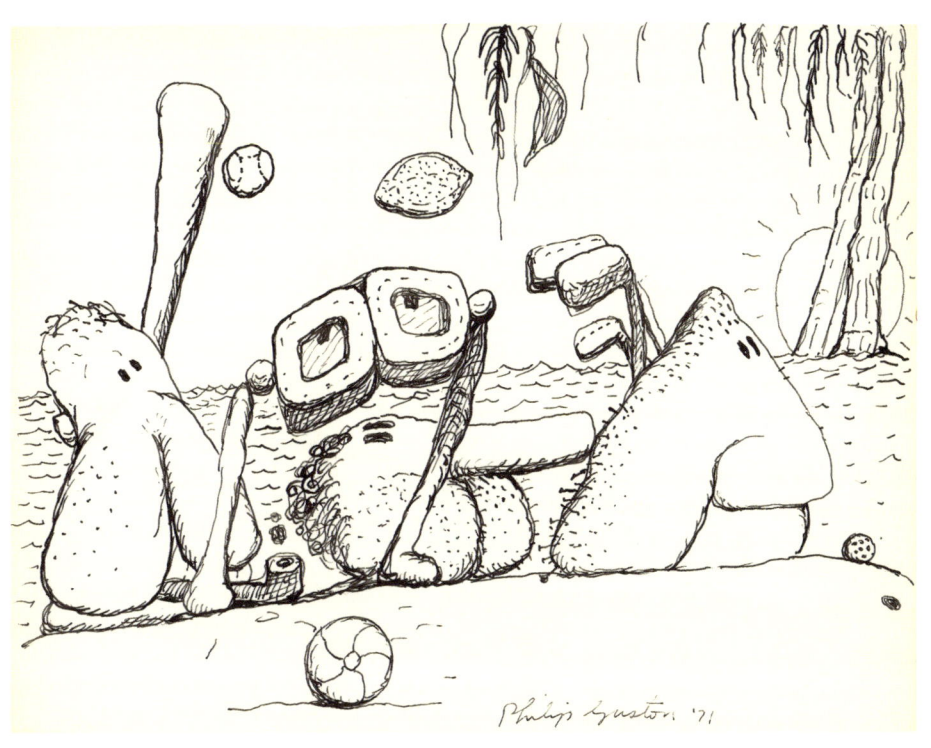

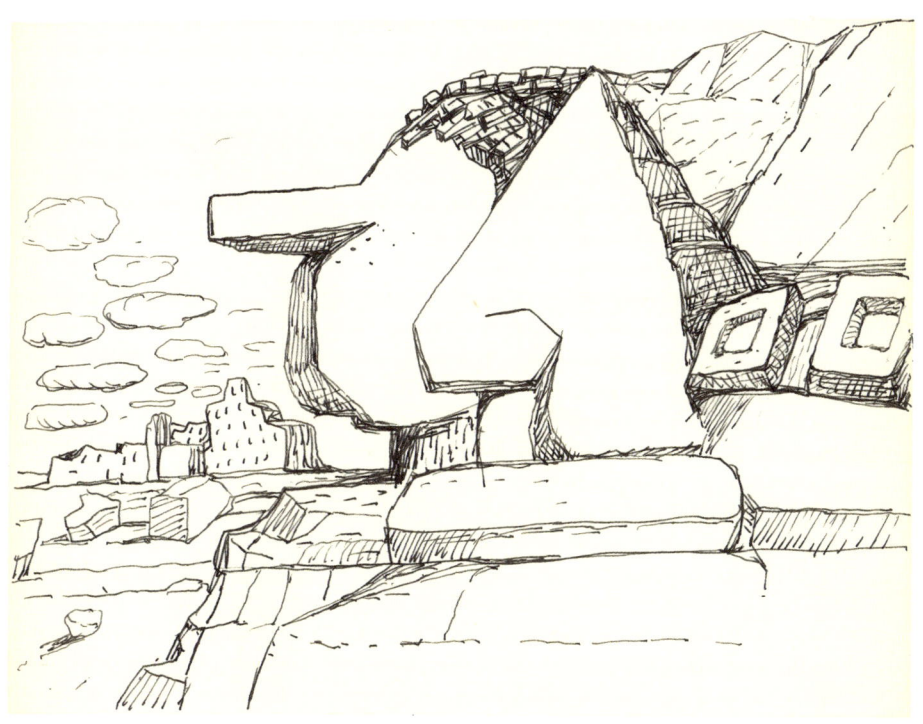

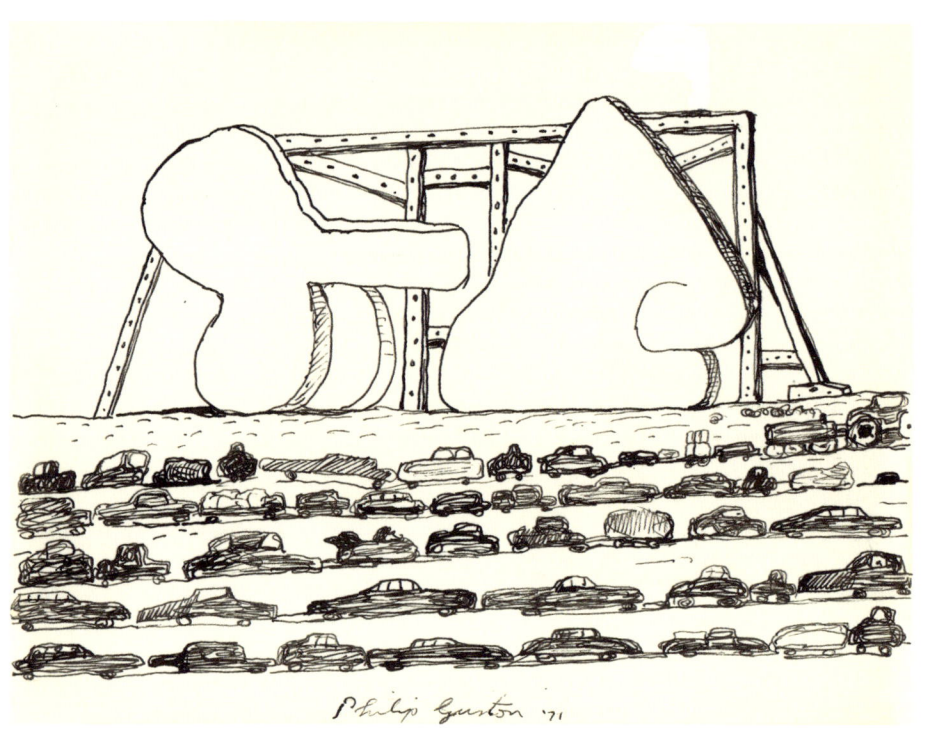

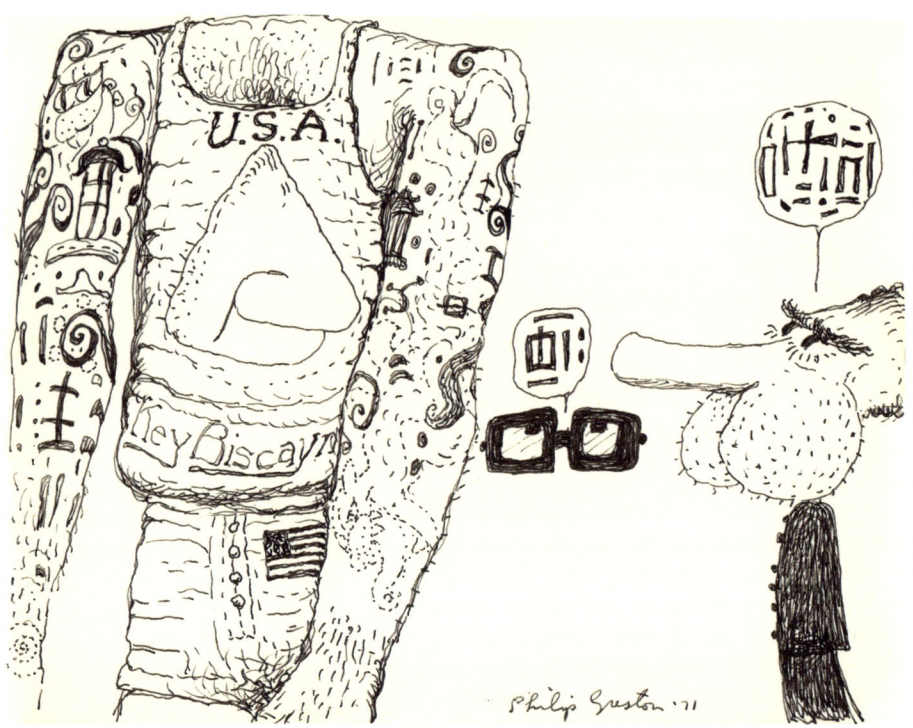

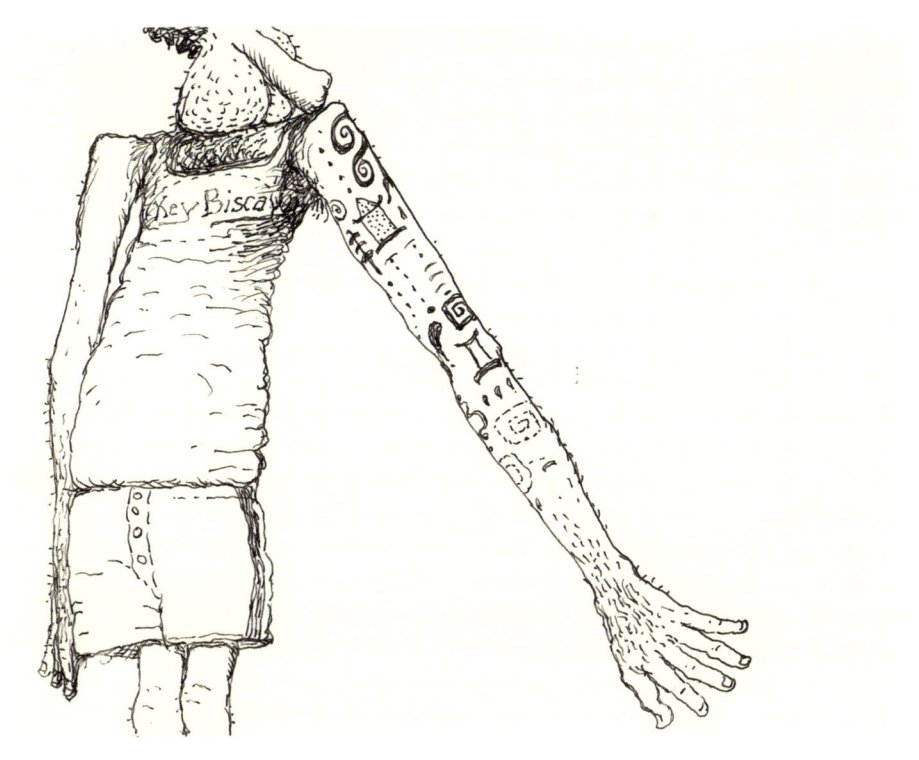

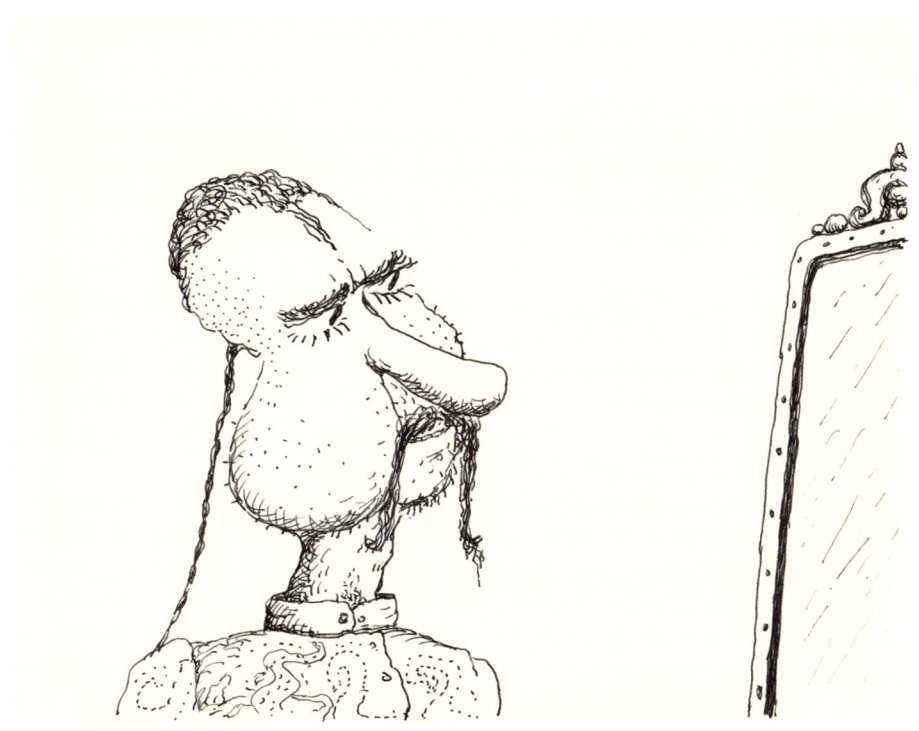

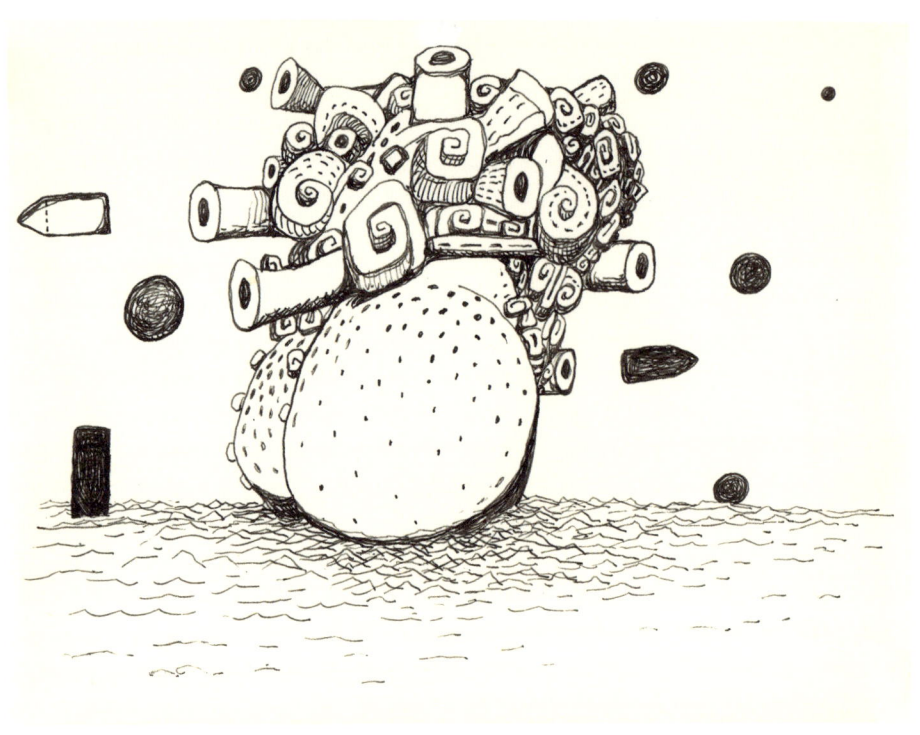

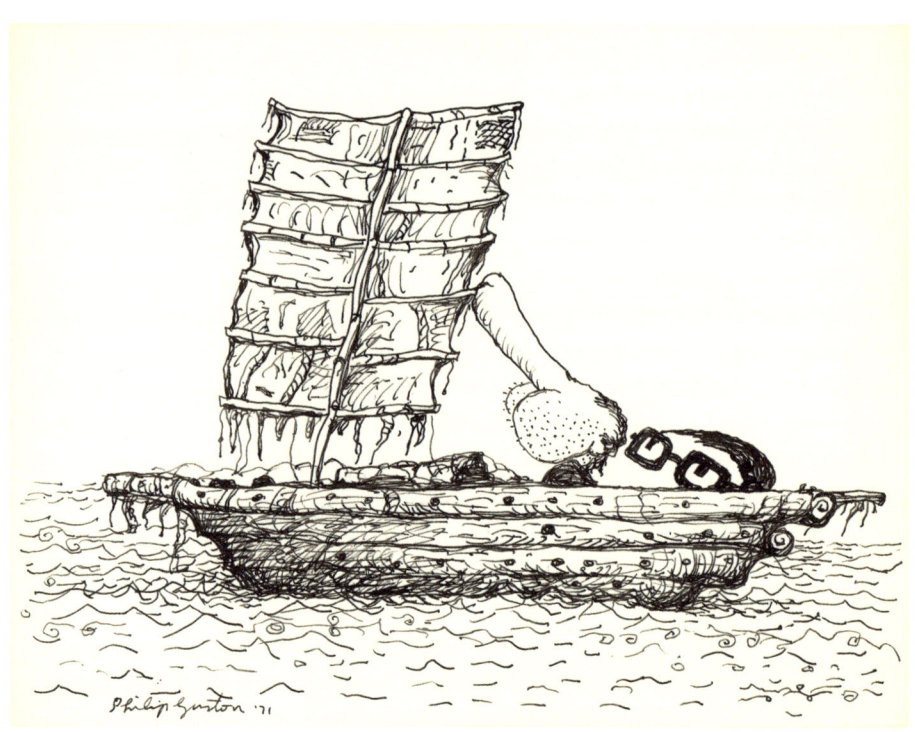

Philip Guston '71

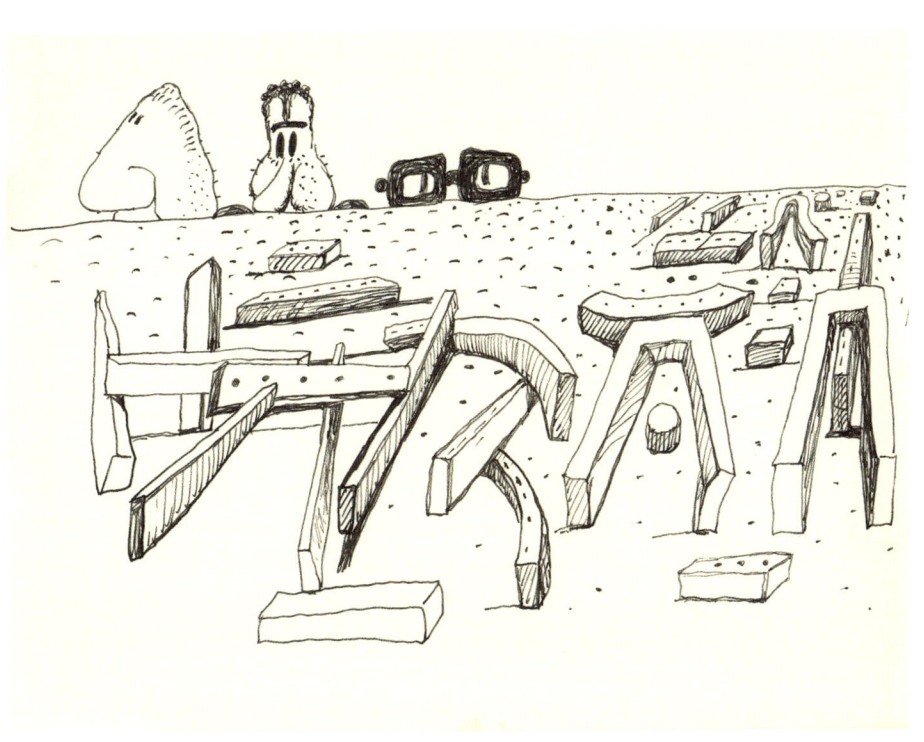

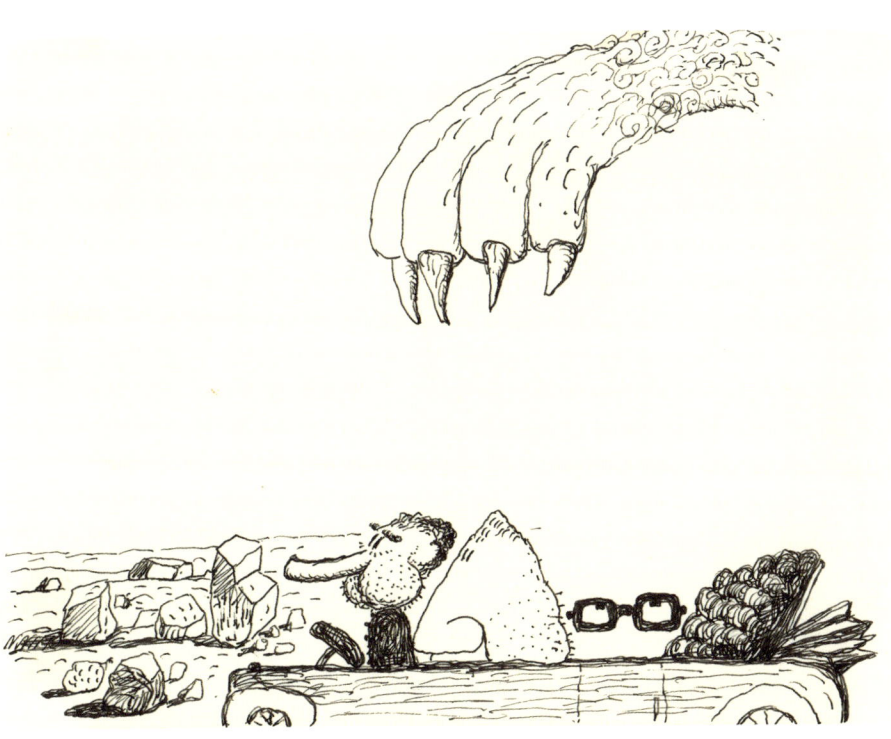

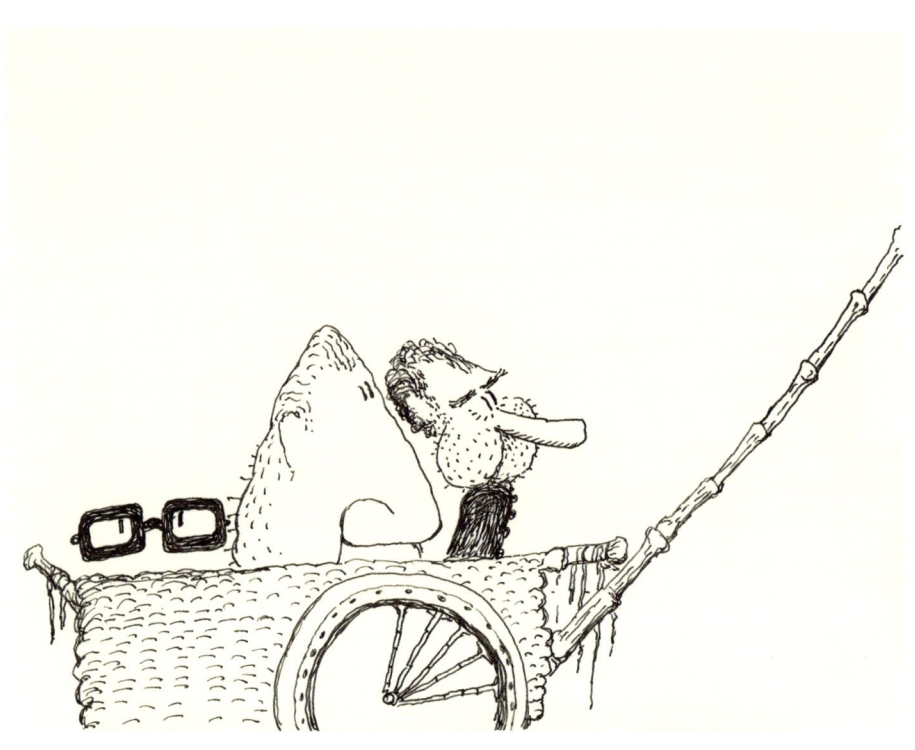

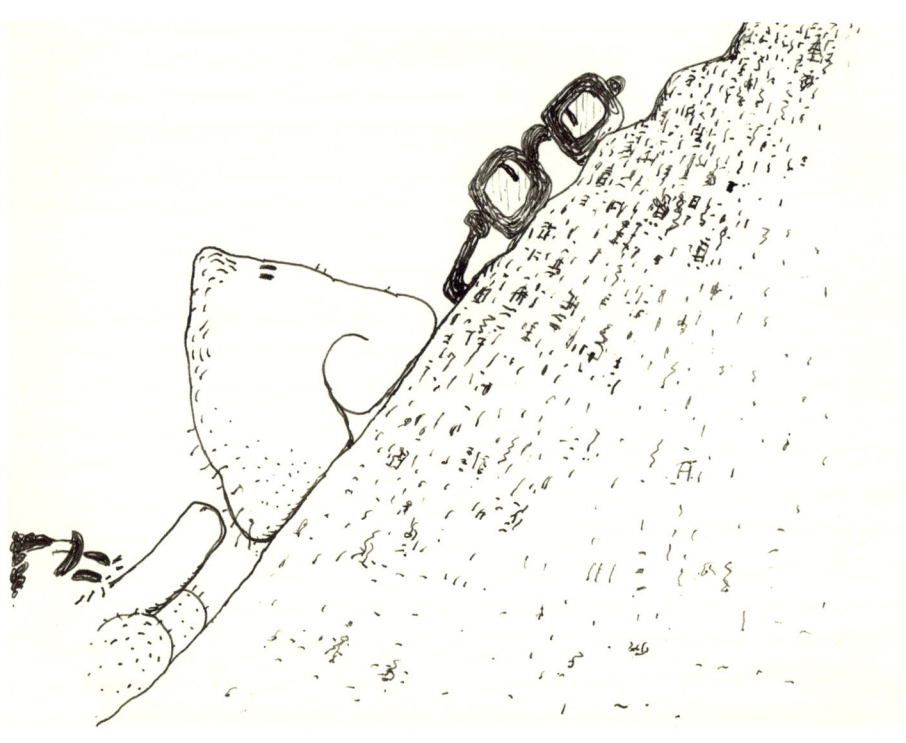

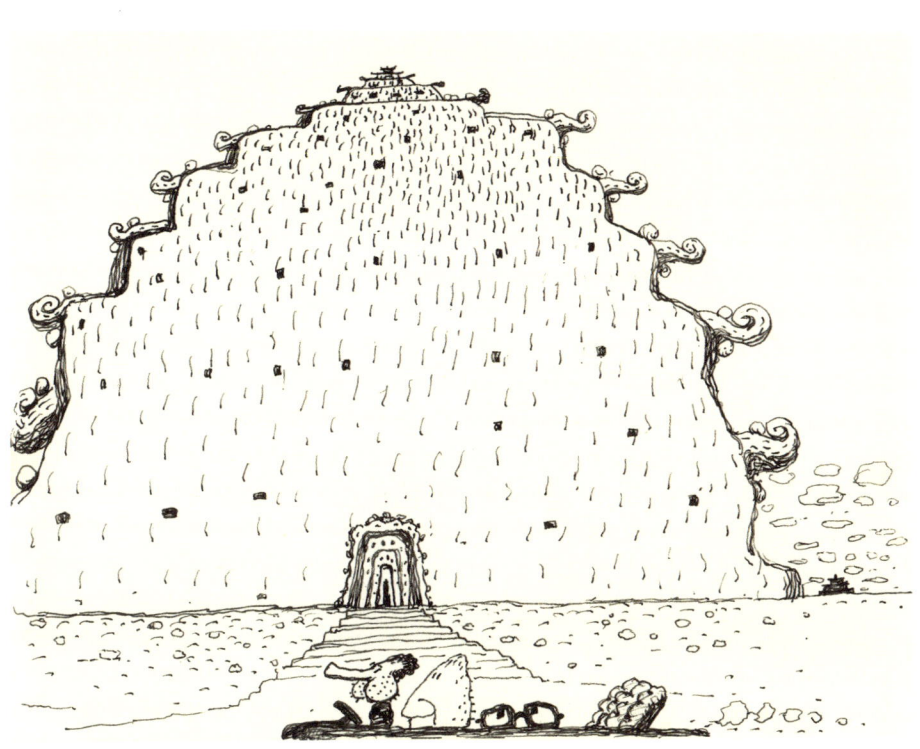

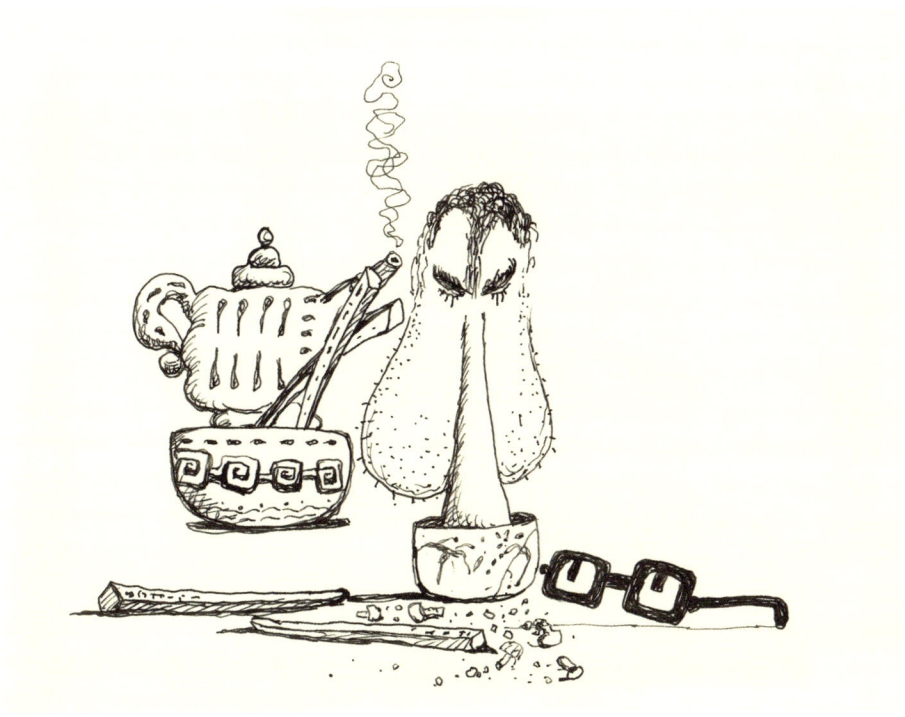

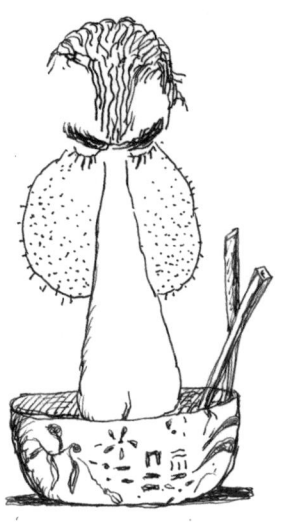

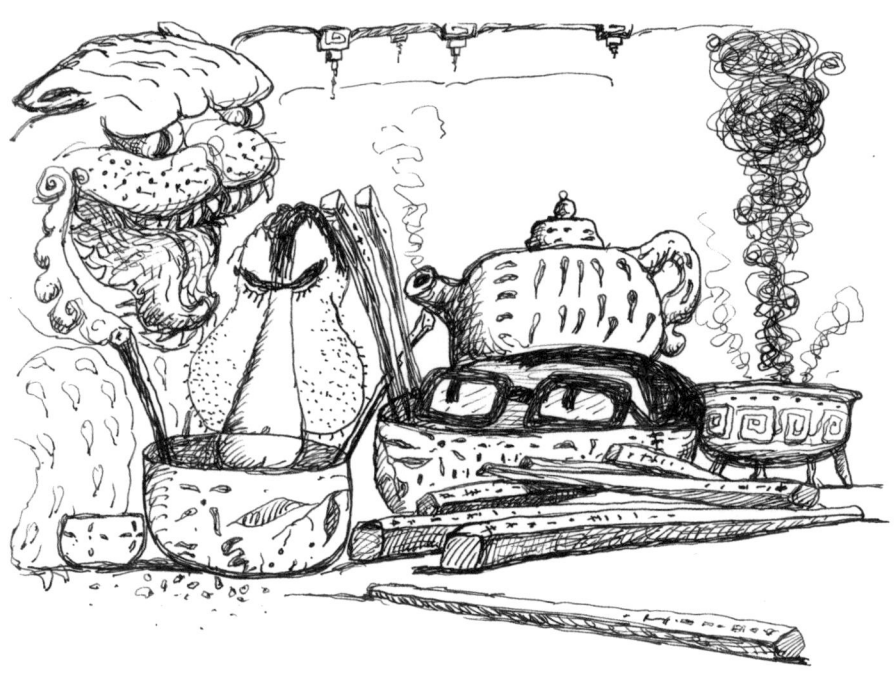

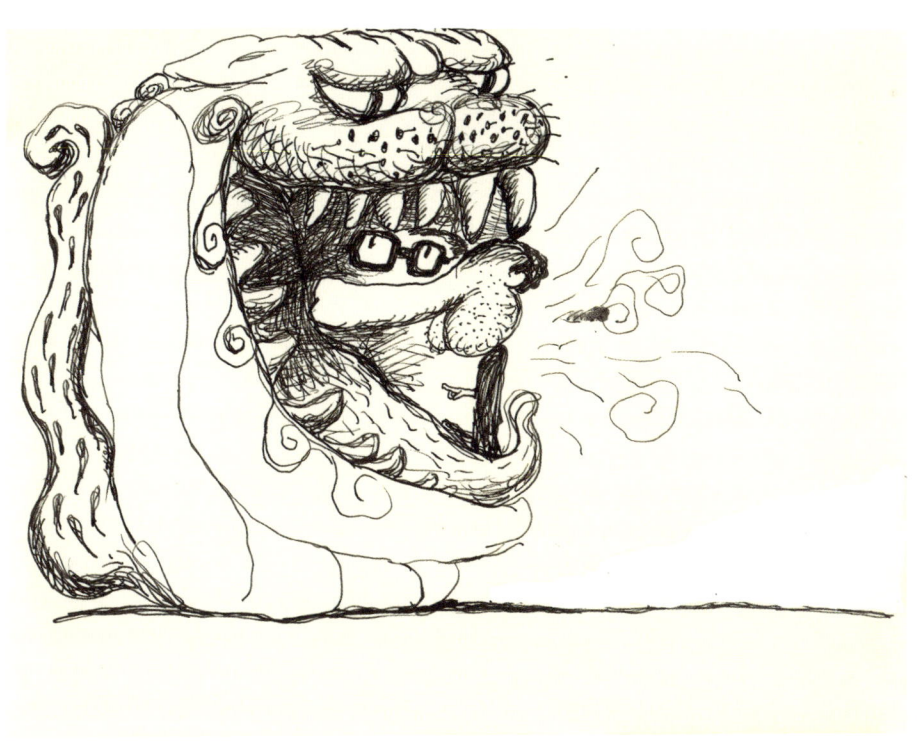

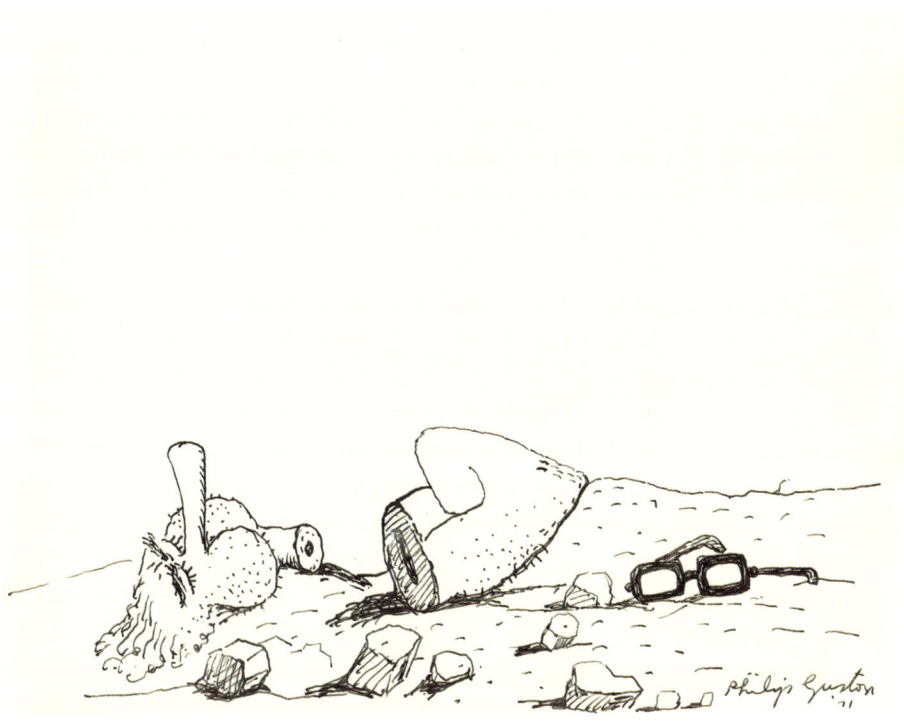

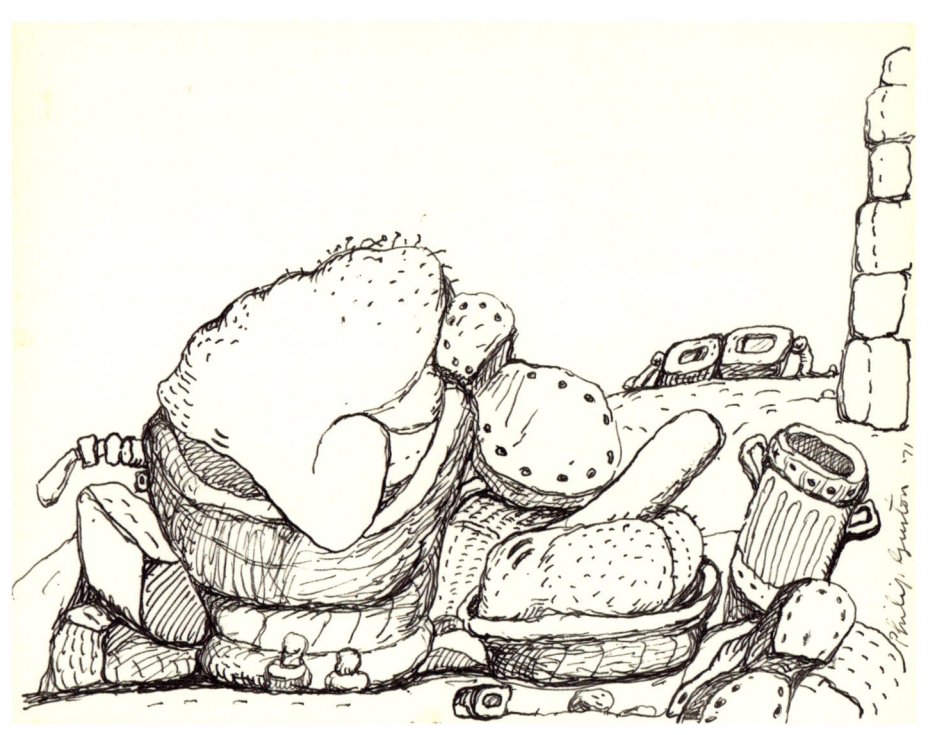

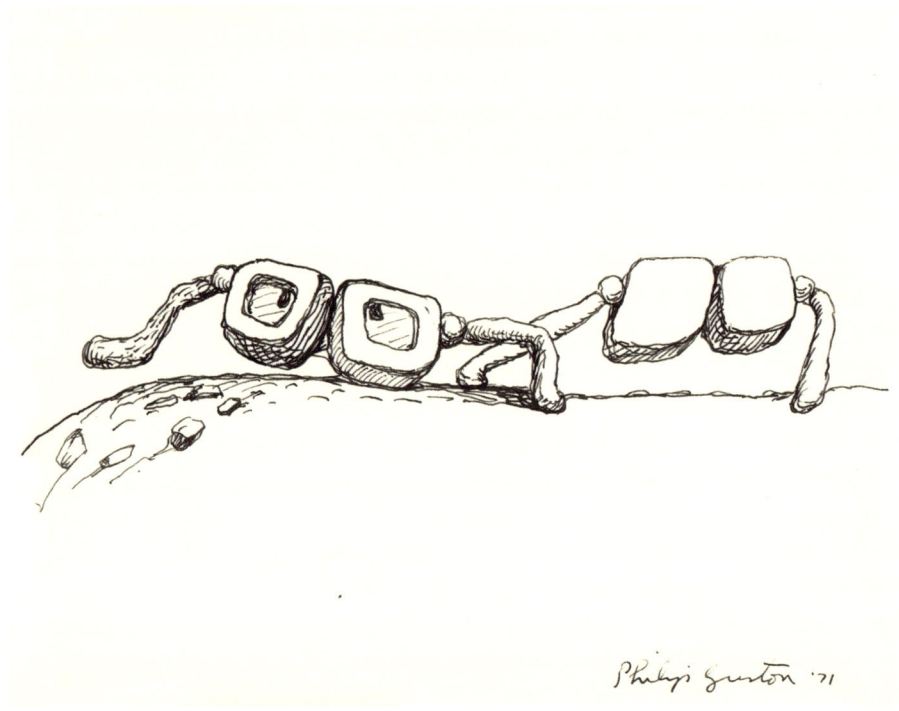

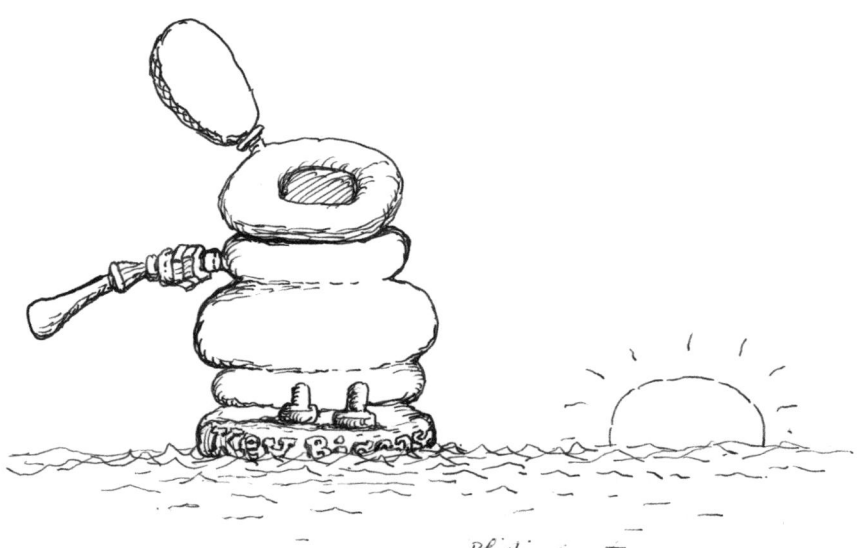

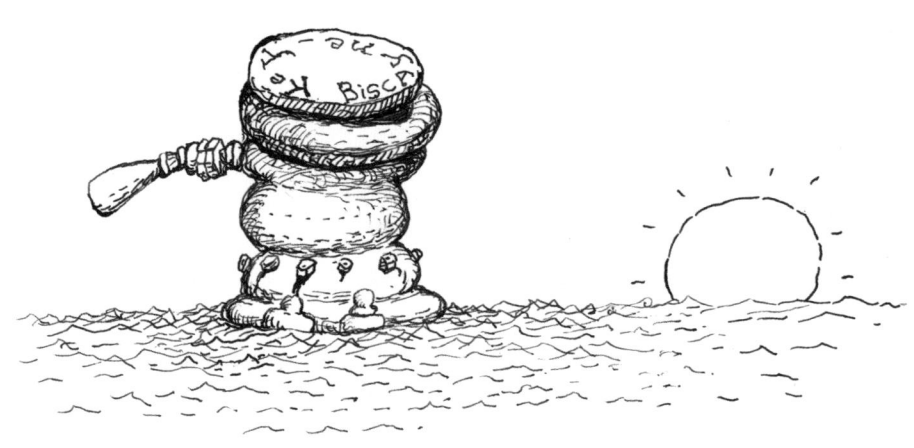

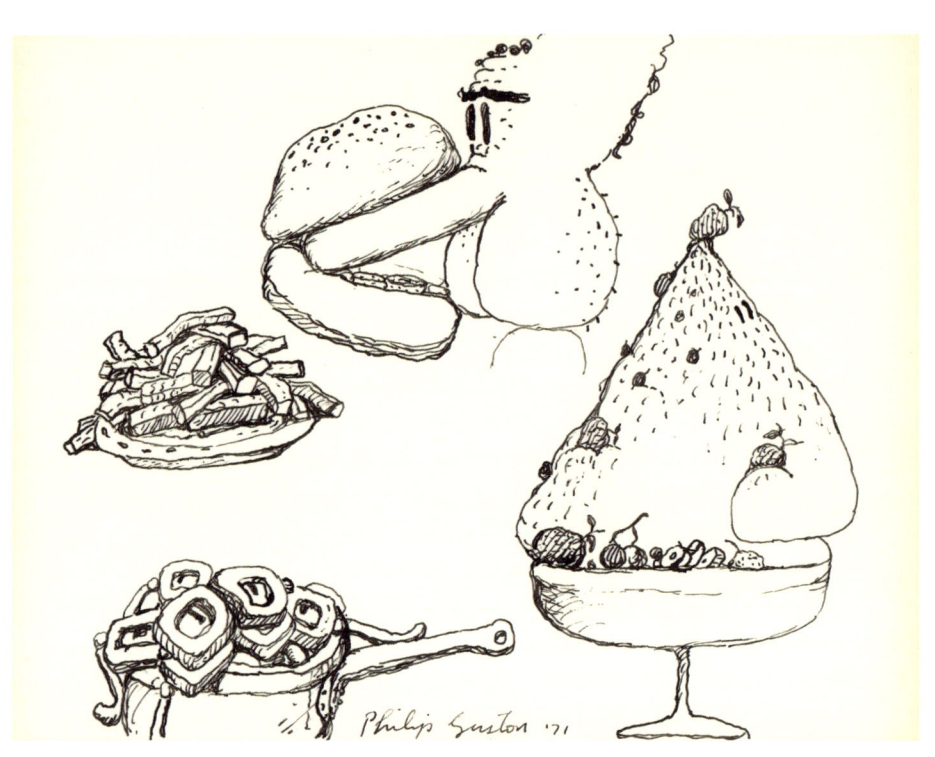

Philip Guston '71

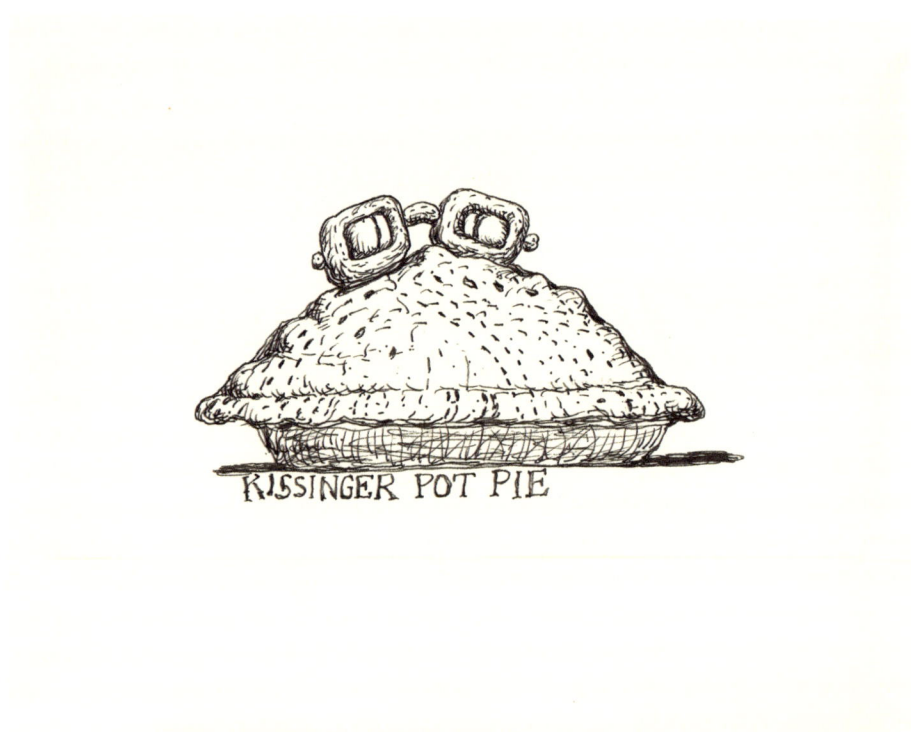

KISSINGER POT PIE

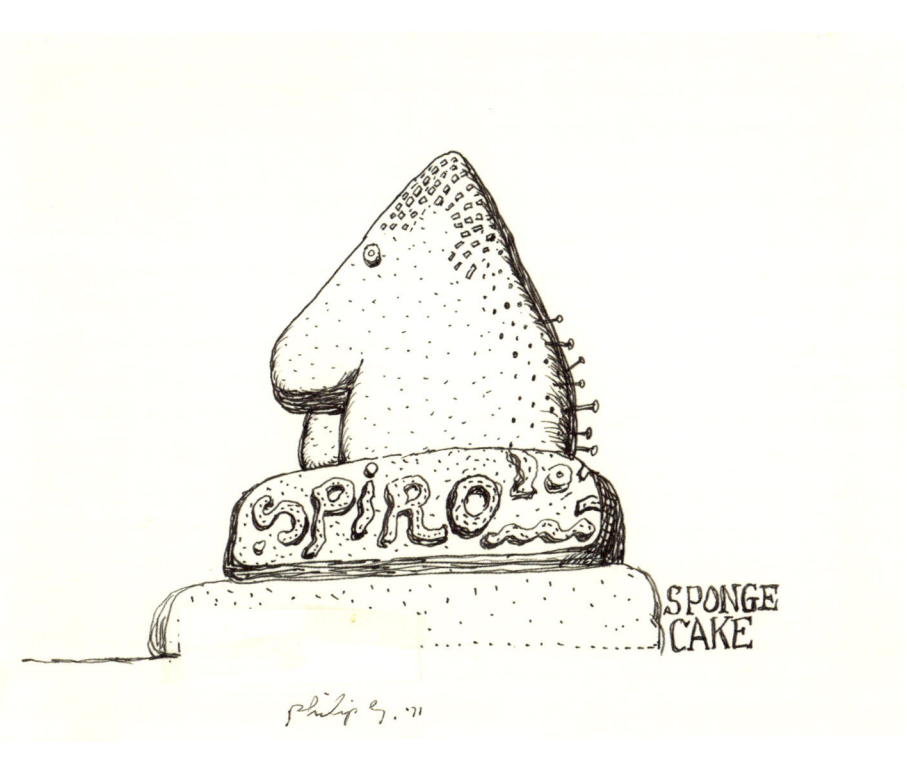

SPONGE
CAKE

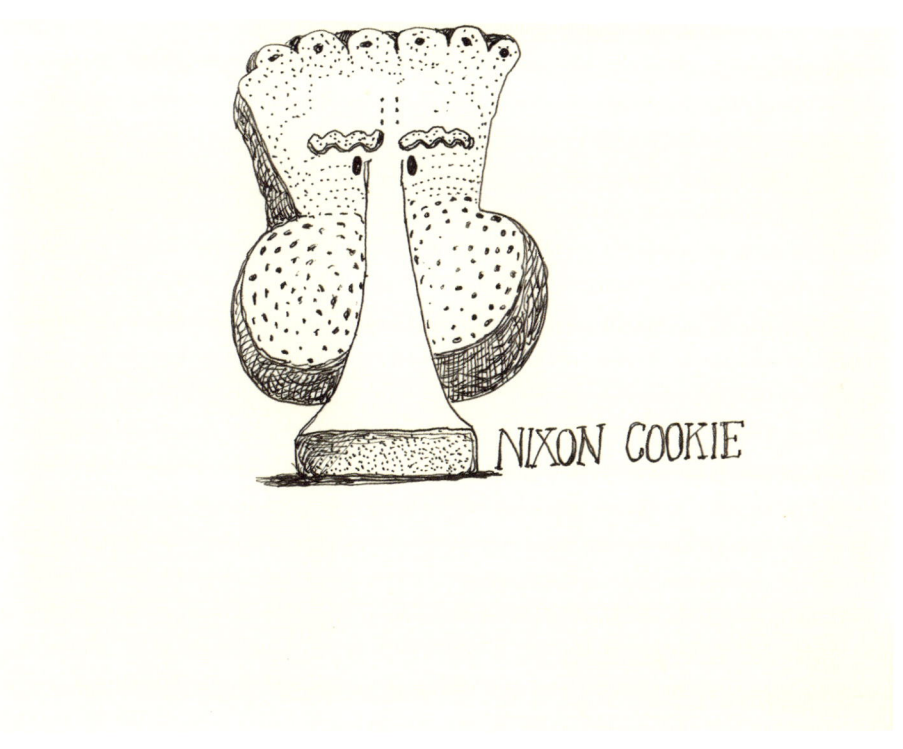

NIXON COOKIE

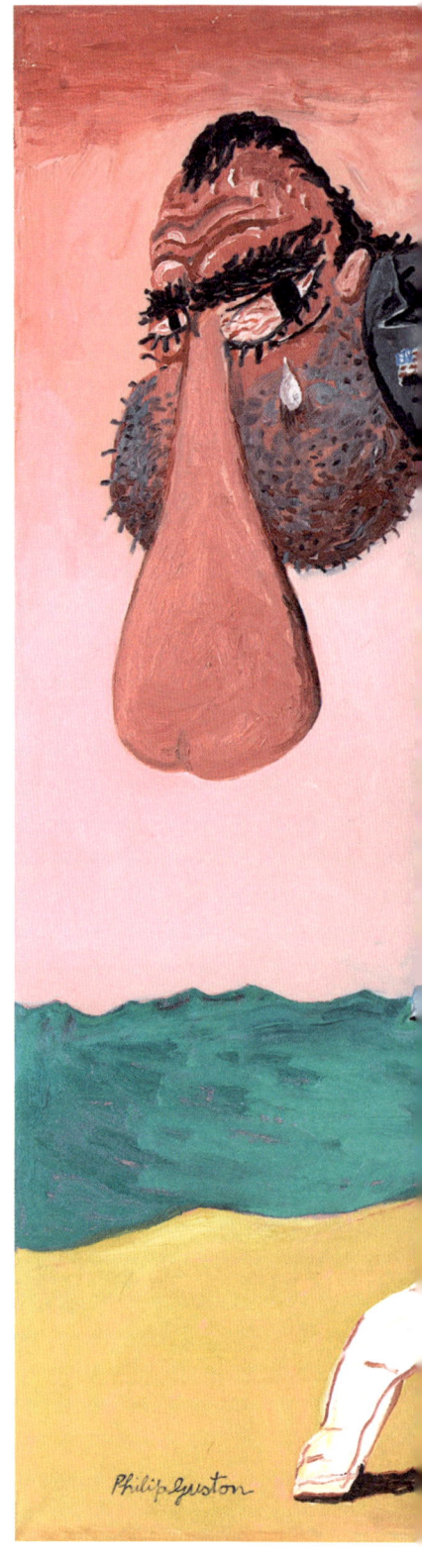

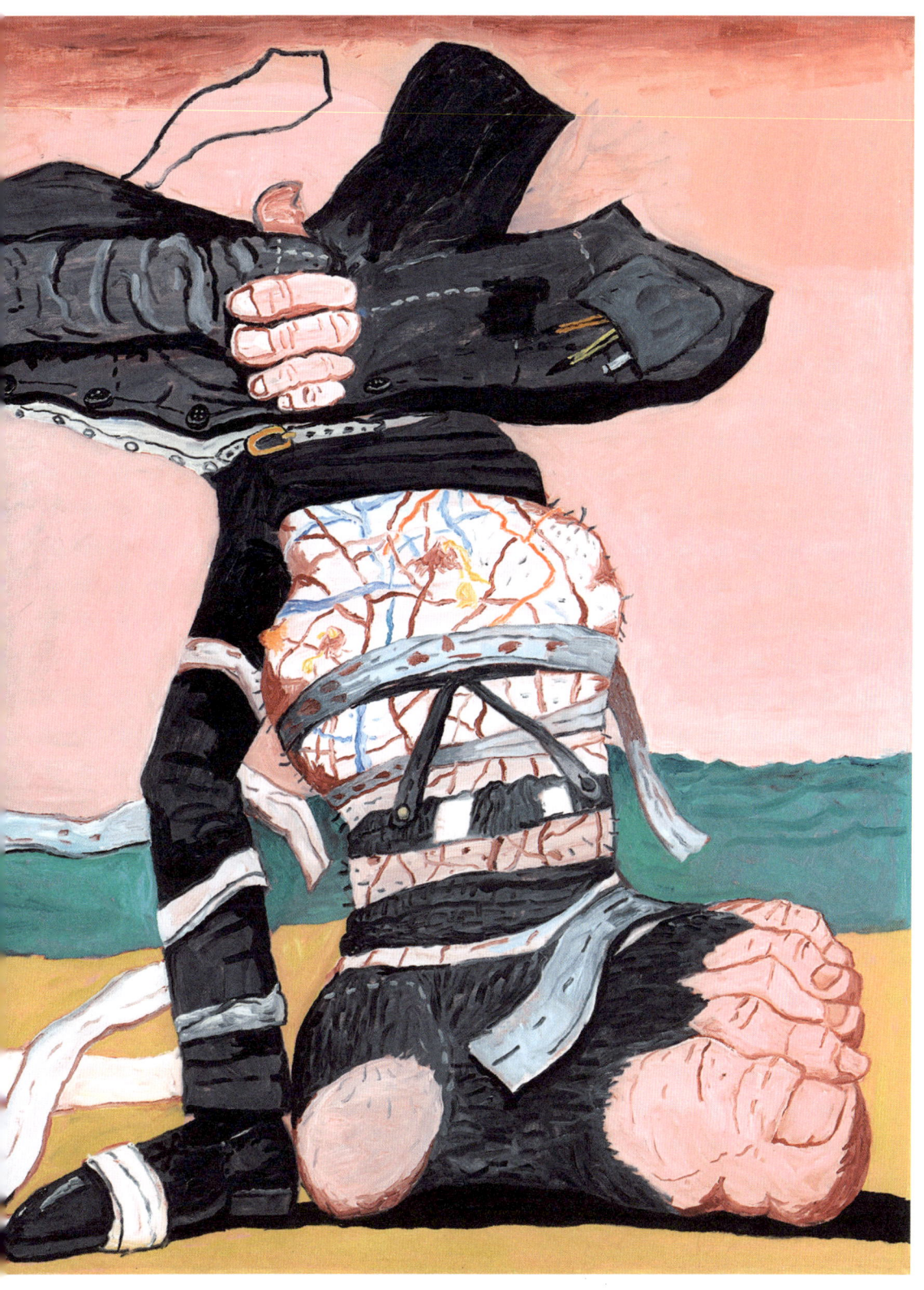

138 — *San Clemente,* 1975. Oil on canvas, 172.72×186.06 cm. Glenstone Museum, Potomac (Maryland)

Philip Roth and
the Grotesque

AGNÈS DESARTHE

In 2008 Philip Roth published his twenty-ninth novel, *Indignation*.[1] It tells the story of Marcus Messner who, to escape the domination of his father, a suspicious and overbearing butcher, enrolls at a university 800 kilometers from his home in Winesburg, Ohio.

Winesburg, Ohio just happens to be the title of a collection of short stories published eighty-nine years earlier, in 1919, by Sherwood Anderson, a pioneer of American expressionism—"a giant," according to William Faulkner.

This knowing nod from Roth to Anderson, at a distance of nearly a hundred years, is anything but trivial. Not only does it tell us something about Roth's taste for literary camaraderie (and camaraderie in general), but it also provides a precious clue to the novelist's vision.

The opening story in *Winesburg, Ohio* is titled "The Book of the Grotesque." In it, we learn from the narrator that it is truths that make people grotesque: the moment a person makes a truth their own, calls it their truth, and tries to live their life by it, they become grotesque and the truth they embraced becomes a lie.

Truth and lies form one of the couples that repeatedly act out their conflict on the stage of the grotesque as conceived by Roth. Loyalty and betrayal are another. But whatever the polarities involved, at the heart of it all lies a critique of conformity, an attack on univocality. Every human group develops its own rules for living together, and these rules that protect its integrity are singled out by the writer as a powerful source of alienation.

THE SELF-PORTRAIT AND ITS DOUBLE

Following in Anderson's footsteps, Roth thus attacks every possible form of convention, whether those of the Jewish petite bourgeoisie in New Jersey, in which he grew up, or of the WASP establishment, with which he collided when he attended Bucknell University, or of the literary world—particularly in probing the mores of an intellectual milieu thronged by his thriving alter egos. For, in the interests of fairness, and to ensure that no one is spared, the creator of Alexander Portnoy scatters avatars of himself throughout his work, the most obvious ones being Nathan Zuckerman, David Kepesh, Peter Tarnopol, and even Philip Roth (who, in *Operation Shylock*,[2] takes the place of the real writer). For Roth, self-portraits are an opportunity to aim the magnifying glass at his own person, showing up idiosyncrasies that are close cousins of the ridiculous. The writer himself is thus the primary incarnation of the grotesque.

In addition to his own doubles, which he subjects to the ordeal of the distorting lens, Roth also depicts his colleagues. Some have seen E. I. Lonoff (*The Ghost Writer*)[3] as a composite portrait of two admired elders, Bernard Malamud and Henry Roth. Saul Bellow stated that he recognized himself in the character of Felix Abravanel, the famous novelist who inspires a mixture of veneration and distrust in Nathan Zuckerman: "The satirist you don't really see till you catch the

1
Indignation, Boston: Houghton Mifflin, 2008.
2
Operation Shylock: A Confession, New York: Simon and Schuster, 1993.
3
The Ghost Writer, New York: Farrar, Straus and Giroux, 1979. Published as *Zuckerman Bound* along with *Zuckerman Unbound*, *The Anatomy Lesson*, and *The Prague Orgy* in 1985, which is the edition referred to here.

commedia dell'arte profile. There's where the derision lives. Head-on he's something of a heartthrob. Bombay black eyes, and so on."[4] But this description also suggests Roth himself; the "Bombay black" eyes could also be his. That would make Abravanel a cross between the adored/dominant master and his respectful/aggressive disciple. Humor serves to maintain the ambivalence of his feelings as well as doubt as to the model's real identity, exploiting the mixed portrait as a way of producing a chimera, one privileged medium of the grotesque: "Like him? No. But impressed, oh yes. Absolutely. It's no picnic there in the egosphere. I don't know when the man sleeps, or if he has ever slept, aside from those few minutes when he had that drink with me."[5] And, further on: "Which isn't to suggest that Felix Abravanel lacked charm. On the contrary, the charm was like a moat so oceanic that you could not even see the great turreted and buttressed thing it had been dug to protect. You couldn't even find the drawbridge. He was like California itself—to get there you had to take a plane."[6] For Roth, the grotesque is a tool of exploration, a way of touching on people's truth while allowing their counter-truth to vibrate like harmonics.

In *The Facts*,[7] presented as an autobiography whose very title indicates a striving for objectivity, the narrative is imbued with a tension created by the interaction between the author and his character, Roth and Zuckerman, the former addressing the latter. The book opens with a long letter from Philip to Nathan which introduces the question that all serious writers ask themselves when handing in their manuscript: is it really a good idea to publish this text? In the one hundred or so pages that follow, we're offered a picaresque, moving and often funny life story. We believe it all. We can perfectly picture Philip as a child hiding in his mother's lap thanks to this scene: "animal-me hearing her dead father's name, the protoplasm-me, boy-baby, and bodyburrower-in-training, joined by every nerve ending to her smile and her sealskin coat."[8] We then observe Philip as a smart, sarcastic young man, playing to the gallery with his mimicry, and later on as a brilliant student who nevertheless suffers a certain isolation at Bucknell: "I was not unaware, especially when I was still fresh from home, that I was a Jew at a university where the bylaws stipulated that more than half the Board of Trustees had to be members of the Baptist church, where chapel attendance was required of lowerclassmen, and where the extracurricular organization for which most Bucknellians seemed to have membership cards was the Christian Association."[9] A few years after that, we find him falling in love with a manipulative *shiksa* (a non-Jewish young woman) who makes his life a living hell. And so on. All these episodes are echoed in Roth's novels.

As reader, we have the impression that we have access to what we might call "the author's truth." But the epigraph, taken from a remark made by Nathan Zuckerman in *The Counterlife*,[10] signals the need for caution: "And as he spoke I was thinking, the kind of stories that people turn life into, the kind of lives that people turn stories back into."[11]

4
Ibid., p. 52.
5
Ibid., p. 53.
6
Ibid., p. 58.
7
The Facts: A Novelist's Autobiography, New York: Farrar, Straus and Giroux, 1988.
8
Ibid., p. 18.
9
Ibid., p. 61.
10
The Counterlife, New York: Farrar, Straus and Giroux, 1986.
11
Epigraph, *The Facts*, op. cit.

The ironic distance literally shatters in the last part of the book, when the recipient of the letter—and therefore of the manuscript we have just perused—replies to the sender. "Dear Roth," starts Zuckerman, who then proceeds to lay into him in a series of attacks, including this one, damning his self-indulgence, which is both the richest and the most cruel: "Speaking of being loved, just look at how you begin this thing. The little marsupial in his mother's seal-skin pouch. No wonder you suddenly display a secret passion to be universally loved. But where, by the way, is the mother after that? It may well be that this incredible animal love that you have for your mother, and that you allude to in only one sentence in the prologue, can't be exposed by you undisguised, but aside from that sealskin coat, there is no mother."[12]

Here is an author who takes his love of amusement, both for himself and for the reader, to the point of absurdity. Someone stands before us and talks to us. And, often this person irritates, worries, disturbs us. Just as we are irritated or disturbed by Guston's self-portraits—a face without a nose, just a giant eye, cigarette hanging from his lips, with a mountain of hobnail shoes behind him, pots of paint and French fries slathered in ketchup (ill. 170). Was it the love of caricature that brought the two artists together? Is it their relationship to truth and its twin, countertruth, that baffles and fascinates?

PHILIP AND PHILIP

Philip Roth met Philip Guston in 1969 in Woodstock, where each in his own way had taken refuge, far from New York. Guston, who was depressive, had just begun to emerge from a long barren spell that followed fame, and, with his wife, had moved into their country home in Maverick Road. Roth, for his part, was on the run from the success of a provocative, risqué, and hilarious novel *Portnoy's Complaint*,[13] which had made some see him as a "crazed penis," as he wrote in "Pictures by Guston," an article originally published in *Vanity Fair* in 1989 then reprinted in *Shop Talk*.[14]

The writer was living in a small rented house two miles from the center, with his love of the moment, a PhD student who liked to watch the sun go down after her day's work. Guston was fifty-six and Roth twenty years younger. They shared a passion for *crapola*, a neologism coined by Guston from the word *crap*. And they were delighted and inspired by the charmless landscape and atmosphere created, as Roth wrote, by "billboards, garages, diners, burger joints, junk shops, auto body shops."

It was during these few years spent in a kind of happy rustic reclusion that Roth wrote *The Breast*,[15] a Kafkaesque variation on the theme of identity and its threatening instability. Guston spontaneously illustrated certain passages of the book in the black ink of comic book writers, and offered the drawings to his neighbor.

12
Ibid., p. 168.
13
Portnoy's Complaint, New York: Random House, 1969.
14
Shop Talk: A Writer and His Colleagues and Their Work, New York: Houghton Mifflin, 2001, pp. 131–38. This article is reproduced on page 127 of this catalogue.
15
The Breast, New York: Holt, Rinehart and Winston, 1972.

BETRAYAL FOR THE SAKE OF FIDELITY

This penchant for satire, which he shared with Guston, came early to Roth. It was a kind of counterweight to his role as a "good"boy (the quotation marks were his) in the family. As he explains in "Writing and the Powers That Be,"[16] he realized that "in our Jewish section of Newark there was nothing much else to be, unless I wanted to steal cars or flunk courses."[17] Raised by a loving father who was eager to integrate, and a tender, protective mother, both second-generation Americans with roots in the Jewish communities of Eastern Europe (Austrian Galicia for his mother, Kyiv for his father), Roth did not consider teenage revolt as an option. Aware of his father's financial difficulties, and of the efforts made by his mother to keep a spotless home where the kitchen floor was so clean that you could eat off it at any time of day, he was on his best behavior. Except verbally, when joshing with his friends: "I associate that amalgam of mimicry, reporting, kibbitzing, disputation, satire, and legendizing from which we drew so much sustenance with the work I now do, and I consider what we came up with to amuse one another . . . to have been something like the folk narrative of a tribe passing from one stage of human development to the next. Also, those millions of words were the means by which we either took vengeance on or tried to hold at bay the cultural forces that were shaping us."[18] Excess, parody, and pranks rose into the gap that this highly intelligent adolescent observed between the anxious, restricted world he grew up in and the confidence of a booming America. In this regard Roth, like many other sons and grandsons of immigrants, was a stranger both in the land where he lived and in his own family. He was deeply torn between loyalty to the ancestral model and curiosity toward a new world—hence the attraction to shiksas, a recurrent theme in his novels, and his piercing criticism of a vacuous and moronic society.

How to inhabit these two conflicting realities? Mocking both his own people and others was a way of surviving. And the grotesque, which is exaggeration, excess served by incredible semantic verve, was the procedure that enabled Roth to write both out of his origins and in a world that ignored and often despised them. Verbal intensity, verging on the comic, enabled him to be faithful, self-perjuring, and treacherous at one and the same time.

However, this practice was the fruit of a transformation. Leaving his adolescence behind him at university, the budding writer penned short stories designed to be "touching," stories in which "The Jew was nowhere to be seen; there were no Jews in the stories, no Newark, and not a sign of comedy—the last thing I wanted to do was to hand anyone a laugh in literature. I wanted to show that life was sad and poignant, even while I was experiencing it as heady and exhilarating. I wanted to demonstrate that I was 'compassionate,' a totally harmless person."[19]

16
Reading Myself and Others, New York: Farrar, Straus and Giroux, 1975.
17
Ibid., p. 4.
18
Ibid., pp. 4–5.
19
The Facts, op. cit., p. 60.

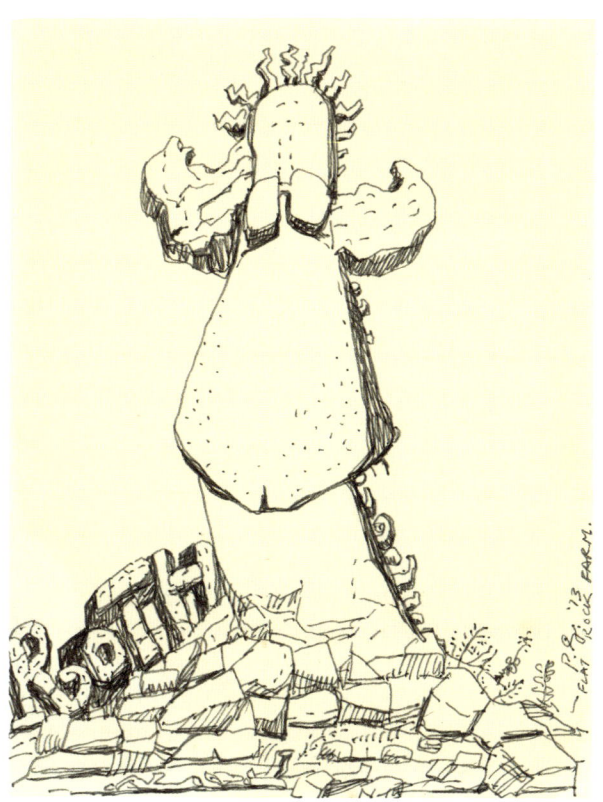

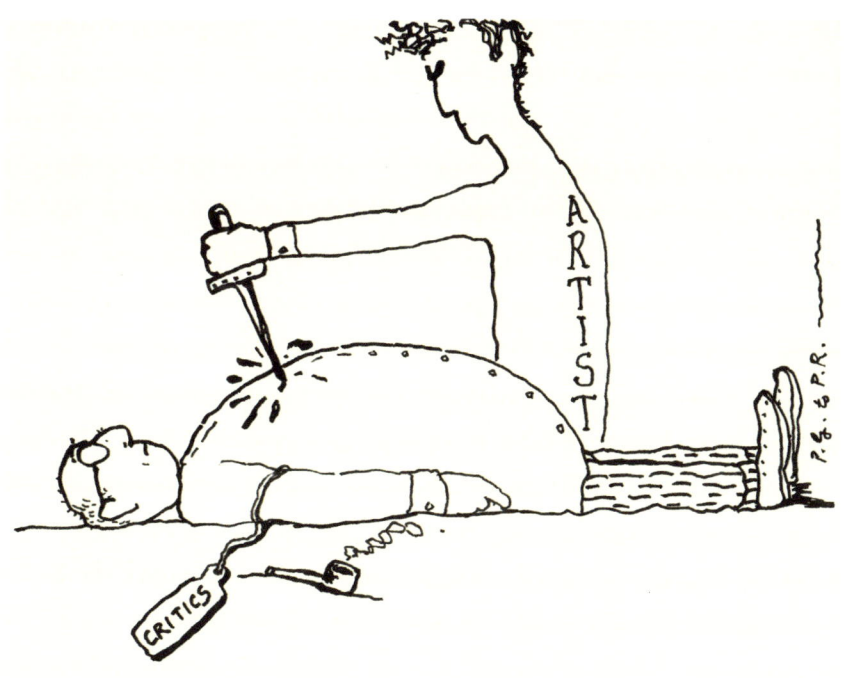

139 — *Caricature of Philip Roth*, 1973. Ink on paper, 27.9 × 21.6 cm
140 — *Untitled (Artist and Critics)*, 1972. Ink on paper, 34.6 × 43.2 cm,
The Guston Foundation, West Hurley (New York)

Soon, though, this self-styled "cuckoo in the Bucknell nest" became aware of the richness of his heritage and changed direction, working with "the playful confidence we had in our Jewishness as an intellectual resource. . . . It seemed less advisable to treat this strain of vulgarity as an impurity to be purged from our speech than to own up to it matter-of-factly, ironically unashamedly, and to take a real, pleasurable satisfaction in what more than likely would have seemed to Henry James to be our unadventitious origins."[20]

It was clear that great men of American letters and overwhelming creators of the canon would not be Roth's major influence. His masters went by the names of Franz Kafka, Nikolai Gogol, and Isaac Babel. From the first two, he took the élan of fantasy, melding the dread created by Kafka's realism with the farcical satire of Gogol. With Babel, he dipped his brush in blood—an image taken from Guston. (ill. 150)

The author of *The Red Cavalry* was the model chosen by the writer and the painter, well before they met. Both had read the book of short stories that Babel based on the journal he kept as war correspondent posted with Budyonny's Cossacks. In the 1920s this violently anti-Semitic elite unit of the Red Army carried out extraordinarily violent pogroms, right in front of the Russian Jewish writer, who applied all his sense of observation and detail into describing these atrocities committed on his fellows. What did Babel feel, living among these cavalrymen heady with barbarism? How far can irony go? How can violence be made bearable?

A keen sense of the absurd prompted Guston to say, echoing Babel's experience: "When the 1960s came along I was feeling split, schizophrenic. The war, what was happening in America, the brutality of the world. What kind of man am I, sitting at home, reading magazines going into a frustrated fury about everything—and then going into my studio to adjust a red to a blue?"[21]

The same questioning can be found in Roth. The grotesque appears as a way of doing justice to reality, a method that may be capable of scrupulously expressing the state of a chaotic world rife with injustice, blindness, and atrocities. Throughout Roth's work, the character of the young conscript who died in Vietnam, a brother or cousin of the main character, is there to force the reader, even in the middle of farce, to remember the magnitude and the cruelty of this war in which the United States was embroiled from 1960s through to the mid-1970s, despite relentless protest at home.

Just as the Guston figures wearing Ku Klux Klan hoods and zipping along in cars with fat cigars in their mouths (ill. 147–149) made a number of viewers uneasy, so many of the characters and situations in Roth's work drew vituperative reactions from readers. The author commented on such tensions in *The Ghost Writer*: "Literary history was in part the history of novelists infuriating fellow countrymen, family, and friends. . . . writers weren't writers, I told myself, if they didn't have the strength to face the insolubility of that conflict and go on."[22]

20
Ibid., p. 115.
21
From an interview given in 1977.
22
The Ghost Writer, op. cit., p. 110.

HOIST WITH HIS OWN PETARD

Beginning with his first book, *Goodbye Columbus*,[23] Roth was the target of accusations from his own milieu. Jews suspected him of being anti-Semitic. "When I speak before Jewish audiences," he says in "Writing about Jews" (*Reading Myself and Others*),[24] "invariably there have been people who have come up to me afterward to ask, 'Why don't you leave us alone? Why don't you write about the Gentiles?'—'Why must you be so critical?'" And, further on: "It is difficult, if not impossible, to explain to some of the people claiming to have felt my teeth sinking in, that in many instances they haven't been bitten at all. Not always, but frequently, what readers have taken to be my disapproval of the lives lived by Jews seems to have to do more with their own moral perspective than with the one they would ascribe to me: at times they see wickedness where I myself had seen energy or courage or spontaneity; they are ashamed of what I see no reason to be ashamed of, and defensive where there is no cause for defense."[25]

Speaking to Kirsty Wark in an interview for BBC Four's *The Review Show* in 2011, Roth tells her that after the publication of *Portnoy's Complaint*, which had whipped up quite a storm in Jewish milieux, his mother asked him ("she was very sweet"): "Philip, *are* you anti-Semitic?" and that he answered with another question: "What do you think?" To which his mother responded, insistently: "No, but why do they say it?" In the end they just laughed about it. Roth was at pains to stress that his parents were adorable: "Even if I was an anti-Semite they would have been proud of me. I would have been the best anti-Semite."[26]

The Ghost Writer contains numerous passages that return to this subject of suspicion. Here, Roth speaks through one of his doppelgangers, Nathan Zuckerman, who is having trouble with his father after the publication of his first short story in a magazine. Zuckerman *père* bewails the lack of gratitude, the fear of what gentiles will think, the difference between American Jews and European Jews, while Zuckerman *fils* defends himself as best he can. The debate culminates in a series of six questions addressed to Nathan by the Wapters, who are friends of his parents. It is difficult to resist the temptation of quoting a few of them: "1. If you had been living in Nazi Germany in the thirties, would you have written such a story? . . . 6. What set of aesthetic values makes you think that the cheap is more valid than the noble and the slimy is more truthful than the sublime? . . . 10 Can you honestly say there is anything in your short story that would not warm the heart of a Julius Streicher or a Joseph Goebbels?"[27]

In this multi-level joke Roth makes this condemnation from his home community one of the main planks of his narrative. But the novel also gives him the opportunity to examine the questions of belonging and identity in a more tragic light. This is illustrated by the dialogue between Amy Bellette (a real or fantasy avatar of Anne

23
Goodbye, Columbus and Five Short Stories, Boston: Houghton Mifflin, 1959.
24
Reading Myself and Others, op. cit., p. 194.
25
Ibid.
26
https://www.bbc.co.uk/programmes/p01ywfw6
27
The Ghost Writer, op. cit., pp. 103–04.

Frank) and one of her teachers, held shortly after the liberation of the camps: "One day after school Miss Giddings took her for a lemon-curd tart at the local tearoom and asked her questions about the concentration camps. . . . 'Terrible,' Miss Giddings said, 'so terrible.' . . . 'Why is it,' the unhappy teacher finally asked, 'that for centuries people have hated you Jews?' Amy rose to her feet. She was stunned. 'Don't ask me that!' the girl said. 'Ask the madmen who hate us!'"[28]

Comedy, as we can see, does not exclude profundity, and this astonishing figure of the European Jewish survivor of the camps whom Zuckerman rightly or wrongly believed to be Anne Frank provides another way into the question of the work's reception.

Roth was frequently accused of misogyny. Today, there is a kind of readership for whom he represents the prototype of the "white male" with his preponderantly masculine characters and women reduced to stereotypes and vital statistics. Drenka in *Sabbath's Theater*[29] is not the only figure to belie this conception. A demanding, earthy lover with an unforgettable physique—"those clay figurines molded circa 2000 B.C."[30]—she is at once endearing and powerful, licentious and ethical: in a word, complex. One might also think of Hope, Lonoff's wife in *The Ghost Writer*, and of her monologue at the end, a veritable indictment of the role of "great man's wife" in which she dismantles, one by one, the mechanisms of male domination and the impunity it enjoys. We may also recall, coming back to Amy Bellette, that avatar of Anne Frank, caught up in a play of reflections between Nathan Zuckerman and Philip Roth, that *The Ghost Writer* was conceived as a monument to the memory of that young woman, an authentic writer of genius, who, stopped by time and history, is too often reduced to her identity as a teenager killed by the Nazis. Roth gives his reader the chance to read or reread extensive passages from the journal of this literary prodigy, which are reproduced in the text.

But it is above all in *Our Gang*[31] that readers will find a rebuttal of this suspicion of misogyny, which thus becomes one among other interpretations of the work, a possible but not necessarily relevant reading, like the conception of his works as tiresomely anti-Semitic.

FROM REALISTIC GROTESQUE
TO VISIONARY GROTESQUE

Jokers always run the risk of being misunderstood, discredited, disavowed, but they cannot resist what draws a smile, as Milan Kundera explains in the interview he gave Roth after his publication of *The Book of Laughter and Forgetting* (reprinted in *Shop Talk*): "I learned the value of humor during the time of Stalinist terror. I was twenty then. I could always recognize a person who was not a Stalinist, a person whom I needn't fear, by the way he smiled. A sense of humor was a trustworthy sign of recognition. Ever since, I have been terrified by a world that is losing its sense of humor."[32]

28
Ibid., pp. 130–31.
29
Sabbath's Theater, London: Vintage Books, 2010.
30
Ibid., p. 5.
31
Our Gang (Starring Tricky and His Friends), London: Vintage Books, 2006.
32
Shop Talk, op. cit., p. 94.

Roth's most politically engaged and wackiest novel is also his most realist, as well as the most feminist imaginable. *Our Gang* opens with a double epigraph comprising passages by Jonathan Swift on the human use of lies and by George Orwell on the debasement of language, but on the next page we come across another foreword, this time in capital letters, which reproduced verbatim a statement made by Richard Nixon in San Clemente on April 3, 1971 on the subject of abortion. "FROM PERSONAL AND RELIGIOUS BELIEFS I CONSIDER ABORTIONS AN UNACCEPTABLE FORM OF POPULATION CONTROL." And, further in: "THE UNBORN HAVE RIGHTS ALSO, RECOGNIZED IN LAW, RECOGNIZED EVEN IN PRINCIPLES EXPOUNDED BY THE UNITED NATIONS."[33]

At the start of the book Trick. E. Dixon, the grotesque double of the incumbent president (Richard Nixon, also known as Tricky Dicky), announces that fetuses are to be granted the vote, justifying himself as follows: "You hear a lot these days about Black Power and Female Power. Power this and Power that. But what about Prenatal Power? Don't they have rights too, membranes though they may be? . . . It would be a tragic irony indeed, and as telling a sign as I can imagine of national confusion and even hypocrisy, if we were willing to send our boys to fight and die in far-off lands so that defenseless peoples might have the right to choose the kinds of government they want in free elections, and then we were to turn around here at home and continue to deny that very same right to an entire segment of our population, just because they happen to live on the placenta or in the uterus, instead of New York City."[34]

In 1971, when asked about satire by a director at Random House who hesitated to publish *Our Gang*, Roth answered: "Political satire isn't writing that lasts. Though satire, by and large, deals with enduring social and political problems, its comic appeal lies in the use made of the situation of the moment. It's unlikely that reading even the best satiric work of another era we feel anything like the glee or the outrage experienced by a contemporary audience."[35] Nearly fifty years later, it might be said that the facts have shown the author of *Portnoy's Complaint* to be wrong.

On November 6, 2024 a terrifying individual with orange skin was elected (for the second time) as head of the U.S. government. The man who, during his first term, advised his fellow citizens to drink bleach in order to cure Covid had managed to convince them that he could restore America's lost grandeur. How was this possible? Listening to Roth's Trick E. Dixon speaking to his "political coach," we may understand better: "Let's not underestimate the imagination of the American people. This may seem like old-fashioned patriotism such as isn't in fashion any more, but I have the highest regard for their imagination and I always have. Why, I actually think the American people can be made to believe anything. These people, after all, have their fantasies and fears and superstitions, just like

33
Epigraph, *Our Gang*, op. cit.
34
Ibid., p. 20.
35
"On *Our Gang*," *Reading Myself and Others*, op. cit., p. 37.

anybody else, and you are not going to put anything over on them simply by addressing yourself to the real problems and pretending that the others don't exist just because they are imaginary."[36]

It's all here, already: the manipulation, the alternative truths, and even the conflict with Denmark. In his mad agitation, Donald Trump wanting to annex Greenland seems like a puppet guided by the same hand as Trick E. Dixon in his passionate, rambling speech to the nation: "I have made it clear to the Pro-Pornography government in Copenhagen tonight that I do not intend to react to any renewed threat to our territorial integrity, to our honor, or to our idealism, with plaintive diplomatic protests. And in order that there should be no misunderstanding of my position, I have ordered the American Seventh Army, stationed in West Germany, to be mobilized in striking position here (points) at the fifty-fifth parallel on the border between Germany and Denmark."[37]

The sublime buffoonery of the satirical novel published last century under the title *Our Gang* is now being borne out by our Ubuesque reality. Fable has become journalistic reportage. It is amazing to find that every page of this old piece of slapstick contains elements from our present. The coarseness, the misogyny, the lack of limits, the excess, everything in the Trump administration, which is so close to Dixon's, evokes Roth's beloved farce. The expression "truth is stranger than fiction" is overused, but here we discover that the phrase suited to the present situation is more "reality is more grotesque than fiction." We can also understand why this book, written, like *The Breast,* during the brief Woodstock interlude, moved Guston to respond with drawings. When lucidity prompts disgust, we ward off despair using representation, which is also denunciation.

It is not surprising that the two Philips recognized each other as kindred spirits. Having offered the writer images of a giant, flabby mammary gland, the painter now gave Roth a jowly and pouchy Trick E. Dixon, as well as penile portraits of his own writerly self. For both men, showing the exposed, exploded body was a way of resisting good taste, the supreme conformism and supreme lie. Lucidity, derision, and self-derision, an irresistible urge to subvert, the subversion of meaning, of the image, of clichés—all these things link the two artists despite the generation between them and their different modes of expression.

What unites them is also, very paradoxically, their modesty. Because, once we are done hooting with laughter and howling with indignation, the grotesque, in the last instance, is a fantastic hiding place. From this perfect shelter whose mirror walls show the reader and viewer their own fun-house image, the artist does occasionally emerge. He braves the outside, without artifice, resulting in pages like the ones in which "the Swede," the main character of *American Pastoral,*[38] weeps for his dead daughter: "He had learned the worst

36
"Tricky Has Another Crisis; or, The Skull Session," *Our Gang,* op. cit., p. 25.
37
"Tricky Addresses the Nation," ibid., p. 83.
38
American Pastoral, Boston: Houghton Mifflin, 1997.

lesson that life can teach—that it makes no sense. And when that happens, happiness is never spontaneous again. . . . he ruthlessly goes on pretending to be [content]. Stoically he suppresses his horror. He learns to live behind a mask. A lifetime experiment in endurance. A performance over a ruin."[39]

39
Ibid., p. 81.

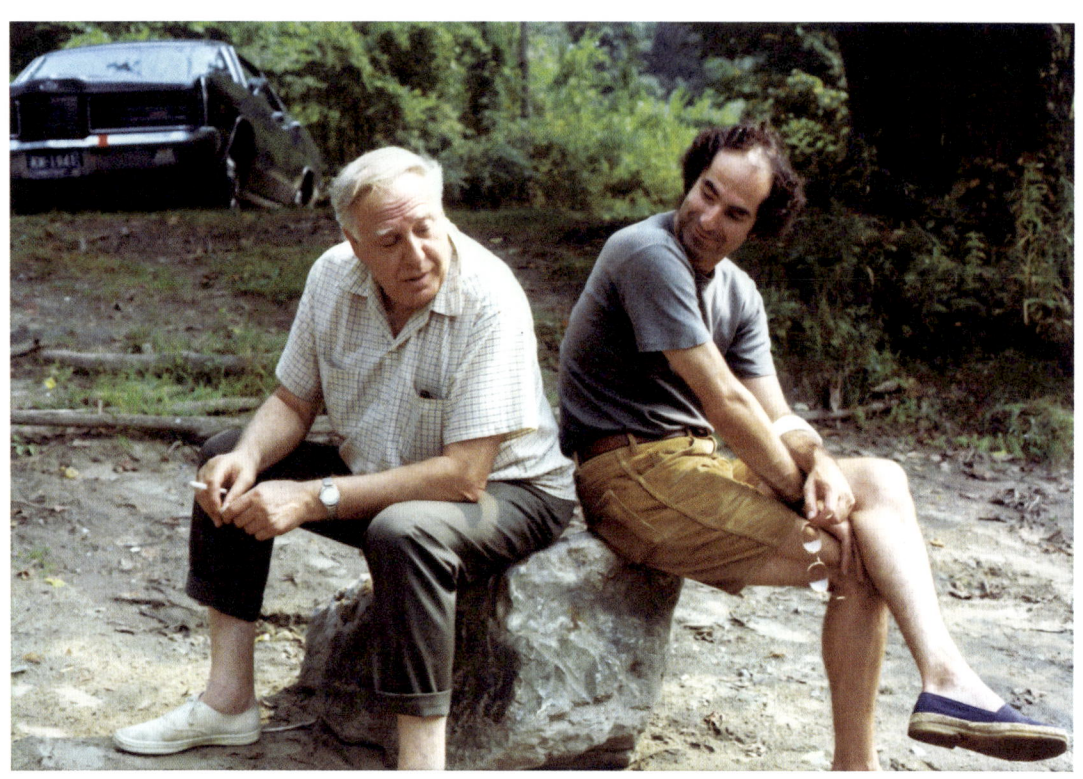

141 — Barbara Sproul, *Philip Guston and Philip Roth*, 1972

PICTURES BY GUSTON
PHILIP ROTH[1]

> "One time, in Woodstock," Ross Feld said, "I stood next to Guston in front of some of these canvases. I hadn't seen them before; I didn't really know what to say. For a time, then, there was silence. After a while, Guston took his thumbnail away from his teeth and said, 'People, you know, complain that it's horrifying. As if it's a picnic for me, who has to come in here every day and see them first thing. But what's the alternative? I'm trying to see how much I can stand.'"
>
> From *Night Studio: A Memoir of Philip Guston* by Musa Mayer,[2] [1989]

In 1967, sick of life in the New York art world, Philip Guston left his Manhattan studio forever and took up permanent residence with his wife, Musa, in their Woodstock house on Maverick Road, where they had been living off and on for some twenty years. Two years later, I turned my back on New York to hide out in a small furnished house in Woodstock, across town from Philip, whom I didn't know at the time. I was fleeing the publication of *Portnoy's Complaint*.[3] My overnight notoriety as a sexual freak had become difficult to evade in Manhattan, and so I decided to clear out—first for Yaddo, the upstate artists' colony, and then, beginning in the spring of 1969, for that small rented house tucked out of sight midway up a hillside meadow a couple of miles from Woodstock's main street. I lived there with a young woman who was finishing a Ph.D. and who for several years had been renting a tiny cabin, heated by a wood stove, in the mountainside colony of Byrdcliffe, which some decades earlier had been a primitive hamlet of Woodstock artists. During the day I wrote on a table in the upstairs spare bedroom while she went off to the cabin to work on her dissertation.

Life in the country with a postgraduate student was anything but freakish, and it provided a combination of social seclusion and physical pleasure that, given the illogic of creation, led me to write, over a four-year period, a cluster of uncharacteristically freakish books. My new reputation as a crazed penis was what instigated the fantasy at the heart of *The Breast*,[4] a book about a college professor who turns into a female breast; it had something to do as well with inspiring the farcical legend of homeless alienation in homespun America that evolved into *The Great American Novel*.[5] The more simplehearted my Woodstock satisfactions, the more tempted I was in my work by the excesses of the Grand Guignol. I'd never felt more imaginatively polymorphous than when I would put two deck chairs on the lawn at the end of the day and we'd stretch out to enjoy the twilight view of the southern foothills of the Catskills, for me unpassable Alps through which no disconcerting irrelevancy could pass. I felt refractory and unreachable and freewheeling, and I was dedicated—perversely overdedicated, probably—to shaking off the vast newfound audience whose collective fantasies were not without their own transforming power.

Guston's situation in 1969—the year we met—was very different. At fifty-six, Philip was twenty years older than I and full of the doubt that can beset an artist of consequence in late middle age. He felt he'd exhausted the means that had unlocked him as an abstract painter, and he was bored and disgusted by the skills that had gained him renown. He didn't want to paint like that ever again; he tried to convince himself he shouldn't paint at all. But since nothing but painting could contain his emotional turbulence, let alone begin to deplete his self-mythologizing monomania, renouncing painting would have been tantamount to committing suicide. Although painting monopolized just enough of his despair and his seismic moodiness to make the anxiety of being himself something even he could sometimes laugh at, it never neutralized the nightmares entirely.

It wasn't supposed to. The nightmares were his not to dissipate with paint but, during the ten years before his death, to intensify with paint, to paint into nightmares that were imperishable and never before incarnated in such trashy props. That terror may be all the more bewildering when it is steeped in farce we know from what we ourselves dream and from what has been dreamed for us by Beckett and Kafka. Philip's discovery—akin to theirs, driven by a delight in mundane objects as boldly distended and bluntly depoeticized as theirs—was of the dread that emanates from the most commonplace appurtenances of the world of utter stupidity. The unexalted vision of everyday things that newspaper cartoon strips had impressed upon him when he was growing up in an immigrant Jewish family in California, the American crumminess for which, even in the heyday of his thoughtful lyricism, he always had an intellectual's soft spot, he came to contemplate—in an exercise familiar to lovers of *Molloy* and *The Castle*—as though his life, both as an artist and as a man, depended on it. This popular imagery of a shallow reality Philip imbued with such a weight of personal sorrow and artistic urgency as to shape in painting a new American landscape of terror.

Cut off from New York and living apart from Woodstock's local artists, with whom he had little in common, Philip often felt out of it: isolated, resentful, uninfluential, misplaced. It wasn't the first time that his ruthless focus on his own imperatives had induced a black mood of alienation, nor was he the first American artist embittered by the syndrome. It was as common among the best as it was among the worst—only with the best it was not necessarily a puerile self-drama concocted out of

egomaniacal delusion. In many ways it was a perfectly justified response for an artist like Guston, whose brooding, brainy, hypercritical scrutiny of every last aesthetic choice is routinely travestied by the misjudgments and simplifications that support a major reputation.

Philip and his gloom were not inseparable, however. In the company of the few friends he enjoyed and was willing to see, he could be a cordial, unharried host, exuding a captivating spiritual buoyancy unmarked by anguish. In his physical bearing, too, there was a nimble grace touchingly at variance with the bulky torso of the heavy-drinking, somewhat august-looking, white-haired personage into whom darkly, Jewishly, Don Juanishly handsome Guston had been transformed in his fifties. At dinner, wearing those baggy-bottomed, low-slung khaki trousers of his, with a white cotton shirt open over his burly chest and the

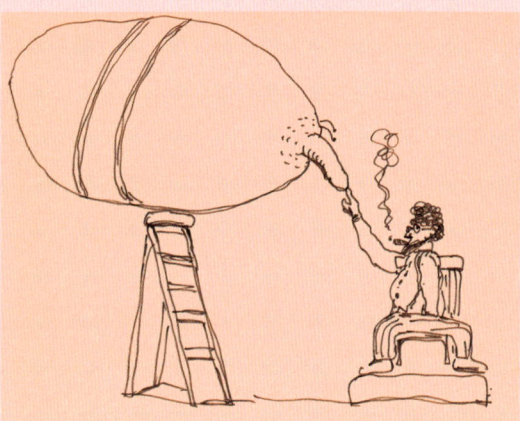

sleeves still turned up from working in the studio, he looked like the Old Guard Israeli politicians in whom imperiousness and informality spring from an unassailable core of confidence. It was impossible around the Guston dining table, sharing the rich pasta that Philip had cooked up with a display of jovial expertise, to detect any sign of a self-flagellating component within his prodigious endowment of self-belief. Only in his eyes might you be able to gauge the toll of the wearing oscillation—from iron resolve through rapturous equilibrium to suicidal hopelessness—that underlay a day in the studio.

What caused our friendship to flourish was, to begin with, a similar intellectual outlook, a love for many of the same books as well as a shared delight in what Guston called "crapola," starting with billboards, garages, diners, burger joints, junk shops, auto body shops—all the roadside stuff that we occasionally set out to Kingston to enjoy—and extending from the flat-footed straight talk of the Catskill citizenry to the Uriah Heepisms of our perspiring president. What sealed the camaraderie was that we liked each other's new work. The dissimilarities in our personal lives and our professional fortunes did not obscure the coincidence of our having recently undertaken comparable self-critiques. Independently, impelled by very different dilemmas, each of us had begun to consider crapola not only as a curious subject with strong suggestive powers to which we had a native affinity but as potentially a tool in itself: a blunt aesthetic instrument providing access to a style of representation free of the complexity we were accustomed to valuing. What this self-subversion might be made to yield was anybody's guess, and premonitions of failure couldn't be entirely curbed by the liberating feeling that an artistic about-face usually inspires, at least in the early stages of not quite knowing what you are doing.

At just about the time that I began not quite to know what I was doing exulting in Nixon's lies, or traveling up to Cooperstown's Hall of Fame to immerse myself in baseball

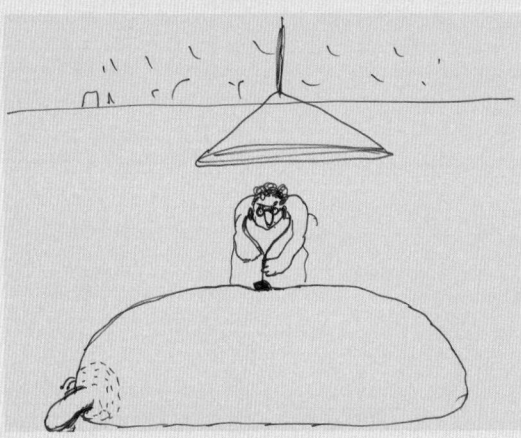

lore, or taking seriously the idea of turning a man like myself into a breast—and reading up on endocrinology and mammary glands—Philip was beginning not quite to know what he was doing hanging cartoon light bulbs over the pointed hoods of slit-eyed, cigar-smoking Klansmen painting self-portraits in hideaways cluttered with shoes and clocks and steam irons of the sort that Mutt and Jeff would have been at home with.

Philip's illustrations of incidents in *The Breast*, drawn on ordinary typing paper, were presented to me one evening at dinner shortly after the book's publication. A couple of years earlier, while I was writing *Our Gang*,[6] Philip had responded to the chapters that I showed him in manuscript with a series of caricatures of Nixon, Kissinger, Agnew, and John Mitchell. He worked on these caricatures with more concentration than he did on the drawings for *The Breast*, and he even toyed with the thought of publishing them as a collection under the title *Poor Richard*. The eight drawings inspired by *The Breast* were simply a spontaneous rejoinder to something he'd liked. The drawings were intended to do nothing other than please me—and did they!

For me his blubbery cartoon rendering of the breast into which Professor David Kepesh is inexplicably transformed—his vision of afflicted Kepesh as a beached mammary groping for contact through a nipple that is an unostentatious amalgam of lumpish, dumb penis and inquisitive nose—managed to encapsulate all the loneliness of Kepesh's humiliation while at the same time adhering to the mordantly comic perspective with which Kepesh tries to view his horrible metamorphosis. Though these drawings were no more than a pleasant diversion for Philip, his predilection for the self-satirization of personal misery (the strategy for effacing the romance of self-pity that stuns us in Gogol's "Diary of a Madman" and "The Nose") as strongly determines the images here as it does in those paintings where his own tiresome addictions and sad renunciations are represented by whiskey bottles and cigarette butts and forlorn insomniacs epically cartoonized. He may only have been playing around, but what he was playing with was the point of view with which he had set about in his studio to overturn his history as a painter and to depict, without rhetorical hedging, the facts of his anxiety as a man. Coincidentally, Philip, who died in 1980 at the age of sixty-six, represents himself in his last paintings as someone who also endured a grotesque transformation—not into a thinking, dismembered sexual gland but into a bloated, cyclopsian, brutish head that has itself been cut loose from the body of its sex.

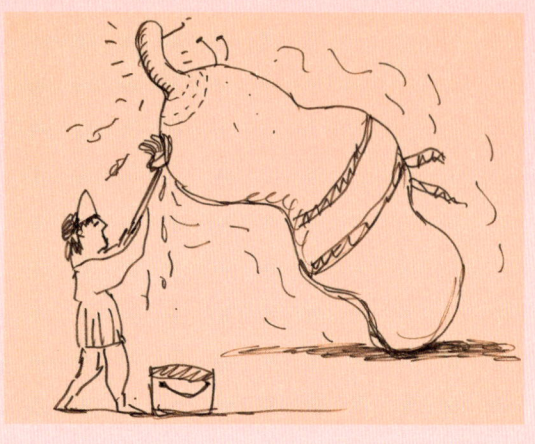

1
This text was first published in *Vanity Fair* in 1989 and then in Philip Roth, *Shop Talk*, Boston: Houghton Mifflin, 2001.
2
Musa Mayer, *Night Studio*, New York: Penguin, 1990, p. 182.
3
Portnoy's Complaint, New York: Random House, 1969.
4
The Breast, Boston: Houghton Mifflin, 1972.
5
The Great American Novel, Boston: Houghton Mifflin, 1973.
6
Our Gang, New York: Random House, 1971.

THOUGHTS
(OR ADVICE TO MYSELF)[1]
PHILIP GUSTON

Sunday, September 27, 1978

I just did a painting which I shall call *The Tomb* or *The Artist's Tomb*. So it is truly a bitter comedy that is being played out. Painting, which duplicates and is a kind of substitute for your life, is lived from hour to hour, day to day. Nothing is stable, all is shifting, changing. There is no such thing as a picture, it is an impossibility and a mirage to believe so. A fantasy the mind makes like having a dogma, a belief. But it won't stay still, remain docile; you can't tame anything into docility, with yourself as the master. Being a lion tamer—that's just circus razzle-dazzle.

Sometimes I spread out all over the canvas, the rectangle of action, and make this unstable and precarious momentary balanced-unbalanced condition. I did this last week. Now, in reverse, yesterday and today, I made a rock, with platforms, steps for my forms to be on, and play out their private drama.

This will remain for a while.

The only thing I have is my radicalism against art. All that abstract shit—museum and art history aesthetics.

What a lie—lie!

The only true impulse is realism. Arty art screws you in the end; always be on guard against it!

If I speak of having a subject to paint, I mean there is a forgotten place of beings and things, which I need to remember. I want to see this place.

I paint what I want to see.

THE APPOINTMENT
(A TRUE STORY)

Once there were two Philips who were friends. One was a very famous writer, a celebrity, the other a painter who had some degree of fame. Philip the Painter, who lived in the mountains and whose solitude was always being interrupted by the telephone, decided to put a stop to this thievery of time. He installed a switch that turns off the ringing telephone. This was a luxurious feeling for him, since he could telephone out to the outside world, but the outside world could not reach him at all.

Philip the Writer, who lived in the City (by preference, he once said, where he could roam the streets at will, eat in foreign restaurants, and taste all sorts of imported delicacies), had been trying to telephone Philip the Painter for six months. Then, after a trip to European cities, Philip the Writer tried again to telephone Philip the Painter. Again without success. Finally, Philip the Writer wrote this letter: "For Christ's sake let your phone ring. The world isn't just shit heads and monsters wanting to disturb you at your sacred foolishness—there's also me, your old pen and brush pal. Call me."

Philip the Painter waited a week before he telephoned Philip the Writer, whose answering service said he was busy and that he would telephone Philip the Painter. But remember, Philip the Painter's telephone couldn't ring, and since he again went back to his "sacred foolishness" in his studio, weeks went by. He received a second letter from Philip the Writer. This time in capital letters. "HOW CAN I CALL YOU BACK IF YOU WON'T ANSWER THE TELEPHONE? HUMANLY IMPOSSIBLE. TECHNOLOGICALLY IMPOSSIBLE. HOPELESS SITUATION, NO?" Then, as if they were secret agents, a designated time was chosen (through a third party, a neighbor) for Philip the Painter to telephone Philip the Writer. Philip the Writer couldn't believe his ears when Philip the Painter called. Philip the Writer pretended he wasn't home when he answered the phone call.

The dilemma was overcome when Philip the Writer agreed to visit Philip the Painter a week later for dinner and some talk. With the stern admonition, however, that since Philip the Writer couldn't telephone Philip the Painter, the appointment had to be firm and definite. This appointment made Philip the Painter more nervous than usual. He never knew from minute to minute how he felt. He couldn't control his moods, which changed like the shape of clouds. The commitment to a definite time of meeting might mean that he would have to telephone Philip the Writer again in order to change the time of the meeting to a future time. Naturally, this made him even more nervous.

This story ends happily, however.

Through a new source of willpower, Philip the Painter overcame his nervousness and was calm as he prepared to entertain his friend, Philip the Writer. This determination was accomplished by the feeling of security that they would spend their evening, during and after dinner, leisurely discussing their mutual nervousness about the time stolen from their work by the world outside. He knew they would exchange their fears of the ringing telephone. Philip the Painter knew that he and Philip the Writer would speak of their miseries and would plan strategies to prevent the frightening theft of time.

There is *no* [underlined three times] relationship between my desires, ambitions, and the needs of a dealer!

The total conformity of painting now that we see is absolutely deadening to my spirits. Its conventionality. Its domesticity.

De Chirico's thought was not willed. It was so perfectly balanced that his forms never seem to have been painted. His walls and shadows, his trains and cookies, his manikins, clocks, blackboards, and smoke. They could all disappear. Yet they appeared. They have known each other for centuries. De Chirico drew aside his curtain, revealing what was always there. It had been forgotten.

Picasso, the builder, re-peopled the earth—inventing new beings. We believe his will.

Marvelous artists are made of elements which cannot be identified. The alchemy is complete. Their work is strange, and will never become familiar.

You can wreck your painting that you believe in by overexamining it—dispel its magic—its spell lost.

Advice to myself: leave it alone.

It should be able to live by itself.

1
This text was first published in Clark Coolidge, ed., *Philip Guston: Collected Writings, Lectures, and Conversations*, Berkeley: University of California Press, 2011, p. 310–13.

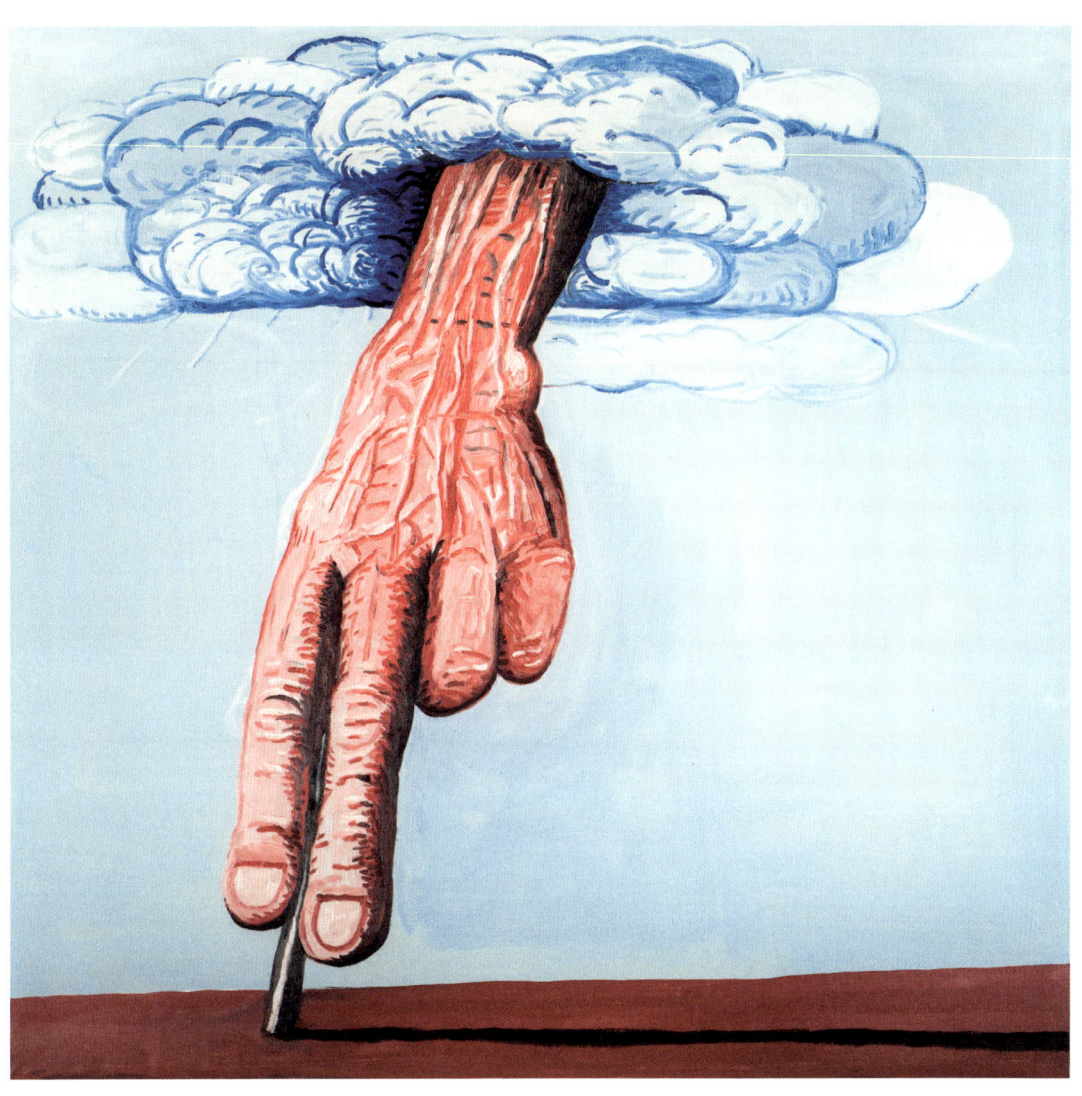

145 − *The Line*, 1978. Oil on canvas, 180.3×186.1 cm

"A Mandarin Pretending to be a Stumblebum"[1]

The retrospective exhibition devoted to Guston's work at the Guggenheim Museum in 1962 confirmed him as a leading exponent of the New York School. After the deaths of Pollock in 1956, Franz Kline in 1962, and Rothko in 1970, Guston emerged as the last proponent of a style of painting that had established the independence and leadership of modern American art. The shock was all the greater when, in October 1970, Guston exhibited his latest works depicting hooded figures in a style reminiscent of comic strips. These recent paintings resolved the split that Guston felt in himself: "The war, what was happening in America, the brutality of the world. What kind of man am I, sitting at home, reading magazines, going into a frustrated fury about everything—and then going into my studio to adjust a red to a blue?"[2] D. O.

[1]
Title of the article published by critic Hilton Kramer in *The New York Times* on October 25, 1970.
[2]
Quoted by Robert Storr, *Philip Guston*, New York: Abbeville Press, 1989, p. 153.

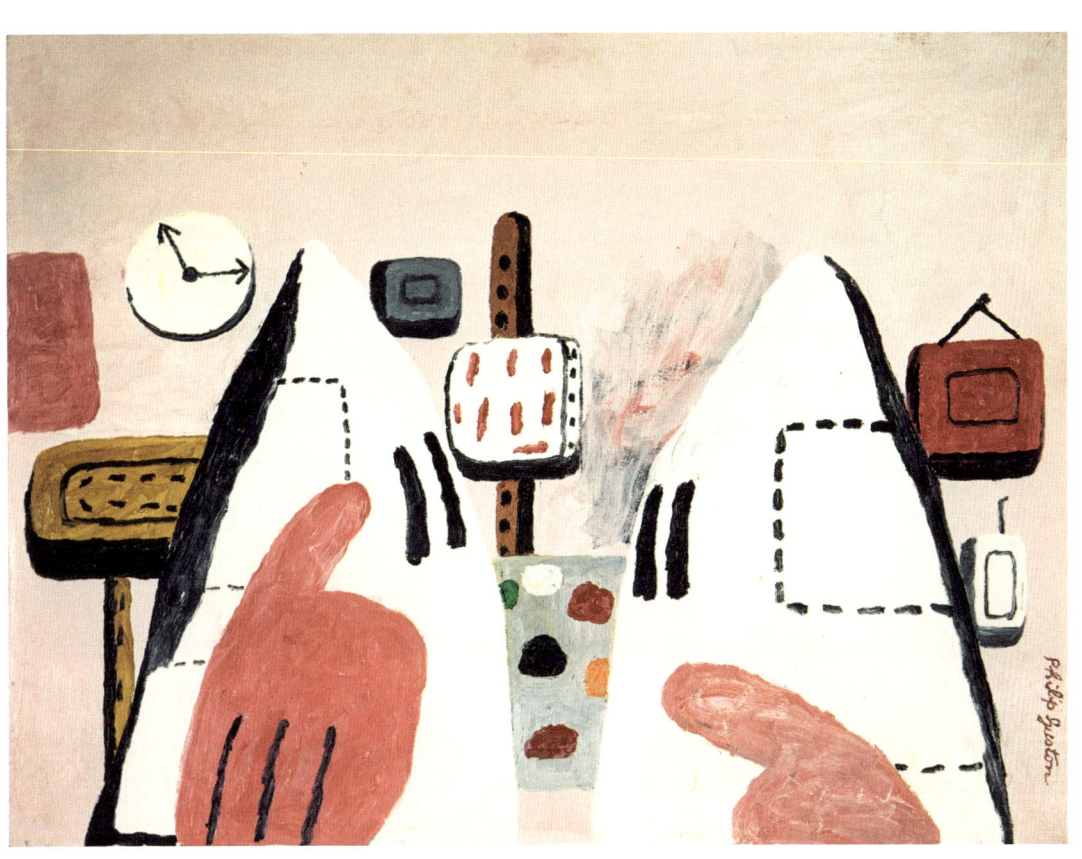

146 — *Discussion*, 1969. Oil on panel, 76.2×101.6 cm. Anne and Joel Ehrenkranz

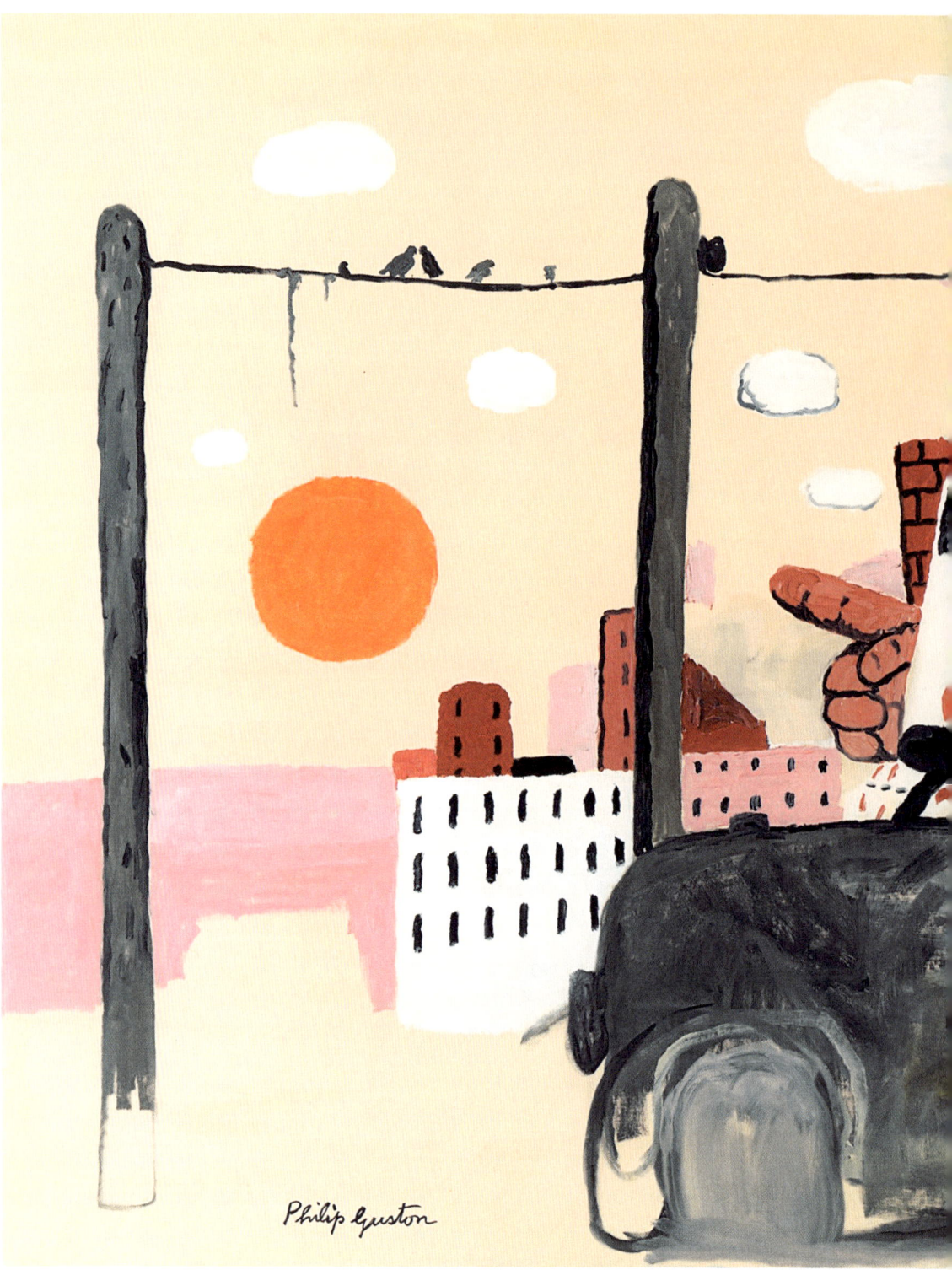

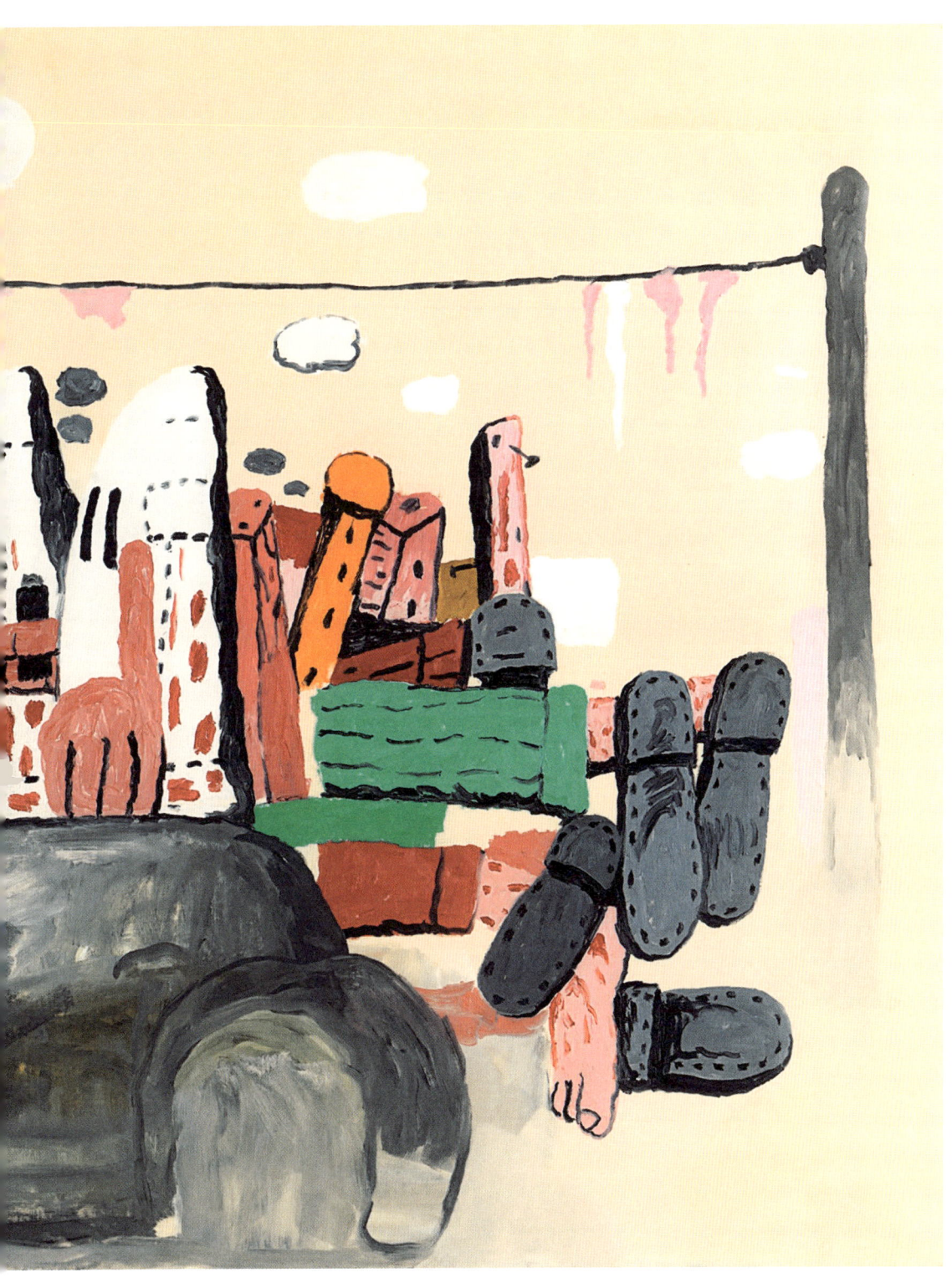

147 — *Dawn*, 1970. Oil on canvas, 170.82 × 274.32 cm.
Glenstone Museum, Potomac (Maryland)

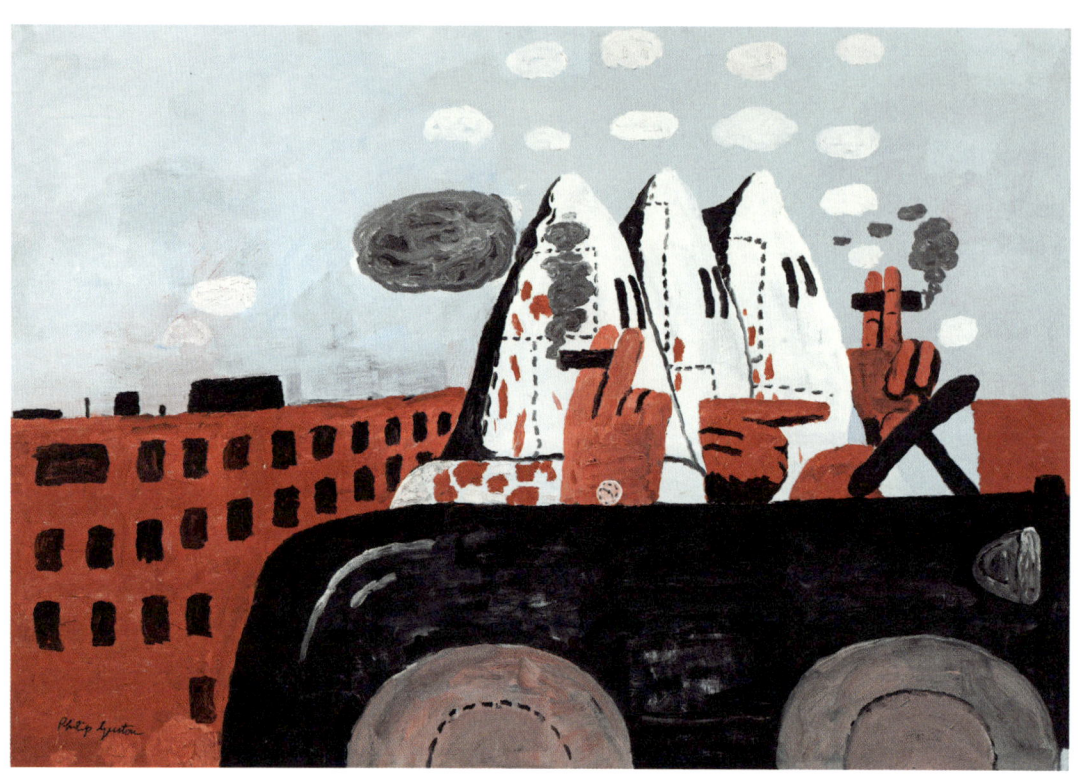

148 — *Riding Around*, 1969. Oil on canvas, 137.2 × 200.7 cm

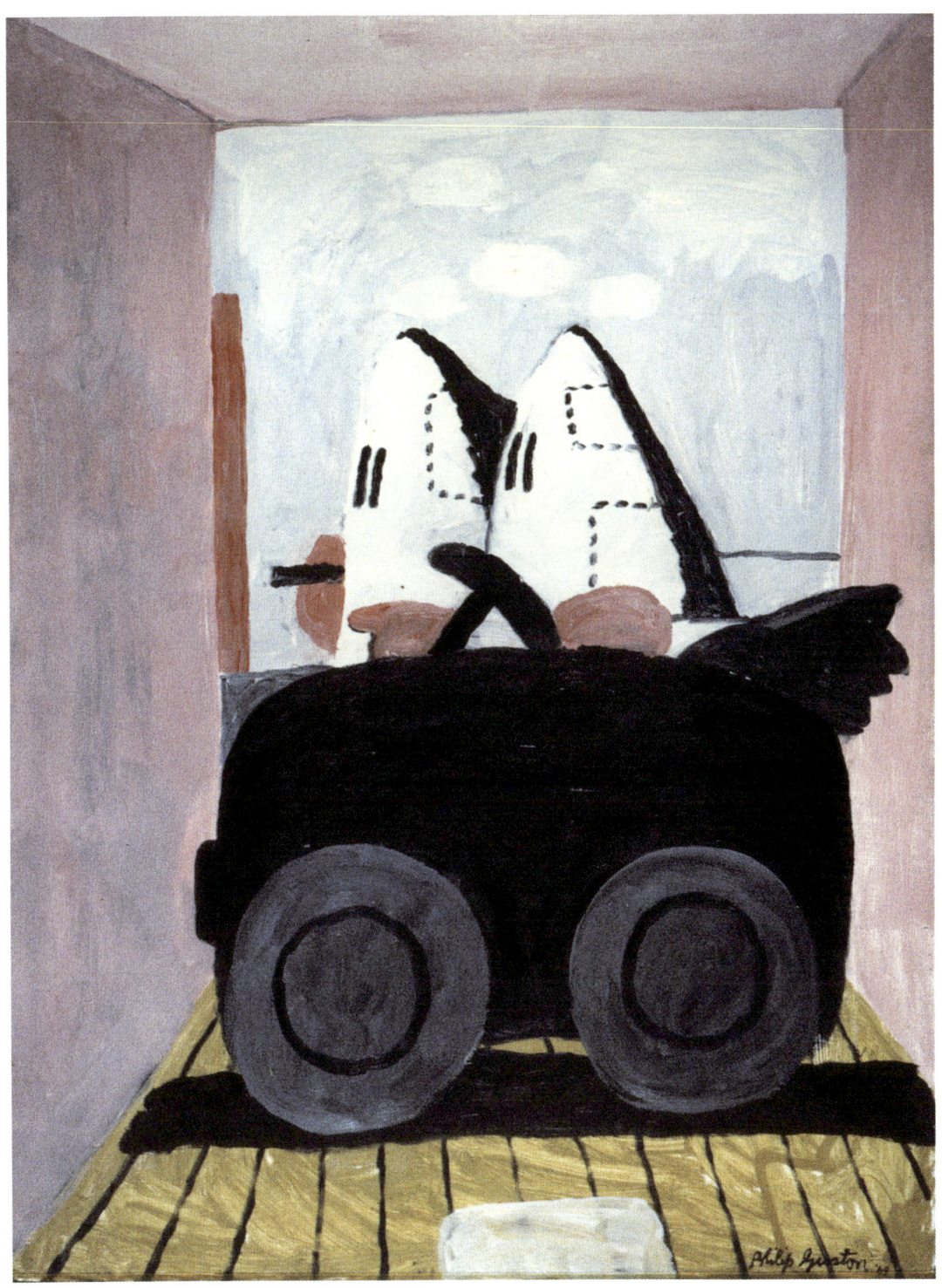

149 — *Out for a Ride*, 1969. Oil on panel, 109.2 × 83.2 cm. Location unknown

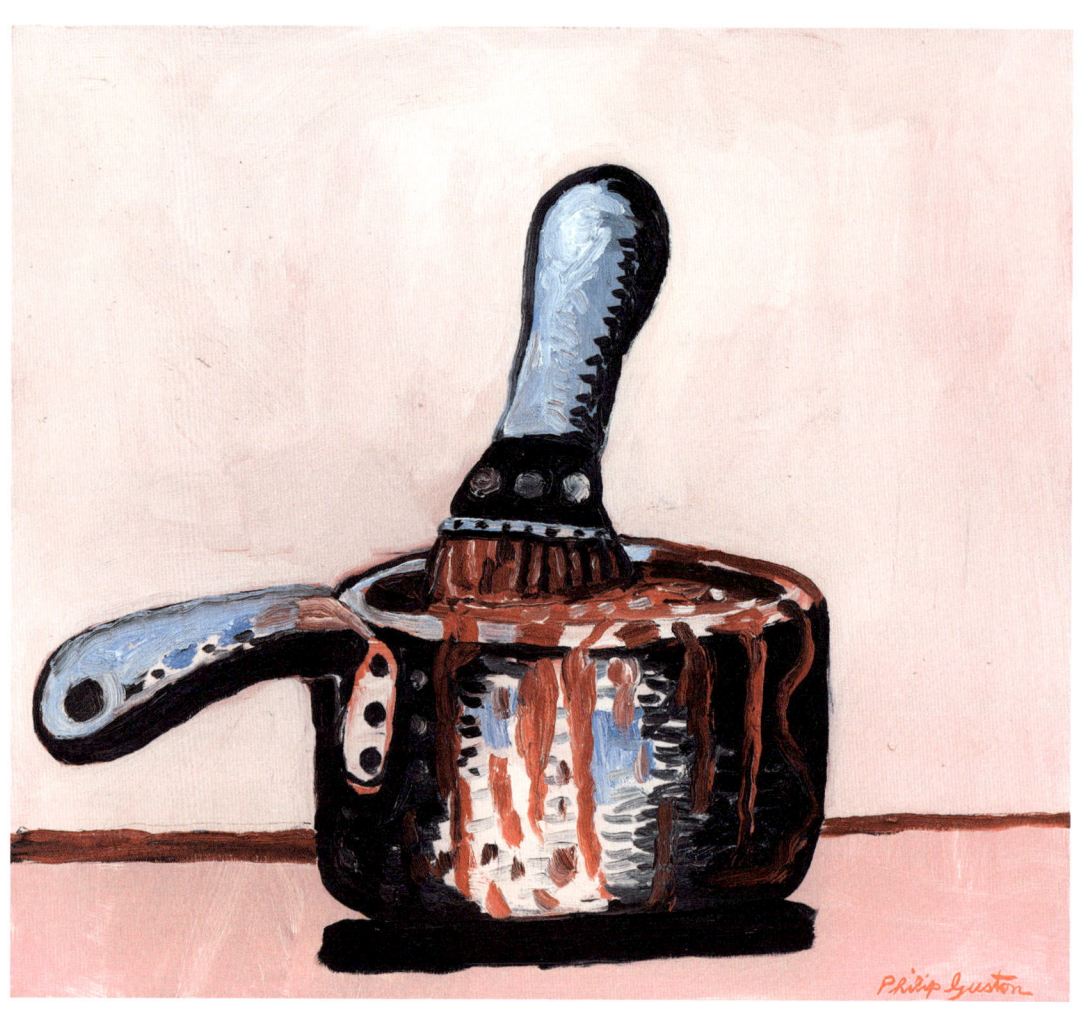

150 — *Large Brush*, 1979. Oil on canvas, 81.3×91.4 cm.
Aaron I. Fleischman Collection, New York

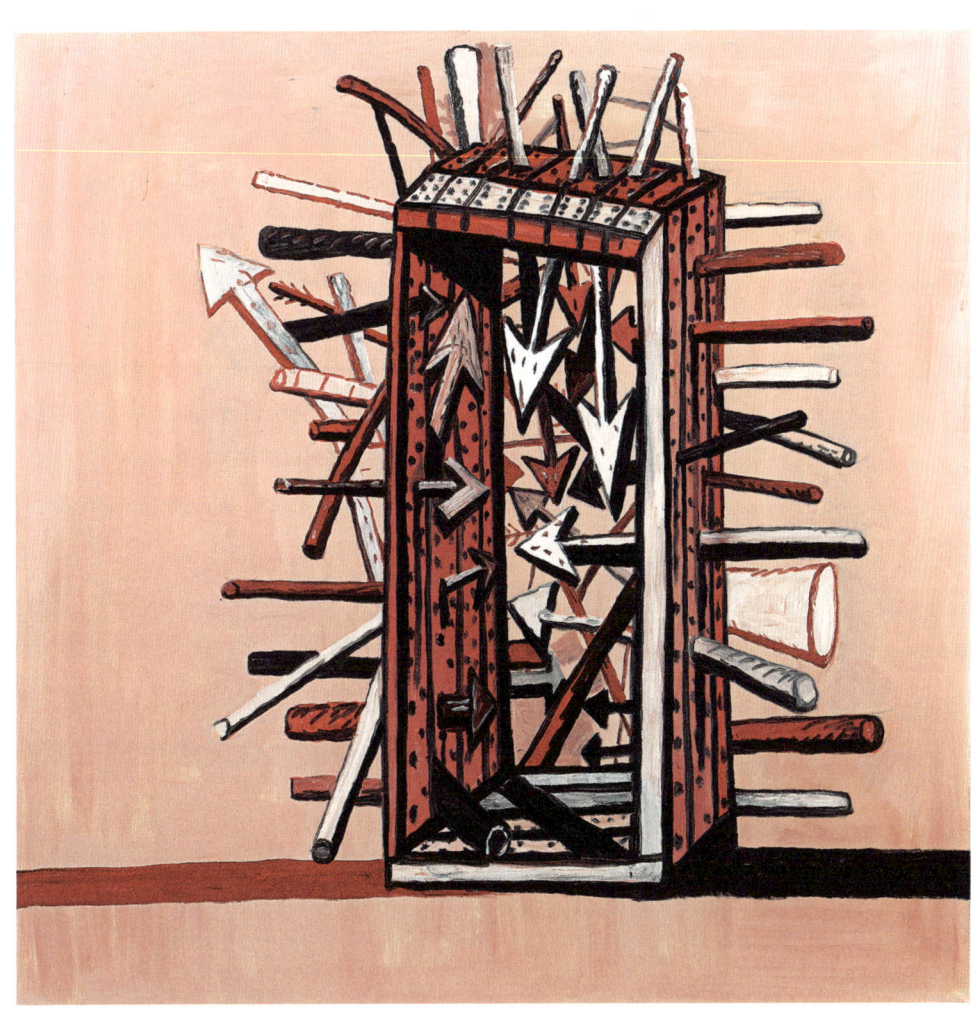

151 — *Martyr*, 1978. Oil on canvas, 174 × 175.9 cm. Private collection

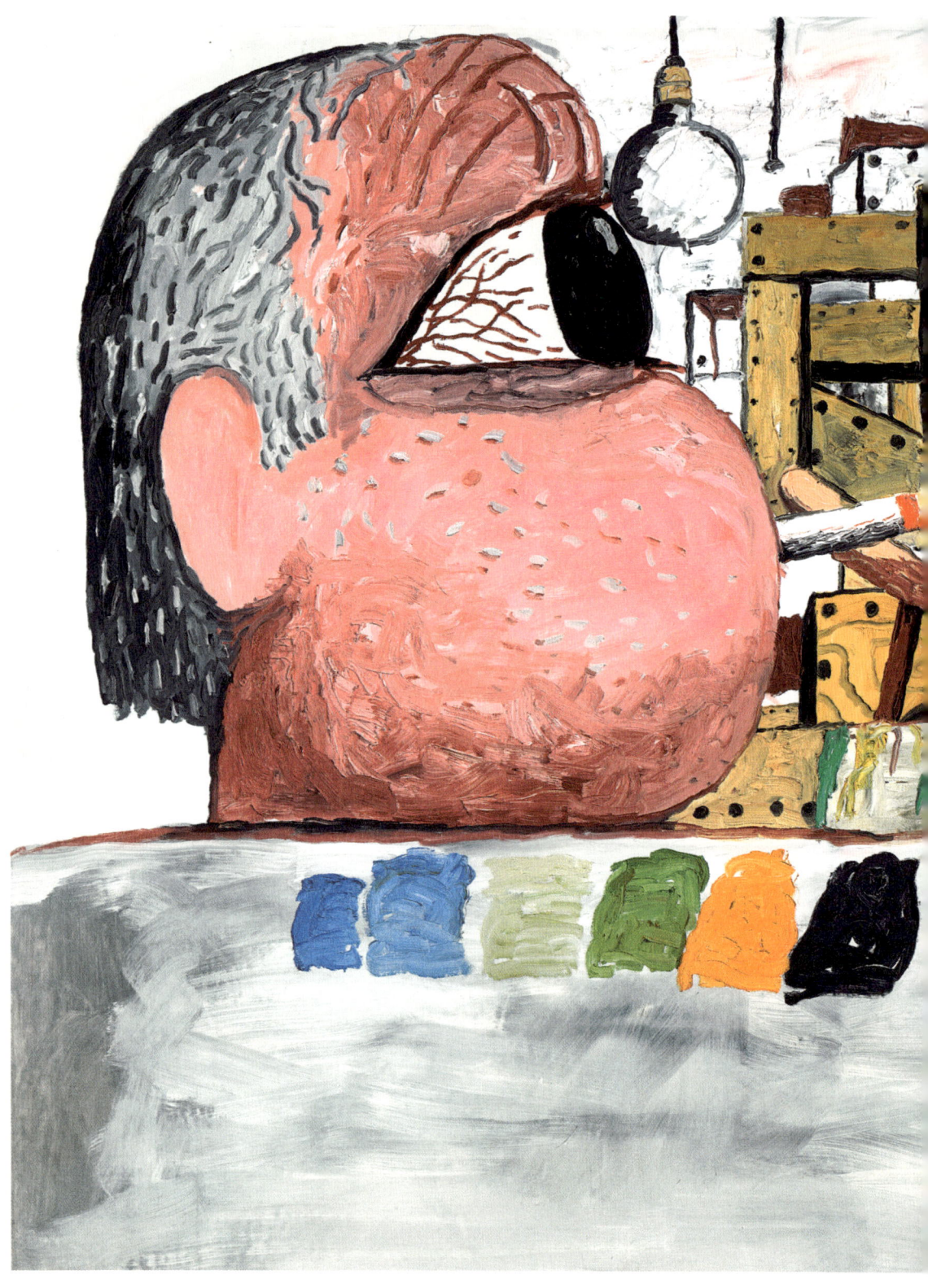

142

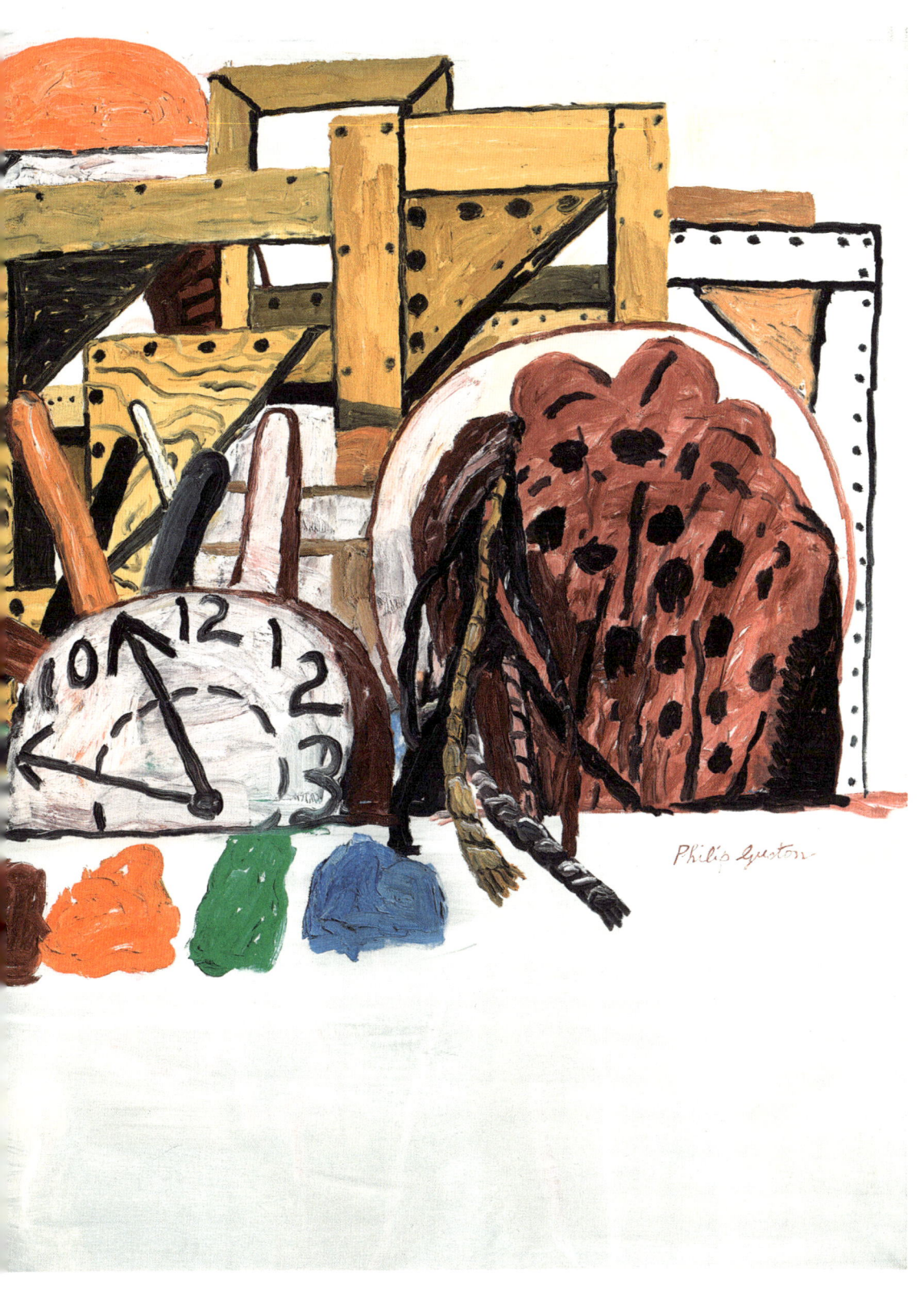

Philip Guston

152 — *Studio Landscape*, 1975. Oil on canvas, 170.2×264.2 cm. Arora Collection, London

Picasso and
the Grotesque

JOANNE SNRECH

The painting shows a woman whose outsize nose is tailored to a body in full frontal view. The faultless alignment of her face, breasts, and navel draw the eye down to the lower body: thighs spread apart, vulva and pubic hair as frankly displayed as the stream of urine flowing onto the sand. The colors are vivid, especially the blue of the sky and sea, which dominate the painting. *La Pisseuse* (Woman Pissing, ill. 153) belongs to Picasso's late period, with the characteristically lively brushwork and curls merging with the paint. The theme, unusual outside of popular imagery, is addressed free of all misgivings and with a certain relish. Shocking in its triviality and in the elevation of the scatological, the sexual, and the "low" to the realm of art—especially that of the painter at the height of his fame in the mid-1960s—this is nonetheless an integral, if little studied, part of a grotesque vein in the Picasso oeuvre. Drawing on a widespread Spanish tradition, Picasso appropriated some of the codes of grotesquerie from his early drawings, in a vein that remained present in the gallery of old men, musketeers, smokers, and painters that appeared in his paintings until his death. More than just an aesthetic of deformation, however, the grotesque appears in his work as a truly radical language: a critique of society, power, and art through humor and the subversion of established forms and norms.

But let us first return to the highly complex notion of the grotesque, whose meaning has evolved over the centuries, and whose defining characteristics include its ambiguity, ambivalence, and ability to exist outside of frameworks and norms. As Victor Hugo pointed out in the preface to his play *Cromwell* (1827), there is only one type of ideal beauty, while the variations and combinations of the grotesque are potentially infinite.[1] The term "grotesque," whose etymological meaning is "cave decorations," appeared during the Italian Renaissance to describe the ornamental paintings decorating the walls and ceilings of the underground chambers (the grottoes) of Nero's *Domus Aurea*, rediscovered around 1480. These "grotesques" feature a learned mix of human and animal forms, together with fruits, flowers, and other vegetation, and embody the idea of a physical in-between, a transformation or a metamorphosis. In literature and theater in particular, the grotesque became a kind of "comic caricature," with the most eloquent examples undoubtedly found in the work of Rabelais and in the *commedia dell'arte*, where it took on some of the attributes with which it is still associated: exaggeration, distortion, laughter, and satire. A carnivalesque dimension, accompanied by a reversal of hierarchies and values. In the early seventeenth century, the term mainly meant "bizarre, extravagant, ridiculous,"[2] while in the nineteenth, in the writings of Victor Hugo and John Ruskin,[3] it took on its fundamental ambivalence and the two opposing poles between which it oscillates: the ridiculous and the terrifying, "the deformed and the horrible" on the one hand, "the comic and the buffoonish"[4] on the other.

1
Victor Hugo, preface to *Cromwell*, Paris, 1827: "Beauty has only one type, ugliness has a thousand."
2
Antoine Furetière, *Dictionnaire universel*, The Hague and Rotterdam: Arnoud and Reinier Leers, 1690.
3
John Ruskin, *The Stones of Venice. Volume the Third. The Fall*, London: Smith, Elder & Co., London, 1853.
4
Victor Hugo, preface to *Cromwell*, op. cit.

These contradictory emotions are at the heart of the questions and investigations raised by the grotesque in the field of art in the twentieth century. Two fundamental works, by Mikhail Bakhtin[5] and Wolfgang Kayser,[6] analyze the various elements that constitute the grotesque. Highlighting images of exaggerated, disproportionate physiques and bodily secretions, Bakhtin emphasizes its exuberance and its carnivalesque laughter as a legacy of medieval popular culture. Kayser, for his part, stresses the darker dimension of the grotesque, and its essential, underlying feeling of fear. Both extend their reflection on the subject to an aesthetic conception of the world and both point up the difficulty of precisely defining this notion, which resists any form of firm categorization. Synthesizing these different elements, art historian Frances Connelly proposes the idea of the grotesque as an image in "flux," whose visual characteristics take on a form either "aberrant" (ranging from disfigurement to monstrosity), "combinatory" (including such archetypal figures as mermaids and minotaurs, hybrid creatures that defy reason and nature), or "metamorphic" (transforming one form or substance into another).[7] Connelly puts forward the theory that the identity of the grotesque lies not so much in its unstable form as in its liberation from a cultural base, thus challenging norms and conventions.

Deformed bodies, inversion, exaggeration, distortion, monstrosity: these are just some of the terms from the lexical field of the grotesque that apply to the Picasso oeuvre, whose taste for satire, excess, provocation, ridicule, and unabashed obscenity is fully in keeping with this aesthetic and, by provoking laughter and freeing itself from seriousness, allows for a desacralization of established values.

MAPPING THE GROTESQUE IN PICASSO

Picasso's sensitivity to the grotesque was fueled early in his career by an interest in the deformation of bodies, itself drawn from several sources intrinsically linked to his youth. First, there was his life in Paris at the turn of the century, and in particular the nightlife for which he developed an insatiable appetite in the early 1900s. This was the case with the cabarets, whose role in the integration of the grotesque into modern German painting has been subtly demonstrated by Pamela Kort: as venues for satirical performances in which artists used black humor and caricature to criticize the society and politics of the time, they allowed the emergence of a subversive form which gradually infiltrated the visual arts.[8] The same goes for Toulouse-Lautrec, whose depictions of nightlife—its rhythms, social interactions, lighting, and costumes—sometimes sculpt bodies almost to the point of monstrousness. Picasso adopted these visual codes, ranging from exaggeration to caricature, to highlight the dark and marginal aspects of the circles he moved in.[9]

During the same period, his interest in the representation of the world of acrobats and other circus performers allowed him to explore

5 Mikhail Bakhtin, *Rabelais and His World*, trans. Hélène Iswolsk, Bloomington: Indiana University Press, 1984.

6 Wolfgang Kayser, *The Grotesque in Art and Literature*, trans. Ulrich Weisstein, New York: Columbia University Press, 1981 [1957].

7 Frances S. Connelly, *The Grotesque in Western Art and Culture: The Image at Play*, New York: Cambridge University Press, 2014 [2012], pp. 8–9.

8 Pamela Kort, *Comic Grotesque: Wit and Mockery in German Art (1870–1940)*, Munich: Prestel, 2004.

9 Paloma Alarcó, "Picasso/Lautrec: Elective Affinities," in Francisco Calvo Serraller and Paloma Alarcó (eds.), *Picasso/Lautrec*, exhibition catalog, Madrid: Museo Thyssen-Bornemisza, 2017.

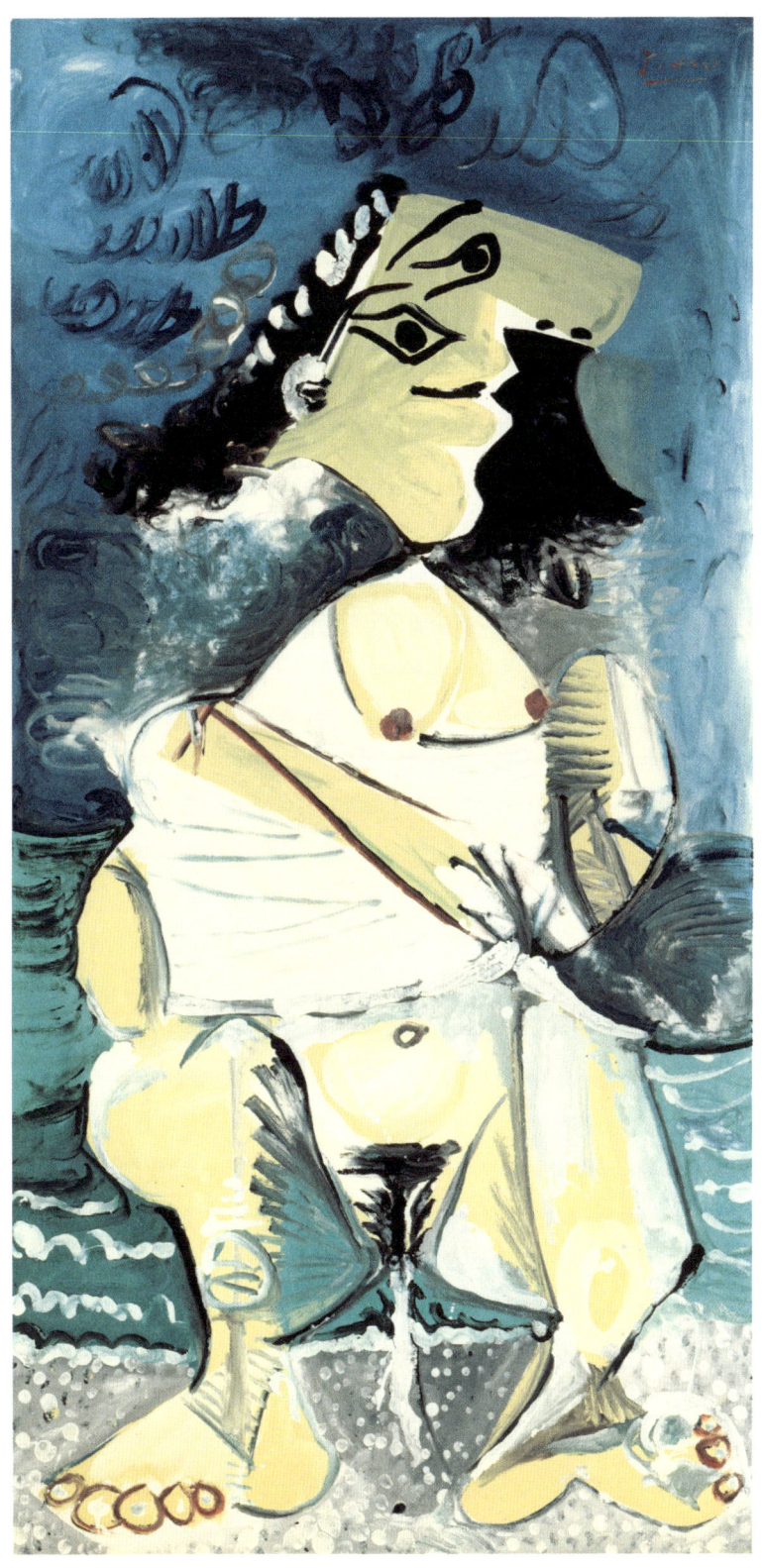

153 — Pablo Picasso, *Woman Pissing*, 1965. Oil on canvas, 194.8 × 96.5 cm.
Centre Pompidou – Musée National d'Art Moderne – Centre de Création Industrielle

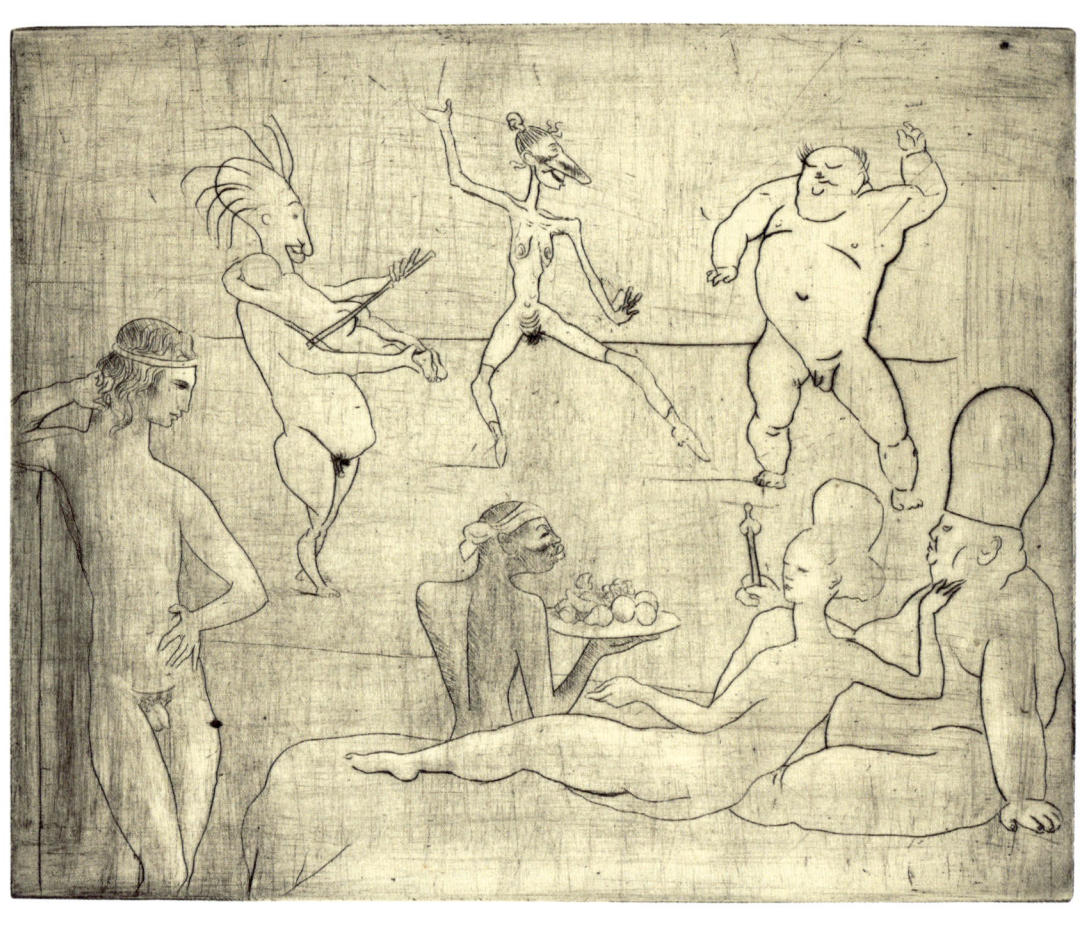

154 — Pablo Picasso, *"The Barbaric Dance" (Before Salome and Herod)*, 1905.
Drypoint on copper, 25×32.8 cm. Musée National Picasso-Paris

a relationship with the body based on the deformation and distortions that these artists prided themselves on, embodying a fragile, marginal humanity far removed from the codes of bourgeois society (ill. 154).

In addition to Parisian life, Picasso's Spanish roots had a strong influence on his grotesque style. From the Baroque tradition to popular imagery, Picasso was the heir to a culture that many critics single out, within the broader European culture, for its unique combination of the grotesque and the comic.[10] Very early on, Picasso had copied Goya's series of engravings *Los Caprichos*, a powerful satire of a late eighteenth-century Spanish society[11] in which the characters' exaggeratedly distorted facial features accentuate their bestial appearance in scenes populated with strange creatures.[12] The drawings made at the Museo del Prado by a young Picasso in 1895 already show his keen interest in Velázquez, particularly the singular figures of the jester and the dwarf,[13] which crop up throughout his career (*Seated Man with a Sword and a Flower,* 1969;[14] *El Bobo*, ill. 155).

This interest in deformities is especially evident in his sketchbooks and various loose pages (ill. 156). Not intended to be seen, these drawings were rather part of his process of reflection and artistic elaboration. In this "image laboratory," as in his Parisian sketchbooks of 1901,[15] we find the various types of personalities who crossed his path, among them cancan dancers, prostitutes, and other more or less caricatured figures.

THE HYBRID FIGURE:
THE ORIGINS OF THE GROTESQUE

These cultural references provided fertile ground for the development of a thoroughgoing grammar of the grotesque. In addition to its terminological complexity, the grotesque invariably conjures up a mixture of forms and realms and their reciprocal porousness. The figures discovered in Nero's *Domus Aurea*, as in Picasso's work, are marked by a focus on ambiguity which blurs any possibility of rational identification. In both cases the fragmentation, reassembly, and fusion of seemingly miscellaneous elements challenge the boundaries between the human, the animal, the vegetable, and the mineral: the body becomes a locus of transformation and indeterminacy, an expression both of pronounced fantasy and a more ambivalent taste for hybridity.

Hybrid figures pop up all over Picasso's work. One of the most iconic examples is probably the flower-woman (ill. 157), who literally recycles the human-plant hybridization common in Renaissance grotesques. In this portrait of Françoise Gilot, the young woman's facial features and spherical breasts are recognizable, while the rest of her body is fused with a plant whose deep green leaves frame her face. Another figure intimately rooted in Picasso's imagination, the omnipresent minotaur is a human-animal hybrid that Picasso interpreted in several ways: in the Vollard series, for example, a bull's head

10
Valeriano Bozal, "Picasso and the Tradition of the Grotesque in Spanish Art," in Brigitte Léal, Laurent Gervereau, and María Teresa Ocaña (eds.), *Picasso: From Caricature to Metamorphosis of Style*, exhibition catalog, Barcelona: Museu Picasso, 2003, pp. 11–23.
11
Lydia Vázquez, "Goya's monsters: Grotesque figurations of a childlike imaginary," *Littérature*, no. 169, 2013, pp. 102–09.
12
See the Museu Picasso in Barcelona, MPB 111.517: "Si quebró el Cantaro." Copy of Goya's *Capricho no. 25.*
13
Francisco Calvo Serraller, "Picasso and the Spanish School," in Anne Baldassari and Marie-Laure Bernadac (eds.), *Picasso and the Masters*, exhibition catalog, Paris: Éditions de la Réunion des Musées Nationaux, 2008, pp. 61–70.
14
Private collection.
15
Musée National Picasso-Paris, MP1990-94 and MP1854. See also all the "sketch" sheets of 1899–1900 in the Museu Picasso in Barcelona.

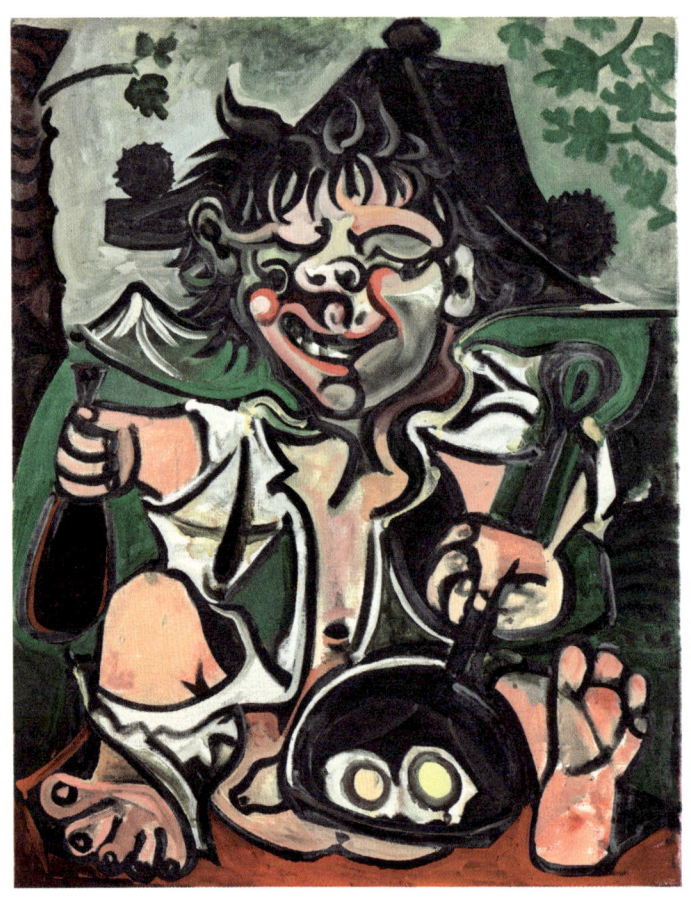

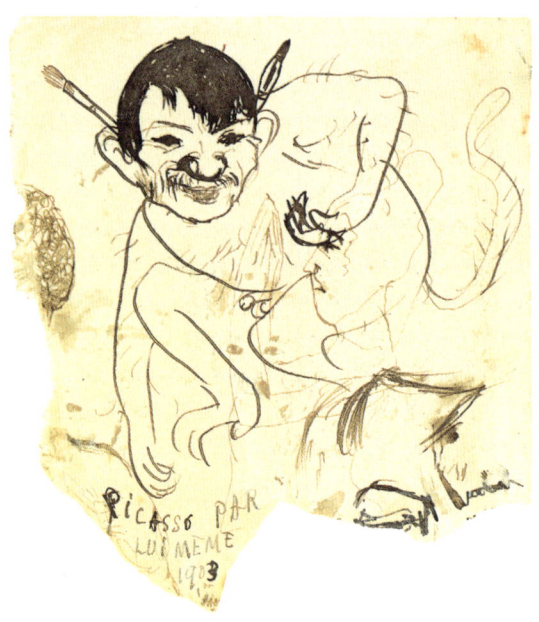

155 — Pablo Picasso, *El Bobo*, 1959. Oil and enamel on canvas, 92×73.2 cm.
Musée National Picasso-Paris
156 — Pablo Picasso, *"Picasso par lui-même,"* 1903. Pen and ink on paper, 11.8×10.7 cm.
Museu Picasso, Barcelona

surmounts a muscular body and appears doubly human through its piteous gaze.[16] The mineral side is not to be outdone, with representations such as *Femme lançant une pierre* (Woman Throwing a Stone)[17] or the series of bathers from 1928–31,[18] in which the female figures seem to be carved out of stone. Taking hybridization even further, Picasso offers a striking variation via the fusion of bodies, in which interpenetration opens up the almost inconceivable possibility of a collective body. Thus, in *Le Baiser* (The Kiss) from 1925 (ill. 163), as later in *L'Étreinte* (The Embrace) from 1970,[19] a single mouth connecting two faces blurs the boundaries of the figure and merges the individual into a creature at once unique and multiple.

This taste for hybridity is not limited to purely formal considerations: in Picasso's work, it is part of a practice of metamorphosis, an all-embracing embodiment of creative power. By exploring the incessant transformation of forms, materials, and meanings, particularly through his use of assemblage, the artist reveals his unfailing capacity for self-reinvention.

THE PICASSO CARNIVAL

In his seminal 1965 work *Rabelais and His World*, Mikhail Bakhtin aptly defines the grotesque as a form of expression that values transformation—the fusion between the human body and the world—but also excess, which the author links to the concept of the carnivalesque, a festive state in which social hierarchies are reversed and transgression is celebrated. With this reversal of norms, the grotesque paves the way for the challenging of established authorities, and the grotesque body, reshaped by humor, vulgarity, and excess as forms of resistance, becomes the primary tool of social criticism. For Rabelais, the grotesque manifested itself in images of exuberant bodies, in bodily metaphors illustrating a worldview in which popular, carnal, and collective life—prominent in Picasso's late period—is valued over an official, rigid, dogmatic culture. The carnival is reflected in his shimmering colors, unbridled energy, excessiveness, and exuberance. Michel Leiris, in his introduction to the catalog devoted to Picasso's final period,[20] says much the same thing when he describes this style, in which "derision" rubs shoulders with "satire," the "violently caustic," and the "caricatural," and the "ironic use of the most unexpected materials" is intimately linked to the desire to "shake things up" and "break with routine." From a visual standpoint, this is reflected in a work like *Homme et femme nus* (Nude Man and Woman, 1965) by a *literal* reversal of one of the figures (the man is upside down), a focus on the genitals, which are perfectly symmetrical in the center of the canvas, deliberately crude drawing, a sketchy superimposition of the figures on the background, with no suggestion of depth, and the artist's gesture clearly visible in the paint through the traces left by the brush in the flat areas of green and gray.

16
Minotaure aveugle guidé par Marie-Thérèse au pigeon dans une nuit étoilée (Blind Minotaur Guided through a Starry Night by Marie-Thérèse with a Pigeon), Musée National Picasso-Paris, MP1982–156.
17
Musée National Picasso-Paris, MP133.
18
Musée National Picasso-Paris, MP106, MP118, MP1058, MP1060.
19
Musée National Picasso-Paris, MP1990–39.
20
Michel Leiris, "Un génie sans piédestal," in Gérard Regnier (ed.), *Le Dernier Picasso (1953–1973)*, exhibition catalog, Paris: Centre Pompidou, 1988, pp. 14–15.

Iconographically speaking, one of the best examples of this carnivalesque vein can be found in the variations on the portrait of Jaime Sabartés, which express the deep bond between the two men over the decades. Picasso regularly dressed Sabartés in the most unlikely costumes, as a decadent poet (1900), a monk (1938), a Golden Age gentleman wearing a ruff (1939), and a faun (1946), and depicted him in situations ranging from the (literally) piddling (*Sabartés aux toilettes* [Sabartés at the Toilet][21]) to the downright crude, notably in a series of small "humorous drawings" from 1957 (ill. 159–162),[22] depicting a veritable "human tragicomedy."[23]

Picasso indefatigably transposed this satirical vein from one medium to another, as in the engravings dedicated in 1968 (ill. 158) to *La Celestina*, the matchmaker in Fernando de Rojas's Spanish Renaissance classic *La Tragicomedia de Calisto y Melibea*, of which there were at least two copies in Picasso's library.[24] His taste for the grotesque is clearly reflected in the objects, works of art, and books in his personal collection. In the vein of society portraits found in Spanish literature and visual culture, whose codes Picasso reproduced quite literally, the engravings echo the *La Célestine* painting (1904) from his Blue Period,[25] which already showed the black-veiled matchmaker as a somewhat monstrous figure. Sixty years later, he would develop the story of this character in the medium of engraving, which allowed him to exploit the grotesque potential of the subject to the full, multiplying scenes and individuals and turning drawing into a narrative tool. Likewise, the freedom afforded by drypoint and Picasso's technical mastery made possible an emphasis on the grotesque nature of certain characters, particularly the courtiers, who gaze lustfully at the young woman in several of the vignettes.[26] Sex is once again the focal point of the composition, recalling its prominence in the grotesque, in line with what Bakhtin identifies as one of the latter's essential attributes: a body in transformation, characterized by the exaggeration of its orifices and its protrusions (mouth, belly, breasts, genitals). In addition to Picasso's late period, the idea of a humorously reshaped body lending itself to a reversal of norms, is present very early on in the artist's work and perhaps initially, more than anywhere else, in his *Demoiselles d'Avignon*.[27]

With their unnatural poses, angular bodies, and grimacing faces, the *Demoiselles* spectacularly subvert the classical theme of the nude. Even more so, with this canvas Picasso sets up a paradoxical juxtaposition of promise and denial: the motif of the bathers or Zeuxis choosing the five young women of Croton to embody the ideal beauty of his Helen—one of the founding myths of art—conjures up the notions of harmony and supernatural beauty, which are disappointed here, just as the promise of sensual pleasure, glimpsed through the naked female body, is contradicted by the aggressive angularity of line, the disintegration of contour, the chromatic dissonance, and the disparity of technique.[28] All this adds up

21
1956, Musées de Reims.
22
All the works mentioned are held in the Museu Picasso in Barcelona. For more information on Picasso's representations of Sabartés, see *Sabartés per Picasso per Sabartés*, Fundació Museu Picasso de Barcelona, 2018.
23
Yannick Courbès, "Quand le texte fait image," in Christelle Manfredi (ed.), *Picasso illustrateur*, exhibition catalog, Tourcoing, MUba Eugène-Leroy; Ghent: Snoeck, 2019, p. 94.
24
Picasso Peintre et graveur, Tome VI. Catalogue raisonné de l'œuvre gravé et des monotypes, Berne: Editions Kornfeld, 1994, p. 199.
25
Musée National Picasso-Paris, MP1989-5.
26
Musée National Picasso-Paris, MP1985-57.
27
Circa 1906–09, MoMA, New York.
28
Ulrich Heimann, *Picassos Kubismus und die Ironie*, Munich: Wilhelm Fink, 1998, p. 120.

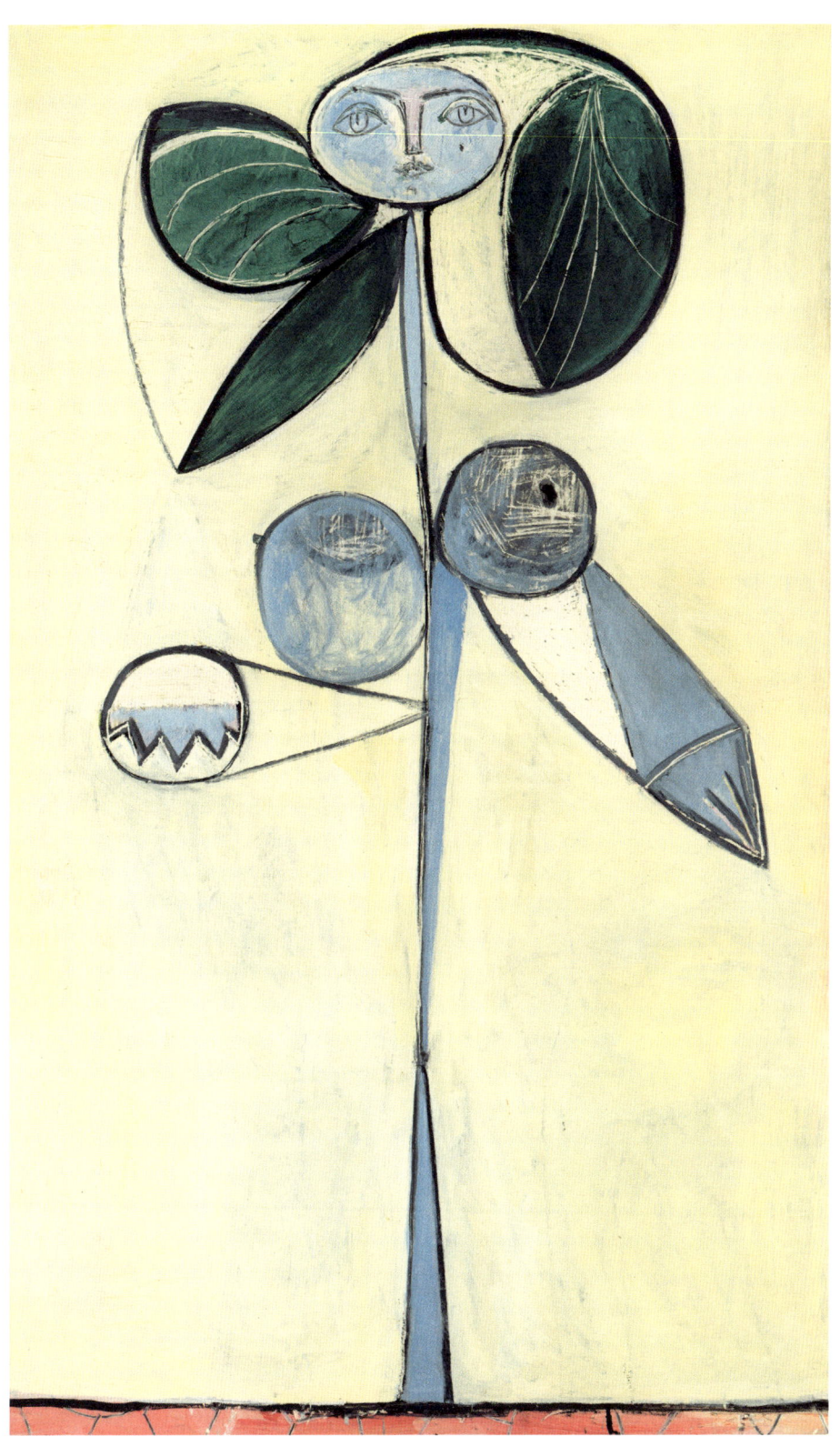

157 — Pablo Picasso, *Woman Flower*, 1946. Oil on canvas, 146×89 cm.
Thomas Ammann Fine Art Gallery, Zurich

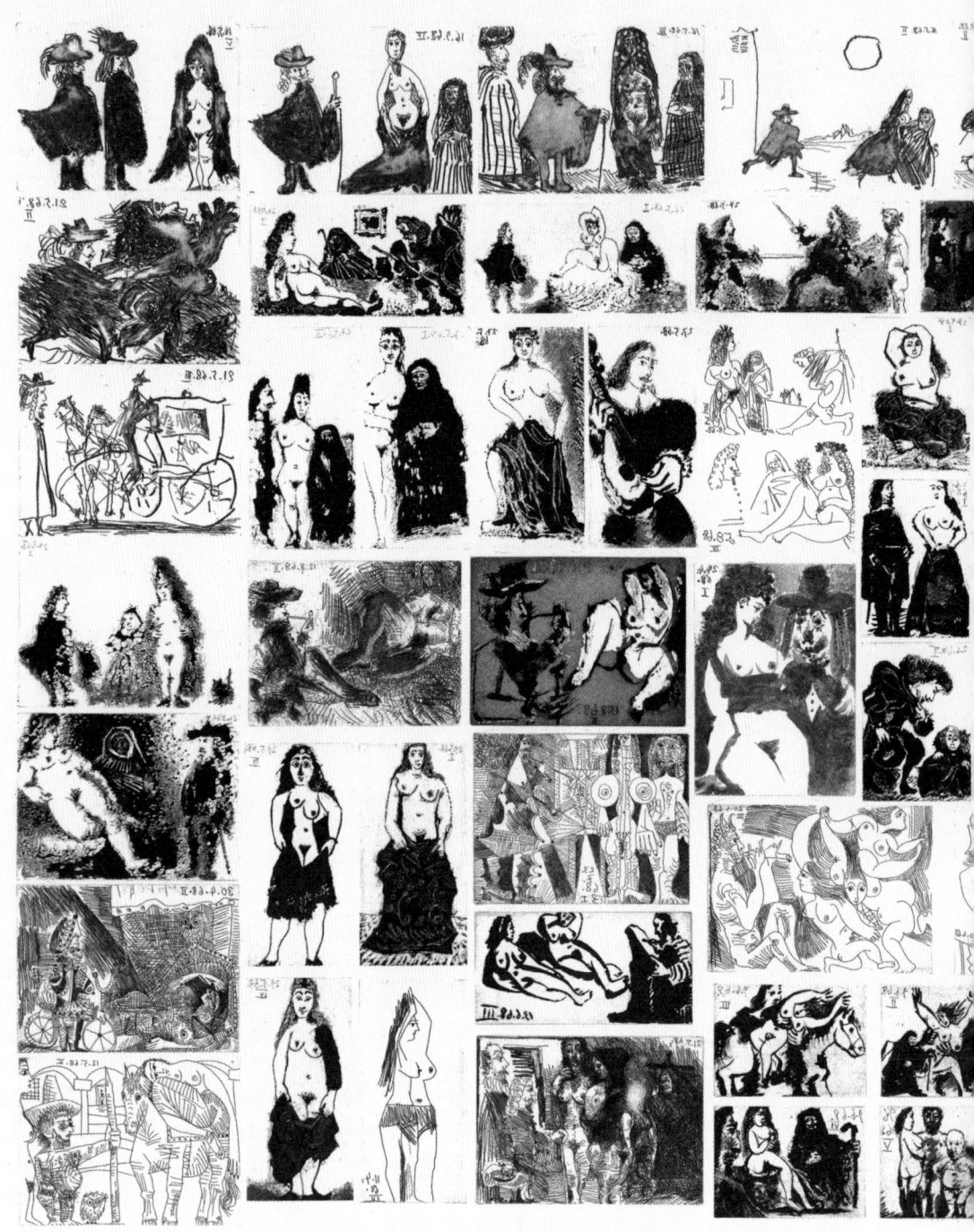

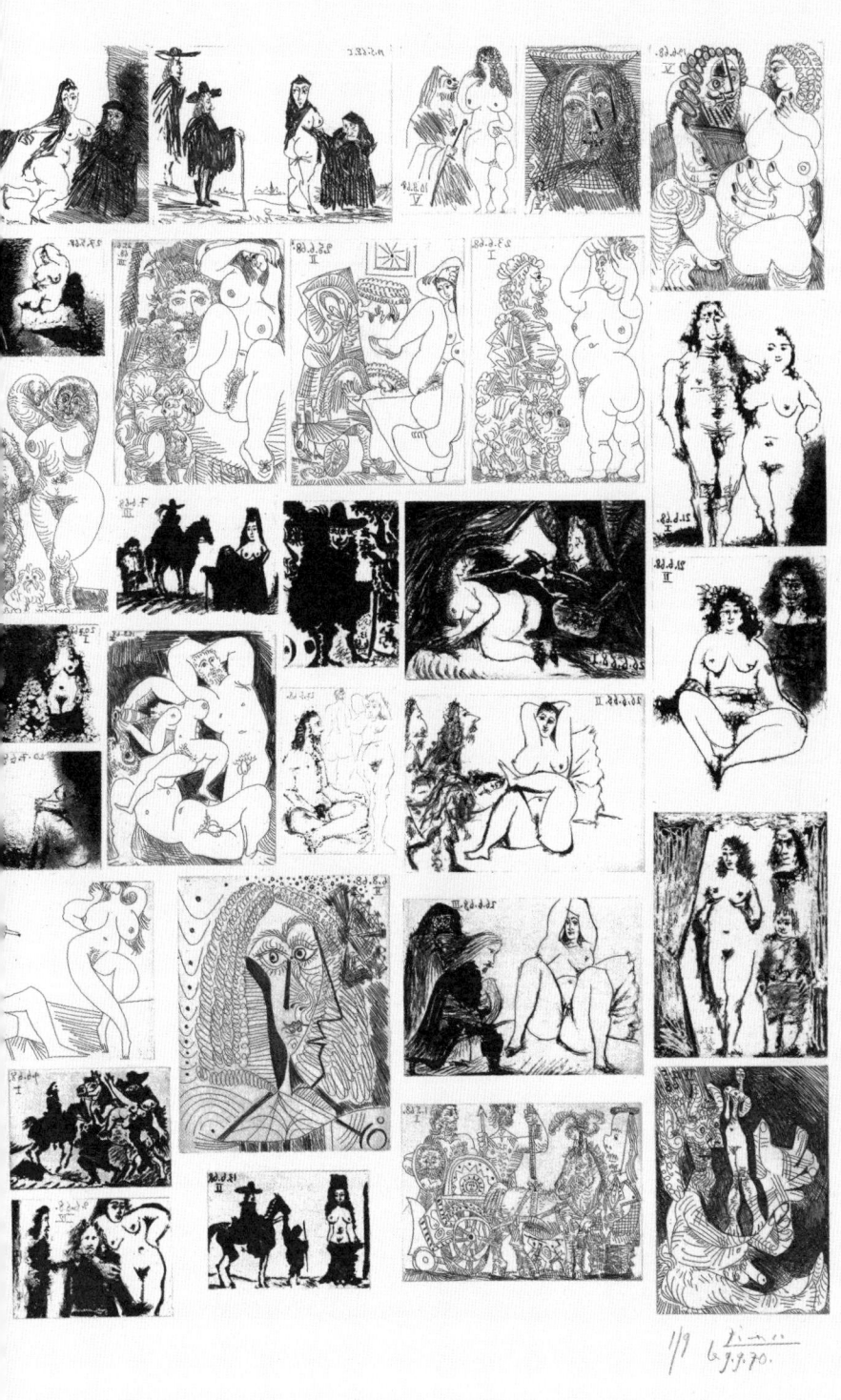

158 — Pablo Picasso, *La Célestine*, 1968. Etching, aquatint, scraping and drypoint on sixty-six copper plates, 74.2×104 cm. Musée National Picasso-Paris

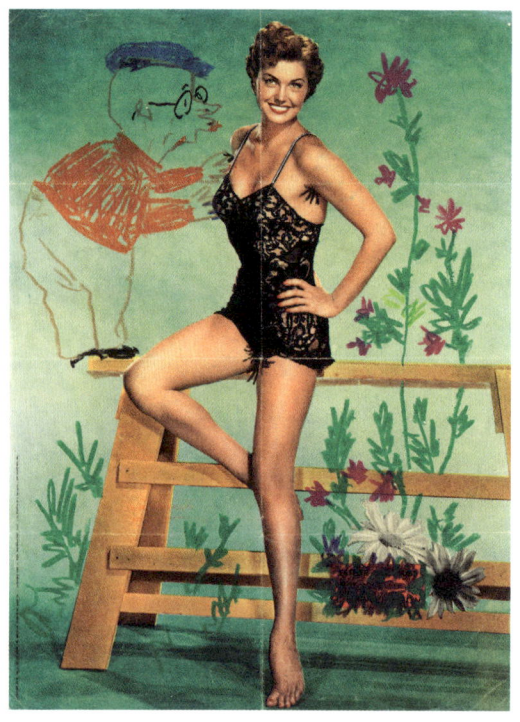

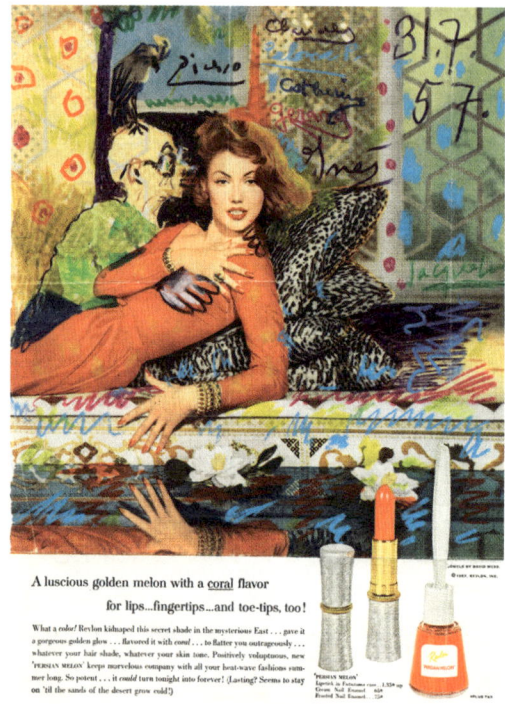

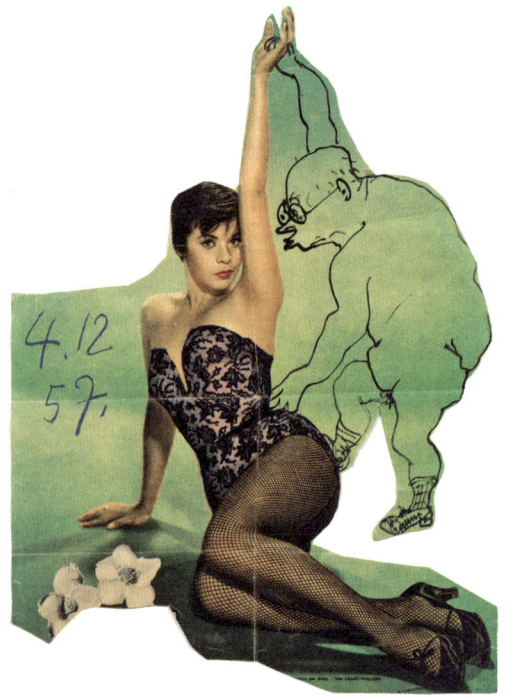

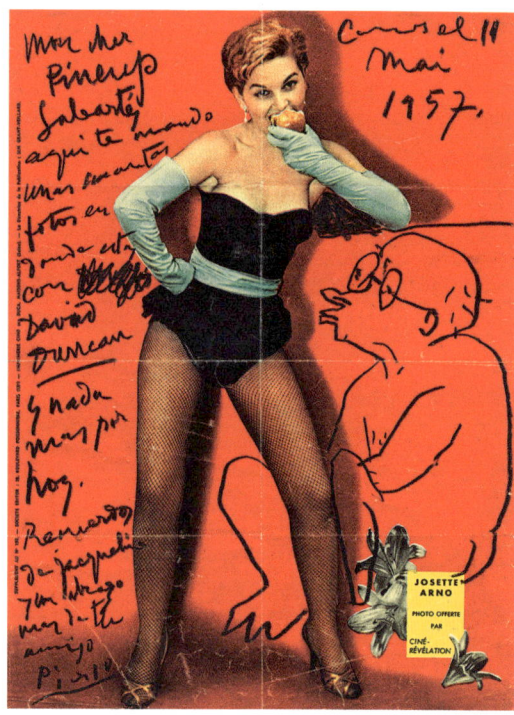

159 — Pablo Picasso, *Humorous composition. Jaime Sabartés and Esther Williams*, 1957. Grease pencils on magazine printed paper, 35.6×26.5 cm. 160 — Pablo Picasso, *Humorous composition. Jaime Sabartés and Gita Hall May*, 1957. Grease pencils on magazine printed paper, 32.4×24.2 cm. 161 — Pablo Picasso, *Humorous composition. Jaime Sabartés and Neile Adams*, 1957. Brush and ink on magazine printed paper cutting, 35.6×26.3 cm. 162 — Pablo Picasso, *Humorous composition. Jaime Sabartés and Josette Arno*, 1957. Black grease pencil on magazine printed paper, 35×26.3 cm.

Museu Picasso, Barcelona

to a monumental snub to the classically normative idea of art and beauty, as the critic Félix Fénéon undoubtedly intuited when he said to the artist, after seeing the painting: "You should be a caricaturist."[29] Picasso denies the viewer everything that the subject and imagery seemed to promise—an erotic feast for the eyes, beauty, universal harmony—with a total transformation into its opposite, into a shock, a representation of that led the gallerist Daniel-Henry Kahnweiler to claim that "everyone thought this painting was crazy or monstrous."[30]

THE GROTESQUE AS A POLITICAL TOOL

The reversal at work in this grotesque carnival and the permeability of the body to the world around it that the artist emphasizes constitute the basic tools of Picasso's political vocabulary. A collection like the engraved plates of *Dream and Lie of Franco* (ill. 165, 166) is one of the most explicit examples of this. In this scathing satire of the Franco regime, Picasso exploits the full potential of its vignette structure in a host of half-comical, half-threatening metamorphoses of a monstrous dictator, a denunciation of tyranny and the absurdity of power. We see Franco riding a ridiculous steed and striking absurd poses, while other vignettes trace the imagery of the disasters of war. In this regard Picasso has been quoted as saying, "I avoided any realism that would have bored and embarrassed me, and I made Franco into a kind of grotesque Picrochole (I read a little Rabelais) drawn by Goya and inspired by Arcimboldo."[31] Interestingly, this Franco on horseback bears a striking resemblance to Don Quixote, and it is hardly surprising that Picasso should turn to the archetypal figure of the picaresque novel, a literary genre which originated in Spain in the sixteenth century and in which the grotesque plays a core part. In Cervantes' novel, the exaggerated, distorted and often comical representation of reality aims at provoking both laughter and reflection, while the gap between the main character's chivalrous ideal and the real world around him, together with his anti-hero attributes, render him at once comical and pathetic.

The war years were conducive to the emergence of a grotesque style close to Kayser's definition, oscillating between horror and laughter. A good example is *Jeune garçon à la langouste* (Young Boy with Lobster, ill. 164), which juxtaposes childlike innocence and physical monstrousness. A smile verging on a grimace is emphasized by the red of the boy's mouth—the only touch of color in the painting—while his grip on the lobster, which he seems almost to be suffocating, creates an undeniable unease in the viewer. The reversal of roles presented here—the child as executioner—reinforces the grotesqueness of the work in its exposing of the absurdity of the situation. Picasso seems to have been perfectly aware of this mechanism, when, in another context, he says, "People need to be woken up. Their way of identifying things, shattered. Unacceptable images have

29
See Roland Penrose's account in *Picasso: His Life and Work*, Berkeley and Los Angeles: University of California Press, 1981 [3rd edition], p. 131.

30
Daniel-Henry Kahnweiler, *Huit entretiens avec Picasso*, Caen: L'Échoppe, 1990.

31
A fascinating quote that traces the ideal genealogy of grotesque imagery, unknown.

to be created. Images that make people foam with rage. That force them to understand that they live in a strange world. A disquieting world. A world different from what they think it is."[32]

This reversal of values can be found in other, perhaps less likely areas of Picasso's work. In *Le Désir attrapé par la queue* (Desire Caught by the Tail), a play written by Picasso in 1941, the text goes beyond mere humor to become a weapon of aesthetic and political resistance. Human and non-human, the characters with absurd names—*Le Gros Pied* (Bigfoot), *La Tarte* (The Pie), *Les Deux Toutous* (The Two Puppies), *L'Angoisse grasse* (Fat Anxiety) and *L'Angoisse maigre* (Skinny Anxiety)—distort reality to reveal its most disturbing and comical aspects, indirectly criticizing the society of the time, marked by Nazi occupation and hardship. Often reduced to objects or body parts, these characters illustrate the dehumanization caused by the conflict. Putting the grotesque to political use, Picasso follows in the footsteps of many artists of the early twentieth century, such as Otto Dix and his *Die Skatspieler* (The Skat Players),[33] who draw on the same mechanisms of a deeply critical, tragic grotesque, a grotesque that shocks in order to challenge.

THE GROTESQUE: CREATING IN THE INTERSTICES

Bakhtin's definition of "grotesque realism" is anchored in the idea of a deformed body that expresses the material conditions of existence and emphasizes the grotesque as above all a movement, "the lowering of all that is high, spiritual, ideal, abstract; it is a transfer to the material level, to the sphere of earth and body in their indissoluble unity."[34] In this context, seeing the grotesque as a merely comic or political force would seem to obscure its most fundamental function as a force for regeneration, a tool for reformation rather than gratuitous deformation. In Picasso's work, as in the commentaries on it, the idea that the driving force behind the creative process lies in transgression of the norm thus elevates the grotesque to a dynamic principle.

In 2003, the introduction to the catalog for the exhibition *Picasso: From Caricature to Metamorphosis of Style* already highlighted the potential misgivings about calling the artist's oeuvre "caricature." Given that the genre was considered insufficiently "noble," there might have been a sense of unease at the idea of reducing Picasso's work to something akin to illustration or the grotesque, with his supporters preferring to refer to "metamorphosis" and humor.[35] In addition to this semantic concern, the lack of studies of the grotesque in Picasso's work reflects the difficulty of defining this shifting concept, which can also be explained by its markedly cultural origins. The grotesque is defined in relation to a norm which obviously evolves over time. Thus the "primitive" aspect of *Les Demoiselles d'Avignon,* at a time when non-Western art objects were not widely circulated, had a far greater subversive power in 1907 than it did

32
Quoted in André Malraux, *Picasso's Mask*, trans. June Guicharnaud and Jacques Guicharnaud, New York: Da Capo, 1994. This translation by John Tittensor.
33
1920, Neue Nationalgalerie, Berlin.
34
Mikhail Bakhtin, *Rabelais and His World*, op. cit., p. 19.
35
Brigitte Léal, María Teresa Ocaña, and Laurent Gervereau, "From Caricature to Metamorphosis of Style," in *Picasso: From Caricature to Metamorphosis of Style*, op. cit., p. 8.

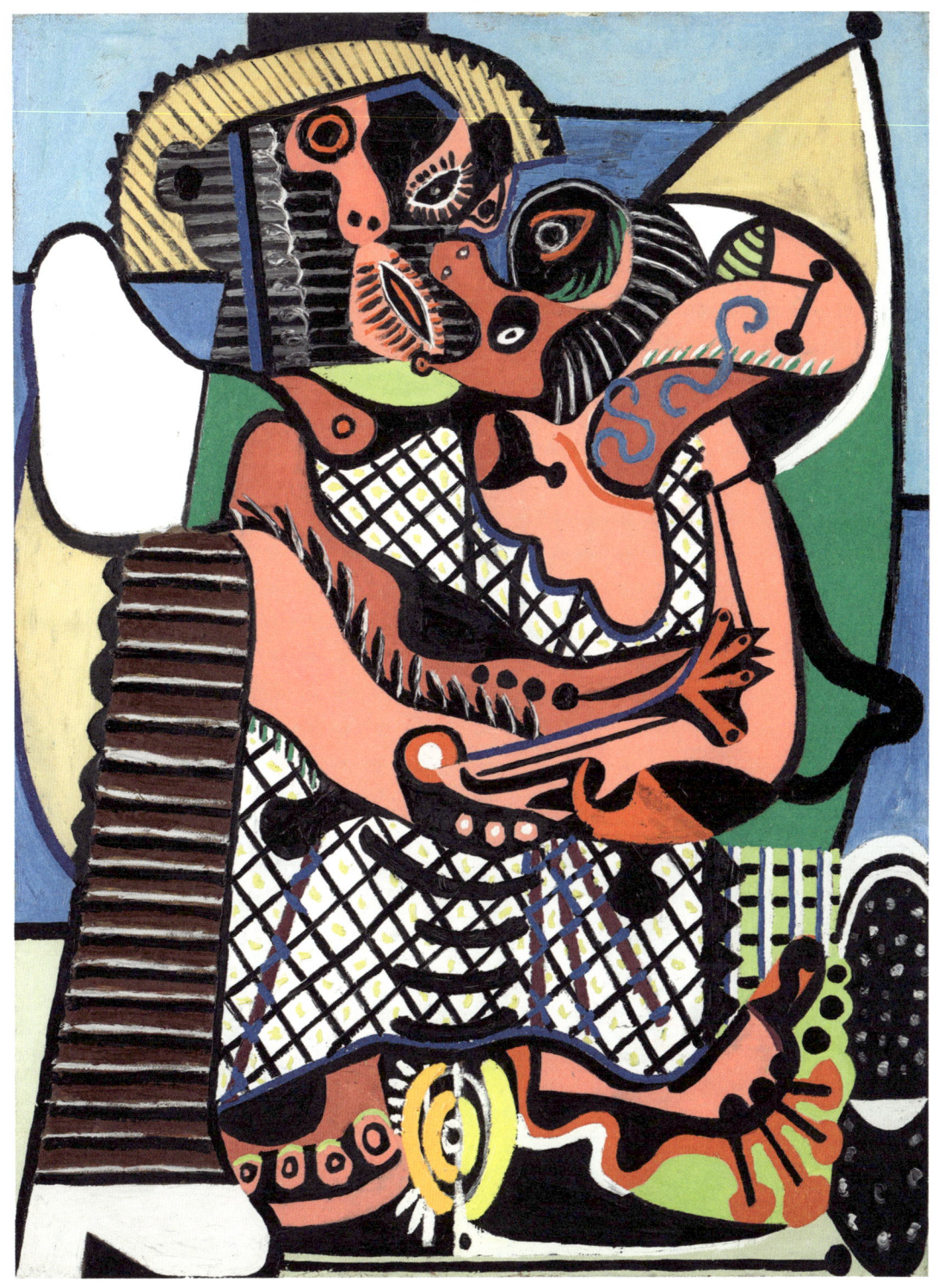

163 — Pablo Picasso, *The Kiss*, 1925. Oil on canvas, 130.5×97.7 cm. Musée National Picasso-Paris

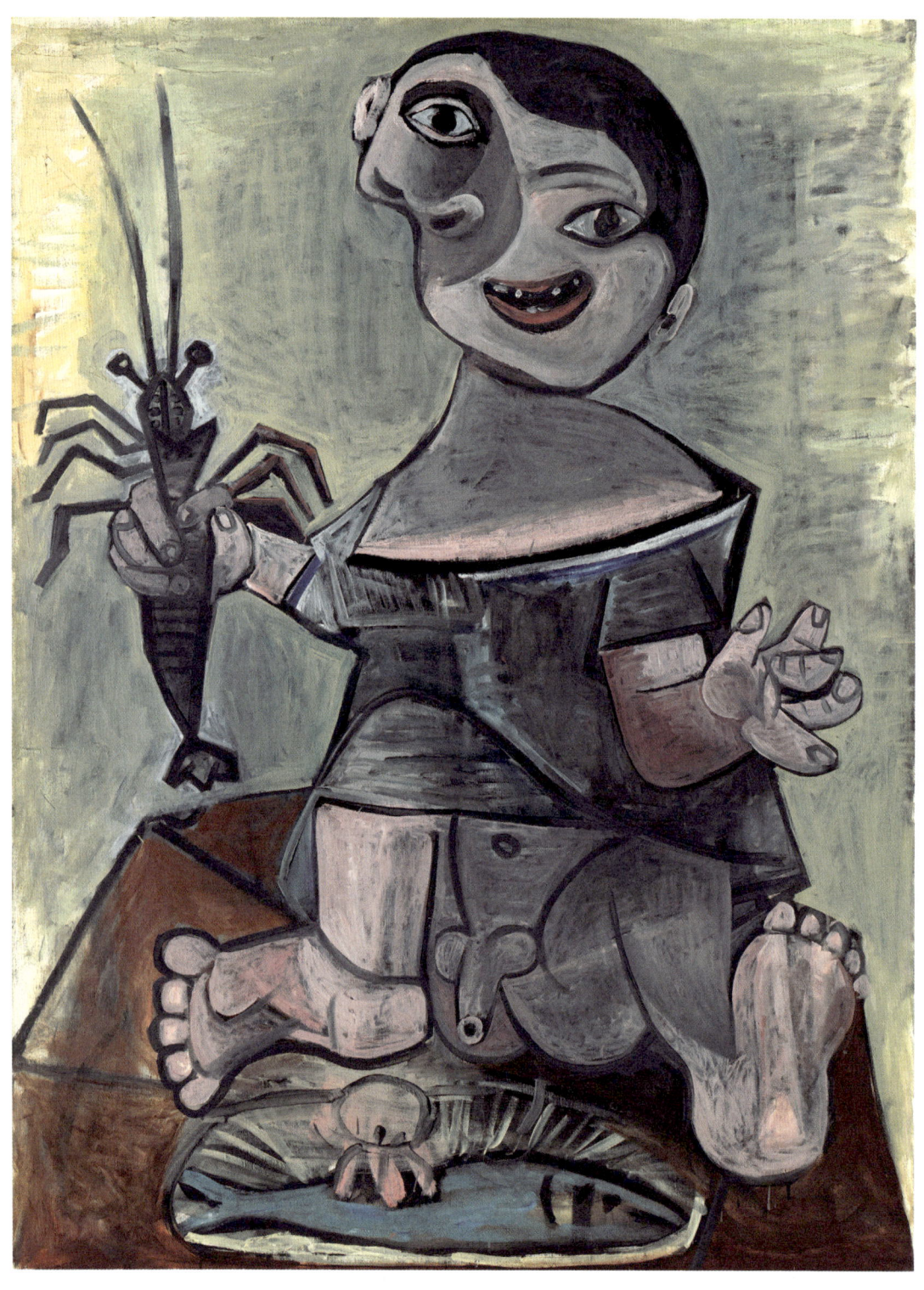

164 – Pablo Picasso, *Young Boy with Lobster*, 1941. Oil on canvas, 130×97.3 cm.
Musée National Picasso-Paris

some decades later,[36] just as Picasso's caricatures of André Salmon, which merge the subject's facial features with the objects he loves and collects, can only regenerate art from the margins as long as the actual objects are considered marginal.[37] Picasso himself endorsed this idea of art as being out of step when he declared, "Art is not the application of a canon of beauty, but what the instinct and the brain can conceive beyond any canon."[38] Thus, with all the "disrespect"[39] that characterizes him, he calls on the viewer to question established norms and consider new forms of representation and resistance.

36
Frances S. Connelly, *The Grotesque in Western Art and Culture*, op. cit., pp. 110–11.
37
Adam Gopnik, "Caricature," in Kirk Varnedoe and Adam Gopnik (eds.), *High and Low: Modern Art and Popular Cuture*, exhibition catalog, New York: Museum of Modern Art, 1990, pp. 130–31.
38
Christian Zervos, "Conversation with Picasso," in Alfred H. Barr, Jr., *Picasso: Fifty Years of His Art*, New York: Museum of Modern Art, 1946, p. 266. Translation based on one by Myfanwy Evans.
39
André Malraux, *Picasso's Mask*, op. cit.

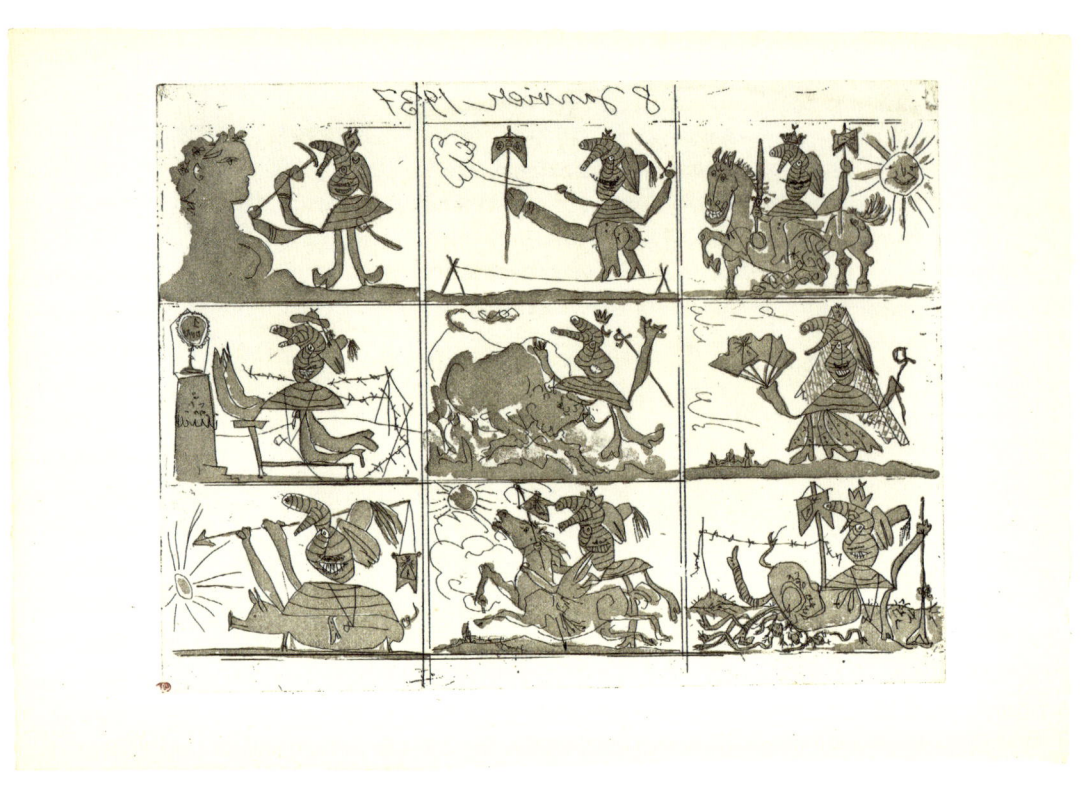

165 — Pablo Picasso, *The Dream and Lie of Franco (plate I)*, 1937. Etching and sugar-lift aquatint on copper, 2nd state, 38.5 × 57.3 cm. Musée National Picasso-Paris

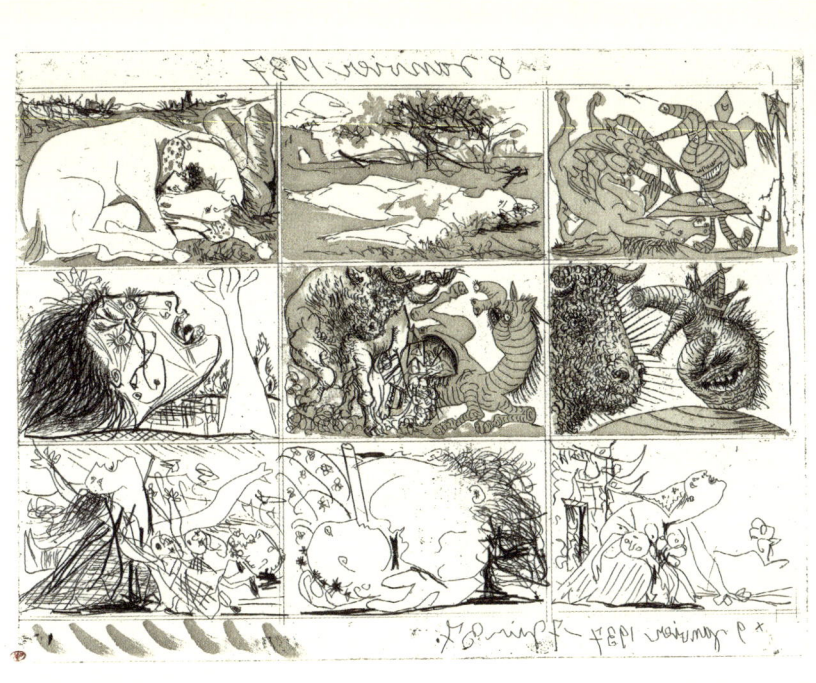

166 — Pablo Picasso, *The Dream and Lie of Franco (plate II)*, 1937. Etching and sugar-lift aquatint with scraping on copper, 5th state, 38.5×57.1 cm. Musée National Picasso-Paris

A tragicomic world

In his Woodstock home, Guston surrounded himself with images of works by Paolo Uccello and Piero della Francesca. The "clarity" he admired in the paintings of della Francesca, the simple and monumental bearing of his figures, the chaos of Uccello's battles, and that of Luca Signorelli's frescoes continued to haunt his paintings. He plunged the dignity of the Old Masters into the burlesque and pathetic soup of his favorite authors. Like Guston's family, Isaac Babel was originally from Odessa, where he joined the revolutionary Red Cavalry and rubbed shoulders with the Cossacks who, not long before, had carried out pogroms against the Jewish communities. In his short story *Red Cavalry* (1926), he translated the tragicomedy of an era whose ideals were shattered against the walls of a derisory prosaic reality. Guston's paintings draw on this dual movement of angelic elevation and realist absurdity. D. O.

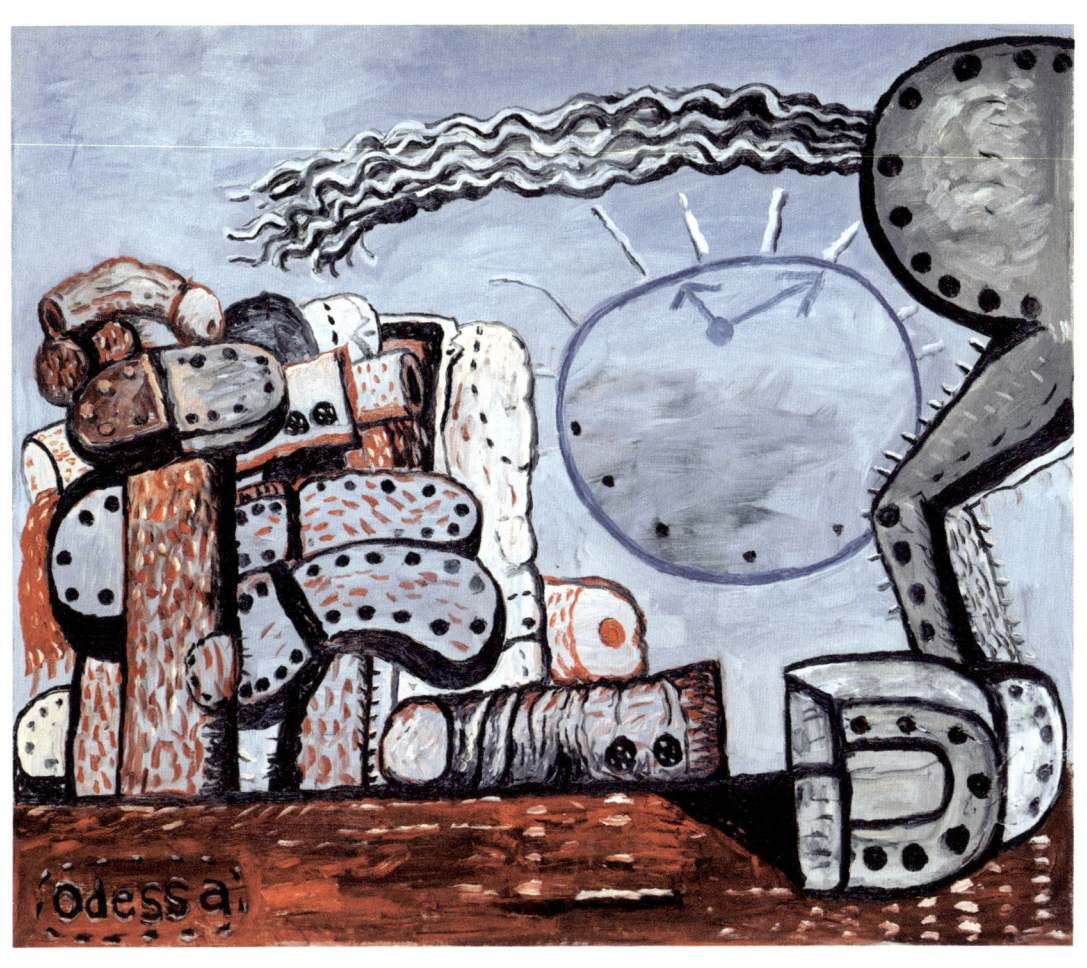

167 — *To I.B.* (Isaac Babel), 1977. Oil on canvas, 170.8 × 203.2 cm. Private collection

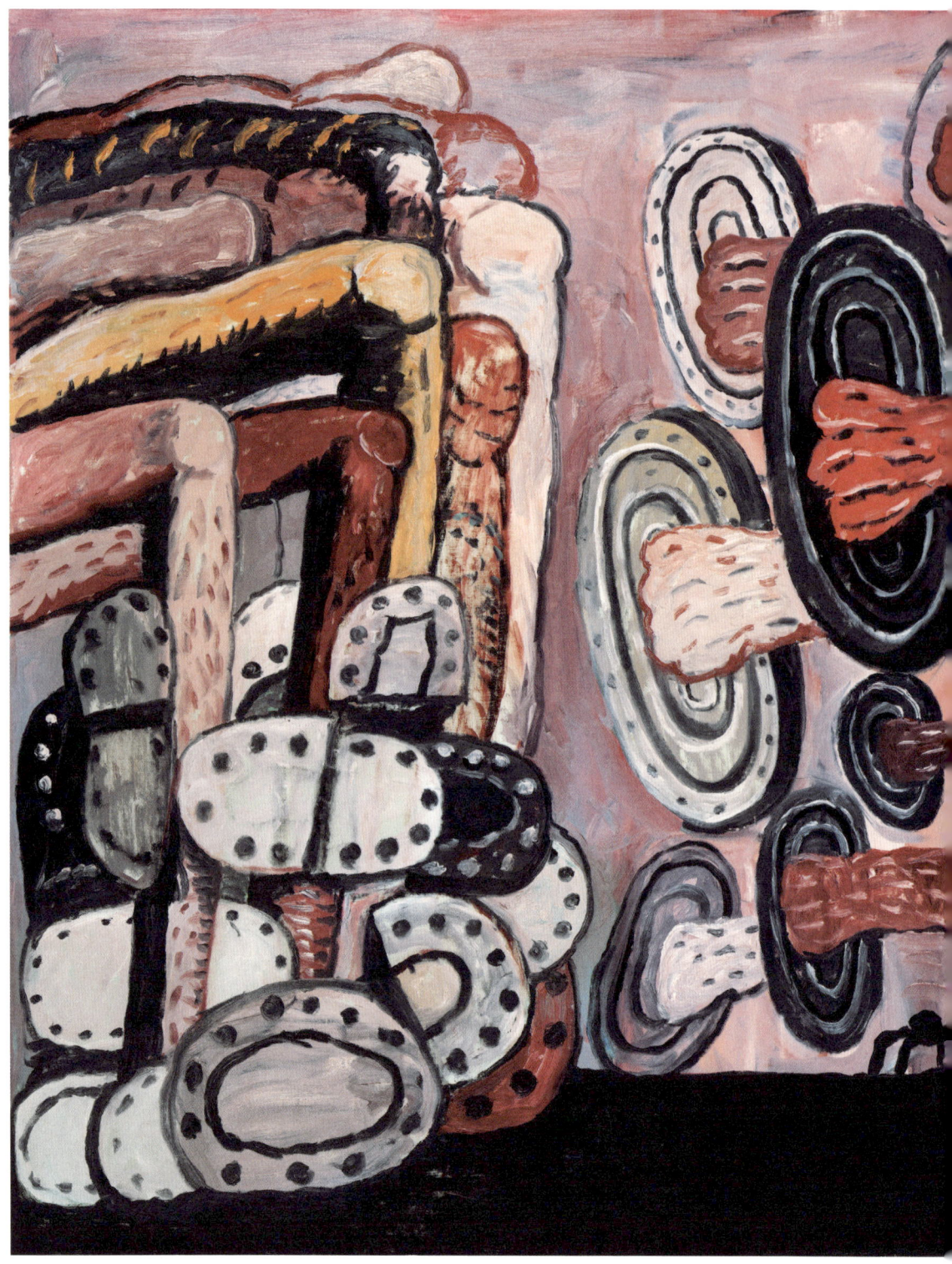

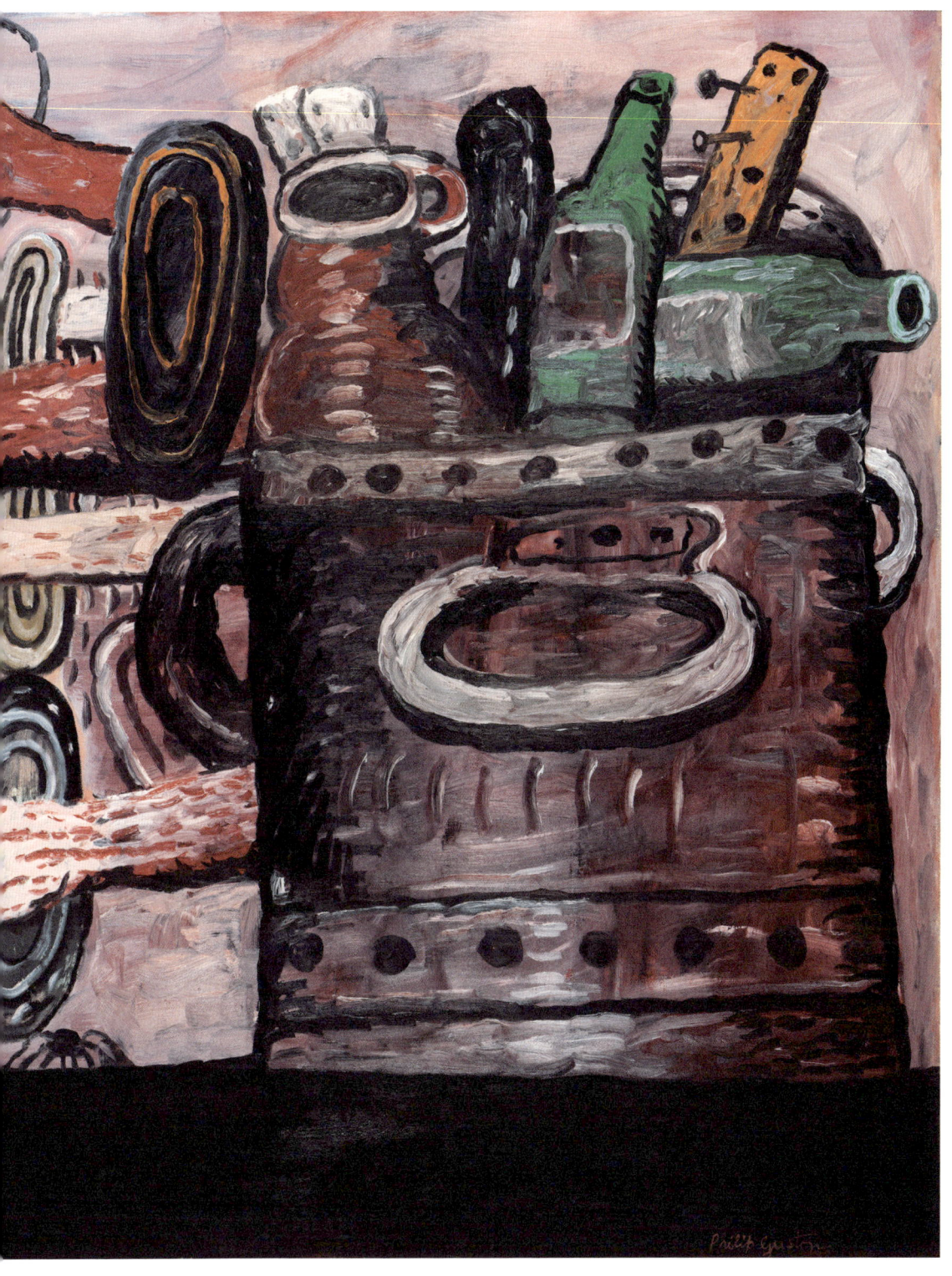

168 — *The Street*, 1977. Oil on canvas, 175.6×281.6 cm. Metropolitan Museum of Art, New York

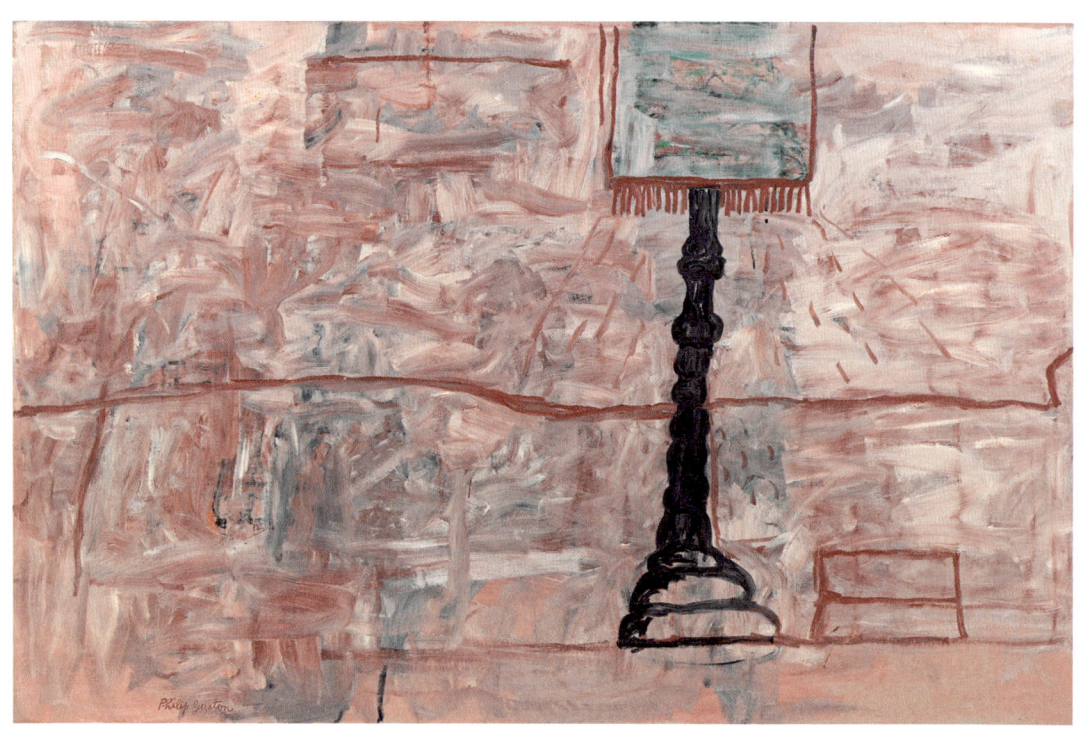

169 — *Lamp*, 1974. Oil on canvas, 171.4×265.4 cm. Pinault Collection

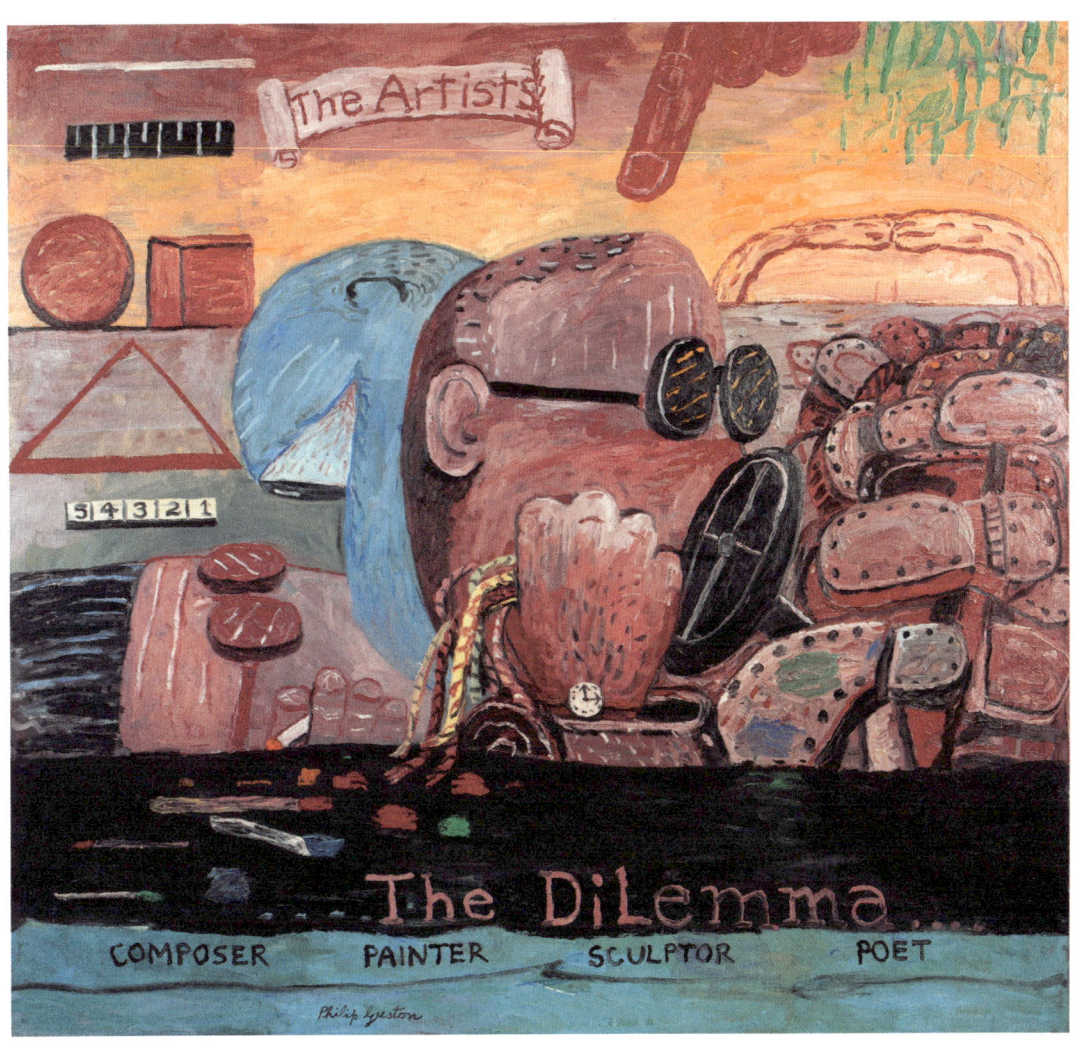

170 — *Allegory*, 1975. Oil on canvas, 172.7×186.1 cm. Saint Louis Art Museum

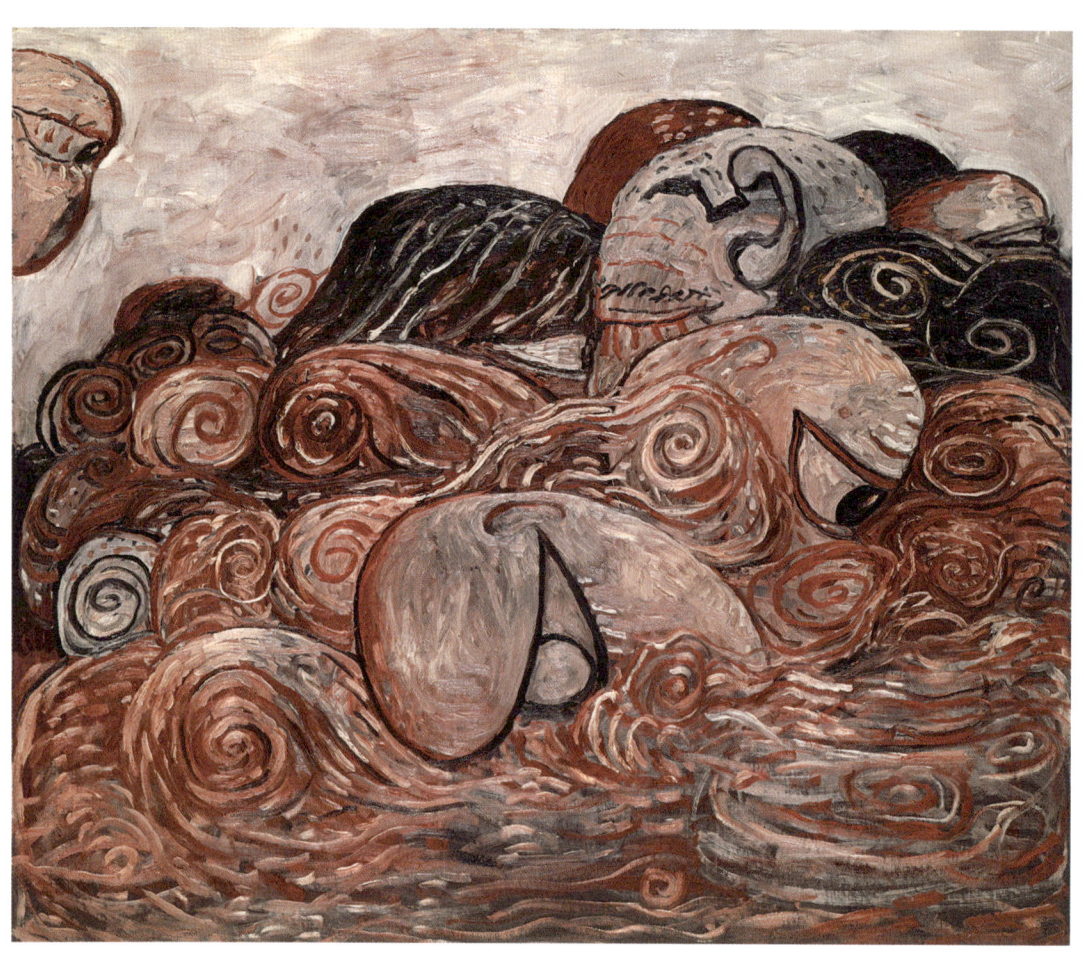

171 — *Deluge III*, 1979. Oil on canvas, 172.7 × 207 cm. Private collection, New York

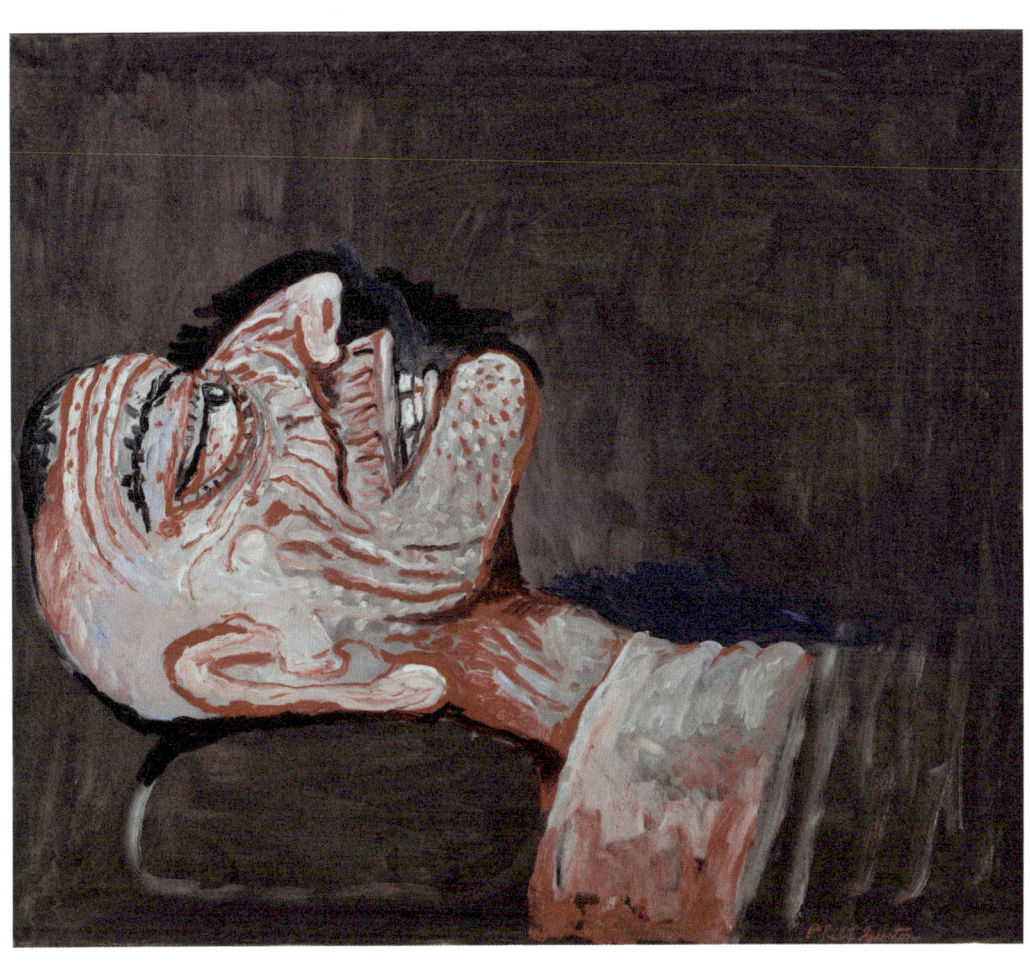

172 — *East Coker-T.S.E.*, 1979. Oil on canvas, 106.7×121.9 cm. MoMA, New York

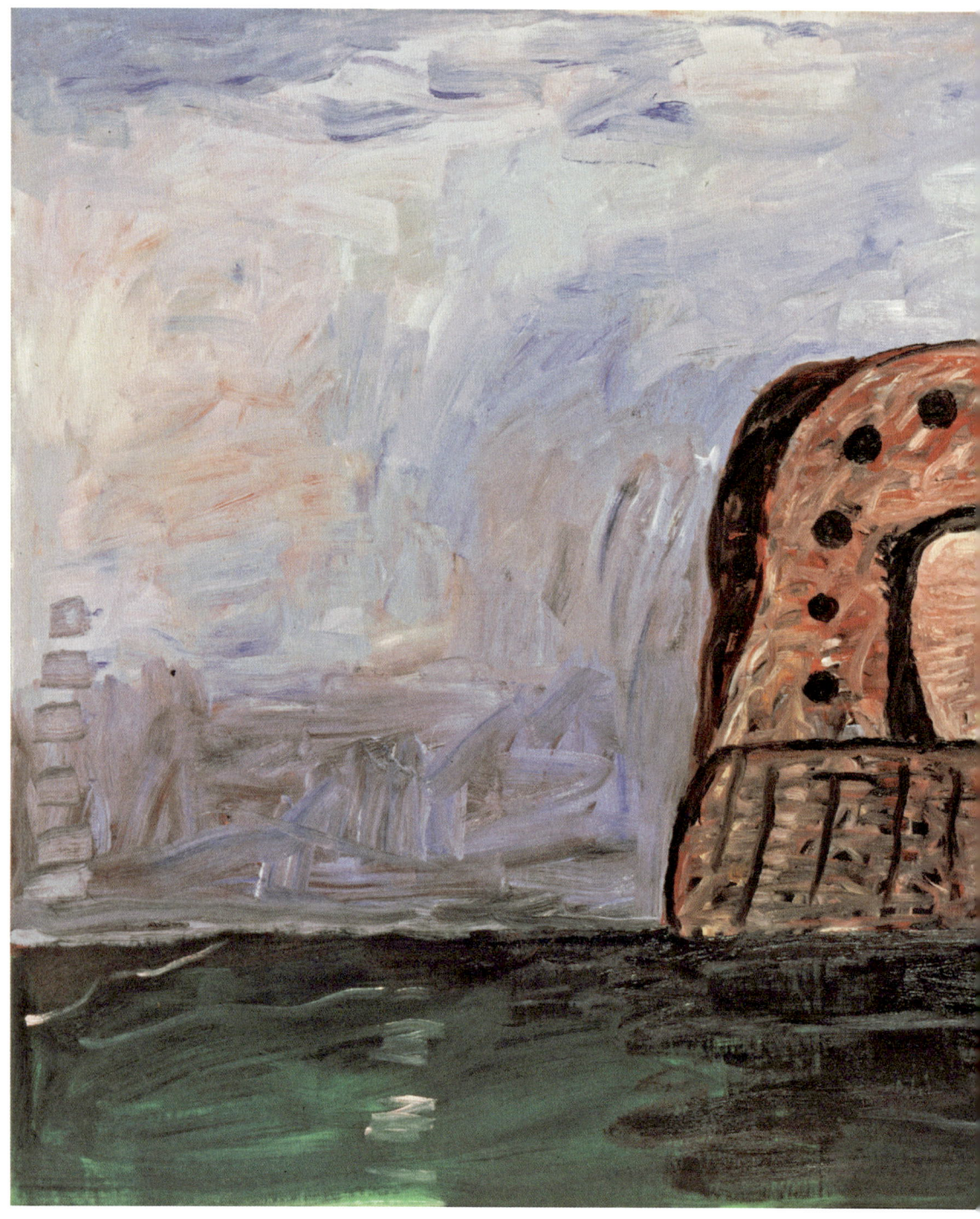

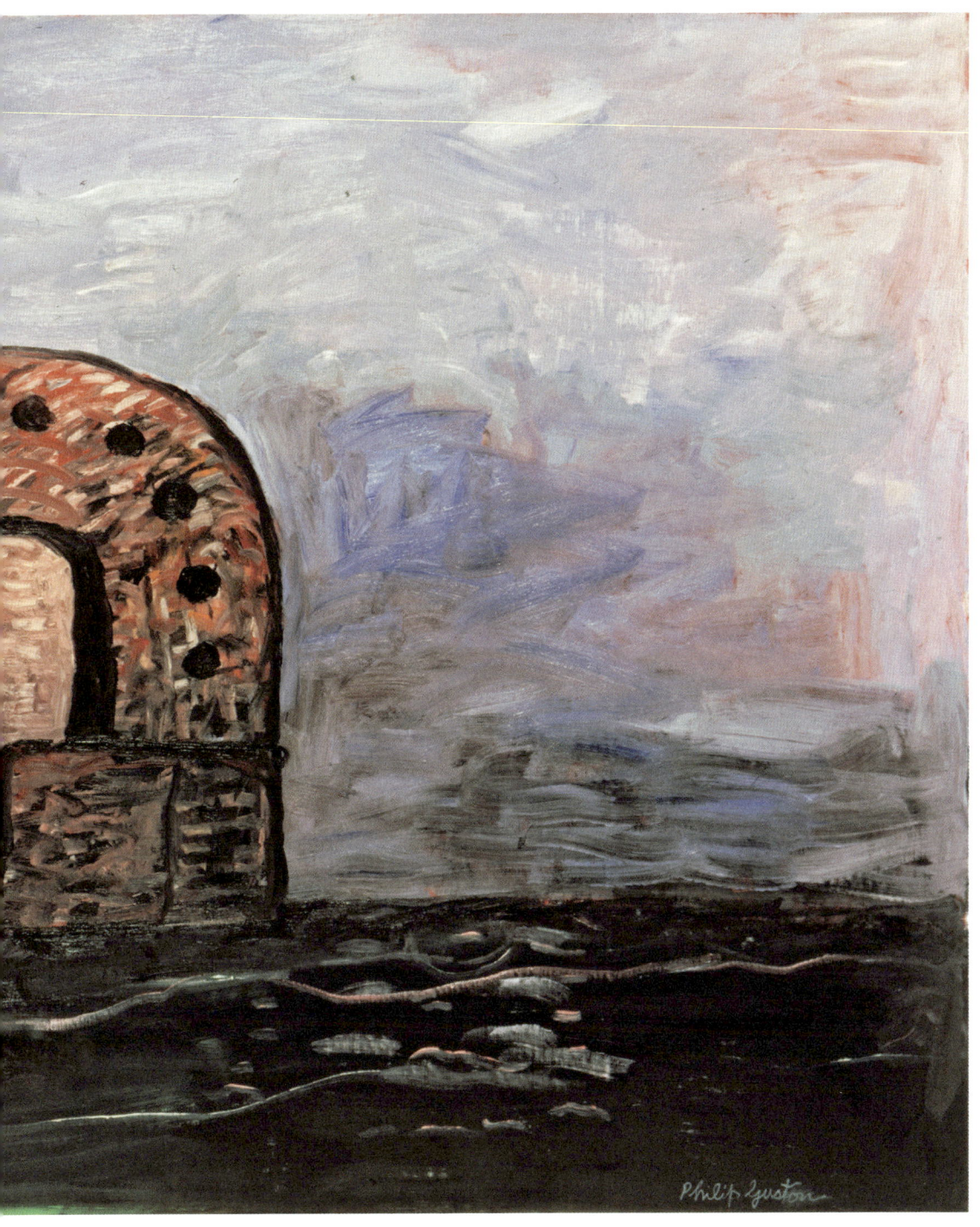

173 — *Black Sea*, 1977. Oil on canvas, 173 × 297.2 cm. Tate, London

Final work

In 1979, Philip Guston suffered a heart attack that forced him to rethink his working method. Gone were the large formats through which he had maintained the link between his painting and the murals of his young days. Sitting at his desk, he began a series of works on paper in which he recapitulated the forms and subjects of his art. At the time when his painting was still abstract, he had dreamed of achieving the freedom and lightness of the Chinese paintings of the Song dynasty (960–1279), made by artists who, after repeating the same gesture over and over again, were able to create a form in which the conscious mind seemed to play no role.

In this series of final works, produced in the year of his death, Guston achieved a state of technical and iconographic grace. The objects he had copied endlessly to enshrine his transition to figurative art emerged from his brush as if they had been painted by the first man, free from any preconceived model, liberated from any idea of art. D. O.

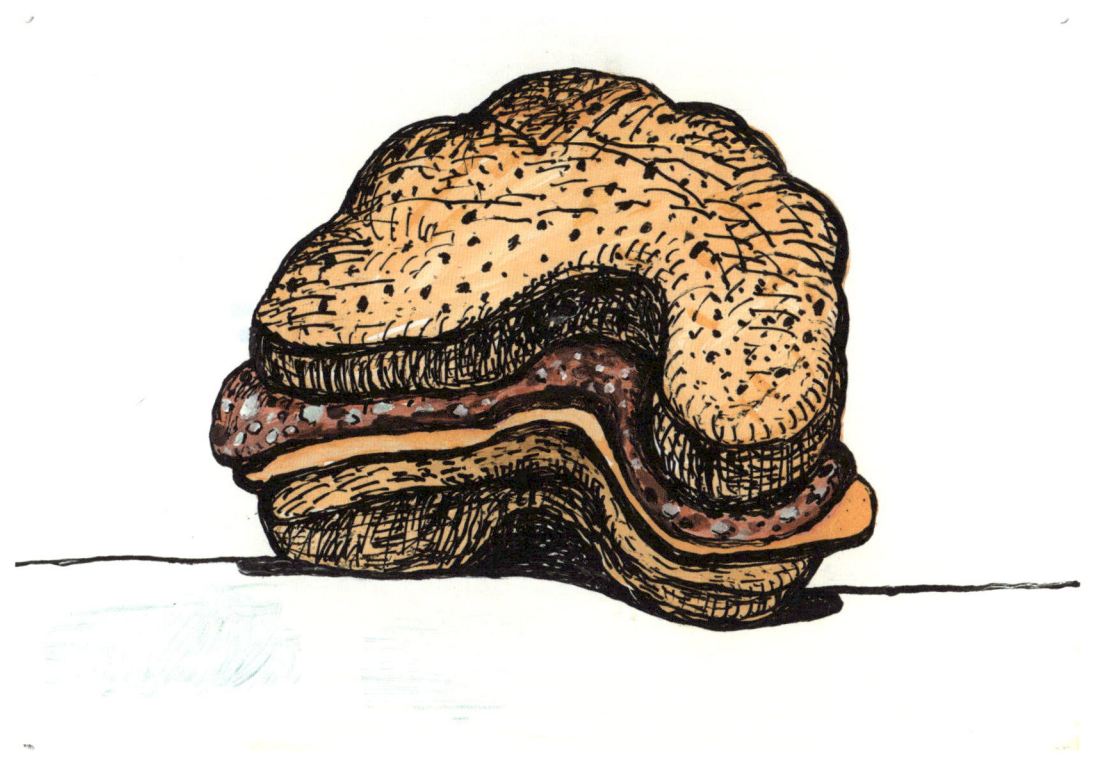

174 — *Untitled,* 1980. Acrylic and ink on illustration board, 50.8×76.2 cm

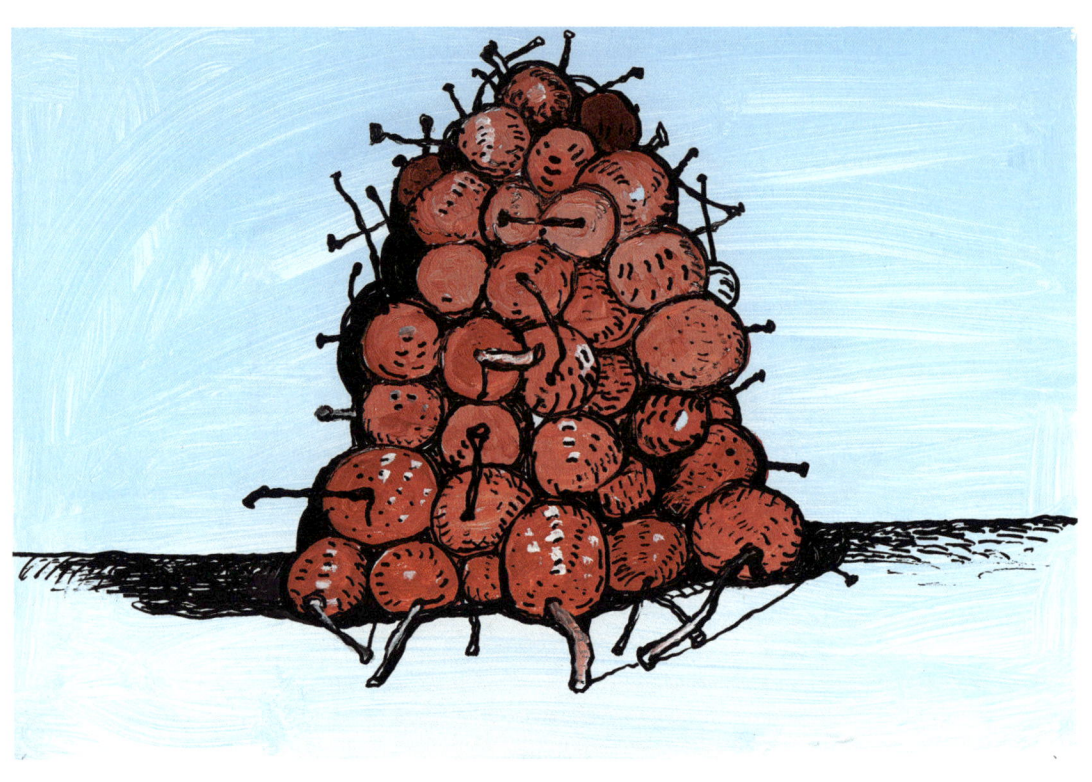

175 — *Untitled*, 1980. Acrylic and ink on illustration board, 50.8×76.2 cm

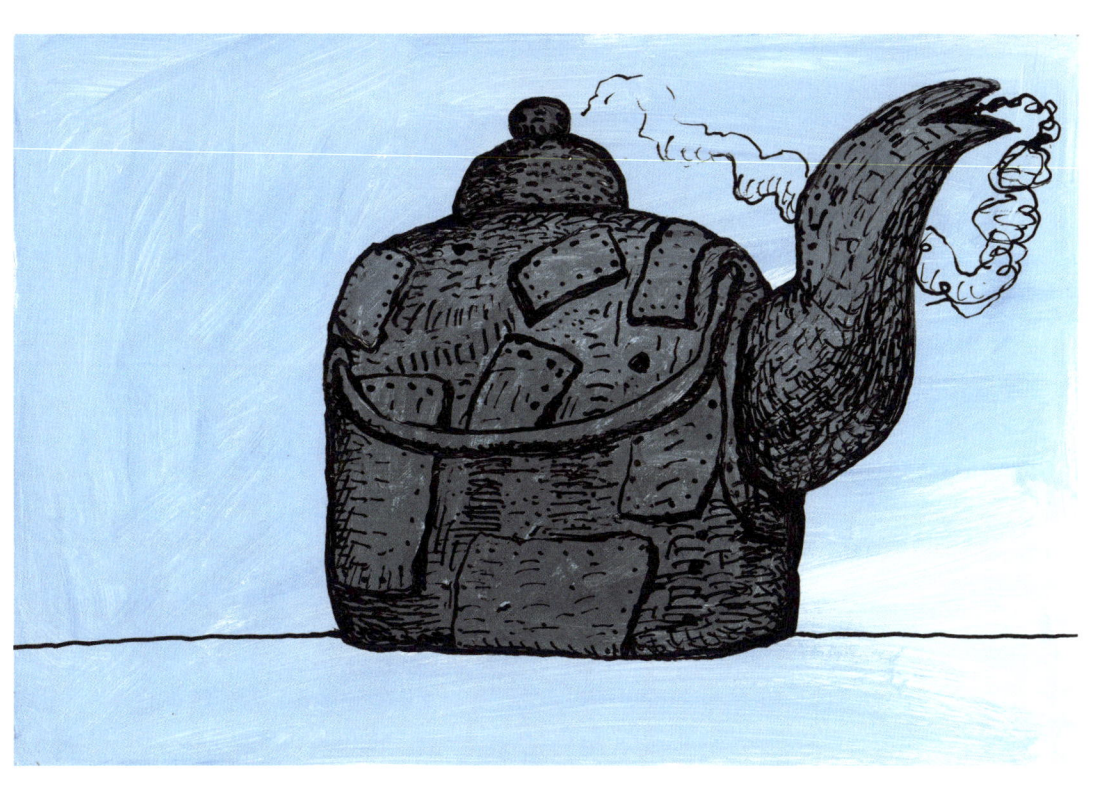

176 — *Untitled*, 1980. Acrylic and ink on illustration board, 50.8×76.2 cm

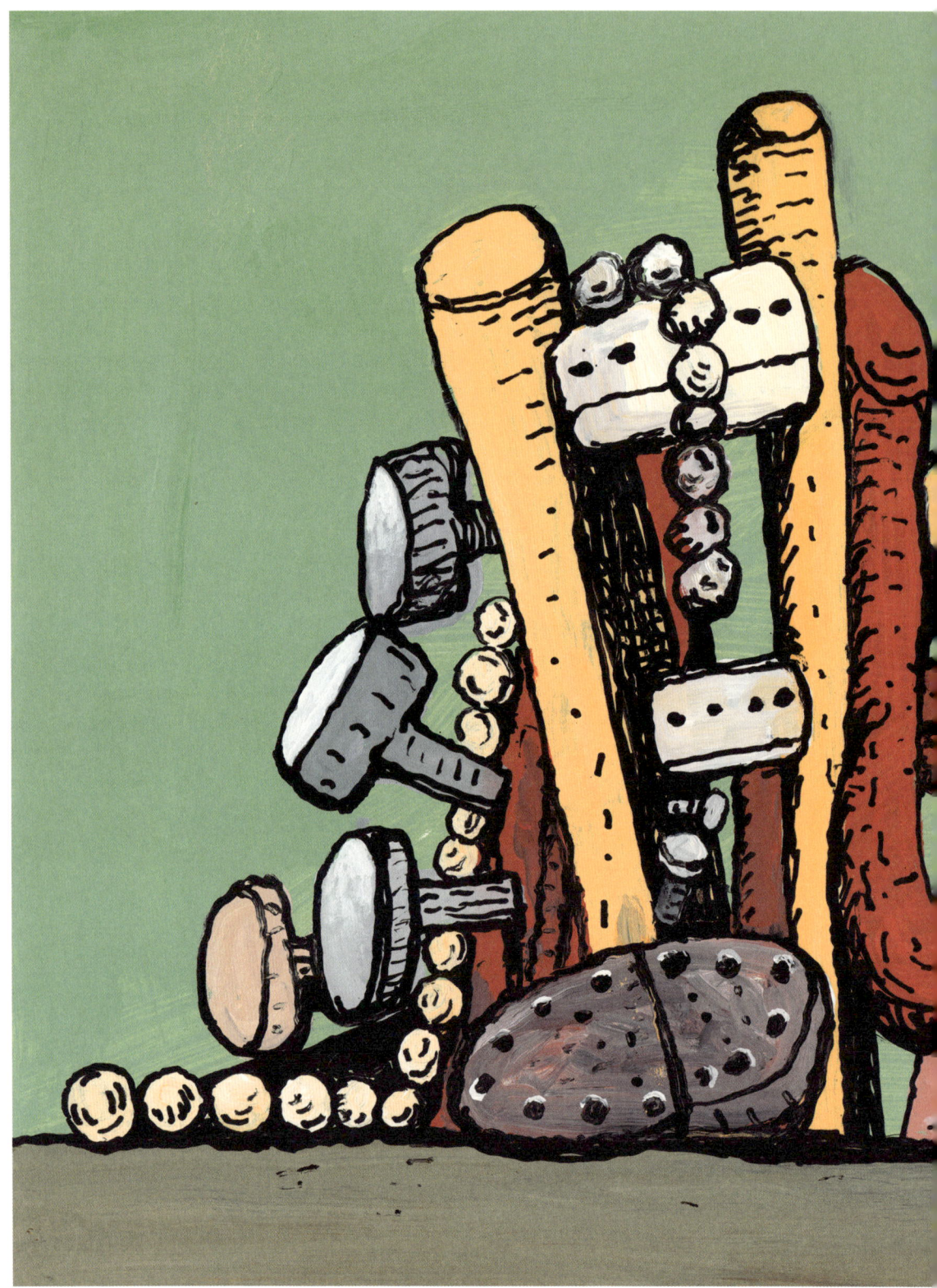

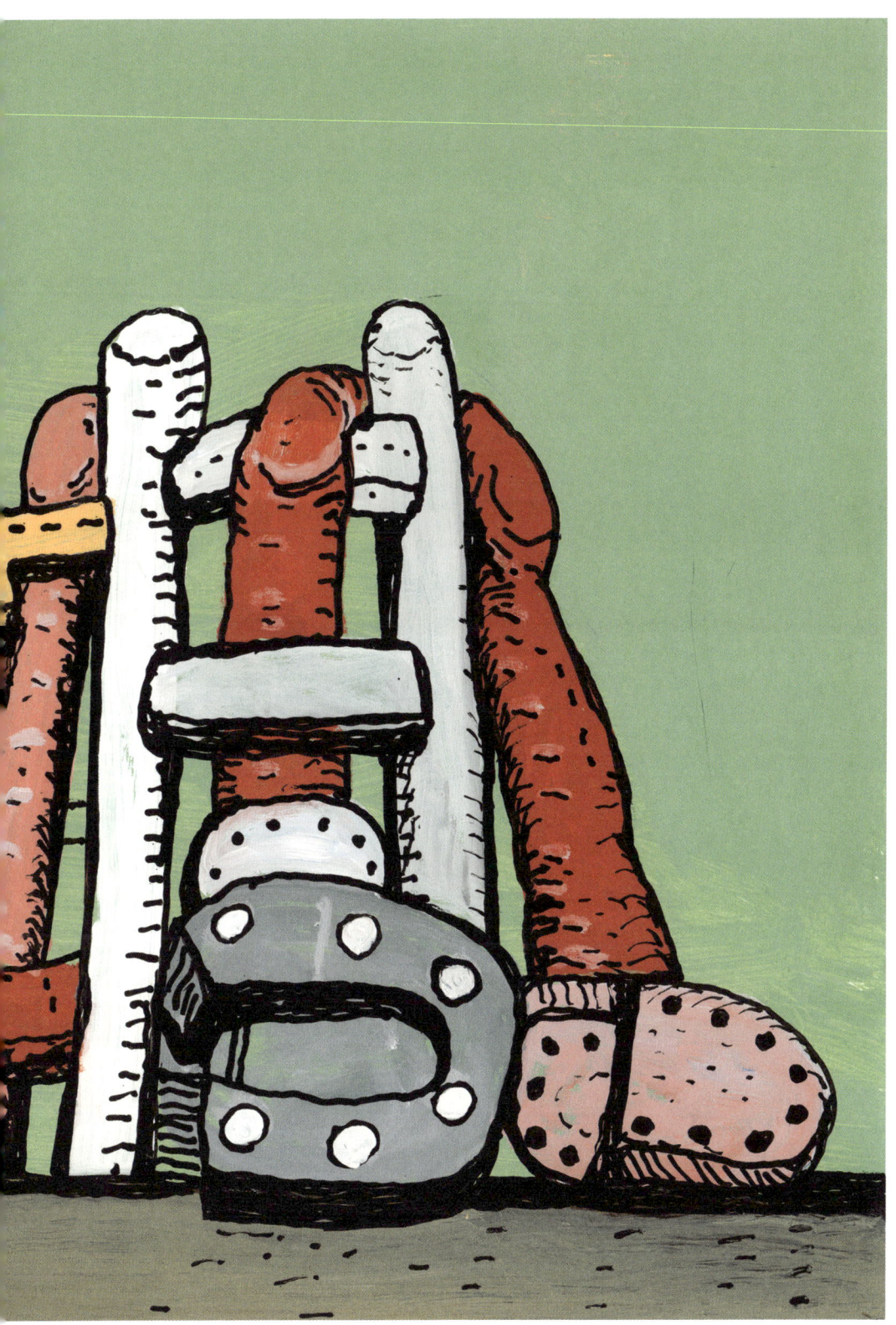

177 — *Untitled*, 1980. Acrylic and ink on illustration board, 50.8×76.2 cm

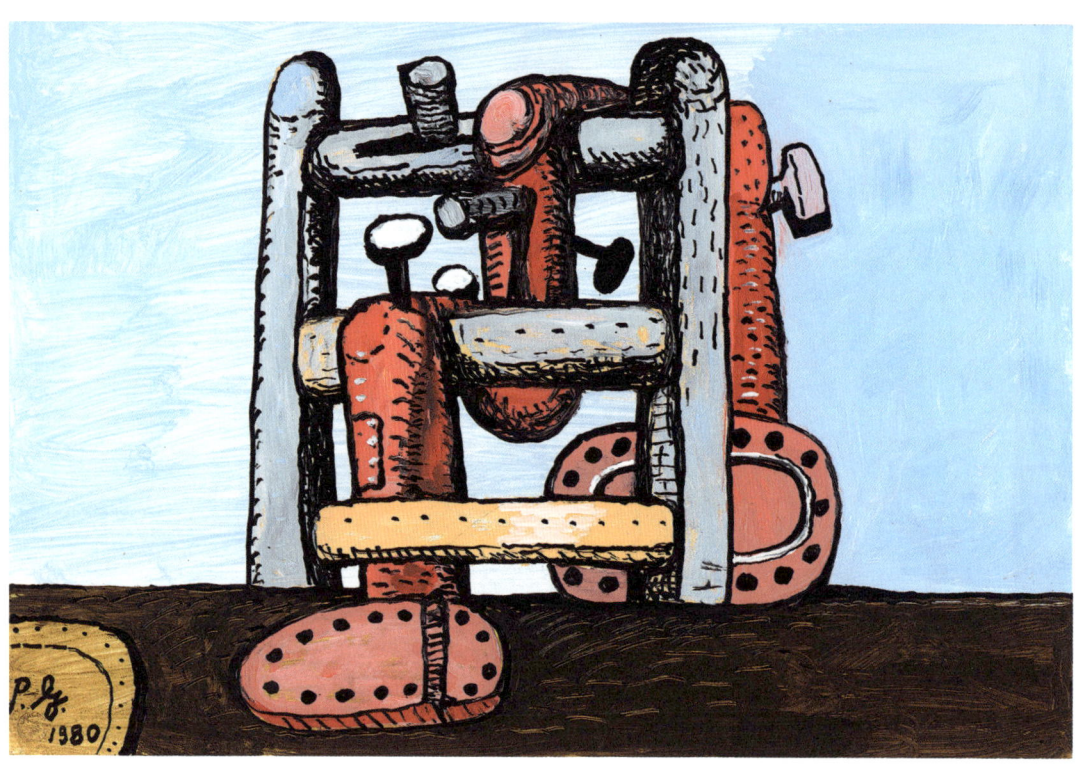

178 — *Untitled*, 1980. Acrylic and ink on illustration board, 50.8 × 76.2 cm

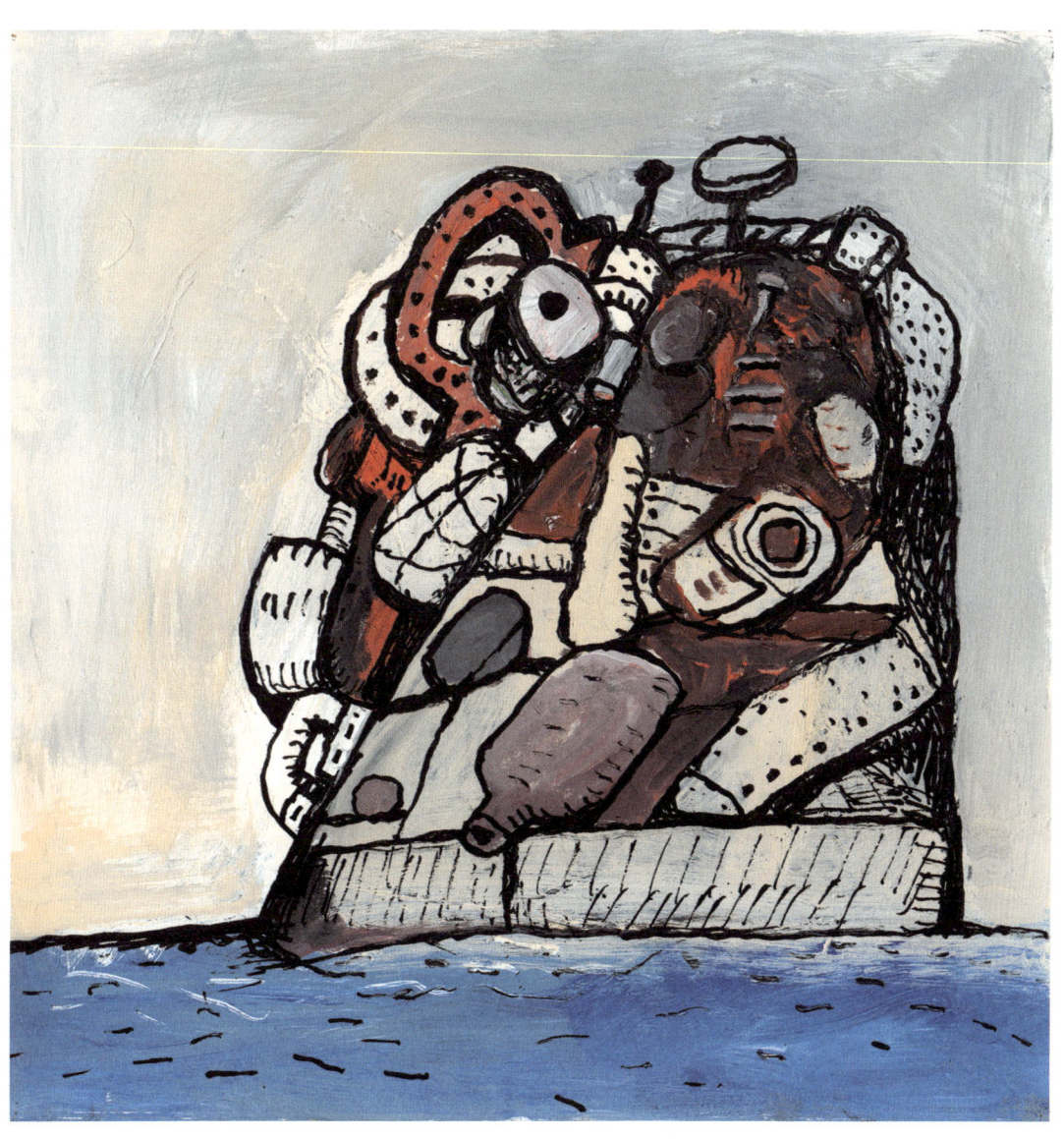

179 — *Untitled*, 1980. Acrylic and ink on paper, 58.4×58.4 cm

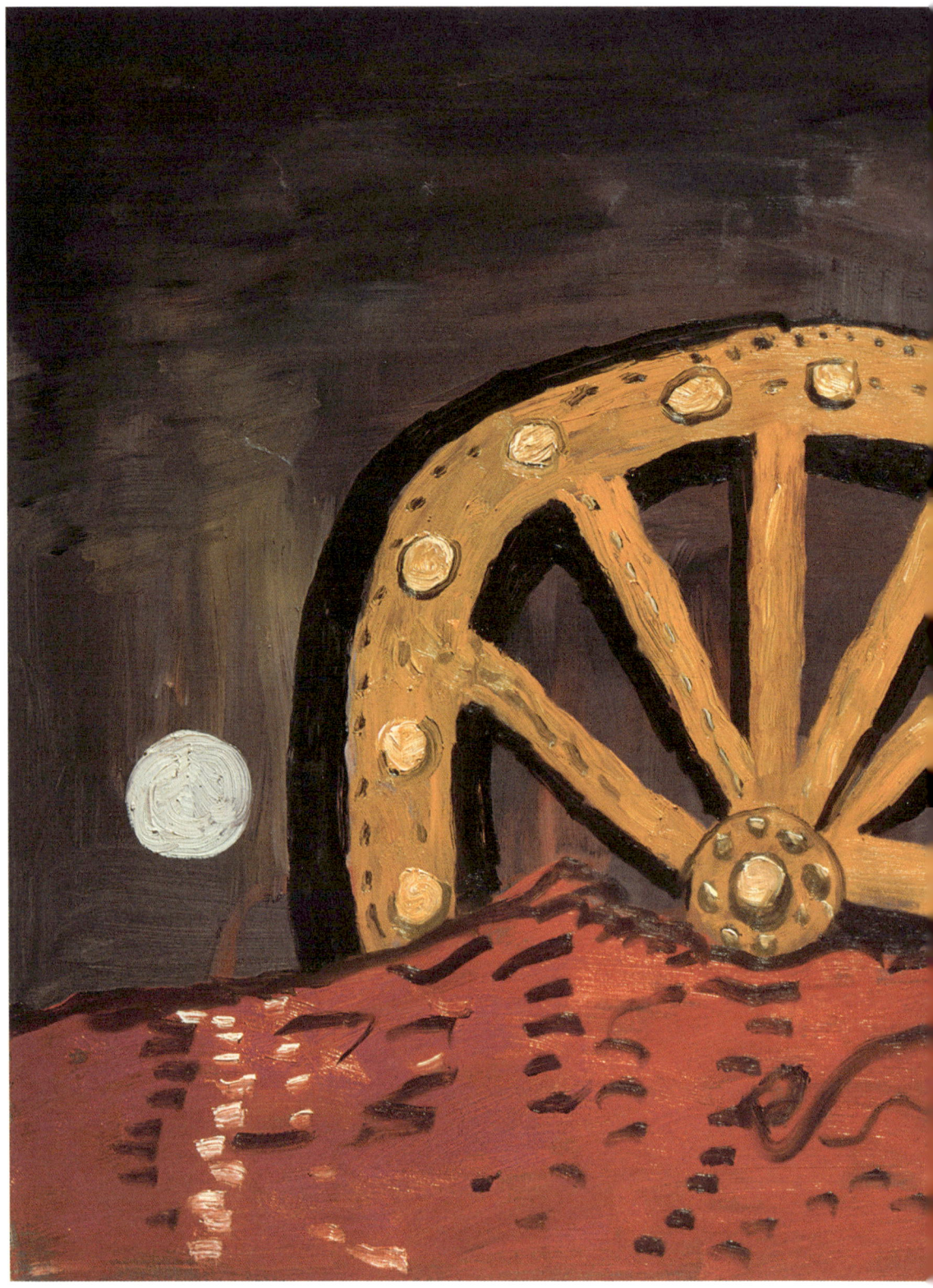

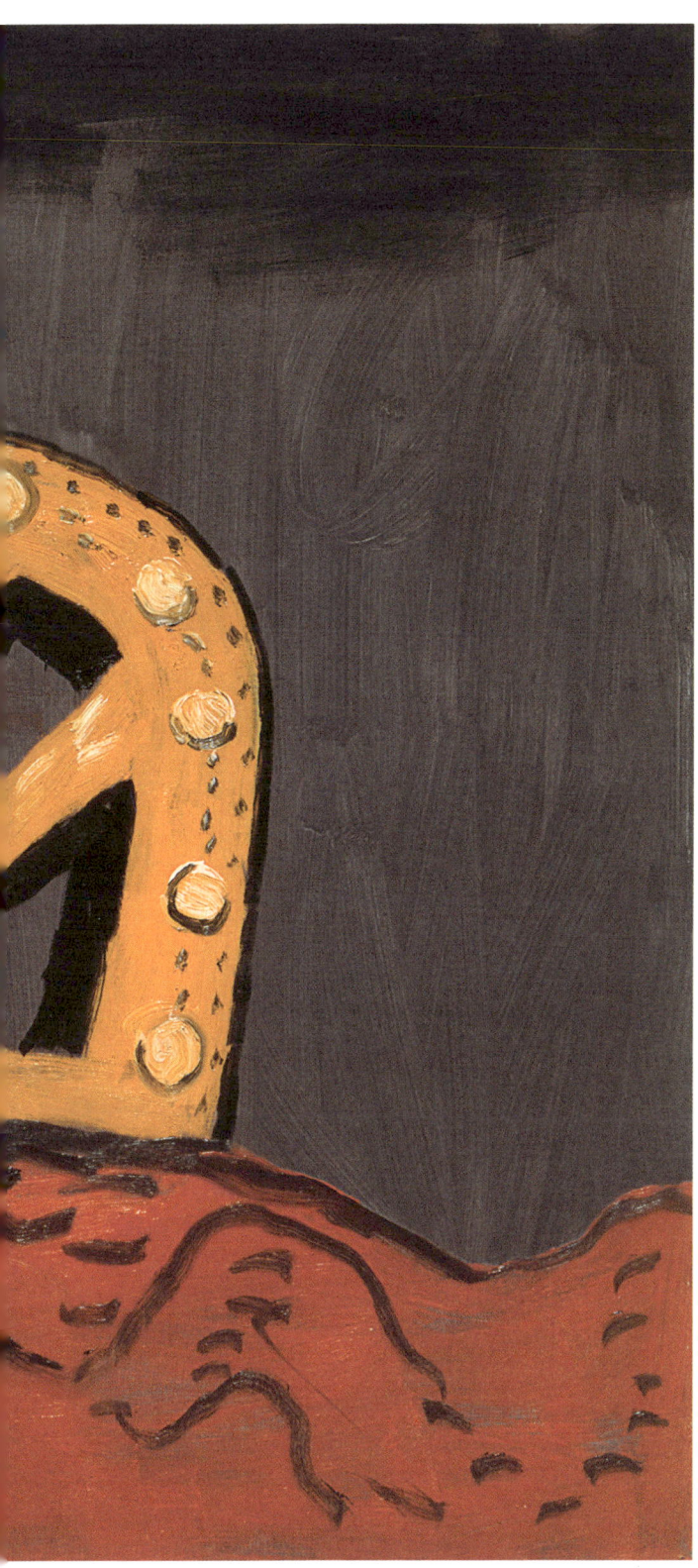

180 — *Wheel*, 1979. Oil on canvas, 121.9×152.4 cm. Private collection

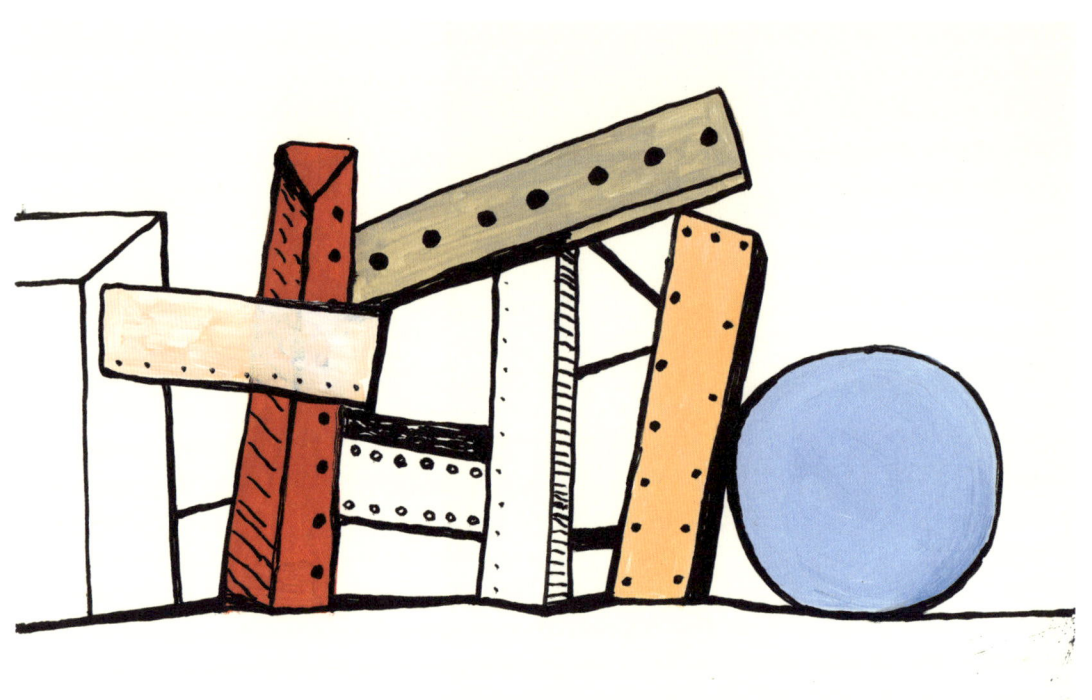

181 — *Untitled*, 1980. Acrylic and ink on illustration board, 50.8×76.2 cm

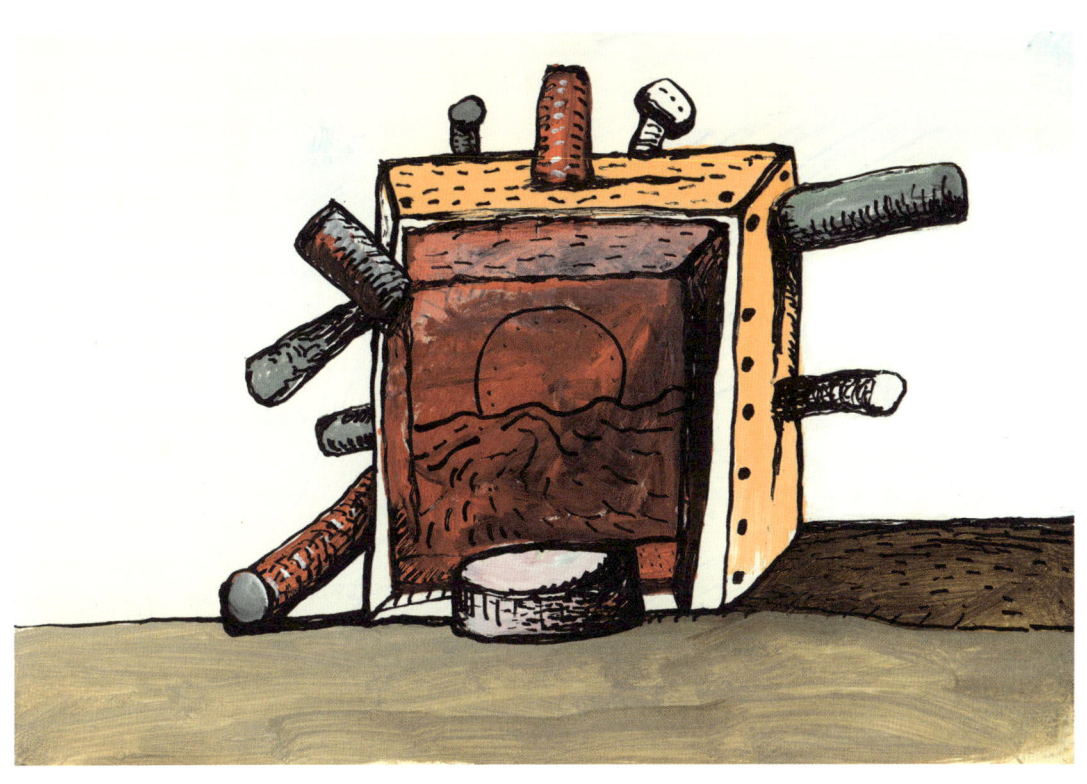

182 — *Untitled*, 1980. Acrylic and ink on illustration board, 50.8×76.2 cm

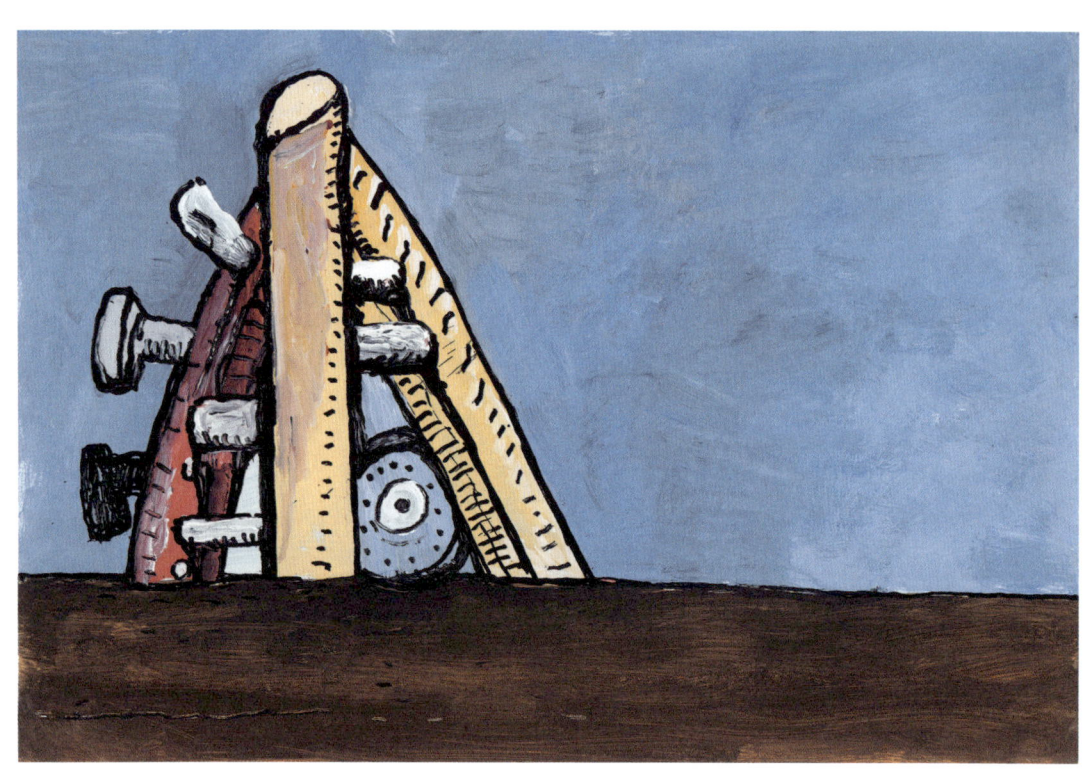

183 — *Untitled*, 1980. Acrylic and ink on illustration board, 50.8 × 76.2 cm

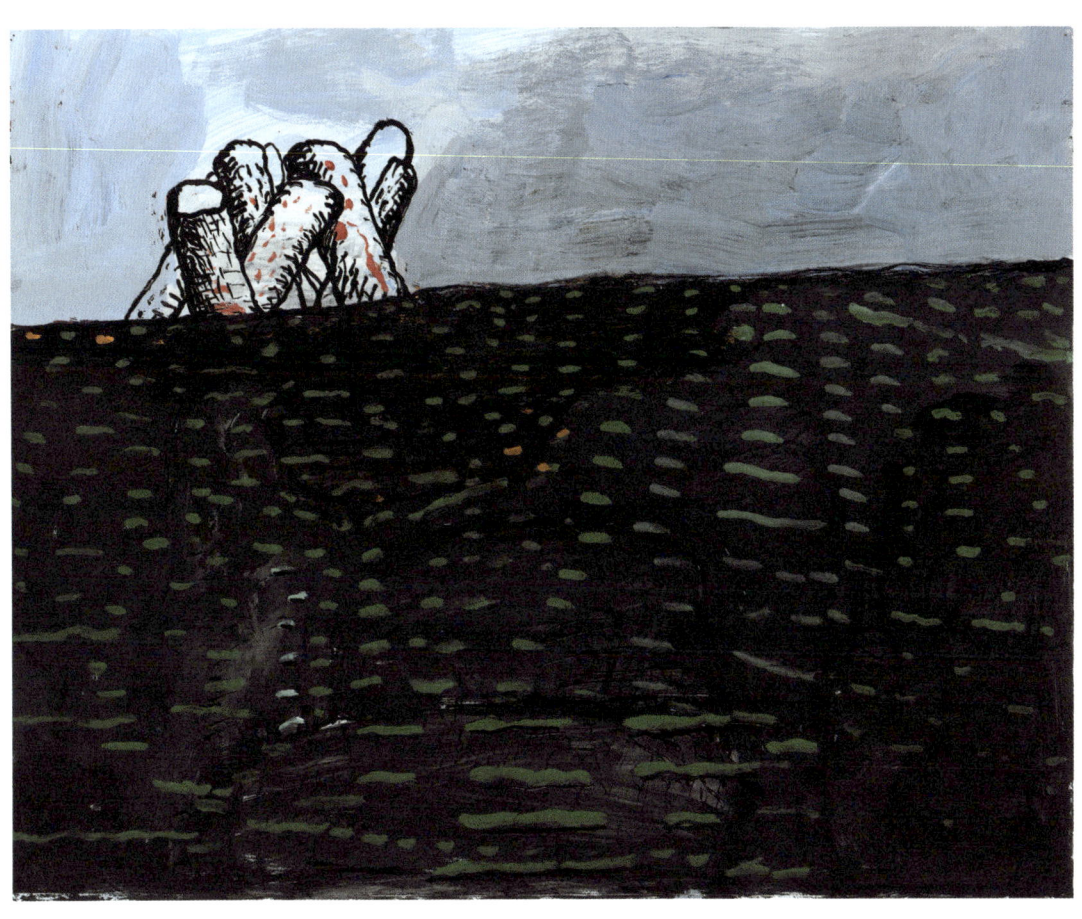

184 — *Untitled*, 1980. Acrylic and ink on illustration board, 58.4×73.7 cm

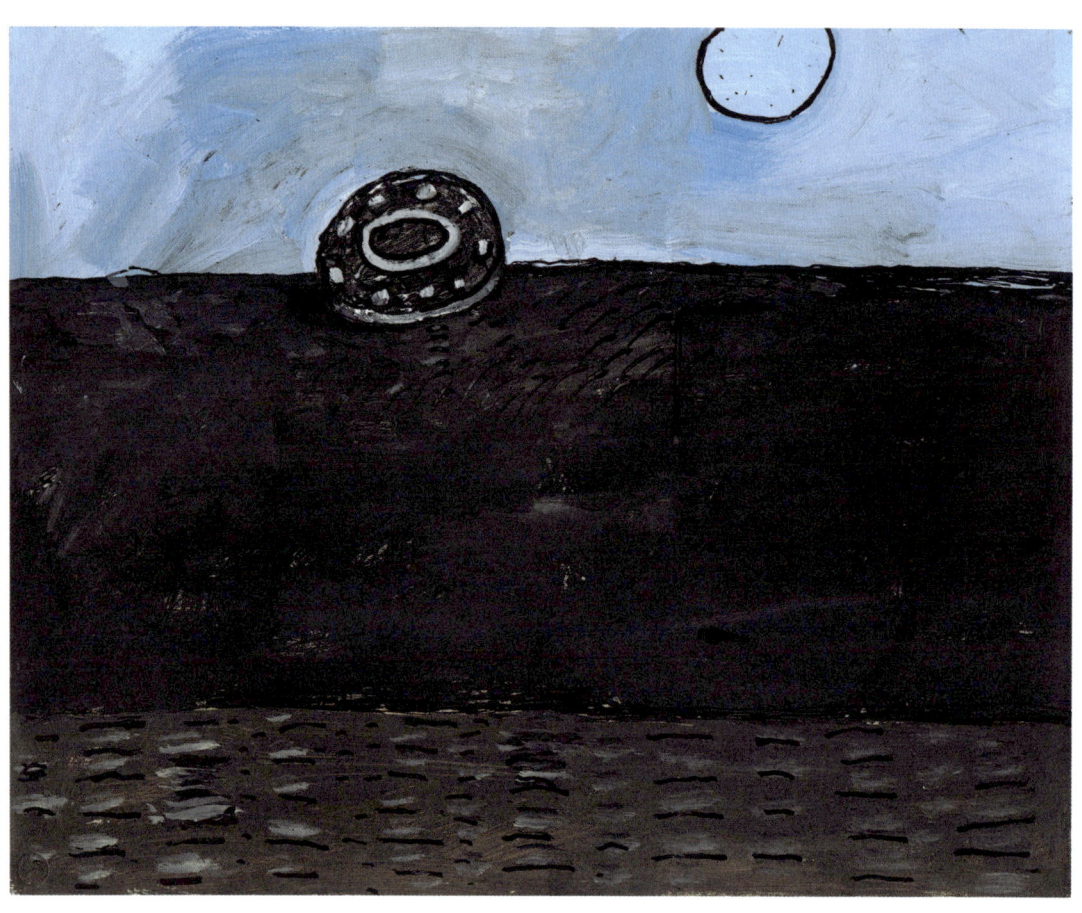

185 — *Untitled*, 1980. Acrylic and ink on paper, 58.4×73.7 cm

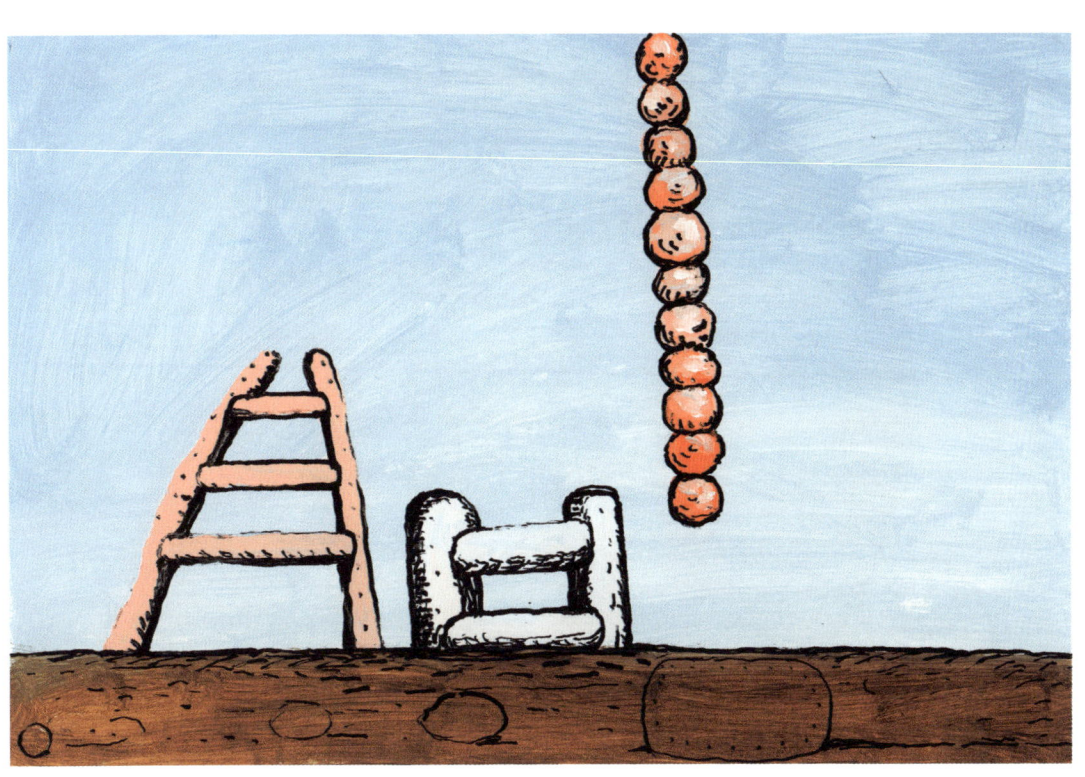

186 — *Untitled*, 1980. Acrylic and ink on illustration board, 50.8×76.2 cm. MoMA, New York

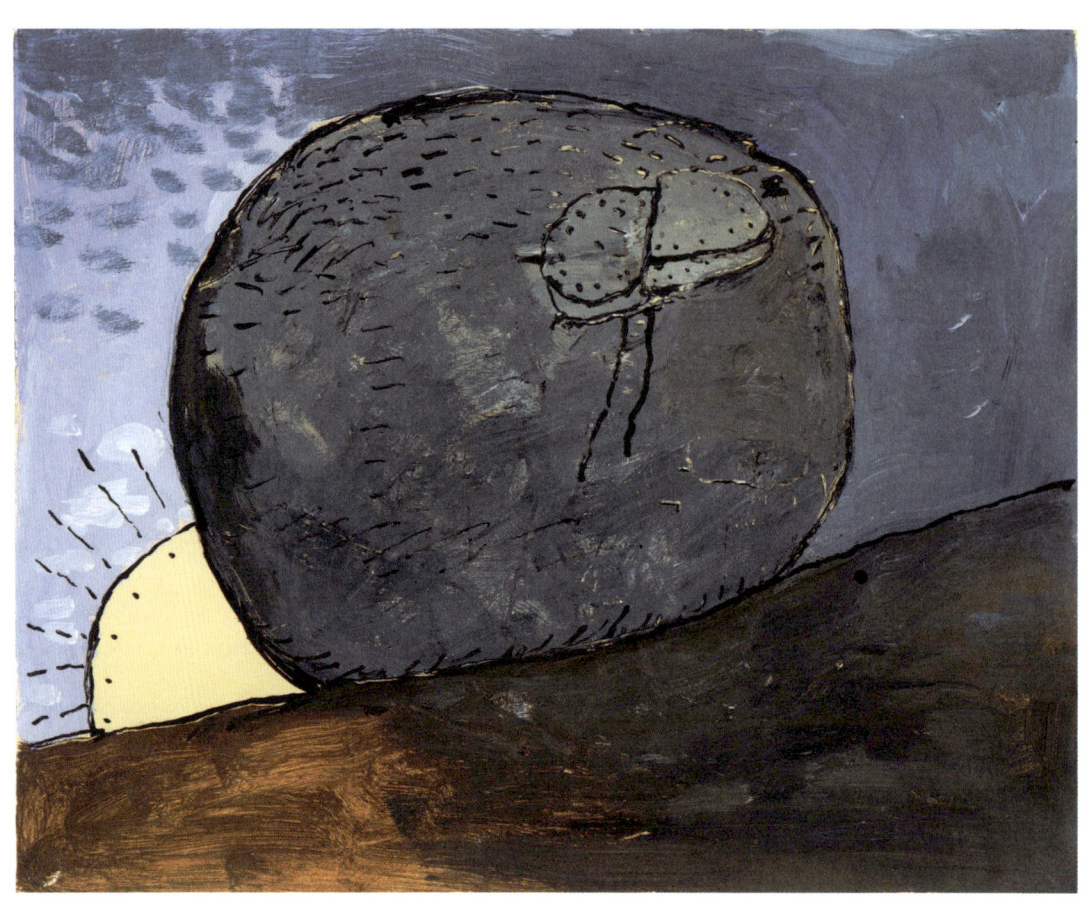

187 − *Untitled*, 1980. Acrylic and ink on paper, 58.3×73.6 cm. MoMA, New York

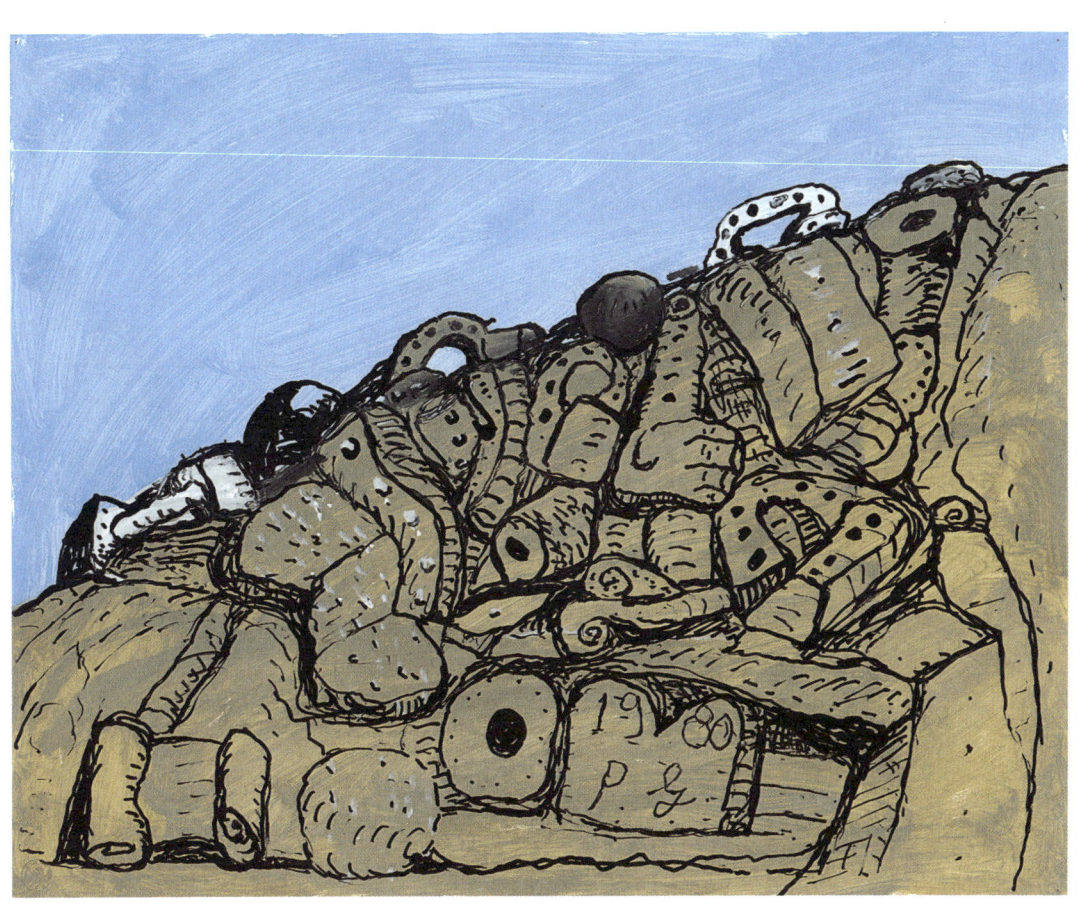

188 — *Untitled*, 1980. Acrylic and ink on paper, 58.4 × 73.6 cm

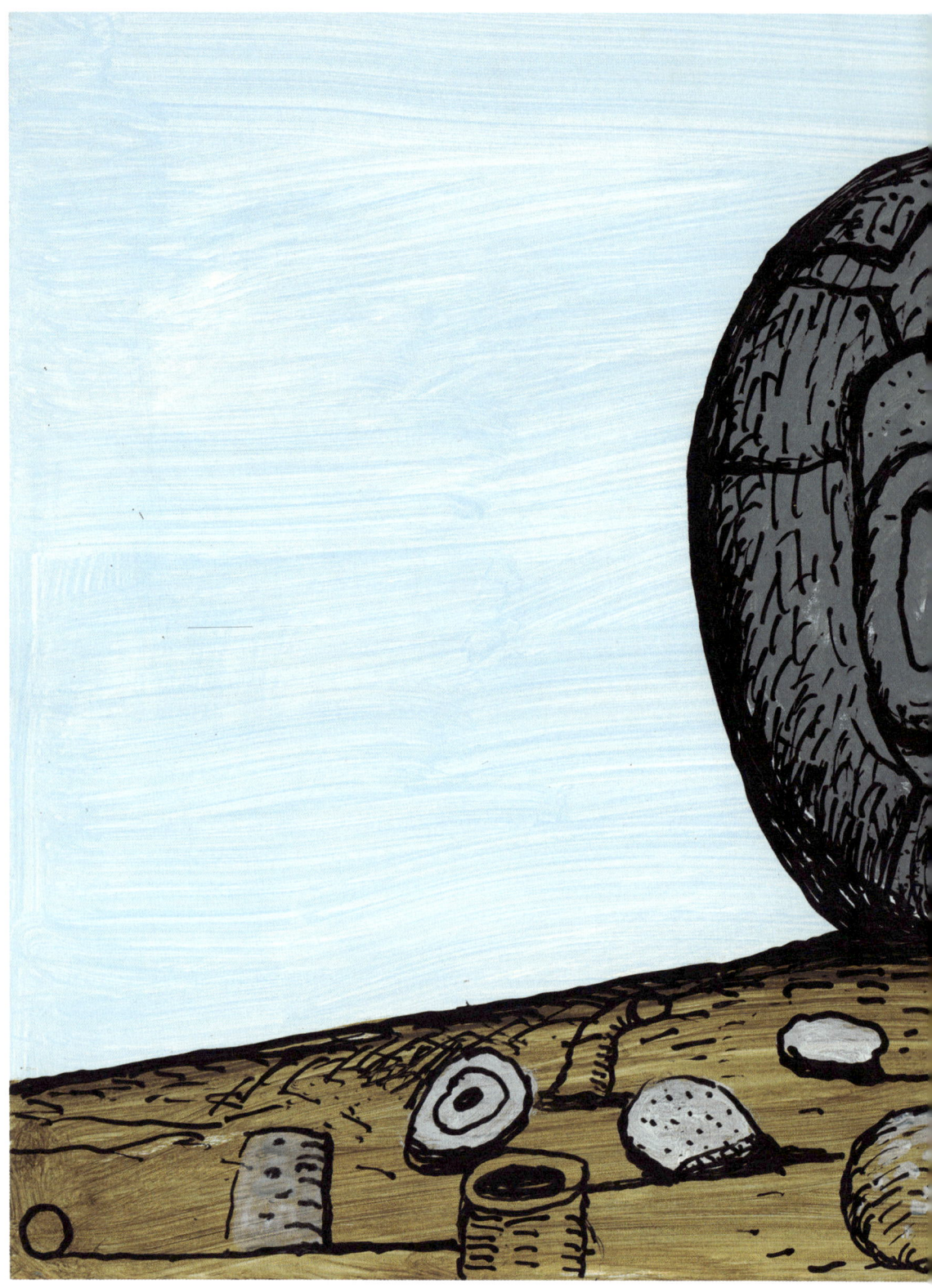

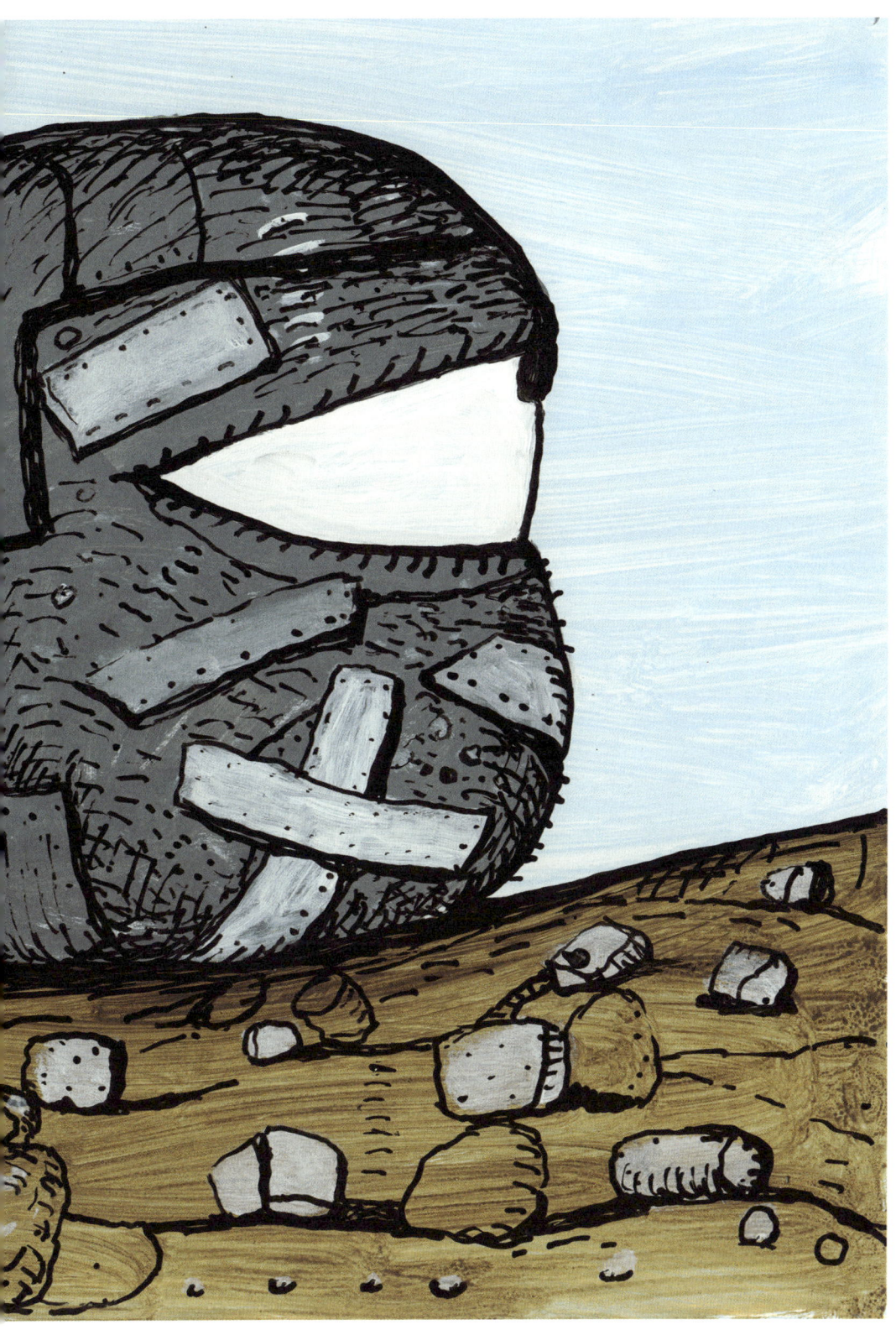

189 — *Untitled*, 1980. Acrylic and ink on illustration board, 50. 8 × 76.2 cm

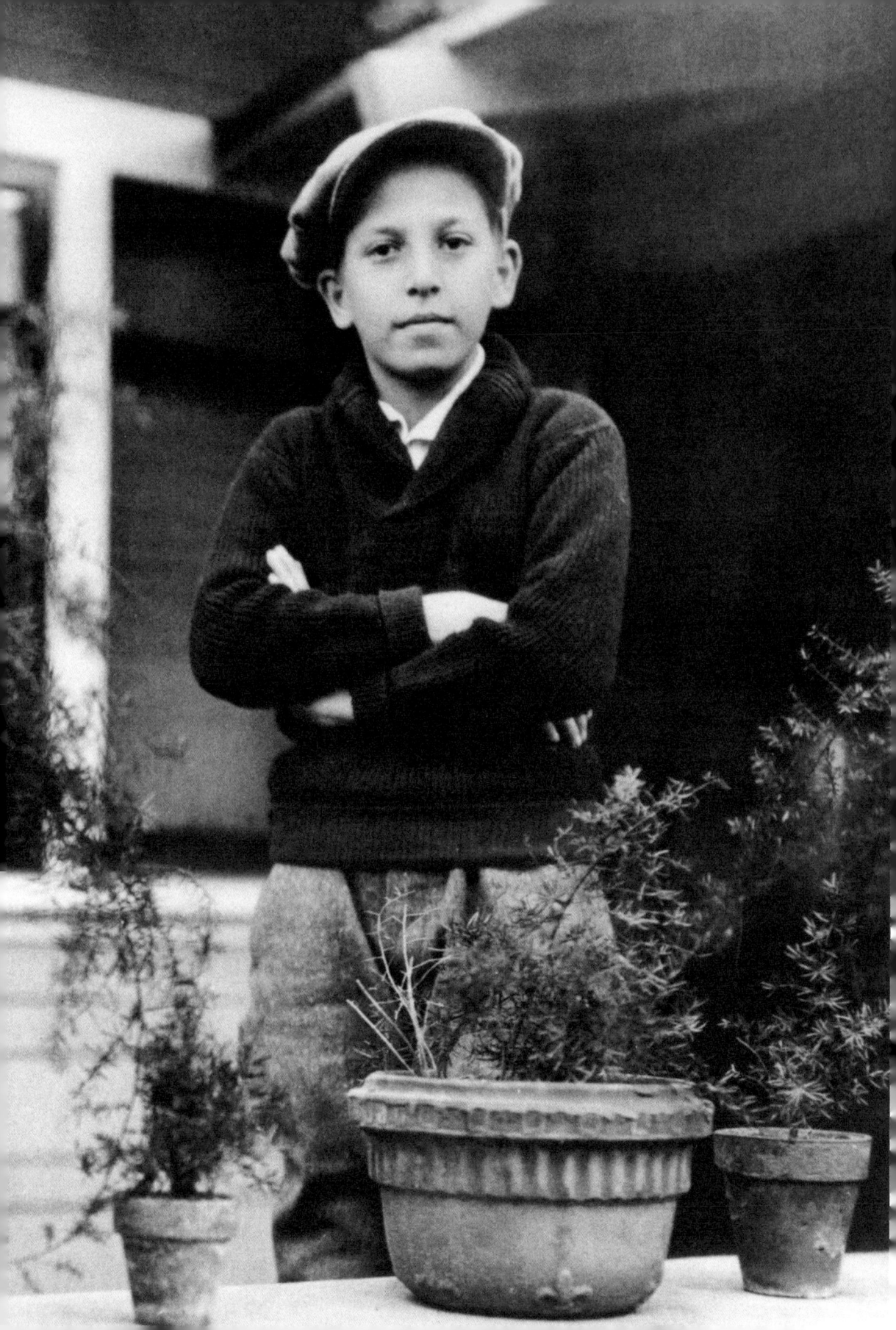

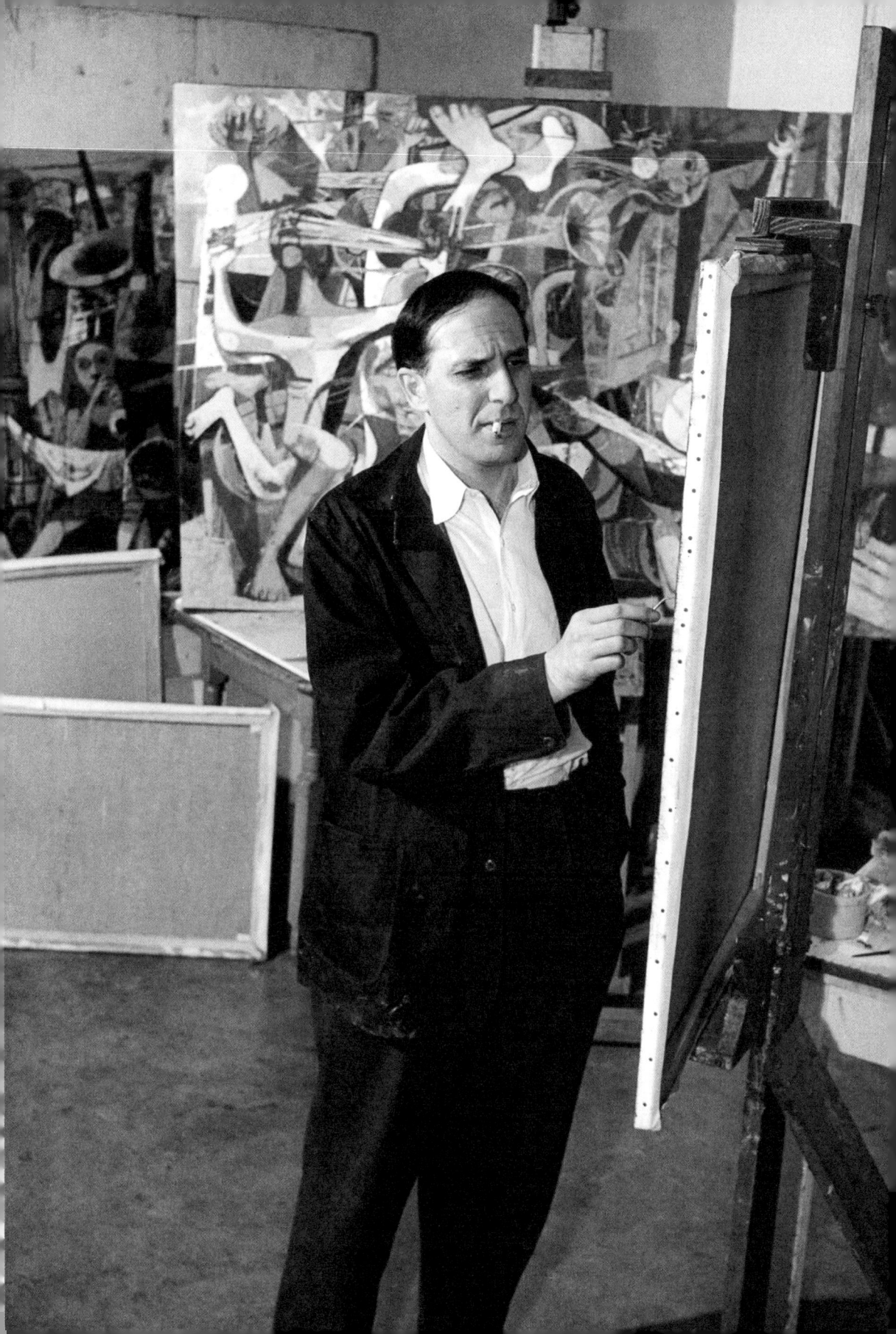

Chronology

DIDIER OTTINGER

pages 194–195
190 — *Philip Guston in Los Angeles*, c. 1923. Courtesy of the Estate of Philip Guston Archives
191 — H. G. Walker, *Philip Guston in his studio in Saint Louis*, for *Life* magazine, 1946
pages 202–203
192 — Walter Auerbach, *Philip Guston in his studio in New York*, c. 1953
193 — Arthur Swoger, *Philip Guston in his studio in New York*, 1957

1913

June 27 – Birth of Phillip Goldstein in Montreal. He is the youngest of seven children born to Leib and Rachel Ehrnlieb Goldstein. His parents, Russian émigrés from Odessa, had been living in Canada since 1905.

1922

The family leaves Canada, moving to Los Angeles.

1923

Suicide of his father, a former railroad engineer in Russia, who could not bear having to work as a junkman in order to survive.

1926

An avid reader of comics, Guston had a particular admiration for *Krazy Kat* by George Herriman and *Mutt and Jeff* by Bud Fisher. For his thirteenth birthday, his mother enrolls him in a cartoon-drawing correspondence course.

1927

He is admitted to the Manual Arts High School in Los Angeles, where Jackson Pollock is a fellow student. Their teacher, Frederick John de St. Vrain Schwankovsky, introduces them to modern art, as well as Hinduist philosophy, of which he was an adept.

1928

With Pollock, Guston is suspended from the Manual Arts High School after drawing and publishing caricatures of the sports staff. He discovers the Mexican muralist movement thanks to the January issue of the magazine *Creative Art*.

1930

He enters the Otis Art Institute in Los Angeles, where he meets the artist and Art student Musa McKim and the painter Reuben Kadish. Disappointed in the program, which he finds traditional, he would leave the Institute three months later: "There I was thinking about Michelangelo and Picasso, and I had to study anatomy and build clay models of torsos."[1]

Kadish introduces him to the painter Lorser Feitelson, who encourages him to take an interest in the work of Uccello, Masaccio, Signorelli and above all Piero della Francesca, and arranges for him to see Walter and Louise Arensberg's modern art collection in 1932. There the artist discovers the paintings of Léger, Picasso, and de Chirico. His drawing *Conspirators* marks the first appearance of a hooded figure in his work. The Mexican painters David Alfaro Siqueiros and José Clemente Orozco are in Los Angeles, where they are painting murals. Guston visits Pomona College, in Claremont (California), in order to meet Orozco, who is painting his mural *Prometheus* there.

1931

Guston has roles as an extra in Hollywood films: "I stormed the Bastille, participated in the fall of Babylon."[2] This experience boosted his interest in cinema. He admired the Soviet films of Alexandr Dovzhenko and Sergei Eisenstein. A short spell working at a large cleaning plant gave him the opportunity to take part in a strike. With the painters Reuben Kadish and Herman Cherry, he attends meetings of the John Reed Club, a Marxist group. All three of them paint murals for the Club. His painting, which represents acts of violence by the Ku Klux Klan, is vandalized (in 1933) by the Red Squad made up of members of the Los Angeles police.

1932

Guston meets with David Alfaro Siqueiros, who has come to paint a mural for the Chouinard Art Institute in Los Angeles.

1934

Thanks to Siqueiros, Guston and Kadish receive a commission to paint a fresco at Maximilian's Palace in Morelia (Mexico). An article is published in *Time* magazine about *The Struggle Against Terrorism* (ill. 29, 36). Siqueiros says: "It is my honest belief that Goldstein and Kadish are the most promising young painters in either the U.S. or Mexico."[3]

1935

Guston joins the Works progress Administration Federal Art Project. With Kadish, he receives a commission for the Los Angeles sanatorium (California) (ill. 31). Phillip Goldstein adopts the name of "Guston."

Winter 1935–36

Based in New York since 1930, Pollock encourages Guston to join him.

1936

Guston moves to New York, where for a short while he shares an apartment with Sande McCoy. He works on various mural projects for the WPA (Works Progress Administration). He becomes friends with Stuart Davis and Willem de Kooning.

1937

Marries Musa McKim.
He paints *Bombardment* (ill. 13), inspired by the bombardment of Spanish towns during the civil war.

1938

Commission from the Treasury Department for a mural in Georgia, *Early Mail Service and the Construction of Railroads*.

1939

Guston paints the façade of the WPA building at the World's Fair in New York. The work, *Maintaining America's Skills* (ill. 28), wins first prize in a competition sponsored by the American Society of Mural Painters, awarded after a vote by visitors to the World's Fair. The government, which is becoming more vigilant with regard to the communist threat and is cracking down on so-called "anti-American" activities, interrupts Guston's work on his fresco *Work and Play* (ill. 32, 34) for the Queensbridge Houses in New York, when inspectors from Washington think they identified the symbols of the sickle and hammer in the tail of a dog.

May – *Guernica*, by Picasso, is exhibited at the Valentine Gallery in New York.

The Max Beckmann exhibition at the Buchholz Gallery in New York makes a big impression on him.

1940

Guston moves to Woodstock, two hours by car from New York, in order to concentrate on his painting: "I wanted to work independently on personal imagery."[4]

1941

Martial Memory (ill. 16), which Guston regards as his first mature statement in painting, features the motif of children fighting.

With his wife Musa, he paints murals for three ships belonging to the President Steamship Lines. Together they paint the murals *Pulpwood Logging* and *Wildlife in the White Mountains* for the Forestry Building, in Laconia (New Hampshire).

He becomes interested in Corot and reads Franz Kafka, Heinrich Wölfflin, Henri Focillon (*The Life of Forms in Art*), Élie Faure, and Erwin Panofsky, whose writings enrich his thinking on forms of allegory.

Guston accepts the post of visiting artist and teacher at the University of Iowa, in Iowa City. "In the solitude of the Mid-West for the first time I was able to develop a personal imagery."[5]

1942

He completes his last mural, for the auditorium of the Social Security building in Washington D.C., *Reconstruction and The Well-Being of the Family* (ill. 33).

1943

Birth of his daughter Musa Jane.

He paints a series of gouaches illustrating military instruction for *Fortune* magazine (ill. 18) and produces a number of drawings for the Naval Air Force.

1945

He paints *If This Be Not I* (ill. 17), the title of which, taken from *Contes de ma mère l'Oye* by Charles Perrault, is suggested to him by his wife, Musa. A synthesis of the lessons of Beckmann and Picasso, the work evokes the theatrical atmosphere of Tiepolo and Watteau.

Guston is awarded first prize in the *Painting in the United States* exhibition, organized by the Carnegie Institute in Pittsburgh (Pennsylvania). He says that the prize-winning work, a portrait titled *Sentimental Moment* (1943–44), is too "literal."

His paintings are exhibited for the first time in New York, at the Midtown Gallery. The tension that had been building for a while between Guston and Pollock explodes at the opening, when the latter accuses him of betraying modernism with paintings that he deemed too traditional.

"In the early days, we all went to each other's shows. Barnett Newman and Mark Rothko and Franz Kline and I, de Kooning too. Now *there* was a group of people who worked *totally* differently. There was a separation there. People talk about 'the New York School' as if it really was a school, but there were a great many differences."[6]

1946

Life devotes a major article to him, titled "Philip Guston: Carnegie Winner's Art is Abstract and Symbolic."

Impatient to leave Iowa City, he accepts the post of art teacher at the Washington University, in Saint Louis (Missouri), where he teaches for two years. Guston sees paintings by Max Beckmann again in local collections.

1947

He is awarded a Guggenheim Fellowship and wins the Altman Prize, National Academy of Design.

Images of legs and shoes with nails appear in his last figurative works. He completes *The Porch*, begun in 1945, in which the compressed figures are marked by the images of the concentration camps that America was discovering. He watches films on the Holocaust. "Much of our talk was about the holocaust and how to allegorize it. . . . [but I] was searching for the plastic condition, where the compressed forms and spaces themselves expressed my feeling about the holocaust."[7]

His figurative art is at a dead-end. "Then followed a year of destroying everything. Everything seemed unsuccessful to me, and I couldn't continue figuration."

Winter – During an intense period devoted to drawings, he begins experimenting with abstraction. He visits New York frequently in order to see his friends (de Kooning, Rothko, Pollock).

1948

Purchase Prize from the University of Illinois, in Urbana. Prix de Rome from the American Academy in Rome. Grant from the American Academy of Arts and Letters.

Autumn – First trip to Europe, where he studies Italian, Spanish, and French art. In Venice, he discovers Titian and Tintoretto; in France, the works of Cézanne and Manet; in Spain, El Greco and Goya. A renewed desire to paint leads him to cut short his trip. He returns to the United States.

1949

Guston moves to New York, keen to benefit from the creative and critical energy that electrifies the artistic milieu. He rents a studio with Bradley Walker Tomlin.

1950

Spring – He works as artist-in-residence at the University of Minnesota in Minneapolis. He participates in evenings at the Cedar Tavern in Greenwich Village, as well as those of the Club in Eighth Street where painters and intellectuals debate artistic issues and their social and political roots. Guston forms a friendship with Robert Motherwell, the composers Morton Feldman and John Cage (whom he met in Rome in 1948), who share his interest in Zen philosophy and existentialism. He reads Beckett, Kierkegaard, and Sartre, becomes a friend of Harold Rosenberg and Thomas B. Hess and, later on, the poet Stanley Kunitz.

He does drawings, producing works that are now completely abstract. Compositions such as *Small Quill Drawing* and *Autumn* evoke Eastern calligraphy.

1951

Red Painting is selected for an exhibition at the Museum of Modern Art. Guston is now one of the leaders of Abstract Expressionism. About *White Painting* (ill. 38), he says: "I wanted to see if I could paint a picture—have a run, so to speak—without stepping back and looking at the canvas ... Instead of walking back, pulling out a cigarette and thinking, to not suspend my own endeavors, but to test myself, to see if my sense of structure was inherent. I would stand in front of the surface and simply keep on painting for three or four hours."[8]

1952

New intense period of drawing (until around 1954). His works, including the drawings *Zone* and *Drawing* (ill. 25), reveal "Mondrianesque" qualities. His gridded compositions testify to a rigorous construction.

1955

He joins the Sidney Janis Gallery, in New York, which represents Abstract Expressionists (Pollock, de Kooning, and Mark Rothko). He would exhibit there regularly up until 1961. For the first time since the Great Depression, Guston manages to live off his work (between 1941 and 1956, he only sold eleven paintings).

1956

Several of his abstract paintings featured in the *12 Americans* exhibition at MoMA, which buys *Painting* from him (1954, ill. 40).

1958

Participates in *The New American Painting*, an exhibition organized by MoMA which travels to Europe. His work impresses Georg Baselitz. A new period of drawings begins. *Head – Double View* and *Forms in Change* display a hint of dissatisfaction with abstraction, heralding a return to figuration.

1959

He receives a grant from the Ford Foundation and wins The Art Institute of Chicago's Flora Mayer Witkowsky Prize. A large number of his drawings and paintings from 1949 to 1958 are exhibited at the São Paulo Biennale and Documenta II in Kassel.

Guston reads Dostoevsky, Camus, Baudelaire, Michaux, Cocteau, and Pasternak, and takes a new interest in Expressionist painters, notably Soutine.

1960

Summer – Guston is one of four artists represented in the American Pavilion at the Venice Biennale. Three-month trip to Europe, including a stay in Italy, where he studies the frescoes of Piero della Francesca again.

1961

Takes part in the *Modern American Drawing* exhibition organized by MoMA, which subsequently travels to Europe and Israel.

1962

Retrospective of his work at the Solomon R. Guggenheim Museum in New York. The exhibition then travels to Amsterdam, London, Brussels, and Los Angeles. He leaves the Sidney Janis Gallery, together with all of the gallery's Abstract Expressionists, in protest at the presence of American Pop Art works in the *New Realists* exhibition (first Pop Art exhibition in New York).

1963

A series of gouaches (including *Departure* and *Dark Form II*) testifies to the figurative orientation of his art. He embarks on several large series of drawings, which he works on simultaneously, alternating for two years between "pure drawings" and representations of everyday objects.

1964

He joins the Marlborough Gallery in New York, which exhibits the Abstract Expressionists.

1965

Guston executes a series of drawings in pencil and ink, in which he creates simplified forms with pure lines. At the end of the year, he stops painting altogether and devotes himself entirely to drawing (until 1968). "Sometimes I know what they [the forms] are.... But if I think 'head' while I'm doing it, it becomes a mess.... I want to end with something that will baffle me for some time."[9]

Art News publishes his remarks about Piero della Francesca in "The Impossibility of Painting."

1966

The Jewish Museum in New York organizes the exhibition *Philip Guston: Recent Paintings and Drawings*, which presents traditional paintings, gouaches, and drawings from 1958 to 1965. In the introduction to the catalog, Guston confides to Harold Rosenberg: "To preconceive an image or even to dwell on an image, and then to go ahead and paint it is an impossibility for me ... it's intolerable—and also irrelevant—because it's too abstract. By that I mean that it's simply and only recognizable. The artist had a thought and then proceeded to paint the thought."[10] Critical opinion is divided.

1967

He returns to Woodstock, this time for good. His daughter Musa says: "Woodstock always remained a place where he could work, his sanctuary, his closet."[11] He has a studio built next-door to his house. His new friends are predominantly poets and writers rather than artists.

1968

Figuration predominates in his work. Guston takes up painting again, capturing everyday objects on small panels. "Looking back, it was as if all the conflicts had come together and been compressed in time, with the force distributed equally between the two alternatives. Only when certain doubts cleared in 1968 and I began feeling more positive about the drawings of the tangible world did I begin to paint again. Finally, only total immersion in painting 'things' settled the issue."[12]

He is increasingly disturbed by the Vietnam War and social conflict in America. His iconography revolves obsessively around Ku Klux Klan hoods, clocks (ill. 197), books, hands, brushes, and irons. "Although Guston clearly meant his new paintings to be interpreted in light of contemporary events, he refrained from the literalness of conventionally partisan art.... Described by the critic Lawrence Alloway as Ubuesque they [the Klansmen] are indeed buffoon bullies."[13]

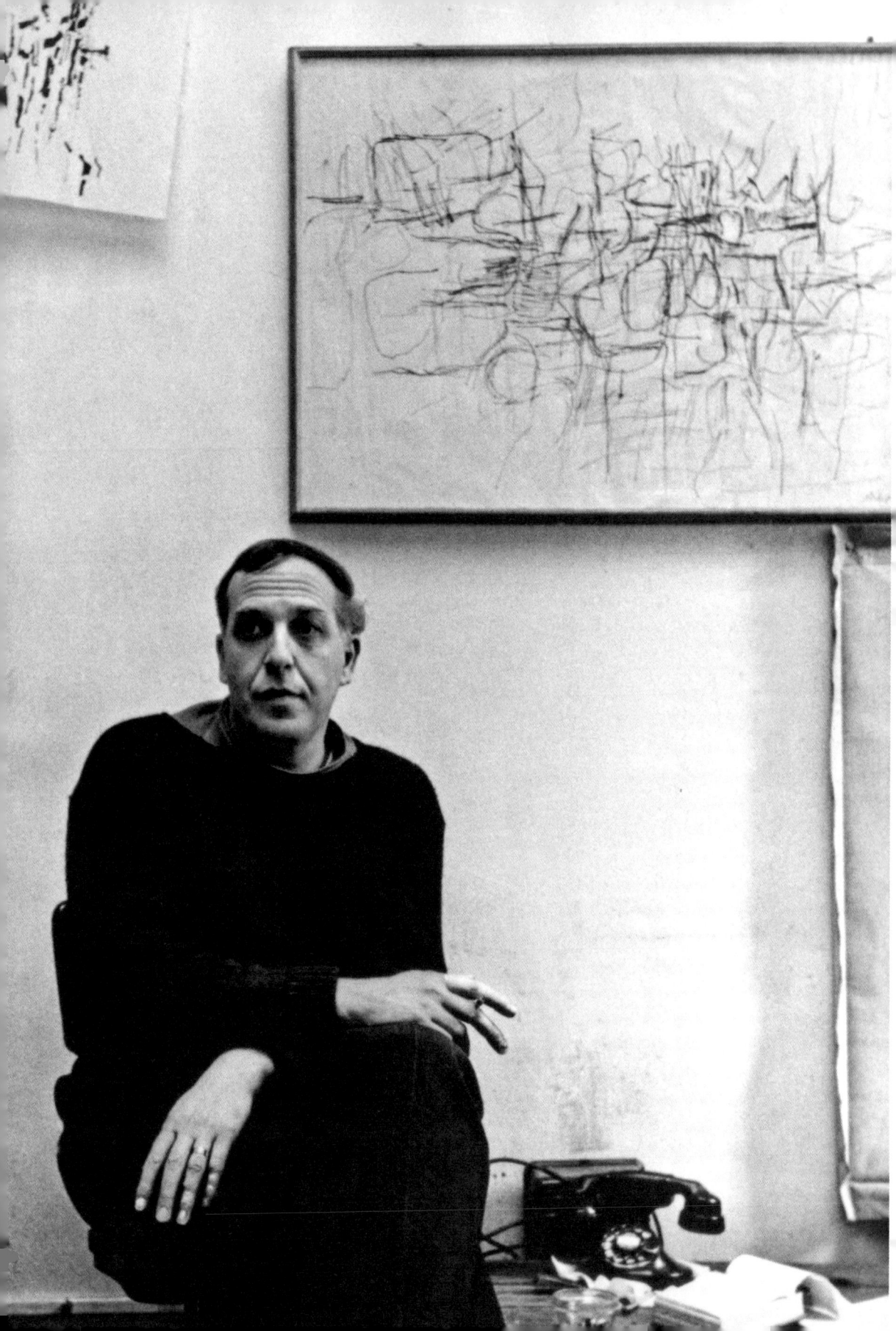

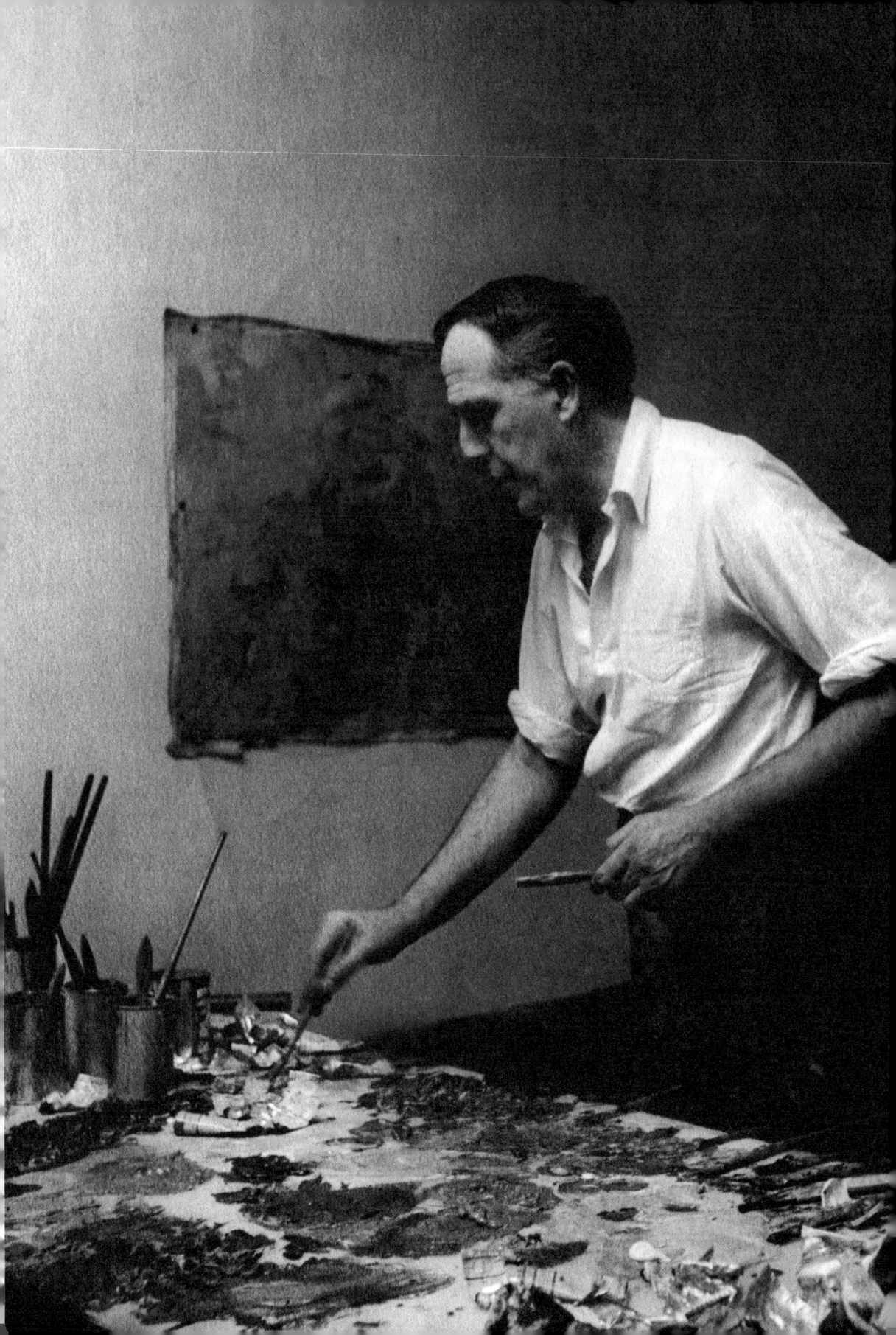

"They are self-portraits. I perceive myself as being behind the hood. In the new series of 'hoods' my attempt was really not to illustrate, to do pictures of the Ku Klux Klan, as I had done earlier. The idea of evil fascinated me, rather like Isaac Babel, who had joined the Cossacks, lived with them and written stories about them. I almost tried to imagine I was living with the Klan What would it be like to be evil? To plan, to plot."[14]

He becomes friends with the poet Clark Coolidge, with whom he shares an interest in Melville, Kafka, and Beckett.

1969

Keen to escape the controversy surrounding his novel *Portnoy's Complaint*, the writer Philip Roth moves to Woodstock. The intellectual fraternity with Guston is immediate. They share the same interest in Russian literature, for what they call "crapola," the kitsch, and popular poor taste. "I got sick and tired of all that purity! I wanted to tell Stories."[15]

1970

Guston is awarded an honorary degree by Boston University.

October – The Marlborough Gallery exhibits primarily figurative paintings from the past two years. Harold Rosenberg writes about the exhibition in the *New Yorker*: "[Guston] has managed to make social comment seem natural to the visual language of postwar painting. Other contemporaries have done political pieces for specific occasions. . . . Guston is the first to have risked a fully developed career on the possibility of engaging art in the political reality. In so doing, he may have given the cue to the art of the nineteen-seventies."[16] The critic of *The New York Times*, Hilton Kramer, is indignant, criticizing Guston for presenting his images as "innocent" and "childlike." The reactions to his exhibition hurt Guston deeply. His friendship with Morton Feldman is shattered. Willem de Kooning is one of the few who understands his evolution toward figuration: "You know, Philip, what your real subject is? It is freedom!"[17] Admitted as a member of the American Academy in Rome, he leaves for Italy, spending nine months in Europe.

1971

Artist-in-residence at the American Academy in Rome, he starts work on the Roma series of more than 100 oils on paper featuring Italian gardens and archeological sites. He travels in Europe (Italy, Sicily, Greece). At the end of the spring, he returns to Woodstock. Philip Roth tells him about the book he is working on, *Our Gang*, in which he lambasts Nixon and his administration, whose misdemeanors are denounced by the American press. Guston produces more than 200 caricatures, 73 of which he groups together under the title *Poor Richard* (ill. 65 to 137).

1972

He is elected a member of the National Institute of Arts and Letters.

Following the lack of commercial success of this exhibition marking a shift towards figuration, he leaves the Marlborough Gallery.

The time has come for Guston to remove the "last mask."[18] The hooded figures give way to the painter's eye and hand. Clocks assume growing importance. Critics still fail to understand Guston, finding his work "crude" and "bizarre." He is depressed and discouraged by so much rejection and incomprehension: "I guess I was shocked the 'official' art world (of *Modern Art!*) could be as bigoted as it was . . . And by now I feel that things really *never* change and that it is pure illusion to ever think that it can . . . I am truly on my own now."[19]

1973

He is appointed art professor at Boston University, where he teaches three days each month, until 1978.

1974

Guston joins the David McKee Gallery in New York founded by David and Renee McKee, formerly associated with the Marlborough Gallery. He begins a series of drawings and paintings, *Smoking in Bed II* and *Head and Bottle*, which depict a bloated figure, with a head without eyes: the painter's alter ego.

After the coup d'état in Chile, he writes: "Our whole lives (since I can remember) are made up of the most extreme cruelties of holocausts. We are the witnesses of the hell. When I think of the victims it is unbearable. To paint, to write, to teach in the most dedicated sincere way is the most intimate affirmation of creative life we possess in these despairing years."[20]

1975

He is awarded the Distinguished Teaching of Art Award by the College Art Association. He explores the theme of the Deluge (until 1976) in such drawings as *Lower Level* and *Current*. He also produces drawings featuring objects from his studio piled up.

1976

His works are exhibited in the *Drawing by Five Abstract Expressionist Painters* exhibition, organized by the Hayden Gallery at the Massachusetts Institute of Technology.

Guston is assailed by imagery that keeps him in his studio day and night. "Time—time! Is it my age or does it really take forty years or more to become an artist?"[21]

1977

His wife Musa has a stroke. Guston is deeply marked by it. The theme of the shield and street fights reappears in *The Street* (ill. 168).

"We are primitives in spite of our knowing. So much preparation for a few moments of innocence—of desperate play. To learn how to unlearn."[22]

1978

The critic Roberta Smith devotes a long essay to Guston in the periodical *Art in America*. She notes the enthusiasm of a new generation for his work. "In some ways, Guston is not only underground, he is a young artist again—perhaps younger than ever before."[23]

At the David McKee Gallery, Guston meets Edward R. Broida, the man who would become his principal collector, whom he would call "my Arensberg."

1979

Suffers a heart attack.

1980

Receives the Creative Arts Award from Brandeis University. Forced to work in small formats, he creates a series of lithographs for the publisher Gemini G.E.L. and produces a series of twenty-six paintings on paper, the culmination of a formal synthesis of familiar motifs.

May – A large retrospective of his works opens at the Museum of Modern Art in San Francisco. "It's a painting show, but it's like a life, you know?"[24]

June 7 – Philip Guston dies of a heart attack in Woodstock.

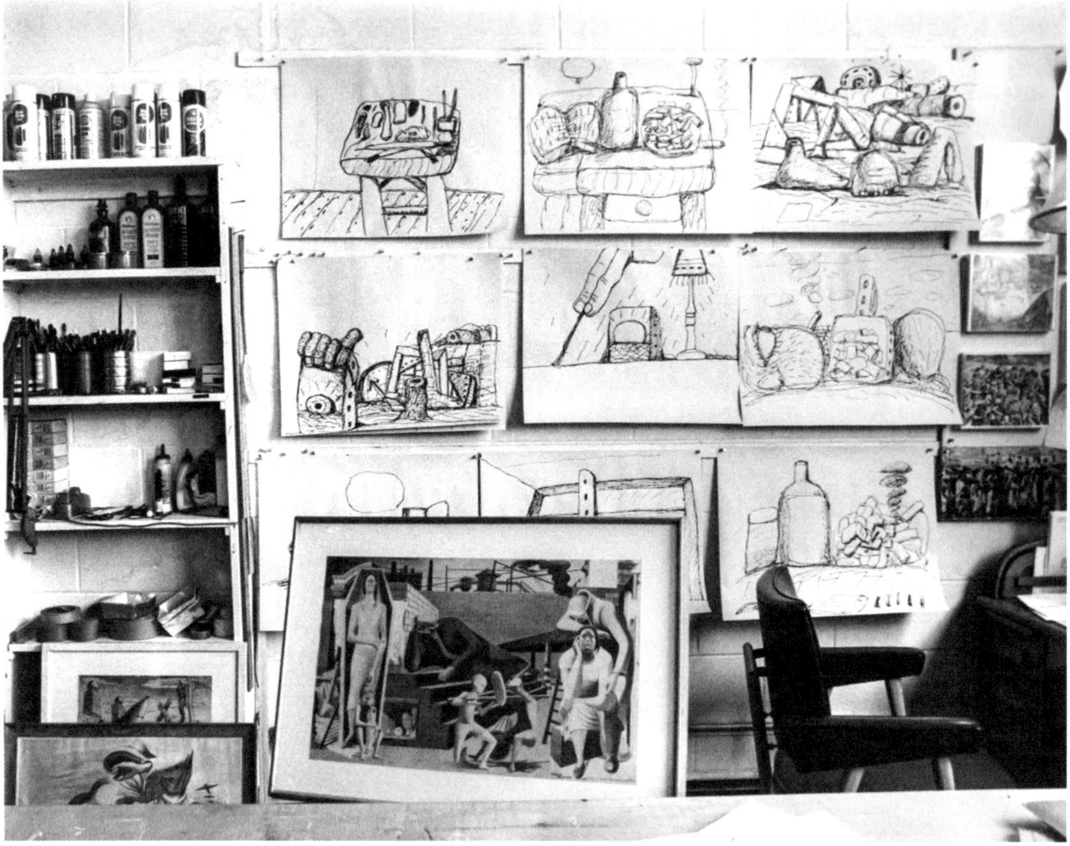

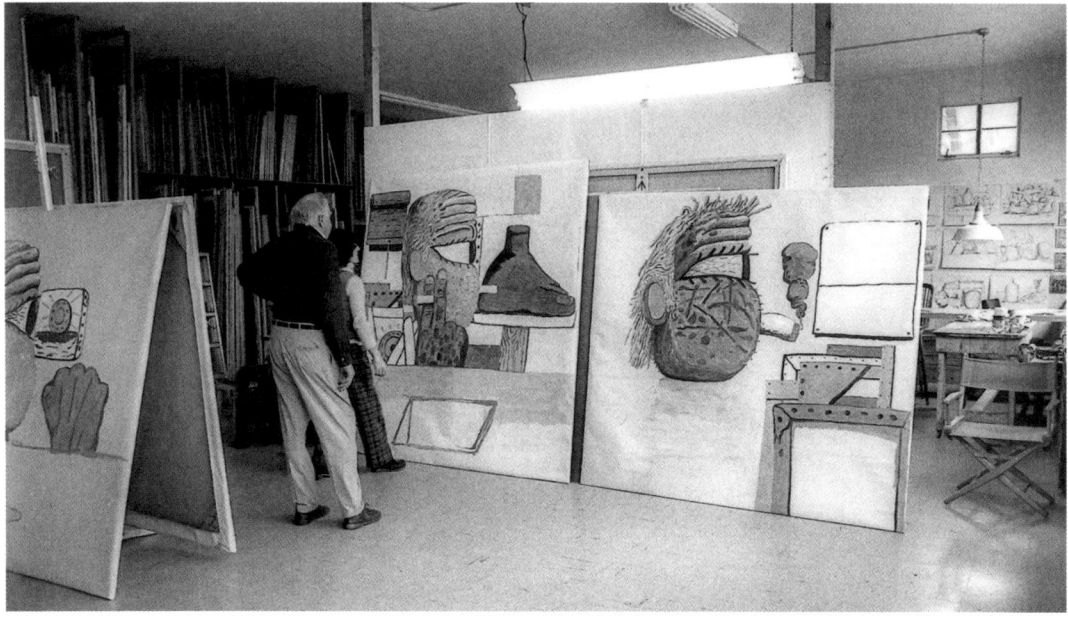

194 — Denise Brown Hare, *Wall of the studio behind the drawing table*, 1975
195 — Denise Brown Hare, *Guston with Dore Ashton in the studio in Woodstock,*
looking at (from left to right) "Spleen," "In the Studio," and "Painter's Head," 1975

1
Quoted in Musa Mayer, *Night Studio: A Memoir of Philip Guston by his Daughter*, New York: Knopf, 1988, p. 14.

2
Ibid., p. 15.

3
David Alfaro Siqueiros, quoted in Mayer, ibid., p. 20.

4
Philip Guston, quoted in Mayer, ibid., p. 32.

5
Philip Guston, quoted in Robert Storr, *Philip Guston*, New York: Abbeville Press, 1986, p. 16.

6
Philip Guston, quoted in Mayer, ibid., p. 64.

7
Philip Guston, quoted in Dore Ashton, *A Critical Study of Philip Guston*, Berkeley: University of California Press, 1990, p. 74.

8
Philip Guston, quoted in Mayer, *Night Studio*, op. cit., p. 49.

9
Philip Guston, quoted in Storr, *Philip Guston*, op. cit., p. 43.

10
Philip Guston, quoted in Ashton, *A Critical Study*, op. cit., pp. 131–32.

11
Mayer, *Night Studio*, op. cit., p. 59.

12
Philip Guston, quoted in Storr, *Philip Guston*, op. cit., p. 47.

13
Storr, ibid., p. 53.

14
Philip Guston, quoted in "Philip Guston Talking," in Nicholas Serota (ed.), *Philip Guston: Paintings, 1969–1980*, exhibition catalog, London: Whitechapel Art Gallery, 1982, p. 52.

15
Quoted in Storr, *Philip Guston*, op. cit., p. 52.

16
Quoted in Storr, ibid., p. 53.

17
Quoted in Storr, ibid., p. 64.

18
Quoted in Ashton, *A Critical Study*, op. cit., p. 127.

19
Quoted in Mayer, *Night Studio*, op. cit., p. 158.

20
Quoted in Ashton, *A Critical Study*, op. cit., p. 177

21
Quoted in Mayer, *Night Studio*, op. cit., p. 179.

22
Ibid., p. 83.

23
Art in America, January-February 1978, pp. 100–05.

24
Comments taken from the film *Philip Guston: a Life Lived* by Michael Blackwood, 1981.

pages 208–209
196 — *Philip Guston with his students at Boston University*, c. 1978.
Courtesy of the Estate of Philip Guston Archives

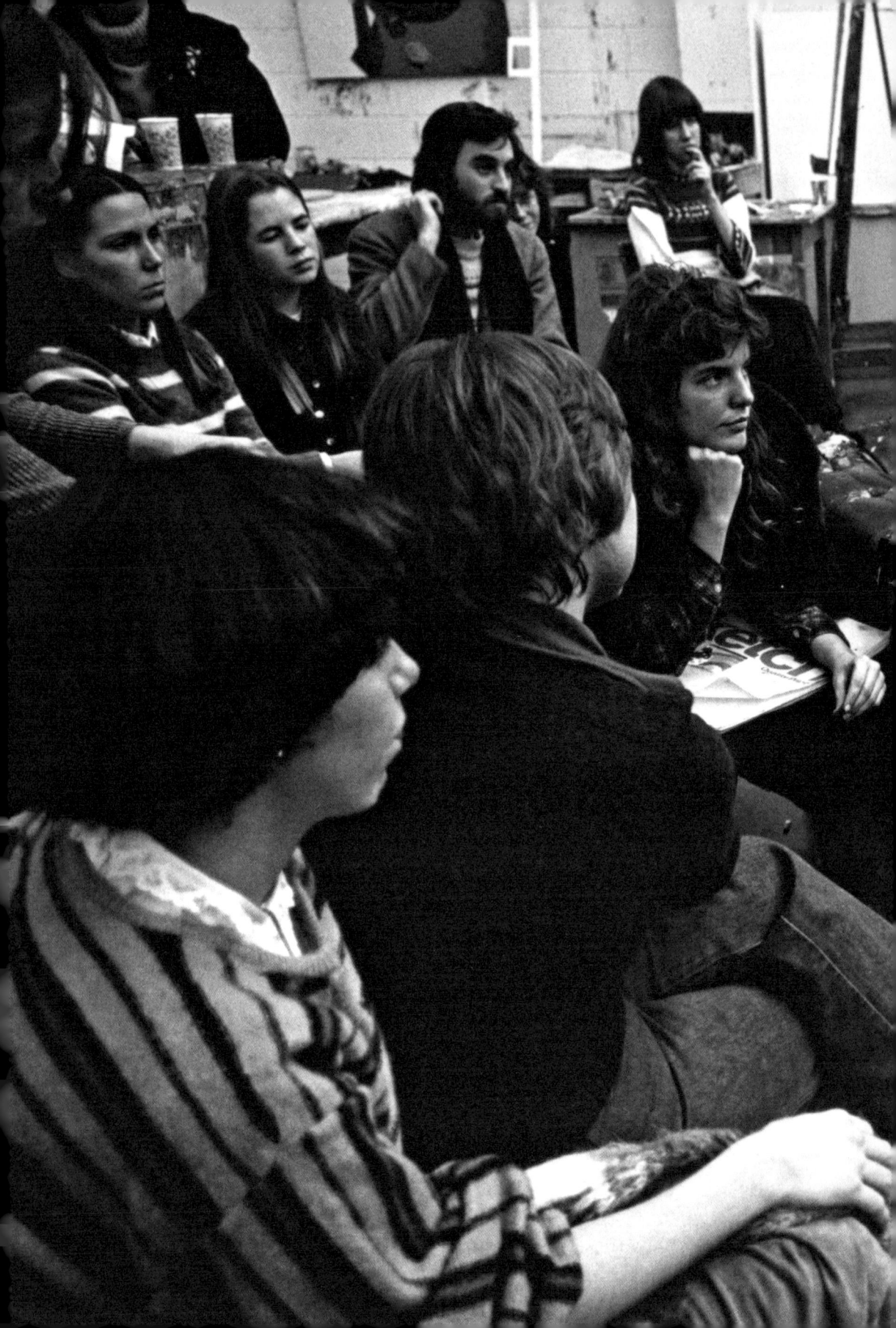

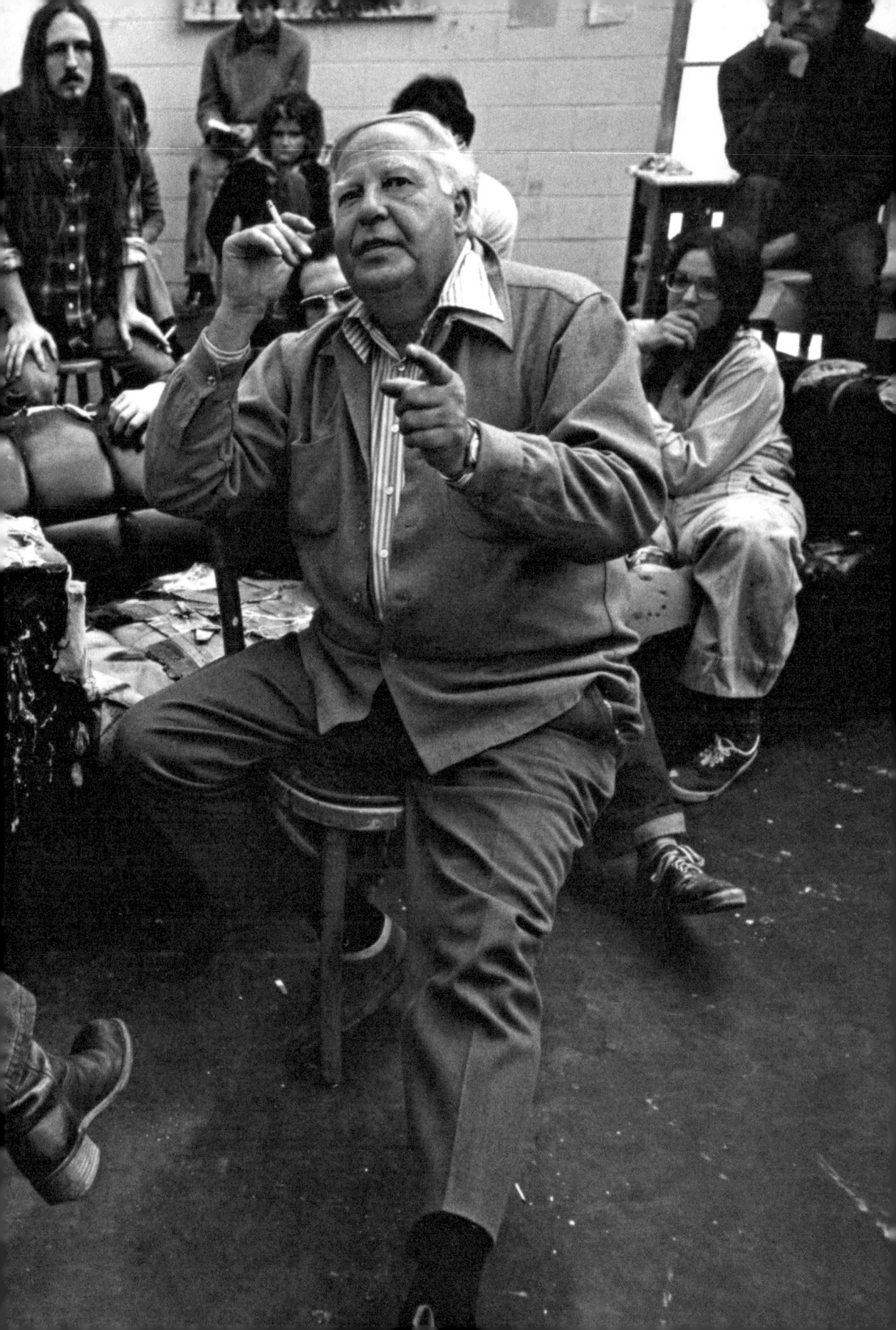

Select bibliography

About Philip Guston

Artist's writings

Philip Guston, *Collected Writings, Lectures, and Conversations*, Berkeley, University of California Press, "Documents of Twentieth-Century Art" series, 2010

Essays

Dore Ashton, *A Critical Study of Philip Guston*, New York, Viking Press, 1976

Blake Bailey, *Philip Roth*, New York, W. W. Norton & Company, 2021

Debra Bricker Balken, *Philip Guston's "Poor Richard,"* Chicago, University of Chicago Press, 2001

Musa Mayer, *Night Studio: A Memoir of Philip Guston by His Daughter*, New York, Penguin Books, 1990

Robert Storr, *Philip Guston*, New York, Abbeville Press, 1986

Robert Storr, *Philip Guston: A Life Spent Painting*, London, Laurence King Publishing, 2020

Exhibitions and catalogs

Philip Guston [official title unknown], Los Angeles, Stanley Rose Gallery, September 1933

Recent Paintings by Philip Guston, New York, Sidney Janis Gallery, February 6 – March 3, 1956

Philip Guston, exh. cat. (New York, Solomon R. Guggenheim Museum, May 2 – July 1, 1962; Amsterdam, Stedelijk Museum, September 20 – October 15, 1962; London, Whitechapel Art Gallery, January 1 – February 15, 1963; Brussels, Palais des Beaux-Arts, March 1–31, 1963; Los Angeles, Los Angeles County Museum, May 21 – June 30, 1963), essay by H. H. Arnason, New York, Solomon R. Guggenheim Museum, 1962

Philip Guston: Recent Paintings and Drawings, exh. cat. (New York, Jewish Museum, January 12 – February 13, 1966), introduction by Sam Hunter, interview with Harold Rosenberg, New York, Jewish Museum, 1966

Philip Guston: A Selective Retrospective Exhibition (1945–1965), exh. cat. (Waltham [Mass.], Rose Art Museum, Brandeis University, February 27 – March 27, 1966), Waltham, Poses Institute of Fine Arts/Rose Art Museum/Brandeis University, 1966

Philip Guston: Recent Paintings, exh. cat. (New York, Marlborough Gallery, October 17 – November 7, 1970), New York, Marlborough Gallery, 1970

Philip Guston: The Last Works, exh. cat. (Washington, D.C., Philips Collection, March 21 – May 24, 1981; Cleveland, Cleveland Museum of Art, June 6 – September 13, 1981; Pittsburgh, Museum of Art, Carnegie Institute, October 10, 1981 – January 3, 1982; New York, David McKee Gallery, January 12 – February 10, 1982), essay by Morton Feldman, Washington D.C., Philips Collection, 1981

The Drawings of Philip Guston, exh. cat. (New York, Museum of Modern Art, September 8 – November 1, 1988; Amsterdam, Museum Overholland, January 14 – March 12, 1989; Barcelona, Centre Culturel de la Fundació Caixa de Pensions, March 30 – May 14, 1989; Oxford, Museum of Modern Art, May 28 – July 23, 1989; Dublin, Douglas Hyde Gallery, August 9 – September 16, 1989; Rome, Galleria Nazionale d'Arte Moderna, October 9 – November 26, 1989), Dublin, Douglas Hyde Gallery, 1989

Philip Guston: Retrospectiva de Pintura, exh. cat. (Madrid, Centro de Arte Reina Sofía, March 1 – May 8, 1989; Barcelona, Palau de la Virreina, May 25 – July 16, 1989; Saint Louis, Saint Louis Art Museum, September 9 – October 22, 1989; Dallas, Dallas Museum of Art), essays by Mark Rosenthal, Robert Storr, Carrie Rickey, Francisco Calvo Serraller, and Dore Ashton, Madrid, Ministério de Cultura, Dirección General de Bellas Artes y Archivos, Centro Nacional de Exposiciones, 1989

Philip Guston (1913–1980). Œuvres sur papier (1975–1980), exh. cat. (Les Sables-d'Olonne, Musée de l'Abbaye Sainte-Croix, June 24 – September 30, 1995), edited by Didier Ottinger, Les Sables-d'Olonne, Musée de l'Abbaye Sainte-Croix, 1995

Philip Guston, Gemälde/Paintings (1947–1979), exh. cat. (Bonn, Kunstmuseum, September 2 – November 1, 1999; Stuttgart, Württembergischer Kunstverein, February 16 – April 24, 2000; Ottawa, National Gallery of Canada, May 12 – July 30, 2000), Ostfildern, Hatje Cantz Verlag, 1999

Philip Guston. Peintures (1947–1979), exh. cat. (Paris, Centre Pompidou, September 14 – December 4, 2000), edited by Didier Ottinger, Paris, Centre Pompidou, 2000

Philip Guston: Nixon Drawings (1971 & 1975), exh. cat. (New York, Hauser & Wirth, November 1, 2016 – January 28, 2017; London, Hauser & Wirth, May 19 – July 29, 2017), edited by Musa Mayer and Sally Radic, New York, Hauser & Wirth, 2017

Philip Guston and the Poets, exh. cat. (Venice, Galleria dell'Accademia, May 10 – September 3, 2017), New York, Hauser & Wirth Publishers, 2017

Philip Guston Now, exh. cat. (Boston, Museum of Fine Arts, May 1 – September 11, 2022; Houston, Museum of Fine Arts, October 23, 2022 – January 15, 2023; Washington, D.C., National Gallery of Art, March 2 – August 27, 2023; London, Tate Modern, October 5, 2023 – February 25, 2024), edited by Harry Cooper, Mark Godfrey, Alison de Lima Greene, and Kate Nesin, Washington, D.C., National Gallery of Art, 2020

Online catalogue raisonné of Guston's work on the website

of the Guston Foundation, URL:
<https://www.gustoncrllc.org/
home/catalogue_raisonne>

Articles

Hilton Kramer, "Art: Abstractions
of Guston Still Further Refined,"
The New York Times, January 15,
1966

Hilton Kramer, "A Mandarin
Pretending to Be a Stumblebum,"
New York Times, October 25,
1970

Film

Philip Guston: A Life Lived
by Michael Blackwood, 1981

Memoirs and essays by Philip Roth

Reading Myself and Others,
New York, Farrar, Straus and
Giroux, 1975

*The Facts: A Novelist's
Autobiography*, New York, Farrar,
Straus and Giroux, 1988

Shop Talk: *A Writer and His
Colleagues and Their Work*,
Boston, Houghton Mifflin, 2001

General works

Dore Ashton, *New York School:
A Cultural Reckoning*, New York,
Viking Press, 1973

Frances S. Connelly, *The Grotesque
in Western Art and Culture: The
Image at Play*, Cambridge and
New York, Cambridge University
Press, 2014 [2012]

Willem de Kooning, *Collected
Writings of Willem de Kooning*,
Madras and New York, Hanuman
Books, 1988

Clement Greenberg, *Art and
Culture. Critical Essays*, Boston,
Beacon Press, 1969

Ulrich Heimann, *Picassos
Kubismus und die Ironie*,
Munich, Wilhelm Fink, 1998

Wolfgang Kayser, *The Grotesque
in Art and Literature*, translated
from the German by Ulrich
Weisstein, New York, Columbia
University Press, 1981 [1957]

Brigitte Léal, Laurent Gervereau,
Maria Teresa Ocaña et al.,
*Picasso: From Caricature to
Metamorphosis of Style*, exh. cat.
(Barcelona, Museu Picasso,
2003), Aldershot, Lund
Humphries / Barcelona,
Museu Picasso, 2003

José Lebrero Stals (ed.), *The
Grotesque Factor*, exh. cat.
(Málaga, Museo Picasso,
October 22, 2012 – February 10,
2013), Málaga, Fundación Museo
Picasso, 2012

Erwin Panofsky et al., *Saturn
and Melancholy. Studies in the
History of Natural Philosophy,
Religion and Art*, Montreal,
Kingston, London, and Chicago,
McGill-Queen's University Press,
2019 [1964]

Gérard Régnier (ed.), *Le Dernier
Picasso (1953–1973)*, exh.
cat. (Paris, Centre Pompidou,
February 17 – May 16, 1988),
Paris, Éd. du Centre Pompidou,
1988

Irving Sandler, *The Triumph of
American Painting: A History
of Abstract Expressionism*,
New York, Praeger Publishers,
1970

Kirk Varnedoe and Adam Gopnik
(eds.), *High and Low: Modern Art
and Popular Culture*, exh. cat.
(New York, Museum of Modern
Art, October 7, 1990 – January 15,
1991), New York, Museum of
Modern Art, 1990

List of illustrations

Philip Guston's paintings each have a number assigned in the catalogue raisonné (CR), which can be consulted on the website of The Guston Foundation: www. gustoncrllc.org/home/catalogue_raisonne.

Prints and drawings

Max Beckmann
(Leipzig, Germany 1884 – New York, United States, 1950)
Spielender Kinder
(Playing Children), 1918
Drypoint on laid paper, 37 × 36.9 cm
Sprengel Museum Hannover,
Hanover, Gr. 1965,92
14 p. 28

Philip Guston
(Montreal, Canada, 1913 – Woodstock, United States, 1980)
Barnett Newman, 1955
Ink on paper, 27.3 × 21 cm
Private collection
Exhibited work, 50 p. 64

Barnett Newman, 1955
Ink on paper, 27.3 × 21 cm
Private collection
Exhibited work, 49 p. 64

Caricature of Philip Roth, 1973
Ink on paper, 27.9 × 21.6 cm
The Guston Foundation,
West Hurley (New York)
Exhibited work, 139 p. 119

Drawing No. 2 (Ischia), 1949
Ink on paper, 27.9 × 38.1 cm
Promised gift of Musa Guston
Mayer to the Metropolitan
Museum of Art
25 p. 36

Elaine de Kooning, c. 1955
Pencil on paper, 27.9 × 21.6 cm
Private collection
Exhibited work, 51 p. 65

Esteban Vicente, c. 1955
Pencil on paper, 24.1 × 16.5 cm
Private collection
Exhibited work, 52 p. 66

Franz Kline, c. 1955
Pencil on paper, 27.9 × 21.6 cm
Private collection
Exhibited work, 46 p. 63

Franz Kline, 1955
Ink on paper, 27.6 × 21.6 cm
Private collection
Exhibited work, 47 p. 64

Franz Kline and Willem de Kooning, c. 1955
Pencil on paper, 22.9 × 15.2 cm
Private collection
Exhibited work, not reproduced

Harold Rosenberg, 1955
Pencil on paper, 24.1 × 16.5 cm
The Guston Foundation,
West Hurley (New York)
Exhibited work, 45 p. 62

Jack Tworkov, c. 1955
Pencil on paper, 24.1 × 16.5 cm
Private collection
Exhibited work, 44 p. 61

Mark Rothko, c. 1955
Pencil on paper, 28 × 21.6 cm
Private collection
Exhibited work, 42 p. 61

Philip Roth, 1973
Ink on paper, 27.9 × 21.6 cm
The Guston Foundation,
West Hurley (New York)
Exhibited work, not reproduced

Poor Richard, 1971
Ink on paper, 26.7 × 35.2 cm
The Guston Foundation, Promised
Gift to the National Gallery of Art,
Washington, D.C.
Exhibited works, 65–137 p. 75–111

Robert Motherwell, c. 1955
Pencil on paper, 26.7 × 20.3 cm
Private collection
Exhibited work, 43 p. 61

Saul Steinberg, c. 1955
Pencil on paper, 28 × 21.6 cm
Private collection
Exhibited work, 41 p. 61

Stanley Kunitz, c. 1955
Ink and pencil on paper,
26.7 × 21.6 cm
Private collection
Exhibited work, 53 p. 67

Study for "Work and Play"
(Study for Queensbridge
Housing Project Mural), 1939
Colored pencil and ink on paper,
38.1 × 62.9 cm
Promised gift of Musa Guston
Mayer to the Metropolitan
Museum of Art
Exhibited work, 34 p. 51

Untitled, c. 1972
Ink on paper, 21.6 × 27.9 cm
The Guston Foundation,
West Hurley (New York)
142–144 p. 128–130

Untitled (Artist and Critics), 1972
Ink on paper, 34.6 × 43.2 cm
The Guston Foundation,
West Hurley (New York)
Exhibited work, 140 p. 119

Willem de Kooning, c. 1955
Ink on paper, 27.9 × 21.6 cm
Private collection
Exhibited work, not reproduced

Willem de Kooning, 1955
Ink on paper, 27.3 × 21.6 cm
Private collection
Exhibited work, 48 p. 64

Pablo Picasso
(Málaga, Spain, 1881 – Mougins,
France, 1973)
Caricature of Henri Delormel,
Paris, [1905]
Ink on paper, 29.7 × 22.7 cm
Bought in 1986
Musée National Picasso-Paris,
MP1986-43 (r)
Exhibited work, 62 p. 73

Caricature of Jaime Sabartés,
Paris, March 4, 1954
Ink and collage on card
with gouache on paper, verso
of a page from a book, 32 × 24.5 cm
Transfer from the Direction
Générale des Douanes et Droits
Indirects, 1981
Musée National Picasso-Paris,
MP1982-1
Exhibited work, 57 p. 70

Caricature of Jaime Sabartés,
Paris, June 27, 1959
Ink on paper, 27 × 21 cm
Dation Pablo Picasso, 1979
Musée National Picasso-Paris,
MP1524
Exhibited work, 58 p. 70

Caricature of Jaime Sabartés,
Paris, 1959
Ink and soft pencil on paper,
21 × 27 cm
Dation Pablo Picasso, 1979
Musée National Picasso-Paris,
MP1525 (v)
Exhibited work, 59 p. 70

Caricature of Jean Cocteau,
Rome, 1917
Gouache on paper, 19.7 × 6.8 cm
Dation Pablo Picasso, 1979
Musée National Picasso-Paris,
MP784
Exhibited work, 55 p. 69

Caricature of Jean Moréas,
Paris, [1905]
Ink on paper, 29.2 × 24.9 cm
Purchased in 1986
Musée National Picasso-Paris,
MP1986-41
Exhibited work, 63 p. 73

Caricature of Léon Bakst,
Rome, 1917
Gouache on paper, 13.9 × 5.7 cm
Dation Pablo Picasso, 1979
Musée National Picasso-Paris,
MP786
Exhibited work, 56 p. 69

Caricature of Sergei Diaghilev,
Rome, 1917–18
Gouache on paper, 8.6 × 6.7 cm
Dation Pablo Picasso, 1979
Musée National Picasso-Paris,
MP787
Exhibited work, 64 p. 74

Caricature (Self-Portrait?),
[Rome-Paris], [1917–18]
Ink on paper, 17 × 8.5 cm
Dation Pablo Picasso, 1979
Musée National Picasso-Paris,
MP855
Exhibited work, 54 p. 68

Dream and Lie of Franco (plate I),
Paris, January 8, 1937
Etching and sugar-lift aquatint
on copper, 2nd state, printed
by Lacourière, 38.5 × 57.3 cm
Dation Pablo Picasso, 1979
Musée National Picasso-Paris,
MP2751
Exhibited work, 165 p. 162

Dream and Lie of Franco (plate II),
Paris, January 8 – June 7, 1937
Etching and sugar-lift aquatint
with scraping on copper, 5th
state, printed by Lacourière,
38.5 × 57.1 cm
Dation Pablo Picasso, 1979
Musée National Picasso-Paris,
MP2754
Exhibited work, 166 p. 163

Humorous composition. Jaime Sabartés and Esther Williams, Cannes, May 23, 1957
Grease pencils on magazine printed paper, 35.6 × 26.5 cm
Gift of Jaime Sabartés, 1964
Museu Picasso, Barcelona, MPB 70.675
159 p. 156

Humorous composition. Jaime Sabartés and Gita Hall May, Cannes, July 31, 1957
Grease pencils on magazine printed paper, 32.4 × 24.2 cm
Gift of Jaime Sabartés, 1964
Museu Picasso, Barcelona, MPB 70.670
160 p. 156

Humorous composition. Jaime Sabartés and Josette Arno, Cannes, May 11, 1957
Black grease pencil on magazine printed paper, 35 × 26.3 cm
Gift of Jaime Sabartés, 1964
Museu Picasso, Barcelona, MPB 70.671
162 p. 156

Humorous composition. Jaime Sabartés and Neile Adams, Cannes, December 4, 1957
Ink and brush on cut-out printed magazine page, 35.6 × 26 cm
Gift of Jaime Sabartés, 1964
Museu Picasso, Barcelona, MPB 70.674
161 p. 156

La Célestine, April 11, 1968 – August 18, 1968
Etching, aquatint, scraping and drypoint on sixty-six copper plates. Printed by Crommelynck, 74.2 × 104 cm
Dation Pablo Picasso, 1979
Musée National Picasso-Paris, MP3053
158 p. 154–155

Mother with Dead Child (IV). Sketch for "Guernica," Paris, 1937
Graphite, gouache, collage and color stick on tracing cloth, 23.1 × 29.2 cm
Legado Picasso, 1981
Museo Nacional Centro de Arte Reina Sofía, Madrid, DE00084
Exhibited work, 12 p. 25

Picasso par lui-même, Paris, 1903
Pen and ink on paper, 11.8 × 10.7 cm
Gift of Pablo Picasso, 1970
Museu Picasso Barcelona, MPB 110.440
156 p. 150

Portrait of Francis Poulenc, Paris, March 13, 1957
Graphite on paper, 54 × 37 cm
Dation Pablo Picasso, 1979
Musée National Picasso-Paris, MP1515
Exhibited work, 60 p. 71

Portrait of Guillaume Apollinaire, Paris, summer 1918
Ink on paper, 13.6 × 87 cm
Dation Pablo Picasso, 1979
Musée National Picasso-Paris, MP497
Exhibited work, 61 p. 72

Still Life on a Pedestal Table in Front of a Window, France, 1919
Gouache and pencil on paper, 49 × 30.9 cm
Partial, fractional and promised gift of Janice and Henri Lazarof (M.2005.70.100)
Los Angeles County Museum of Art, Los Angeles
22 p. 35

The Artist before his Canvas, Paris, March 22, 1938
Charcoal on canvas, 130 × 94 cm
Dation Pablo Picasso, 1979
Musée national Picasso-Paris, MP172
Exhibited work, 4 p. 8

"The Barbaric Dance" (Before Salome and Herod), Paris, autumn – winter 1905
Printer: Eugène Delâtre, Paris (France)
Drypoint on copper. Printed by Delâtre, 25 × 32.8 cm
Dation Pablo Picasso, 1979
Musée National Picasso-Paris, MP1904
154 p. 148

Paintings

Philip Guston
(Montreal, Canada, 1913 – Woodstock, United States, 1980)
Allegory, 1975
Oil on canvas, 172.7 × 186.1 cm
Saint Louis Art Museum, Funds given by the Shoenberg Foundation, Inc. and Mr. and Mrs. Robert Shoenberg, by exchange 8:1990
CR P75.023
170 p. 169

Black Sea, 1977
Oil on canvas, 173 × 297.2 cm
Purchased 1982
Tate, London, T03364
CR P77.018
Exhibited work, 173 p. 172–173

Bombardment, 1937
Oil on Masonite, diam. 106.7
Gift of Musa and Tom Mayer
Philadelphia Museum of Art, Philadelphia, 2011-2-1
CR P37.0001
Exhibited work, 13 p. 27

Dawn, 1970
Oil on canvas, 170.82 × 274.32 cm
Glenstone Museum, Potomac (Maryland), GF2016.076
CR P70.019
Exhibited work, 147 p. 136–137

Deluge III, 1979
Oil on canvas, 172.7 × 207 cm
Private collection, New York
CR P79.006
171 p. 170

Discussion, 1969
Oil on panel, 76.2 × 101.6 cm
Anne and Joel Ehrenkranz
CR P69.100
146 p. 135

East Coker-T.S. E., 1979
Oil on canvas, 106.7 × 121.9 cm
Gift of Musa Guston, 1991
The Museum of Modern Art,
New York, 364.1991
CR P79.038
Exhibited work, 172 p. 171

Gladiators, 1940
Oil and pencil on canvas,
62.2 × 71.4 cm
Gift of Edward R. Broida
The Museum of Modern Art,
New York, 701.2005
CR P40.008
15 p. 28

If This Be Not I, 1945
Oil on canvas, 107.3 × 140.3 cm
University purchase,
Kende Sale Fund, 1945
Mildred Lane Kemper Art
Museum, Washington University
in Saint Louis, WU 3766
CR P45.001
17 p. 31

John Reed Club Panel, c. 1931
Fresco, dimensions unknown
Destroyed in February 1933
CR P31.004
8 p. 20

Lamp, 1974
Oil on canvas, 171.5 × 265.4 cm
Pinault Collection
CR P74.006
169 p. 168

Large Brush, 1979
Oil on canvas, 81.3 × 91.4 cm
Aaron I. Fleischman Collection,
New York
CR P79.055
Exhibited work, 150 p. 140

Martial Memory, 1941
Oil on canvas, 101.9 × 81.9 cm
Saint Louis Art Museum,
Eliza McMillan Trust 115:1942
CR P41.001
16 p. 31

Martyr, 1978
Oil on canvas, 174 × 175.9 cm
Private collection
CR P78.017
Exhibited work, 151 p. 141

Mother and Child, c. 1930
Oil on canvas, 101.6 × 76.2 cm
Promised gift of Musa Guston
Mayer to the Metropolitan
Museum of Art
CR P30.001.1
Exhibited work, 7 p. 19

Out for a Ride, 1969
Oil on panel, 109.2 × 83.2 cm
Collection unknown
CR P69.111
149 p. 139

Painting, 1952
Oil on canvas, 121.9 × 129.5 cm
The Muriel Kallis Steinberg
Newman Collection, Gift
of Muriel Kallis Newman, 2006
The Metropolitan Museum of Art,
New York, 2006.32.25
CR P52.005
Exhibited work, 39 p. 58

Painting, 1954
Oil on canvas, 160.6 × 152.7 cm
Philip Johnson Fund, 1956
The Museum of Modern Art,
New York, 7.1956
CR P54.001
Exhibited work, 40 p. 59

Riding Around, 1969
Oil on canvas, 137.2 × 200.7 cm
Promised gift of Musa Guston
Mayer to the Metropolitan
Museum of Art
CR P69.120
148 p. 138

San Clemente, 1975
Oil on canvas, 172.72 × 186.06 cm
Glenstone Museum, Potomac
(Maryland), GF2016.075
GR P75.033
Exhibited work, 138 p. 112–113

Sanctuary, 1944
Oil on canvas, 56.2 × 91.1 cm
Promised gift of Musa Guston
Mayer to the Metropolitan
Museum of Art
CR P44.003
21 p. 32

Self Portrait, 1944
Oil on canvas, 66 cm × 45.7 cm
Promised gift of Musa Guston
Mayer to the Metropolitan
Museum of Art
CR P44.002
20 p. 32

Sleeping, 1977
Oil on canvas, 213.4 × 175.3 cm
Promised gift of Musa Guston
Mayer to the Metropolitan
Museum of Art
CR P77.008
Exhibited work, 2 p. 2

Studio Landscape, 1975
Oil on canvas, 170.2 × 264.2 cm
Arora Collection, London
CR P75.019
Exhibited work, 152 p. 142–143

Sunday Interior, 1941
Oil on canvas, 96.5 cm × 61 cm
Private collection
CR P41.004
19 p. 32

Tall Book, 1968
Acrylic on panel, 50.8 × 45.1 cm
Promised gift of Musa Guston
Mayer to The Metropolitan
Museum of Art
CR P.68.047
3 p. 6

The Actors V, 1962
Oil on paper mounted on panel,
76.2 × 101.6 cm
Private collection, London
CR P62.003
26 p. 40

The Line, 1978
Oil on canvas, 180.3 × 186.1 cm
Promised gift of Musa Guston
Mayer to the Metropolitan
Museum of Art
CR P78.020
145 p. 133

The Porch II, 1947
Oil on canvas, 158.8 × 109.2 cm
Museum purchase, Munson
Museum of Art, 48.26
CR P41.005
23 p. 35

The Street, 1977
Oil on canvas, 175.6 × 281.6 cm
Purchase, Lila Acheson Wallace
and Mr. and Mrs. Andrew Saul
Gifts, Gift of George A. Hearn,
by exchange, and Arthur Hoppock
Hearn Fund, 1983
The Metropolitan Museum of Art,
New York, 1983.457
CR P77.038
Exhibited work, 168 p. 166–167

The Studio, 1969
Oil on canvas, 121.9 × 106.7 cm
Promised gift of Musa Guston
Mayer to the Metropolitan
Museum of Art
CR P69.106
Exhibited work, 5 p. 9

The Tormentors, 1947–48
Oil on canvas, 103.84 cm × 153.67 cm
Gift of the artist, 1982
San Francisco Museum
of Modern Art
CR P48.001
24 p. 36

To I.B. (Isaac Babel), 1977
Oil on canvas, 170.8 × 203.2 cm
Private collection
CR P77.033
167 p. 165

Untitled, 1968
Acrylic on panel, 76.2 × 81.3 cm
Dr. Corinne M. Flick Collection,
London
CR P68.015
197 p. 224

Untitled, 1980
Acrylic and ink on paper,
58.3 × 73.6 cm
Promised gift of Musa Guston
to the Metropolitan Museum of Art
CR P80.024
Exhibited work, 183 p. 186

Untitled, 1980
Acrylic and ink on illustration
board, 50.8 × 76.2 cm
Promised gift of Musa Guston
Mayer to the Metropolitan
Museum of Art
CR P80.003
Exhibited work, 181 p. 184

Untitled, 1980
Acrylic and ink on illustration
board, 50.8 × 76.2 cm
Promised gift of Musa Guston
Mayer to the Metropolitan
Museum of Art
CR P80.004
Exhibited work, 181 p. 184

Untitled, 1980
Acrylic and ink on illustration
board, 50.8 × 76.2 cm
Promised gift of Musa Guston
Mayer to the Metropolitan
Museum of Art
CR P80.006
Exhibited work, 176 p. 177

Untitled, 1980
Acrylic and ink on illustration
board, 50.8 × 76.2 cm
Promised gift of Musa Guston
Mayer to the Metropolitan
Museum of Art
CR P80.007
Exhibited work, 174 p. 175

Untitled, 1980
Acrylic and ink on illustration
board, 50.8 × 76.2 cm
Promised gift of Musa Guston
Mayer to the Metropolitan
Museum of Art
CR P80.008
Exhibited work, 175 p. 176

Untitled, 1980
Acrylic and ink on paper,
58.4 × 58.4 cm
Promised gift of Musa Guston
Mayer to the Metropolitan
Museum of Art
CR P80.009
Exhibited work, 179 p. 181

Untitled, 1980
Acrylic and ink on illustration
board, 50.8 × 76.2 cm
Gift of Musa Guston
The Museum of Modern Art,
New York, 318.1989
CR P80.011
186 p. 189

Untitled, 1980
Acrylic and ink on illustration
board, 50.8×76.2 cm
Promised gift of Musa Guston
Mayer to the Metropolitan
Museum of Art
CR P80.012
Exhibited work, 178 p. 180

Untitled, 1980
Acrylic and ink on illustration
board, 50.8×76.2 cm
Promised gift of Musa Guston
Mayer to the Metropolitan
Museum of Art
CR P80.014
Exhibited work, 177 p. 178–179

Untitled, 1980
Acrylic and ink on illustration
board, 50.8×76.2 cm
Promised gift of Musa Guston
Mayer to the Metropolitan
Museum of Art
CR P80.017
Exhibited work, 182 p. 185

Untitled, 1980
Acrylic and ink on paper,
57.2×74.9 cm
Promised gift of Musa Guston
Mayer to the Metropolitan
Museum of Art
CR P80.020
Exhibited work, 27 p. 45

Untitled, 1980
Acrylic and ink on paper,
58.4×73.7 cm
Promised gift of Musa Guston
Mayer to the Metropolitan
Museum of Art
CR P80.021
Exhibited work, 184 p. 187

Untitled, 1980
Acrylic and ink on paper,
58.4×73.7 cm
Promised gift of Musa Guston
Mayer to the Metropolitan
Museum of Art
CR P80.022
Exhibited work, 185 p. 188

Untitled, 1980
Acrylic and ink on paper,
58.3×73.6 cm
Gift of Musa Guston
The Museum of Modern Art,
New York, 620.1987
CR P80.024
187 p. 190

Untitled, 1980
Acrylic and ink on illustration
board, 50.8×76.2 cm
Promised gift of Musa Guston
Mayer to the Metropolitan
Museum of Art
CR P80.025
Exhibited work, 189 p. 192–193

Untitled, 1980
Acrylic and ink on paper,
58.4×73.6 cm
Promised gift of Musa Guston
Mayer to the Metropolitan
Museum of Art
CR P80.026
Exhibited work, 188 p. 191

*Untitled (Preliminary Study
for "Reconstruction and
The Well-Being of the Family")*,
c. 1940
Fresco, 32.1×171.1 cm
Promised gift of Musa Guston
Mayer to the Metropolitan
Museum of Art
CR P.40.001
Exhibited work, 33 p. 50–51

Wheel, 1979
Oil on canvas, 121.9×152.4 cm
Private collection
CR P79.035
180 p. 182–183

White Painting II, 1951
Oil on canvas, 127×129.2 cm
Private collection, London
CR P51.004
38 p. 57

*Work and Play (Queensbridge
Housing Project Mural)*, 1940
Casein-glyptol tempera on gesso,
1219.2×175.3 cm
Queensbridge Community Center
of the Queensbridge Houses
CR P40.007
32 p. 50

Pablo Picasso
(Málaga, Spain, 1881 –
Mougins, France, 1973)
El Bobo, Vauvenargues,
April 14–15, 1959
Oil and enamel on canvas,
92×73.2 cm
Dation Maya Ruiz-Picasso, 2021
Musée National Picasso-Paris,
MP2021-6
155 p. 150

Horse Head. Sketch for "Guernica,"
Paris, 1937
Oil on canvas, 65×92 cm
Museo Nacional Centro de Arte
Reina Sofía, Madrid, DE00119
Exhibited work, 11 p. 25

Still Life with a Bull's Head,
Cannes, May 25 – June 9, 1958
Oil on canvas, 162.5×130 cm
Dation Pablo Picasso, 1979
Musée National Picasso-Paris,
MP213
Exhibited work, not reproduced

The Kiss, Juan-les-Pins,
summer 1925
Oil on canvas, 130.5×97.7 cm
Dation Pablo Picasso, 1979
Musée National Picasso-Paris,
MP85
163 p. 159

Woman Flower, 1946
Oil on canvas, 146×89 cm
Thomas Ammann Fine Art
Gallery, Zurich
157 p. 153

Woman Pissing, 1965
Oil on canvas, 194.8×96.5 cm
Donation of Louise and Michel
Leiris (Paris) in 1984
Centre Pompidou – Musée National
d'Art Moderne – Centre de Création
Industrielle, Paris
153 p. 147

Young Boy with Lobster, Paris,
June 21, 1941
Oil on canvas, 130 × 97.3 cm
Dation Pablo Picasso, 1979
Musée National Picasso-Paris,
MP189
164 p. 160

Diego Rivera (Guanajuato,
Mexico, 1886 – Mexico City, 1957)
Man, Controller of the Universe
or *Man in the Time Machine*
Replica of the fresco rejected
and destroyed by the Rockefeller
Center, 48.5 × 114.5 cm
Palacio de Bellas Artes, Mexico
City
10 p. 22–23

David Alfaro Siqueiros
(Chihuahua, Mexico, 1896 –
Cuernavaca, 1974)
Street Meeting, 1932
Fresco, 731.5 × 579.1 cm
Chouinard Art Institute (today
the Chouinard Foundation),
Los Angeles, California
9 p. 20

Film

Michael Blackwood (Germany,
Breslau [today Wrocław, Poland],
1934 – New York, United States,
2023)
Conversations with Philip Guston,
2003
Film in color, length: 45 min
Exhibited work, not reproduced

Publications

Isaac Babel
(Odessa, Russian Empire, 1894 –
Moscow, Russia, 1940)
Cavalerie rouge, original French
edition, Paris, Gallimard, 1959
Musée National Picasso-Paris,
BIB014379
Exhibited work, not reproduced

Contes d'Odessa, original French
edition, Paris, Gallimard, 1967
Musée National Picasso-Paris,
BIB014380
Exhibited work, not reproduced

Nicolas Gogol
(Sorochintsy, Russian Empire,
1809 – Moscow, Russia, 1852)
Le Nez, original French edition,
Paris, Éditions Allia, 1835
Musée National Picasso-Paris,
BIB014385
Exhibited work, not reproduced

Le Manteau, original French
edition, Hérault, Culturea, 2024
Musée National Picasso-Paris,
BIB014386
Exhibited work, not reproduced

Franz Kafka
(Prague, Czech Republic, 1883 –
Kierling, Austria, 1924),
La Métamorphose, original French
edition, Paris, Gallimard, 1938
Musée National Picasso-Paris,
BIB014383
Exhibited work, not reproduced

Philip Roth (Newark, United
States, 1933 – New York, United
States, 2018), *Portnoy's Complaint*,
original American edition,
New York, Random House, 1969
Musée National Picasso-Paris,
BIB014414
Exhibited work, not reproduced

Our Gang, original American
edition,
New York, Random House, 1971
Musée National Picasso-Paris,
BIB014384
Exhibited work, not reproduced

Tricard Dixon et ses copains,
original French edition, Paris,
Gallimard, 1972
Musée National Picasso-Paris,
BIB014381
Exhibited work, not reproduced

The Breast, original American
edition, Boston/New York,
Houghton Mifflin, 1972
Musée National Picasso-Paris,
BIB014347
Exhibited work, not reproduced

Le Sein, original French edition,
Paris, Gallimard, 1975
Musée National Picasso-Paris,
BIB014378
Exhibited work, not reproduced

Sabbath's Theater, original
American edition, Boston/
New York, Houghton Mifflin, 1995
Musée National Picasso-Paris,
BIB014387
Exhibited work, not reproduced

Le Théâtre de Sabbath, original
French edition, Paris, Gallimard,
1997
Musée National Picasso-Paris,
BIB014382
Exhibited work, not reproduced

Magazines

Cover of *Americana: A Magazine
of Pictorial Satire*, April 1933
Courtesy of the Robert D. Farber
University Archives & Special
Collections Department, Brandeis
University
6 p. 14

Fortune, "The Air Training
Program," February 1944,
p. 146–152, 174
Advanced Fighter Training
and *The Air Training Program
(Advanced Pilot Training)*, 1943
Original gouaches in paper,
76.2 × 60.3 cm (left-hand page) and
37.8 × 55.6 cm (right-hand page)
Private collection
18 p. 31

Vanity Fair, "Novelist Philip Roth
and the painter Philip Guston
shared a fascination with the
'crapola' of modern life, BREAST
BARING, by Philip Roth,"
October 1989, p. 94–96
Musée National Picasso-Paris
Exhibited work, not reproduced

Photographs

Walter Auerbach
(Karlsruhe, Germany, 1908 – ?)
*Philip Guston in his studio
in New York*, c. 1953
192 p. 202

Denise Browne Hare
(1924–1997)
*Guston with Dore Ashton
in the studio in Woodstock,
looking at (from left to right)
"Spleen," "In the Studio,"
and "Painter's Head,"* 1975
195 p. 206

*Wall of the studio behind
the drawing board*, 1975
194 p. 206

David Robbins
(New York, United States,
1907–1981)
*Chlorinated rubber paint
on cement by Philip Guston
"Work the American Way
(Maintaining America's Skills),"*
1939
CR P39.003
28 p. 47

Barbara Sproul
Philip Guston and Philip Roth,
1972
141 p. 126

Arthur Swoger (1912–2000)
*Philip Guston in his New York
studio*, 1957
193 p. 203

H. Walker
*Philip Guston in his studio
in Saint Louis*, 1946
Photograph for *Life* magazine
191 p. 195

Edward Weston
(Highland Park, Illinois, United
States, 1886 – Big Sur, California,
United States, 1958)
Philip Guston, 1930
1 p. 1

Unidentified photographer
*Musa Guston in front
of "Reconstruction and
The Well-Being of the Family,"
oil painting for the Social
Security Building*, c. 1940
Courtesy of the Estate
of Philip Guston Archives
37 p. 54–55

*Philip Guston and Reuben Kadish,
sitting in a doorway, under
their fresco representing
Physical Groth of Men,
at the City of Hope sanatorium
in Duarte (California)*, c. 1936
Courtesy of the Estate
of Philip Guston Archives
31 p. 49

*Philip Guston, Reuben Kadish
and their friend Jules Langsner
before the mural "The Struggle
Against Terrorism,"* 1935
Fresco
Museo Regional Michoacano,
Morelia, Mexico
29 p. 48

*Philip Guston sketching a fresco
for the World's Fair in New York*,
February 15, 1939
Black and white print, 20 × 26 cm
Archives of American Art,
Smithsonian Institution, 2139
35 p. 52

*Philip Guston with his students
at Boston University*, c. 1978
Courtesy of the Estate
of Philip Guston Archives
196 p. 208–209

*Philip Guston working on
"Untitled (Mural on Navigation,
for Naval Preflight Training),"*
1942–43
Courtesy of The Estate
of Philip Guston Archives
30 p. 49

*Reuben Kadish, Jules Langsner,
Philip Guston, and Gustavo
Corona before the fresco
"The Struggle Against Terrorism,"
in Morelia, Mexico*, c. 1934–35
Courtesy of the Estate
of Philp Guston Archives
36 p. 53

Young Philip in Los Angeles,
c. 1923
Courtesy of the Estate
of Philip Guston Archives
190 p. 194

Index of names

A

Adams, Neile (born 1932) **156**
Agnew, Spiro Theodore (1918–1996) 129
Anderson, Sherwood (1876–1941) 115
Apollinaire, Guillaume (1880–1918) **72**
Arendt, Hannah (1906–1975) 33
Arensberg, Louise (1879–1953) 197
Arensberg, Walter (1878–1954) 16, 197
Arnason, H. H. (1909–1986) 37
Arno, Josette (1933–2013) **156**
Ashton, Dore (1928–2017) **206**
Auerbach, Walter (1877–1950) **196**

B

Babel, Isaac (1894–1940) 38, 120, 164, 204
Bakhtin, Mikhail (1895–1975) 146, 151, 152, 158
Bakst, Léon (1866–1924) **69**
Baselitz, Georg (born 1938) 200
Baudelaire, Charles (1821–1867) 39, 200
Baziotes, William (1912–1963) 33
Beckett, Samuel (1906–1989) 128, 200, 204
Beckmann, Max (1884–1950) 26, **28**, 29, 33, 198, 199
Bellow, Saul (1915–2005) 115
Benjamin, Walter (1892–1940) 38
Biddle, George (1885–1973) 21
Brach, Paul (1924–2007) 37
Broida, Edward R. (1933–2006) 205
Bruce, Edward (1879–1943) 24
Budyonny, Semyon Mikhailovich (1883–1973) 120

C

Cage, John (1912–1992) 33, 34, 56, 200
Cahill, Holger (1887–1960) 24
Camus, Albert (1913–1960) 43, 200
Cervantes Saavedra, Miguel de (1547–1616) 157
Cézanne, Paul (1839–1906) 199
Chagall, Marc (1887–1985) 16
Cherry, Herman (1909–1992) 197
Cocteau, Jean (1889–1963) **69**, 200
Coolidge, Clark (born 1939) 204
Corona, Gustavo (1899–1991) **56**
Corot, Camille (1796–1875) 198

D

Dante, Alighieri (1265–1321) 16
Davis, Stuart (1892–1964) 24, 198
De Chirico, Giorgio (1888–1978) 17, 29, 132, 197
Delormel, Henri (1878–1948) **73**
Diaghilev, Sergei (1872–1929) **73**
Diderot, Denis (1713–1784) 13
Dix, Otto (1891–1969) 158
Dostoevsky, Fyodor (1821–1881) 39, 200
Dovzhenko, Alexander Petrovich (1894–1956) 16, 197
Duchamp, Marcel (1887–1968) 16
Dürer, Albrecht (1471–1528) 29

E

Eisenstein, Sergei Mikhailovich (1898–1948) 16, 197
El Greco (1541–1614) 199
Ernst, Max (1891–1976) 30

F

Faulkner, William (1897–1962) 115
Faure, Élie (1873–1937) 198
Feitelson, Lorser (1898–1978) 16, 17, 197
Feldman, Morton (1926–1987) 34, 37, 39, 56, 200, 204
Feld, Ross (1947–2001) 13, 127
Fénéon, Félix (1861–1944) 157
Fisher, Bud (1885–1954) 60, 197
Focillon, Henri (1881–1943) 34, 198
Franco Bahamonde, Francisco (1892–1975) 5, 24, 74, 157, **162**, **163**
Frank, Anne (1929–1945) 122

G

Gilot, Françoise (1921–2023) 149
Goebbels, Joseph (1897–1945) 121
Gogol, Nikolai (1809–1852) 120, 129
Goldstein, Leib (1878–1923) 197
Goldstein, Rachel, née Ehrnlieb (1878–1949) 197
Golschmann, Vladimir (1893–1972) 30
Gorky, Arshile (1904–1948) 24, 30
Gottlieb, Adolph (1903–1974) 24
Goya, Francisco de (1746–1828) 42, 149, 157, 199
Greene, Stephen 30
Grosz, George (1893–1959) 15

H

Hall, Gita May (1933–2016) **156**
Hare, Denise Brown **206**
Herriman, George (1880–1944) 5, 15, 60, 197
Hess, Thomas B. (1920–1978) 200
Hood, Raymond (1881–1934) 21
Hugo, Victor (1802–1885) 145

J

James, Henry (1843–1916) 120
Janis, Sidney (1896–1989) 12

K

Kadish, Reuben (1913–1992) 16, 18, **48**, **49**, **56**, 197, 198
Kafka, Franz (1883–1924) 5, 29, 39, 120, 128, 198, 204
Kahnweiler, Daniel-Henry (1884–1979) 157
Kayser, Wolfgang (1906–1960) 146, 157
Kierkegaard, Søren (1813–1855) 200
Kissinger, Henry (1923–2023) 129
Klee, Paul (1879–1940) 38
Kline, Franz (1910–1962) 37, 38, **63**, **64**, 134, 199
Kooning, Elaine de (1918–1989) **65**
Kooning, Willem de (1904–1997) 11, 24, 30, 34, 37, 38, 39, 56, **64**, 198, 199, 200, 204
Kramer, Hilton (1928–2012) 37, 38, 204
Krishnamurti, Jiddu (1895–1986) 16
Kundera, Milan (1929–2023) 122
Kunitz, Stanley Jasspon (1905–2006) **67**, 200

L

Langsner, Jules (1911–1967) **48**, **56**
Léger, Fernand (1881–1955) 197
Leiris, Michel (1901–1990) 151
Lenin, Vladimir Ilyich Ulyanov
(1870–1924) 18, 21
Lorenzetti, Ambrogio (13..?–1348)
33
Lorenzetti, Pietro (1280?–1348?)
33

M

Malamud, Bernard (1914–1986) 115
Mallarmé, Stéphane (1842–1898)
16
Mandelstam, Nadezhda Yakovlevna
(1899–1980) **41**
Manet, Édouard (1832–1883) 199
Marx, Karl (1818–1883) 18
Masaccio (1401–1428?) 33, 197
Masson, André (1896–1987) 30
Matisse, Henri (1869–1954) 21
Matta, Roberto (1911–2002) 30
McKee, David (born 1937) 12, 205
McKee, Renee (born 1940) 5, 205
McKim, Musa (1908–1992) 29, **56**,
127, 197, 198, 199, 205
Melville, Herman (1819–1891) 204
Michaux, Henri (1899–1984) 200
Michelangelo (1475–1564) 16, 17,
60, 197
Mitchell, John Newton (1913–1988)
129
Mondrian, Piet (1872–1944) 33,
39, 56
Moréas, Jean (1856–1910) **73**
Motherwell, Robert (1915–1991) 11,
61, 200

N

Nero (37–68) 145, 149
Newman, Barnett (1905–1970) **64**,
199
Nixon, Richard M. (1913–1994) 5,
15, 74, 123, 129, 204

O

Obregón, Álvaro (1880–1928) 17, 21
Orozco, José Clemente (1883–1949)
17, 26, 46, 197
Orwell, George (1903–1950) 123

P

Panofsky, Erwin (1892–1968) 29,
198
Pasternak, Boris Leonidovič
(1890–1960) 200
Perrault, Charles (1628–1703) 29,
199
Picasso, Pablo (1881–1973) 5, **8**, 15,
16, 17, 21, 24, **25**, 26, 29, 30, **35**,
41, **68**, **69**, **70**, **71**, **72**, **73**, 74, 132,
144, 145, 146, **147**, **148**, 149, **150**,
151, 152, **153**, **154**–**155**, **156**, 157,
158, **159**, **160**, 161, **162**, **163**, 197,
198, 199
Piero della Francesca (1416?–1492)
16, 17, 29, 33, 39, 43, 60, 164, 197,
200
Pollock, Jackson (1912–1956) 16, 18,
21, 30, 34, 37, 38, 56, 134, 197,
198, 199, 200
Pollock, Sanford Leroy McCoy,
as Sande (1909–1963) 198
Poulenc, Francis (1899–1963) **71**
Pulitzer Jr., Joseph (1913–1993) 33

R

Rabelais, François (1494?–1553)
145, 151, 157
Reed, John (1887–1920) 17
Rivera, Diego (1886–1957) 16, 17, 21,
22–**23**, 26
Robbins, David (1907–1981) **47**
Rojas, Fernando de (1465?–1541)
152
Roosevelt, Franklin D. (1882–1945)
18, 21, 24
Rosenberg, Harold (1906–1978) 33,
34, 37, **62**, 200, 201, 204
Roth, Henry (1906–1995) 115
Roth, Philip (1933–2018) 5, 13, 15,
39, 41, 42, 43, 74, 114–130, 204
Rothko, Mark (1903–1970) 11, 24,
33, 37, 56, **61**, 134, 199, 200
Rousseau, Henri, as Le Douanier
Rousseau (1844–1910) 16
Ruskin, John (1819–1900) 145

S

Sabartés, Jaime (1881–1968) **70**,
152, **156**
Salmon, André (1881–1969) 161
Sartre, Jean-Paul (1905–1980) 200
Schelling, Friedrich Wilhelm
Joseph von (1775–1854) 42
Schwankovsky, Frederick John
de St. Vrain 16, 197
Signorelli, Luca (1441?–1523) 42,
164, 197
Siqueiros, David Alfaro (1896–1974)
17, 18, **20**, 26, 46, 197, 198
Soutine, Chaïm (1893–1943) 200
Sproul, Barbara **126**
Steinberg, Saul (1914–1999) **61**
Still, Clyfford (1904–1980) 33
Streicher, Julius (1885–1946) 121
Suzuki, Daisetsu (1870–1966) 34
Swift, Jonathan (1667–1745) 123
Swoger, Arthur (1912–2000) **196**

T

Tiepolo, Giambattista (1696–1770)
29, 199
Tintoretto (1518?–1594) 199
Titian (1489?–1576) 199
Tolegian, Manuel (1911–1983) 18
Tomlin, Bradley Walker (1899–1953)
33, 200
Toulouse-Lautrec, Henri de
(1864–1901) 146
Trump, Donald (born 1946) 124
Tworkov, Jack (1900–1982) **61**

U

Uccello, Paolo (1397?–1475) 164,
197

V

Van Gogh, Vincent (1853–1890) 34
Velázquez, Diego (1599–1660) 149
Vicente, Esteban (1903–2001) **66**

W

Walker, H. G. **196**
Watteau, Antoine (1684–1721) 29,
199
Weston, Edward (1886–1958) **2**
Williams, Esther (1921–2013) **156**
Wölfflin, Heinrich (1864–1945) 198
Wood, Grant (1891–1942) 29

This book is published in conjunction with the exhibition *Philip Guston. The Irony of History*, at the Musée National Picasso-Paris, October 14, 2025 to March 1, 2026.

Exhibition

Curators
Didier Ottinger
General heritage curator,
Centre Pompidou,
Musée National d'Art Moderne –
Centre de Création Industrielle,
Paris and Joanne Snrech
heritage curator,
Musée National Picasso-Paris

Production
Louise Rivet

Exhibition design
Joris Lipsch (Studio Matters)

Graphic design
Floriane Lipsch-Pic,
Claire Cambier (Studio Matters)

Lighting design
Vyara Stefanova, Pierre Franiatte
(Aura Studio)

President
Cécile Debray

Director
Julien Sérignac

Collections and education
Sébastien Delot, director

Production
Sophie Daynes-Diallo, director

Communications and outreach
Leslie de Ferran-Lechevallier,
director

Resources and finance
Pierre Vialle, director

Building services, operations, security and systems information
Lila Dida, director

The president of the Musée National Picasso-Paris would like to express her most sincere gratitude to Musa Mayer, Sally Radic and the entire team of the Guston Foundation.

We would like to express our heartfelt thanks to all of the directors of the public and private institutions and the collectors who, through their loans, have contributed to the organization of this exhibition:

Spain

Museo Nacional Centro de Arte Reina Sofía, Madrid
Mr. Manuel Segade Lodeiro, director

United Kingdom

Tate Modern, London
Karin Hindsbo, director

United States

Glenstone Museum, Potomac
Emily Wei Rales, director

Philadelphia Museum of Art, Philadelphia
Sasha Suda, director and CEO

The Guston Foundation, West Hurley
Sally Radic, executive director

The Metropolitan Museum of Art, New York
Max Hollein, director

The Museum of Modern Art, New York
Christophe Cherix, director

Private collections

Aaron I. Fleischman Collection,
New York
Arora Collection, London

We express our deepest gratitude
to all of the lenders who wished
to remain anonymous.

We extend our warmest thanks
to all of the museum teams, and
in particular to Elisa Cucchiaro,
Sarah Dalquier, Sonia Descamps,
Léo Fontaine, Marion Glère,
Audrey Gonzalez, Céline Isabel,
Charlotte Lannoy, Hermann
Mulenda, Naëma Stamboul,
Aurélia Thyreau.

The Guston Foundation, and
the artist's daughter Musa Mayer,
have generously supported
the exhibition, and have entrusted
to the museum the entire series
of *Nixon Drawings* as well as some
previously unseen works.

GUSTON
The Guston Foundation

The exhibition was also
generously supported by
Mme Renee McKee, as well
as François-Xavier and
Natasha de Mallmann.

Catalogue

Musée Picasso-Paris

Managing editor
Annie Dufour,
ad.édition, for the Musée
National Picasso-Paris

**Editorial coordinator
and picture researcher**
Nadège Plan, for the Musée
National Picasso-Paris

Éditions Gallimard

Édition
Nathalie Bailleux,
editorial director
Giovanna Citi-Hebey,
editorial manager
Natércia Pauty,
department assistant

Artistic director
Anne Lagarrigue,
artistic director
Pascal Guédin,
coordinator art books

Production
Amélie Airiau,
production manager

Press office
Béatrice Foti
assisted by Laetitia Copin

Co-edition
Mathilde Barrois,
head of co-editions
assisted by Coline Briand

**Translation from French
into English**
Charles Penwarden
Ros Schwartz
John Tittensor
Bernard Wooding

Copy-editing
Bernard Wooding

Graphic design and layout
Line Célo
assisted by Chloé Debossu

Photoengraving
Les Artisans du Regard

Photographic credits

Cover, 3, 7, 20, 25, 27, 33, 34, 41–53, 65–137, 139, 140, 142–144, 174–179, 181–185, 188, 189: digital image © The Guston Foundation • 1: photograph by Edward Weston: © Center for Creative Photography, Arizona Board of Regents • 2, 5, 21, 148, 151: photo by Genevieve Hanson, courtesy of Hauser & Wirth and The Guston Foundation • 4: © GrandPalaisRmn (Musée National Picasso-Paris)/Adrien Didierjean • 6: Courtesy of the Robert D. Farber University Archives & Special Collections Department, Brandeis University • 8: photograph by Floyd H. Faxon • 9: The Chouinard Foundation • 10: © Schalkwijk, dist. GrandPalaisRmn/image Schalkwijk Archive • 11, 12: © Photographic Archives Museo Nacional Centro de Arte Reina Sofía • 13: © Philadelphia Museum of Art, dist. GrandPalaisRmn/image Philadelphia Museum of Art • 14: © BPK, Berlin, dist. GrandPalaisRmn/Aline Gwose/Michael Herling • 15, 40, 172, 186, 187: Digital image, The Museum of Modern Art, New York/Scala, Florence • 16, 170: Courtesy of the Saint Louis Art Museum • 17: Mildred Lane Kemper Art Museum, Washington University in St. Louis • 18, 26, 29, 31, 32, 36–38, 146, 149, 150, 167, 171, 180, 190, 196: Courtesy of The Estate of Philip Guston Archives • 19, 145: photograph by Keldon Polacco, courtesy of The Guston Foundation • 22: Digital Image © 2025 Museum Associates/LACMA. Licensed by Dist. GrandPalaisRmn/image LACMA • 23: © Munson-Williams Proctor Arts Institute, Dist. GrandPalaisRmn/image Munson-Williams Proctor Arts Institute • 24: San Francisco Museum of Modern Art/photograph: Ben Blackwell • 28: photograph by David Robbins • 30: Archives of American Art, Smithsonian Institution • 39, 168: © The Metropolitan Museum of Art, Dist. GrandPalaisRmn/image MMA • 54–56, 60, 64, 163: © GrandPalaisRmn (Musée National Picasso-Paris)/Mathieu Rabeau • 57, 61: © GrandPalaisRmn (Musée National Picasso-Paris)/Gabriel De Carvalho • 58, 59, 62, 63, 154, 164: © GrandPalaisRmn (Musée National Picasso-Paris)/Adrien Didierjean • 138, 147: Photo: Christopher Burke © The Estate of Philip Guston, courtesy Hauser & Wirth • 141: photograph by Barbara Sproul • 150: Adam Reich • 152: photo courtesy of Christies Images Limited • 153: © Centre Pompidou, MNAM-CCI, Dist. GrandPalaisRmn/image Centre Pompidou, MNAM-CCI • 155: © GrandPalaisRmn (Musée National Picasso-Paris)/Rachel Prat • 156, 159–162: Museu Picasso, Barcelona. Photo: Fotogasull • 157: Artothek/© Succession Picasso/DACS, London 2025/Bridgeman Images • 158: © GrandPalaisRmn (Musée National Picasso-Paris)/Adrien Didierjean, Mathieu Rabeau • 165, 166: © GrandPalaisRmn (Musée National Picasso-Paris)/Sylvie Chan-Liat • 169: Image courtesy the Estate of Philip Guston and Hauser & Wirth • 173: © Tate, London, Dist. GrandPalaisRmn/Tate Photography • 191: photograph by H.G. Walker for *Life* magazine • 192: photograph by Walter Auerbach: © Walter Auerbach, courtesy Robert Mann Gallery • 193: photograph by Arthur Swoger: © Arthur Swoger Estate • 194, 195: photograph by Denise Browne Hare • 197: photograph by Stefan Altenburger, courtesy of Hauser & Wirth and The Guston Foundation.

For all works by Philip Guston: © The Estate of Philip Guston
For all works by Pablo Picasso: © Succession Picasso 2025
For all works by Reuben Kadish: Courtesy of the Reuben Kadish Art Foundation
For the work by David Alfaro Siqueiros and the work by Diego Rivera: © Adagp, Paris, 2025 and © 2025 Banco de México Diego Rivera Frida Kahlo Museums Trust, Mexico, D.F./Adagp, Paris

In accordance with intellectual property laws, a comprehensive search to find the rights-holders of the images was carried out. Unfortunately, some have not been found. We apologize to them and invite them to make themselves known to the publisher.

Text credits

Philip Roth, "Pictures by Guston" © Philip Roth, 2001. Originally published in Philip Roth, *Shop Talk*, Boston, New York, Houghton Mifflin, 2001. Reprinted by permission of The Random House Group Limited (for the United Kingdom and the Commonwealth) and HarperCollins Publishers (for the United States of America and Canada) // *Thoughts (or Advice to Myself)* and *The Appointment (a True Story)* by Philip Guston, © The Estate of Philip Guston/published in *Philip Guston, Collected Writings, Lectures, and Conversations*, Berkeley, Los Angeles, London, University of California Press, 2011

© Musée national
Picasso-Paris, 2025
5, rue de Thorigny
75003 Paris
www.museepicassoparis.fr

© Éditions Gallimard,
Paris, 2025
5, rue Gaston-Gallimard
75007 Paris
www.gallimard.fr
magasin@gallimard.fr

This catalogue's paper is made from natural, renewable, recyclable fibers, produced from sustainably managed forests.

Paper (interior):
Munken Lynx 120 gr/m²

Printed in August 2025
by Graphicom in Verona
Printed in Italy

Legal deposit: October 2024
ISBN: 978-2-07-312810-2
672173

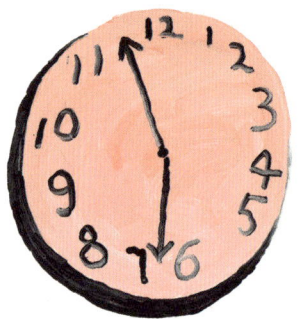

197 — *Untitled*, 1968. Acrylic on panel, 76.2 × 81.3 cm.
Dr. Corinne M. Flick Collection, London

Front cover
Philip Guston, *The Studio*, 1969, oil on canvas, 121.9 × 106.7 cm. Promised Gift of Musa Guston Mayer to the Metropolitan Museum of Art

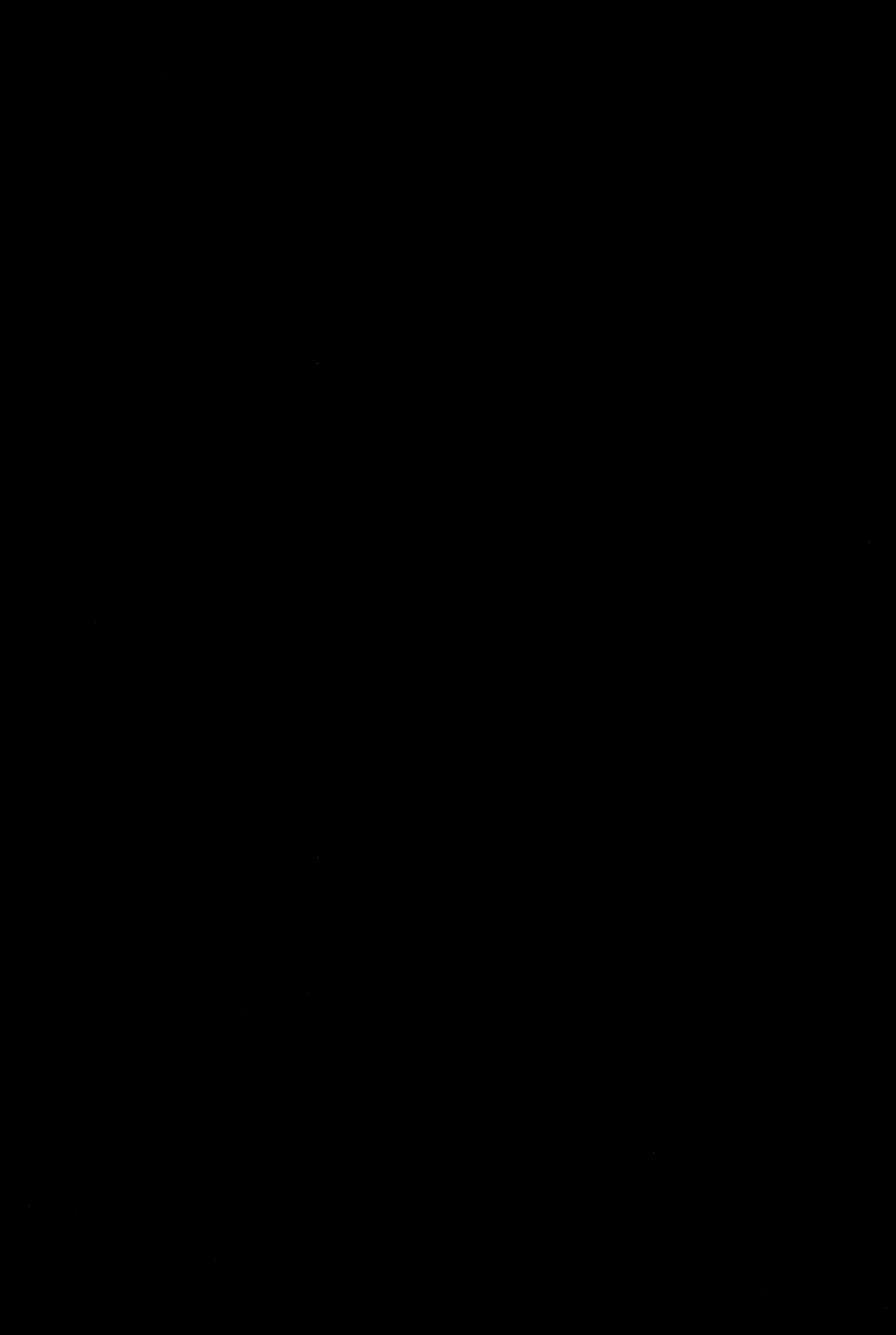